JEFFERSON DAVIS'S FINAL CAMPAIGN

MERCER UNIVERSITY

MERCER UNIVERSITY PRESS

Endowed by

TOM WATSON BROWN

and

THE WATSON-BROWN FOUNDATION, INC.

JEFFERSON DAVIS'S FINAL CAMPAIGN

Confederate Nationalism and the Fight to Arm Slaves

PHILIP D. DILLARD

MERCER UNIVERSITY PRESS | *Macon, Georgia*

2017

MUP/ H928

Published by Mercer University Press
1501 Mercer University Drive
Macon, Georgia 31207

9 8 7 6 5 4 3 2 1

Books published by Mercer University Press are printed on acid-free paper that meets the requirements of the American National Standard for Information Sciences—Permanence of Paper for Printed Library Materials.

ISBN 978-0-88146-605-8
Cataloging-in-Publication Data is available from the Library of Congress

Contents

Acknowledgments vii

Introduction 1
Chapter 1: Evolving Ideals 6

Phase I: Dwindling Men to the Fall of Savannah 21
Chapter 2: An Astonishing Notion 23
Chapter 3: Radical Measures 46
Chapter 4: A Shout in the Night 68

Phase II: Savannah to the Hampton Roads Conference 93
Chapter 5: With Us or Against Us 95
Chapter 6: A Matter of Necessity 122
Chapter 7: No Need to Choose 153

Phase III: Hampton Roads to Appomattox 183
Chapter 8: A Reasonable Sacrifice 185
Chapter 9: All for Independence 203
Chapter 10: A Last Resort 230

Conclusion 259
Chapter 11: Independence or Slavery? 261
Bibliography 277
Index 281

Acknowledgments

Many people have contributed to the successful completion of this work. First, I am indebted to my faculty mentors, Emory Thomas and John Boles. Dr. Thomas introduced the topic to me in a graduate writing seminar at the University of Georgia. He sparked my desire to be a Civil War scholar and guided me through my early explorations of Confederate Nationalism. Upon my arrival at Rice University, Dr. Boles helped me to expand the project both geographically and theoretically. His wise counsel and steadfast support have been invaluable both as a graduate student and as a historian. This project gained in both depth and complexity under his direction. Second, I benefitted tremendously from the support and comradeship of my Rice graduate peers to include: Randal Hall, Paul Levengood, Mathew Thompson, and Charles Israel. Each helped me frame my understanding of the American South. Third, I received incredible assistance from many kind and thoughtful librarians and archivists. I will never forget the knowledgeable staff at the University of Georgia Main Library and Fondren Library at Rice University. They cheerfully filled countless requests and often made helpful suggestions of new avenues to explore. I suspect that I may have worn out more than my share of microfilm machines in both libraries. I could not have completed this work without the assistance of the staff at the Papers of Jefferson Davis. Editor Lynda Crist provided keen insights as I researched in the Davis Papers office. Mary Dix and Ken Williams also generously shared their knowledge of Davis and the workings of the Confederate government. I also attained valuable assistance while researching at the Dolph Brisco Center for American History at the University of Texas, the Galveston and Texas History Center at the Rosenberg Library, Alderman Library at the University of Virginia, the Library of Virginia, the Virginia Historical Society, and Carrier Library at James Madison University.

I also received considerable encouragement and support from my colleagues at James Madison University. Skip Hyser, Steve Guerrier, and Gabrielle Lanier have helped me become a better teacher and better scholar. I have benefitted tremendously from their example and friendship. I have been blessed with many outstanding students who, through their questions and in discussions, have caused me to think more deeply about the American

South and the Confederacy. In particular, I must acknowledge the contributions of Mark Ehlers, Nathan Ryalls, Ashley Schmidt, Jim Schruefer, and Kelsey Ostergren. I want to express my deep appreciation to the History Department, the College of Arts and Letters, and the Office of Research and Scholarship for their financial support of this volume.

Finally, I must express my most heartfelt gratitude to my family. My father and mother, Philip and Carolyn Dillard, taught me to love learning and to persevere even when all seemed lost. I can never repay my many debts to them. My children, Rachel and Tommy, have pushed me to be a better father and a better man. They have listened to too many discussions of Civil War topics and visited too many historical sites to think I have anything left to say. Rachel and Tommy were quite young when this project started and now, at publication, are strong, independent adults. I am very proud of them. I could not have written this volume without the selfless assistance of my wife, Peggy. She is an outstanding historian in her own right, but she is also an exceptional archivist and thoughtful editor. Peggy offered not only unceasing encouragement but also important insights about the war and a keen eye for detail. I will never be able to thank her enough for all her love and support.

Introduction

Too often, traditional histories of the American Civil War have focused on armies and generals and forgotten that civilian society also experienced the war. Similarly, social historians have painted pictures of the nineteenth-century South and scarcely noticed that a major military struggle occurred. Maris Vinovskis noted this glaring gap in Civil War historiography in an article in the *Journal of American History* in 1989 and James McPherson echoed this lament in 1992.[1] Jason Phillips, Stephanie McCurry, and Drew Faust among others have stepped forward in recent years to bridge this chasm. The issue of arming slaves fits squarely in this gap between traditional military history and social history, yet few historians have considered the issue seriously. The debate over the use of black soldiers brought forth tensions in Confederate society along not only racial but also class, gender, and regional lines. By examining the views of Virginians, Georgians, and Texans concerning arming the slaves, a clearer picture of the Confederacy, the role of slavery in Southern society, and the depth of Confederate nationalism emerges.

How could a nation built with slavery as its foundation choose to end the institution in the name of self-preservation? In her study of Confederate Nationalism, Drew Faust contends that southerners undertook a "self-conscious process" for creating a new nation with many unforeseen consequences. "Independence and war," she argues, "reopened unfinished antebellum debates, intensified unresolved pre-war conflicts, and subjected some of the most fundamental assumptions of the Old South to public scrutiny." As in the American Revolution, the army served as a crucial cauldron for the formation of national identity. The Confederate debate over arming slaves was conducted not only in Congress but also in discussions in small communities across the South. In each arena, the opinions of soldiers played a crucial role. Public discussion of black men in gray uniforms brought forth

---

[1] Maris Vinovskis, "Have Social Historians Lost the Civil War? Some Preliminary Speculations," *Journal of American History* 76 (June 1989): 34–58; James McPherson, "Foreword," in *Divided Houses: Gender and the Civil War*, ed. Catherine Clinton and Nina Silber (New York: Oxford University Press, 1992) xiii–xvii.

long-hidden divisions between planters, yeoman farmers, and poor whites. Many common soldiers felt that planters had not lived up to their obligations as patriarchs. Starving soldiers' wives, the draft exemptions for slave owners, and planter resistance to the military use of slaves produced powerful arguments for a rich man's war and a poor man's fight. The war may have begun as a conservative attempt to avoid change, but the hard war that both sides adopted in the final years of the conflict revolutionized not only battlefield tactics but also the objectives of the war.

This work will demonstrate the rich complexity of political and social change during a period most historians want to portray as utterly simple. Without question, the American Civil War was fought over the issue of slavery. All other issues dividing North and South would have been open to compromise, but slavery and cotton and the economic foundation they represented were absolutes in the Antebellum South. As Alexander Stephens had so ineloquently suggested in 1861, the cornerstone of this economic and political world rested upon the belief that the African slave was innately inferior to the white man. From the early 1830s, the Abolitionist challenge to this worldview had frightened white southerners and prevented them from seriously discussing or debating the merits of the "peculiar institution."

Most historians have dismissed Jefferson Davis's efforts to promote arming slaves as simply a desperate act of a failing leader. In contrast, Robert Durden, in *The Gray and the Black: The Confederate Debate on Emancipation*, presents a well-crafted, superbly organized survey of the documents concerning the debate over new roles for the slave in the war effort. Focusing primarily on the views expressed in Richmond, Durden presents an excellent picture of the political struggle to arm the slaves. Although commending the courage of Davis, Lee, and others who attempted to modify slavery, he argues strongly that most southerners lacked the "intelligence, imagination, and moral courage" necessary to emancipate the slaves.[2] While presenting considerable support for this conclusion from the Richmond papers, Durden fails to follow consistently the debate outside the capital. Despite his astute observations about the attitudes prevalent in Richmond, he leaves the reader wondering what the common people of the Deep South and Trans-

[2] Robert F. Durden, *The Gray and the Black: The Confederate Debate on Emancipation* (Baton Rouge: Louisiana State Press, 1972) 287.

Mississippi South thought about arming the slaves and eventually emancipating them.

Only five additional historians have attempted to address these perplexing questions in significant depth. In *Southern Negroes: 1861–1865*, Bell Wiley provides an excellent narrative detailing the course of the efforts to place slaves in the Confederate army. Unfortunately, he fails to question how the acceptance of black regiments into the army reflected changes in public war aims or attitudes toward the Confederate nation. In contrast, in *Why the South Lost the Civil War*, Richard Beringer and his co-authors focus almost exclusively upon the debate over war aims. Without following the evolution of the debate closely, they summarily dismiss the idea that independence could ever have replaced slavery as the South's primary war goal. Instead, they argue that independence served only to cover, and thus obscure, other subconscious reasons. Although "resentment, guilt, and disillusionment" may have played a part in the reappraisal of Confederate war aims, these authors too quickly deny the revolutionary impact of war upon individuals and nations.[3]

Approaching from a different angle, Clarence Mohr in *On the Threshold of Freedom: Masters and Slaves in Civil War Georgia*, presents the most complete examination of the debate in the Deep South. Looking beneath the planter elite, he discovers class appeals swirling through Georgia and attracting considerable yeoman support. "Arguments directed at Georgia's plain folk," Mohr notes, "promoted black enlistment as a means of equalizing wartime hardships by placing heavier burdens on slaves and their owners."[4] Although recognizing the debate as a "search for Southern identity and a quest for national purpose," Mohr focuses upon the views of black Georgians and addresses the intriguing question of whether the slaves would have fought for the South.[5] In contrast to many historians who have assumed that all slaves felt an automatic sense of loyalty to the North, he contends that black wartime "loyalty" to both sides was always conditional. Disillusionment with Union officers, family concerns, personal relationships with indi-

---

[3] Richard E. Beringer et al., eds., *Why the South Lost the Civil War* (Athens: University of Georgia Press, 1986) 391.

[4] Clarence Mohr, *On the Threshold of Freedom: Masters and Slaves in Civil War Georgia* (Athens: University of Georgia Press, 1986) 275–76.

[5] Ibid., 275.

vidual whites, and uncertainty over the war's outcome often combined to make individual decisions difficult.[6] In *Black Confederates and Afro-Yankees in Civil War Virginia,* Ervin Jordan, Jr. attempts to demonstrate the diversity of roles played by black Virginians.[7] Jordan does not explore the stakes in the Confederate debate of emancipation but, rather, examines the Afro-Virginians drawn to the southern cause. Unfortunately, Jordan vastly oversells his case for black Confederate patriotism. Little of the realism of Mohr's "conditionally loyal" Georgians surfaces in Jordan's account.

Most recently, Bruce Levine in *Confederate Emancipation: Southern Plans to Free and Arm Slaves during the Civil War* attempts to answer a number of key questions: Why were black troops proposed? What did the plan say about the motives behind secession? And would slaves have been willing to fight for the Confederacy? Like most historians, Levine bases his arguments upon the accounts of political and economic elites. Further, he assumes that convictions expressed in the secession crisis or in the first days of the war remained constant to the bitter end. He asserts that Davis cynically promoted emancipation with the hope that white southern elites would be able to set the terms of black freedom. Levine finds little evidence that Confederate political leaders or planters had been transformed by the war. Based upon his reading of post-war memoirs and the notorious Black Codes, he argues the Confederate leadership had never wavered in their racial ideas, never intended to offer real emancipation, and could not envision a Confederate nation attained with black assistance. This conclusion assumes that all southerners maintained faith with the planters who stoutly resisted arming and freeing slaves.[8]

Unfortunately, these outstanding books fail to present a clear picture of what the common men and women of the South thought about arming the slaves and what they hoped to gain from the war. What did the average men and women of Virginia, Georgia, and Texas think about this crisis? Did these southerners want to arm the slaves? Could they envision a Confederacy without slavery? At this final crossroads of the war, did southerners consider

---

[6] Ibid., 291.

[7] Ervin Jordan, Jr., *Black Confederates and Afro-Yankees in Civil War Virginia* (Charlottesville VA: University Press of Virginia, 1995) xi, 309.

[8] Bruce Levine, *Confederate Emancipation: Southern Plans to Free and Arm Slaves during the Civil War* (Oxford: Oxford University Press, 2006) 152–60.

the preservation of slavery or southern independence to be the primary Confederate war aim?

This study began as an attempt to answer such questions by examining the debate in two Georgia cities. As I read the Macon and Augusta newspapers, the depth of the arguments presented for and against arming slaves intrigued me. Editorials explored all facets of the question, but the letters from often-anonymous newspaper readers proved captivating. I started to expand my survey of the issue by examining all Georgia cities that avoided Union occupation and maintained a viable newspaper throughout the war. Large cities like Columbus with a population of nearly 8,000 appear as do small farm towns like Blakely. Having completed my study of Georgia, I felt I needed to test my tentative conclusions in other areas outside the Deep South. Texas provided an interesting contrast because no serious military threat ever appeared there. Again, I sought out both large and small city newspapers. Houston and Galveston played key roles in the Texas debate but so did smaller towns like Marshall and Bellville. Unlike the Georgians, Texans approached the questions about war aims and slavery much as they had in 1861. The issues discussed remained constant but the attitudes displayed by Georgians clearly illustrated the impact of hard war. Finally, I attempted to explore the debate in Virginia. Few Virginia locales remained unoccupied during the entire November to March period. Therefore, I focused upon ideas expressed in the capital, at the Confederate bastion of Lynchburg, and in the Shenandoah Valley. By exploring the debate as it unfolded in Virginia, Georgia, and Texas, differences between regions emerged. Further, the examination of small towns as well as better known cities allowed for an appraisal of the depth of the debate. Finally, by looking for common southerners who held neither high government office nor military position, a clearer picture of the importance of slavery within white southern society emerged.

1

Evolving Ideals

From the first shots at Fort Sumter, a few southern leaders had expressed interest in the idea of black men serving in Confederate gray. Although spurred to war by the belief that Abraham Lincoln intended to disrupt and eventually destroy slavery, the Confederate armies quickly found that they could not function without black assistance. White soldiers marching off to war took numerous slaves with them, and at military encampments these slaves assumed duties as musicians as well as cooks and personal servants. Similarly, Confederate leaders requested and received from slaveholders the temporary assistance of slave laborers to begin defensive preparations. With the army, slaves built bridges, dug trenches, and performed many menial tasks. As body servants and as impressed laborers, these black men fit the roles assigned to them by traditional southern ideology. They labored under the direction of their masters or men detailed as military overseers and for the most part undertook tasks not unlike those performed on the plantation.[1]

Like the Lincoln administration, the Confederate government had taken a series of incremental steps during the war, ever expanding the wartime roles accorded to slaves. Building on their success at utilizing slaves as short-term military laborers, a few southerners suggested that bondsmen could make even larger contributions to the war effort. Most notably, the free people of color in New Orleans, in the afterglow of secession, had formed the Louisiana Native Guards, an African-American unit with African-American officers. Although the Confederate government declined to accept this regiment into the Confederate army, the state of Louisiana maintained the unit

[1] While many historians mention the southern use of slaves with the army, the strongest discussion of the Confederate use of black labor is presented in the very well researched work of Jaime Martinez. Jaime Amanda Martinez, *Confederate Slave Impressment in the Upper South* (Chapel Hill: University of North Carolina Press, 2013).

as a militia outfit. Subsequently, when Confederate leaders ordered the evacuation of New Orleans in April 1862, the Native Guards remained in the city and offered their services to the Union forces under Benjamin Butler. The Lincoln administration hesitated for the moment, but within a year, the Native Guards saw action as Union soldiers. The shifting loyalties of the unit illustrated well the Confederate dilemma over black troops. If the Confederacy rejected their assistance, the Union might use them. Even so, many southerners feared that military service would unsuit the black veterans for renewed servitude once the war was over. As the war raged on, the Confederacy felt increasing pressure to follow the example of the Union and to expand the scope of black service in the war effort.

Confederate leaders often stressed the ties between the revolution of 1776 and the revolution of 1861, but few southerners found reason to cheer on 4 July 1863. That morning, Ulysses S. Grant led his victorious troops into Vicksburg and began to feed the starving citizens. Having surrendered, John Pemberton's ragged southern troops received their paroles and headed home. With the capture of the Confederate citadel, Union steamboats ranged the full length of the Mississippi River within a week. In Pennsylvania, Robert E. Lee held his men in defensive positions along Seminary Ridge, hoping that George Meade would hurl his troops across the open fields that George Pickett and his men had so fatefully crossed the day before. All day long the rains poured down upon the southern troops, but Meade did not accept Lee's challenge. In the evening, Lee's weary soldiers withdrew from their forward positions and began an arduous forced march back across the Potomac River into Virginia. The twin campaigns of May through June 1863 both culminated on 4 July with staggering losses for the southern armies. The Confederacy found itself divided by the largest river on the continent, thus wrecking an already weak southern communication and supply system. As important as the loss of Pemberton's entire force, the horrific losses in officers and men suffered by the Army of Northern Virginia in the three days of fighting at Gettysburg deprived that army of the capability to assume the initiative. The Confederate forces in Virginia remained lethal but could no longer seriously threaten to take the war to the North. While a few southerners no doubt recalled that George Washington had often faced similar trying circumstances, many began to search for new ways to fill the gray ranks.

In this hour of southern despair, the Alabama legislature debated and approved a series of resolutions designed to free additional white men to enter the front lines. Noting the large number of soldiers assigned as clerks, quartermasters, and laborers in government factories, the legislators argued that the army needed to better husband its resources: "Our army has been greatly reduced on account of the numberless details of soldiers to labor in Government workshops and other places…performing such work as can be and is usually rendered by slaves." The white men in question had been drafted into the army and then ordered to perform some war essential task in lieu of immediate field service. With conscription laws already quite broad, the legislature hoped to reform army policies that allowed many to remain in the rear. "In the opinion of this body," the Alabama legislators wrote, "slaves should be required by the Confederate States to take the places of all those soldiers who are detailed to labor in the places herein mentioned."[2] If detailed men could be replaced by slaves, southern combat power would rise proportionately and offset the losses resulting from the Vicksburg and Gettysburg defeats. This moderate proposal to employ slaves with the army, like the use of impressed black laborers on defensive positions, did not challenge southern ideas about slavery. Even so, the Alabama legislature took a significant step forward as it cautiously suggested that the South might learn from the North's success with black troops:

> In view of the fact that the Government of the United States has determined to put in the field negro soldiers, and are enlisting and drafting the slaves of the people of the South, this General Assembly submits for the consideration of Congress the propriety and policy of using in some effective way a certain percentage of the male slave population…to perform such services as Congress may by law direct.

---

[2] This legislative proposal was based on the assumption that these "detailed men" were performing common labor. Many of these white men were talented craftsmen with long experience in industry. The Confederacy had cast a wide draft net, but the government had found that taking too many skilled men led to reduced production. For example, Joseph Anderson of Richmond's Tredegar Iron Works soon found the Confederate army asking him to return to industry rather than remaining on the battlefield. The assumption that there were many white men detailed to mundane tasks by the army would remain popular in the South until the end of the war.

The Alabamans never specifically stated which tasks, beyond the realm of menial labor, they hoped slaves would perform. Although set aside after the Confederate victory at Chickamauga in September 1863, the Alabama resolutions clearly illustrate that southerners were prepared to consider modifying the slave's role in the war effort.[3]

In August 1863, recommendations for black troops arrived in Richmond from other sources as well. For instance, Secretary of State Judah P. Benjamin received a letter from an acquaintance in Alabama who strongly urged the immediate enlistment of slaves as soldiers. In response, the secretary listed several practical arguments against the step. First, he contended that the government would have to purchase the troops at tremendous cost, estimated at $200,000 for each 1,000-man regiment. If purchased by the government, the secretary further argued, the slave-soldiers would eventually pose a difficult question for the new nation: "The Government…must either sell the slaves after the war, which would be a most odious proceeding after they had aided in gaining our liberties, or must free them to the great detriment of the country." Second, if slave-soldiers were hired at the going rates rather than purchased, the poor whites, the secretary astutely noted, would be enraged to find that a slave was worth thirty dollars a month but a white man only eleven. Third, he questioned the fidelity of the blacks if tempted by Union emissaries along the front lines. Finally, Benjamin asserted that slaves toiling in factories, on railroads, and in mines encompassed all that could be safely taken out of the fields and yet maintain adequate crop production. "This is the field for negro labor," the secretary concluded, "to which they are habituated, and which appears at first sight to be altogether less liable to objection, than to imitate our enemies by using them in military organizations." None of Benjamin's objections stressed pro-slavery ideology but, rather, focused on specific practical impediments to the scheme.[4]

Secretary Benjamin also received a letter concerning arming slaves from Henry Hotze, a Confederate agent in London. On 26 September 1863, Hotze reported that northern newspapers had made a sensation in Great

[3]United States War Department, *The War of the Rebellion: A Compilation of the Official Records of the Union and Confederate Armies,* Series 4, Vol. 2 (Washington: U.S. Government Printing Office, 1900) 767.

[4] "Judah Benjamin to B.H. Micou," in Robert D. Meade, *Judah P. Benjamin: Confederate Statesman* (New York: Oxford University Press, 1943) 289–91.

Britain by suggesting that the South might arm 500,000 slaves. "If the alternative were once forced upon us," Hotze conceded, "of choosing between independence and the maintenance of our domestic institution, I...say that we are now prepared to pay even this fearful price." The agent expressed considerable surprise that "we had found ourselves so suddenly and so terribly in want of men" and questioned if the slaves could not be equally well utilized in some other capacity: "I should rejoice to see a general impressment of the able-bodied slave population, and believe that at least 200,000 might be employed as teamsters, etc., in the Army, and as workmen in the foundries, mines, and workshops." Despite his personal opinions, the Confederate diplomat readily acknowledged the positive impact of such a step on Confederate foreign relations: "In treating the reported measure not only as possible but even probable, they [southern supporters in Europe] made the greatest step yet made toward blunting the sharp edge of the unreasoning hostility to our institutions." Anti-slavery feeling, Hotze warned Benjamin, remained strong in Britain but was even stronger in France, where slavery was seen as a transgression of the French ideal of liberty. If the South hoped to win popular support for recognition, Hotze argued, some such step to modify slavery would be needed.[5] The depth of European interest in the Confederacy arming its slaves surprised southern diplomats and planted a seed of hope that if needed as a final resort, emancipation might purchase recognition.

Dramatic defeats had sparked the discussion of black troops in August and September 1863, but the inability of Union forces to capitalize upon their successes allowed the embers to cool. While civilian leaders quickly turned to other matters, Confederate military leaders viewed the coming spring campaigns of Grant and Sherman with considerable concern and, therefore, sought new sources to fill their thinning ranks. Looking out at the depleted regiments of the Army of Tennessee encamped at Dalton, Georgia, Major General Patrick Cleburne noted a grave change in troop morale: "Our soldiers can see no end to this state of affairs except in our own exhaustion; hence, instead of rising to the occasion, they are sinking into a fatal apathy,

---

[5] Harry K. White, ed., *Official Records of the Union and Confederate Navies in the War of the Rebellion,* Series 2, Vol. 3 (Washington: U.S. Government Printing Office, 1922) 915–16.

growing weary of hardships...which promise no results." This specter of defeat, Cleburne contended, foreshadowed the loss of not only slavery but also homes, liberty, and even southern manhood. Far from a bastion of strength, the general considered slavery the South's chief weakness: "It is our vulnerable point, a continued embarrassment, and in some respects an insidious weakness. ... To prevent raids we are forced to scatter our forces, and are not free to move and strike like the enemy." Born in Ireland and a veteran of the British army, Cleburne had come to the South as a young adult and never fully accepted the pro-slavery ideas of his neighbors. Owning no slaves himself, Cleburne was prepared to consider all options to continue the struggle. Having arrived at these stark conclusions about the morale of the army and the value of slavery, Cleburne struggled to find a way to turn the tables on the Union armies.[6]

In December 1863 Cleburne consulted with fellow officers and penned a memorial addressed to Jefferson Davis that suggested placing black troops in the Confederate army: "We propose...that we immediately commence training a large reserve of the most courageous of our slaves, and further that we guarantee freedom within a reasonable time to every slave in the South who shall remain true to the Confederacy." Arming and freeing the slaves, Cleburne asserted, would win world approval, "deprive the North of moral and material aid," and ensure numerically equal armies to those of the Union. Further, he argued it would help to cement the relationship between the planter class and the rank and file of the army: "It would remove forever all selfish taint from our cause and place independence above every question of property." Unlike many southerners, the well-respected general conceded that black troops could be effective:

> The negro slaves of Saint Domingo [sic], fighting for their freedom, defeated their white masters and the French troops sent against them. The negro slaves of Jamaica revolted, and under the name of Maroons held the mountains against their masters for 150 years; and the experience of this war has been so far that half-trained negroes have fought as bravely as many half-trained Yankees.

---

[6] United States War Department, *Official Records,* Series 1, Vol. 52, Part 2, 586–92; Craig L. Symonds, *Stonewall of the West: Patrick Cleburne and the Civil War* (Lawrence: University of Kansas Press, 1997) 9–25.

Common humanity as well as the need to ensure the new soldier's fidelity, the general argued, demanded a high price: "If we are to arm and train him and make him fight for the country in her hour of dire distress, every consideration of principle and policy demand [sic] that we should set him and his whole race who side with us free." By freeing all the slaves, Cleburne hoped to outbid the Union army for the black soldier's services: "We can give the negro not only his own freedom, but that of his wife and child, and can secure it to him in his old home." Finally, the general concluded his memorial by calling for an immediate discussion of the proposal's merits: "Negroes will require much training; training will require time, and there is danger that this concession to common sense may come too late."[7]

The officer corps of the Army of Tennessee discussed Cleburne's proposal in a series of meetings, with a number, including three general officers, agreeing to sign the document. But many like William H.T. Walker, Patton Anderson, and William Bate were stunned by the tenor of Cleburne's recommendations, and hard feelings resulted. General Clement Stevens of South Carolina strongly denounced Cleburne's ideas and attacked Colonel James Nisbet directly, who spoke for the memorial: "I am astonished at you! You are demoralized!" Stevens continued, "If slavery is to be abolished, then I take no more interest in our fight. The *justification* of slavery is the *inferiority* of the Negro. If we make him a soldier we concede the whole question." Unlike his opponents, Cleburne (and many of his supporters) came from Arkansas where slavery did not dominate the economy as fully as it did in other parts of the South. Further, the fighting that had occurred in Arkansas had thoroughly disrupted the institution and had convinced many that slavery's days were numbered. Their bold conclusions about the suitability of slaves for military service challenged a key element in the Confederate faith and caused many slaveholding officers like Stevens to feel threatened. Army commander Joseph E. Johnston learned of Cleburne's memorial and citing its civilian nature, refused to send it to Richmond. Despite the new commander's decision, three residents in Dalton attempted to address the slave-soldier issue in the capital.[8]

---

[7] *Official Records*, Series 1, Vol. 52, Part 2, 586–92.

[8] James C. Nisbet, *Four Years on the Firing Line,* ed. Bell I. Wiley (Jackson TN: McCowat-Mercer Press, 1963) 172–73; "Isham G. Harris to Jefferson Davis," 16 January

First, in December 1863 General Thomas C. Hindman (also from Arkansas) wrote a letter under a pseudonym to the *Memphis Appeal*, then a refugee in Atlanta, advocating the immediate enlistment of slaves in the army. At the same time, he drafted a bill for black Confederate troops that he entrusted to a congressman who promised to introduce it in the House of Representatives. Realizing that the measure had no chance in Congress, the congressman presented it informally to the military committee, where it quietly died. Second, on 12 January General William Walker went behind Joe Johnston's back to send a copy of the memorial to Jefferson Davis. "My strong convictions," he declared, "that the further agitation of such sentiments and propositions would ruin the efficacy of our army and involve our cause in ruin and disgrace constitute my reasons for bringing the document before the Executive." Finally, former Tennessee Governor Isham Harris sent a similar letter to Davis in which he speculated about the measure's support in the army and expressed his hope that "it [Cleburne's memorial] may be smothered so as not to gain publicity." In this manner, Davis learned of Cleburne's proposal and subsequently ordered Johnston "to avoid all publicity" and thereby end "all discussion and controversy respecting or growing out of it." Secretary of War James Seddon issued direct orders to Benjamin Cheatham, Cleburne, and Hindman to stop all agitation of the idea of black troops. Even though Cleburne's distinguished battlefield record merited promotion to corps command, Seddon and Davis passed over his name three times in the following year to select less qualified men. Davis and his advisors astutely understood that the South was not yet ready to debate arming and freeing the slaves. Although Cleburne's initiative effectively died in the commander's pocket, it remained an option in Davis's mind.[9]

Despite the bold initiative of Cleburne, few southerners seriously considered arming and freeing the slaves in early 1864. On 16 January, General Hindman temporarily abandoned the idea of arming slaves and wrote the president recommending a more palatable use of the black population: "If negroes were allowed as teamsters, cooks, hospital attendants, laborers, and

---

1864, in *The Papers of Jefferson Davis,* vol. 10, ed. Lynda Crist (Baton Rouge: Louisiana State University Press, 1999) 178. Symonds, *Stonewall of the West,* 181–201.

[9] "Letter from Gen. Hindman," *Austin State Gazette*, 3 May 1865, 3; *Official Records*, Series 1, Vol. 52, Part 2, 595; "Isham G. Harris to Jefferson Davis," 16 January 1864, *The Papers of Jefferson Davis,* 10:78.

for the pioneer companies of divisions, and engine[er] companies of the Army, it would swell our ranks, *at once*, about *20.000* [sic] men." Two weeks previously, General Johnston had written Davis advocating the same employments of slaves, but he expected the measure to release only from ten to twelve thousand white men for field service. Hindman's and Johnston's views mirrored the president's hopes to bring slaves into the army on a permanent basis. The Confederate Congress complied on 17 February 1864 when it approved a bill for the long-term impressment of 20,000 slaves to act as laborers with the army. Although this measure had a smaller impact than Cleburne's proposal contemplated, it was a significant step toward the Confederate use of black soldiers. Despite the resolutions of the Alabama legislature, the letters from diplomats in Europe, and Cleburne's bold memorial, most Confederates had not yet reached the point where they were ready to consider the sacrifice of slavery.[10]

In an address to the people, released by Congress in February 1864, the Confederate leadership clearly reaffirmed that they had entered the conflict to protect slavery from a party "hostile to the South and her institutions": "These States withdrew from the former Union and formed a new Confederate alliance as an independent Government, based on the proper relations of labor and capital." Further, the Congressmen argued that the North must meet both southern war aims to attain peace: "We can only repeat the desire of the people for peace, and our readiness to accept terms consistent with the honor and dignity and independence of the States and compatible with the safety of our domestic institutions." This initial period of discussion concerning the potential of slaves to aid the southern war effort remained strictly limited to government officials, but it set the stage for a full discussion of the merits of slavery during the final months of the war. The defeats at Vicksburg and Gettysburg had shaken the very foundations of the South, but the institution of slavery had not yet fallen from its throne.[11]

The Confederate debate over arming and freeing the slaves did not originate in a single moment of desperation in the final months of the war.

---

[10] "Thomas C. Hindman to Jefferson Davis," 16 January 1864, and "Joseph E. Johnston to Jefferson Davis," 2 January 1864, *The Papers of Jefferson Davis*, 145; Emory Thomas, *The Confederate Nation, 1861–1865* (New York: Harper and Row, 1979) 260.

[11] *Official Records,* Series 4, Vol. 3, 129–31.

Just as Union policy toward slavery evolved in 1861 and 1862, Confederate military and civilian leaders struggled with themselves and each other in 1863 and early 1864 as they attempted to define what it meant to be a southerner. Confederate identity had always been fragile, but proposals that included the sacrifice of slavery to attain independence pushed Confederates into uncharted territory. The deliberate reevaluation of slavery began in the aftermath of the defeats at Vicksburg and Gettysburg. Like northern discussions of emancipation in the summer of 1862, this first southern dialogue mainly involved civilian and military leaders. Cleburne's bold proposal to arm the slaves startled many southern leaders who respected the general's battlefield accomplishments but could not understand his lack of attachment to slavery. Obviously, Cleburne's Irish background was a large reason behind his differing views, but one must wonder how many non-slaveholding soldiers shared the general's willingness to sacrifice all for victory. Although shelved for the moment, battlefield events would force a significant reassessment at the end of the 1864 military campaigns.

Jefferson Davis opened his final campaign with his annual address to Congress on 7 November 1864. As he reviewed the South's dire military situation, President Davis challenged the Confederate Congress and the people generally to reevaluate the importance of slavery. In contrast to most southern leaders, he acknowledged that slaves had two relationships to the state—one as a person and one as property. Like Cleburne and Hindman, Davis insisted that additional manpower must be found. The slave population, he insisted, must be employed to greater effect. To his mind, black southerners could be asked and expected to help win the war. Stopping short of calling for black troops immediately, the president strongly asserted that their use would be far preferable to defeat and reunion. If the South chose to create a greater role for the slave in the Confederacy, they would be choosing independence rather than slavery as their primary war aim. The Confederacy would thus strive to become a new nation shaped by the war rather than a continuation of the Old South. By selecting Davis's revolutionary ideas, southerners would be replacing the plantation South with new social, political, and economic foundations. The scope of Davis's arguments illustrates well the transcendent power of warfare to transform peoples and nations. Although military necessity forced this reconsideration, clearly Jefferson Davis had concluded that the war demanded that they sacrifice slavery and the worldview that supported it.

The battlefield for Davis's final campaign was not fought with Grant in Petersburg or with Congress in Richmond but, rather, in the heads and in the hearts of his countrymen. Local newspapers provide the clearest reflection of the mood of the southern people as they grappled with Davis's ideas and struggled to define a new role for the slave in the war effort. Southern newspapers reported developments that provoked and fueled the debate, attempted to lead public opinion with editorials, and served as sounding boards for public opinion as they printed numerous letters to the editors. Although public sentiment is usually elusive and was especially so during the nineteenth century, these newspapers provide overwhelming evidence that by the spring of 1865, many southerners strongly supported the arming of slaves. In addition, private letters and diaries shed considerable light upon the evolving opinions of many Virginians, Georgians, and Texans. An examination of these private papers, as well as of the news items, editorials, and letters to editors published in the newspapers, offers a clearer picture of the transformation of public opinion engendered by the debate to arm the slaves.

In the wake of Davis's speech, several standard arguments emerged across the South against slave-soldiers. First, the Confederate constitution explicitly prohibited the central government from interfering with slavery. Pro-slavery stalwarts claimed that if the government freed even menial laborers assigned with the army, it would be a violation of the constitution. Second, many considered the debate a confession of moral weakness. How could a society that decreed slavery the best possible world for the slave free any slaves without appearing hypocritical? Third, large planters claimed the slave contributed more through agriculture than he ever could on the battlefield. Fourth, some feared it would be a powerful stimulant to northern recruiting while demoralizing the southern troops. Fifth, many feared that by deserting the concept of slavery they would be giving up the cause so many had died to maintain.

In response the proponents of the measure stressed the idea that if the slaves did not fight for the Confederacy, they would end up fighting against it as Union soldiers. Further, they argued that common decency demanded that people who would risk their children for the cause must likewise surrender their property. Such a concept, they believed, would discredit the idea that the struggle had become a rich man's war and a poor man's fight, thus stemming the tide of southern deserters. Finally, they proclaimed that while slavery might have brought on the war, southern heroes had not died for the institution of slavery but for the noble cause of independence and self-government.[12] These arguments both for and against southern black troops resonated not only in besieged Virginia and Georgia but also in unthreatened Texas.

Unparalleled in its depth, the Confederate debate over arming slaves reached across region and class lines to produce a thorough discussion of the merits of slavery. Jefferson Davis and Judah Benjamin astutely recognized that they could not radically transform the social relations between white and black southerners without gaining the approval and, for it to be successful, the enthusiastic support of the vast majority of both slaveholding and non-slaveholding whites. Therefore, they contacted influential local leaders across the South and asked them to energize local discussions of arming the slaves. These administration efforts and startling Union victories in December brought forth a tremendous number of responses from common citizens attempting to find a path to victory. Soldiers, editors, and common citizens entered and fully participated in the discussions over the role of slaves in the war effort.

Three key events propelled the debate: President Jefferson Davis's annual address to Congress in November 1864, the defeats at Nashville and Savannah in December 1864, and the failure of the Hampton Roads peace conference in February 1865. These three events initiated three distinct phases in the debate about arming the slaves. With each phase, many men and women evolved and adapted opinions as events approached a crisis. Thoughtful citizens examined their goals for the war, weighed the value of slavery, and attempted to define what sacrifices they were willing to make to gain independence.

Davis's final campaign falls naturally into these three phases. The first phase encompasses the president's proposal and its initial reception. Starting with President Davis's modest request for 40,000 slaves to serve with the army as noncombatants, the Confederacy moved quickly in November and

---

[12] Confederate Constitution Article 1, Section 9, in Thomas, *The Confederate Nation*, 313; "Items of Interest," *Houston TriWeekly Telegraph*, 30 December 1864, 3.

December 1864 to a national debate about arming the slaves. The news reports, editorials, and letters to editors of the papers show the common men and women of the South cautiously entering the national dialogue. Although this phase encompasses the period of Sherman's march to the sea, the full effect of this bold campaign did not emerge until after the capture of Savannah. News items served mainly to establish the ideological parameters of the discussion and provided a backdrop for the formation of local opinion. Private letters, newspaper editorials, and letters to editors not only reflect differences of opinion within the states but also show many southerners reassessing their own views about slavery, independence, and the purpose of the war.

General William T. Sherman's long, destructive march through Georgia ended with the capitulation of Savannah on 21 December and sent doubt and despair racing through the southern countryside. On 16 December, Union General George Thomas destroyed the army of Tennessee at Nashville, leaving the Confederacy without a creditable field force in the West. News of the two great defeats struck many southern citizens hard and produced a most sobering Christmas season. In response to these reverses, Davis stepped up his efforts as the campaign entered a new, second phase provoked by the military necessity to meet the threat posed by Sherman and Thomas. The despair arising from the great Union victories added new and potent fuel to the fire of the slave-soldier debate. Almost immediately the public dialogue shifted from a theoretical question of whether the slaves should ever be armed to a very practical discussion of how necessary it was to arm them now. If southerners chose not to let slaves wear Confederate gray, where could the provost marshals and conscription officers find a sufficient number of white men to stem the tide? Editors and individual citizens accepted this shift to necessity as an obvious reflection of the deteriorating conditions around them.

In January and early February 1865 southerners weighed the value of slavery and attempted to determine what sacrifices they must make to achieve victory. News reports in Central and Southwestern Georgia underscored the gravity of the situation, but no immediate Union threat emerged. Similarly, no new threats emerged in Texas. In contrast, General Ulysses S. Grant's determined stance outside Petersburg and Sherman's march through South Carolina contributed significantly to a growing feeling in Virginia and in Eastern Georgia that it had now become necessary to arm the slaves. In many communities, editors surrendered the opinion-shaping initiative to local citizens who were writing to the papers to suggest the bold ideas that could meet the emergency. In the letters to editors, one can clearly see the peculiar institution of slavery beginning to slip from its preeminent position in the southern mind. During this second phase of the campaign, the importance of southern independence to the individual men and women of Virginia, Georgia, and Texas became apparent.

The final phase of Davis's campaign to arm black troops and thus change the South's war aims opened with the return of the unsuccessful Confederate peace commissioners from Hampton Roads. The administration's efforts to force resolution of the issue began in earnest on 9 February with Secretary of State Judah P. Benjamin's speech to Congress, in which he demanded passage of the bill to arm the slaves. With the armies desperately in need of men, Benjamin declared that the Confederacy must employ every means available to prevent defeat. From Benjamin's speech to final passage of the act to arm the slaves on 13 March, the debate raged fiercely as Congress and the people attempted to determine the sacrifices necessary to preserve the southern way of life.

Southerners in all sections of the Confederacy—Upper South, Deep South, and Trans-Mississippi West—seriously considered the introduction of black men into the army. Virginia, Georgia, and Texas provide an interesting and informative comparison because each area experienced the war differently. The long debate about arming the slaves forced the common men and women of the Confederate South to examine the very depths of their souls. Despite the desperate situation, these southerners explored the proposal to arm the slaves and its long-term implications fully. As the debate unfolded, individual men and women struggled with each other and within themselves to decide what it meant to be a southerner. In this final crisis of the Civil War, the vast majority of Virginians, Georgians, and even some Texans discovered that slavery could be sacrificed much more easily than southern independence.

Phase I

Dwindling Men to the Fall of Savannah

2

An Astonishing Notion

In the fall of 1864 the bitter wind of military defeat whipped through the Confederacy and fanned an open, often-heated debate concerning the introduction of slaves into the Confederate army. As long as the gray lines had held firm, no one had to choose between slavery and independence. Stunning Union victories and thinning army ranks in the fall of 1864 forced southerners to decide what they held most dear. The resulting debate about arming the slaves caused the common citizens of the South to ask again why they were fighting. Was slavery truly the "cornerstone" of the southern way of life? From November 1864 to March 1865, the Confederacy and its citizens conducted an open, thorough debate to define the role of the slave in the Confederate war effort. In the process, they weighed the value of slavery and defined the sacrifices they would make to achieve independence. During this period of national soul-searching, white southerners quickly turned from a simple debate of arming their slaves to a thorough discussion of emancipation.

The coordinated campaigns of Grant in Virginia and William T. Sherman in Georgia allowed little time for reflection as the northern generals sorely pressed the southern armies. Yet, in early September, after the fall of Atlanta and the stabilization of the lines at Petersburg, Confederate civilian and military leaders began a search for new manpower sources for the armies. Governor Henry Allen of Louisiana first raised the issue in the fall of 1864. On 26 September Allen wrote to Davis and proclaimed that the situation demanded radical steps: "The time has come for us to put into the army every able-bodied negro man as a soldier. This should be done immediately." The slave, Allen contended, could not avoid service: "He must play an important part in the war. He caused the fight, and he will have his portion of the burden to bear." The governor conceded that the new recruits would demand their freedom in return, but he concluded that black Confederates would make good troops: "We have learned from dear-bought experience that negroes can be taught to fight. … They will make much better soldiers with us than against us and swell the now depleted ranks of our armies." Cut off from the remainder of the Confederacy and driven from his capital, the Louisiana governor could not ignore the darkening military situation. Black Union troops garrisoned New Orleans and Baton Rouge and had performed well during the battle at Port Hudson and during the Red River campaign. Allen saw little hope to reverse the new nation's military fortunes without following the Union's lead by freeing and enlisting a significant portion of the slave population. Unintended for publication, Allen's frank assessment of the situation stirred many when the Union army captured and published his bold epistle in support of arming the slaves. After Allen's letter appeared in northern newspapers in late September, southerners began to again discuss arming slaves. The captured letter demonstrated that true patriots could advocate radical measures in support of the war without running serious risk of being considered traitors.[1]

Confederate leaders appear to have been thinking along the same lines. On 29 September, Ordinance Chief Josiah Gorgas assessed the military situation favorably, in his diary, with one exception: "We are better off now than we were two years ago. … The only point against us is the Scarcity of men to fill up our armies. This must be met by placing negroes in ranks and giving them their freedom." Three days later, Gorgas noted Philip Sheridan's recent victories in the Shenandoah Valley and the inability of the southern armies to replace their losses: "Our loss will probably reach one-half that [of the Union] say 10 or 12 hundred, but even this disparity will ultimately ruin us. … There is no help I fear except to use negroes." Slavery could be sacrificed, Gorgas concluded, if it could secure southern independence. The first step, he suggested had already been taken: "The opening wedge to this use of Slaves is found in [the] law of last Congress conscribing 20,000 for cooks, teamsters &c. The next thing will be to put them in as Soldiers giving them their freedom." On 6 October Gorgas again confided his ideas for modifying slavery to his diary. Confederate troops scheduled to serve for the duration of the war, he reported, had begun "to look upon themselves as doomed men." Using black troops, Gorgas speculated, would

[1] *Official Records*, Series 1, Vol. 41, Part 3, 774.

allow the government to set a maximum period of combat service and would permit skilled white workers to return to their professions rather than remaining in the trenches, thus relieving some pressure on the white male population. Hardened by years of trying to produce arms and ammunition in a country with a tiny industrial base, Gorgas evaluated the southern situation and the dire alternatives realistically and concluded that the slave's role in the war must be significantly expanded for the Confederacy to continue the fight.[2]

As Gorgas contemplated steps the government should take, the *Richmond Enquirer* opened the public discussion of arming slaves in an editorial that appeared on 6 October 1864. Nathaniel Tyler, the editor of the *Enquirer*, began the piece by calling for the prompt enforcement of the "law of Congress for the employment of negroes in the army as teamsters &c." Toward the bottom of the column, Tyler dramatically shifted his focus concerning the military use of slaves from a discussion held between government officials and military officers to a debate held in the wider public arena: "The question of making soldiers of negroes, of regularly enlisting them and fighting them for their safety as well as our own, must have presented itself to every reflecting mind." If it had, most reflecting minds had chosen to express themselves only in private venues. Tyler did not say that black troops must be enlisted immediately, but he clearly argued that such a step would not be the worst possible course: "Whenever the subjugation of Virginia or the employment of her slaves as soldiers are alternative propositions, then certainly we are for making them soldiers, and giving freedom to those negroes who escape the casualties of battle." The *Enquirer* concluded the editorial with a call for the purchase, enlistment, and manumission of 250,000 black troops and asserted that "neither negroes nor slavery will be permitted to stand in the way of the success of our cause." Although discussions of arming the slaves continued to flourish in private circles, this bold *Richmond Enquirer* editorial allowed the common citizens of the South for the first time to participate in the national debate over the importance of slavery.[3]

---

[2] Josiah Gorgas, *The Journals of Josiah Gorgas 1857–1878,* ed. Sarah W. Wiggins (Tuscaloosa: University of Alabama Press, 1995) 134–36.

[3] "The general order…," *Richmond Enquirer*, 6 October 1864, 2.

In the first year of the war, many political observers had considered the *Enquirer* the voice of the Davis administration. This relationship dissolved after Nathaniel Tyler returned from the army to resume his duties as editor. In particular, the *Enquirer* angered Davis as it vilified the conduct of Secretary of State Judah Benjamin in 1863. Why, then, did the *Enquirer* champion a measure that many identified with Davis and Benjamin? The paper itself claimed that patriotism and common sense demanded the sacrifice of slavery. Even if a politician had guided the formation of the 6 October editorial, the paper adopted the policy as its own and printed a second strong endorsement of slave-soldiers on 18 October. The issues at stake, the *Enquirer* proclaimed, are more exalted than the mere preservation of slavery: "The liberty and freedom of ourselves and of our children, the nationality of our country, the right of enjoying any kind of property...are involved in this struggle." Two weeks later, letters from both an opponent and a proponent of black troops appeared in the *Enquirer*. One praised the paper's stance while the other questioned the sincerity of the editor's ideas: "Can it be possible that a Southern man...would recommend a law which at one blow levels all distinctions, deprives the master of a right to his property, and elevates the negro to an equality with the white man?" Both letter writers conceded that by enduring the same hardships and facing the same trials, the relationship between southern blacks and southern whites would be changed forever. Tyler, by his forceful editorials at the *Enquirer*, meant to force the South to face the contradictions inherent in the southern worldview. The cracks in southern society had been papered over for much of the previous century, but now as the Confederacy faced utter defeat, the *Enquirer* begged southerners to rethink their racial values as they attempted to determine the relative importance of slavery and independence.[4]

In the following weeks several Virginia newspapers responded to the *Enquirer*'s call for a wider discussion of the slave's role. On 8 October, the *Lynchburg Virginian* reprinted the *Enquirer* editorial and added a strong piece in support of black troops: "Negroes fighting for the soil upon which

[4] J. Cutler Andrews, *The South Reports the Civil War* (Pittsburgh: University of Pittsburgh Press, 1970) 27; "The proposition to extend...," *Richmond Enquirer*, 18 October 1864, 2; "A Soldier" and "South," "Negro Conscription," *Richmond Enquirer*, 4 November 1864, 2.

they were raised; for the homes of those with whom they have grown up...could surely be made as efficient as the negro soldiers of the invader. And they could as well be spared to feed the insatiate appetite of war."

Editor Charles Button of the *Virginian* urged Congress to take up the matter and thus allow the Confederate army to continue the struggle on nearly equal terms: "We believe that an army of two hundred thousand able-bodied slaves of the better class, could be organized and induced to fight for their freedom on the Southern side of this question." Button, an old Whig, welcomed the discussion of black troops and called on the press to direct popular attention to the topic. Across town, the *Lynchburg Republican* on 2 November pronounced itself "completely appalled [and] dumfounded" by the discussion of arming blacks in Richmond and in its own backyard. "The South," the *Republican* trumpeted, "went to war to defeat the designs of the abolitionists, and behold! in the midst of the war, we turn abolitionists ourselves!" The Democratic editor asserted that arming slaves meant not only the end of slavery but also the destruction of the South's racial caste system. Back in the capital, the *Richmond Whig*, like many of its peers, considered the *Enquirer*'s position ill-advised and ignored the issue editorially. Even so, the *Whig* followed the course of the slavery discussions and published a letter from Mayor John Monroe of New Orleans that stressed the merits of slave-soldiers. Noting the use of black soldiers in the British West Indian regiments and the success of the United States with black troops, Monroe concluded that these examples ought to "convince the most bitterly prejudiced that, under sufficient incitement...the negro will fight as well, at least, as the Yankee." As with all who seriously considered arming slaves, Monroe contended that freedom alone could gain the new recruits' fidelity. These provocative opinions expressed in Lynchburg and Richmond prepared Virginians to enter the larger debate that began in November.[5]

The public debate that had begun in Richmond inspired others to broach the issue privately. On 17 October, the governors of Virginia, North Carolina, South Carolina, Georgia, Alabama, and Mississippi met in Augusta, Georgia, and discussed a number of measures to increase the size of

[5] Charles Button, "Lead Editorial," *Lynchburg Virginian*, 8 October 1864, 1; "Shall We Arm the Negroes?", *Lynchburg Republican*, rep. in *Richmond Sentinel*, 2 November 1864, 1; John Monroe, "A Possibility of the Future," *Richmond Whig*, 5 October 1864, 1.

the armies. Unity of effort was a major theme, with even Governor Joseph E. Brown of Georgia and Governor Zebulon Vance of North Carolina agreeing to push legislation to facilitate the employment of one state's militia in defense of another state. With Governor William Smith of Virginia in the chair, the governors agreed to a series of resolutions to be relayed to the president and the Confederate Congress. Decrying military inefficiency, the governors expressed considerable displeasure with the provost marshal system that challenged civilian liberties and made many southern cities appear like armed camps: "We respectfully and earnestly request that the Confederate authorities will send to the field every able-bodied man…whose place can be filled by either disabled officers and soldiers, senior reserves, or negroes." This step, Brown and Vance hoped, would send more men to the front as it decreased the Confederate presence in their cities. The placement of Confederate troops in communities across the South to enforce the draft and to constantly check for deserters caused many southerners to feel that the central government was expending too many military resources trying to enforce unpopular laws instead of fighting the Union army. The threat to civil liberties appeared quite real to many, though not as severe as Governors Brown and Vance sometimes suggested. While a few white men might thus be made available for combat service, Governor Smith led his less-willing peers to consider more practical steps. Having very different experiences of the war, the six governors agreed to a vaguely worded statement concerning the slave's role in the war effort:

> The course of the enemy in appropriating our slaves who happen to fall into their hands to purposes of war seems to justify a change of policy on our part, and whilst owners of slaves under the circumstances should freely yield them to their country, we recommend to our authorities, under proper regulations, to appropriate such part of them to the public service as may be required.

These six Confederate leaders had debated new roles for the black population but had not reached a clear consensus on the steps to be taken. As the debate over arming slaves mounted, each of the governors present in Augusta provided a differing account of the "change of policy" contemplated. Under intense pressure from slave owners in their home states, Governors Charles Clark of Mississippi and Thomas Watts of Alabama came to support the version of Vance and Brown that claimed the governors had agreed to increasing the number of black laborers with the army but never meant to suggest black troops or emancipation. Smith of Virginia resolutely contended that the governors had considered placing rifles in the hands of slaves. Despite its avowed purpose of unity, the governors' conference sparked controversy among the state executives and suggested to the citizens of the South that the idea of black Confederate troops—though controversial—now merited the attention of key political figures. No one could still claim that the idea remained unthinkable.[6]

As Congress assembled in Richmond, the representatives began to consult with government officials and each other about ways to meet the ever-larger Union armies. On 24 October, Congressman William P. Miles of South Carolina wrote Robert E. Lee to canvas his views on arming slaves. As chairman of the Military Committee of the House, Miles would control the course of legislation on black troops, but in his letter the congressman conceded that Lee's opinion on the topic would play a crucial role in congressional deliberations. Lee responded within a week and suggested that slaves must be used, unsettling Miles, who had hoped that the general would help to stifle the discussion of slave-soldiers. Admitting that he had significant reservations about the impact of black troops on the nation's "political and social system," Miles asked several additional questions to sound the depth of Lee's commitment to the idea: "In a purely military point of view, can the negro in our armies effectually aid us in our struggle? And has the time arrived when our arms-bearing white population can no longer resist the tide of invasion?" Finally, Miles asked Lee how far the South must go to stave off defeat: "Suppose Congress were to authorize the organization of large bodies of sappers & miners, composed of negroes, say fifty or sixty thousand in all, and see how it will work. ... Would not this suffice for the next campaign?" With Miles arriving for the opening of Congress, Lee probably addressed these additional questions in person. No written reply ever arrived. Interestingly, Lee's adjutant, Walter H. Taylor, had written his fiancée in late September and expressed significant reservations about arming black troops. While Lee had endorsed the concept of black men in gray to Miles, many who surrounded the commander were not yet convinced:

---

[6] *Official Records*, Series 4, Vol. 3, 735–36; "The Governors in Council," *Richmond Whig*, 24 October 1864, 1.

"We also propose to make the negroes serviceable & some advocate placing them in the ranks—making soldiers of them—but for this I am not yet quite ready," Taylor opined. Even among those who felt the Union threat most keenly, the formation of black units remained a controversial decision.[7]

The concept of arming slaves clearly made Miles uncomfortable. He had hoped to find an ally in the Confederate hero, but instead he had found someone who, through his advocacy of this measure, could bring the issue to center stage and probably force its passage. Subsequently, Miles did not reveal what he had learned of Lee's views but instead attempted to slow the slave-soldier bill in committee. Like George Washington in the Revolution, Lee revered the principle of the civilian control of the military and studiously avoided making public statements of a political nature. Yet, the correspondence with Miles demonstrates that Lee had formed a strong commitment to arming slaves even prior to Davis's public speculations on the subject. The general no doubt discussed the issue with the president, but Lee did not publicly express his support for black troops until the final stages of the debate when his influence was desperately needed to shift votes in Congress.

In the period from the fall of Atlanta on 2 September to Davis's message to Congress on 7 November, southern leaders reopened the arguments concerning arming the slaves. The grinding campaigns of Grant and Sherman in the summer of 1864 significantly reduced the Southern armies and caused many to rethink their opposition to radical measures. Governor Allen of Louisiana and Josiah Gorgas showed the growing convictions of men who dealt with the deficiencies of the Confederacy on a daily basis. With the vast majority of his state occupied, Allen could see no alternative to black soldiers. Likewise, Gorgas recognized the need for more men on the front, but also understood that if he sent additional skilled white men from the ordinance factories, the armies would soon find that the men they had did not have anything to fight with. The bold words of the *Enquirer* rang out like a cry in the night, resonating not only in the capital but also across the South. As the items in the Lynchburg papers showed, relatively obscure people held strong views for and against arming slaves. Somewhat surprisingly, the variance of opinions expressed by the Lynchburg editors and the letter writers to

---

[7] William Porcher to Robert E. Lee, 24 October 1864 and 3 November 1864, quoted in Durden, *The Gray and the Black*, 135–37.

the *Richmond Enquirer* mirrored the diversity of opinion in official circles. In this period of ferment, realistic leaders began to voice their fears about the state of the nation and ventured comments about ways to modify the slave's role in the war effort. Confronting an increasingly bleak military situation, the president monitored the shifting opinions of his countrymen as he sought to discover a means to reverse the course of the war.

Drawing upon the ideas of Patrick Cleburne, Henry Allen, and others who had spurred the Confederacy to reevaluate the role of slaves in the war effort, Jefferson Davis opened a national debate over arming the slaves with his annual address to Congress on 7 November 1864. While proposing legislation on many subjects, Davis requested "the enrollment of 40,000 negroes to be employed as pioneer and engineer laborers." This proposal would have drawn little comment if Davis had stopped there, but the president claimed that although a slave was property, he or she also bore an obligation to the state as a person. Arguing that while employed by the army the slave's role as a person took precedence over his status as property, Davis contended that the government must purchase the slaves so serving and free them at the end of their service: "The policy of engaging to liberate the negro on his discharge, after service faithfully rendered seems to me preferable to that of granting immediate manumission, or that of retaining him in servitude." This new proposal far exceeded the previous practice of impressing slaves for limited periods.[8]

Even as the president advocated a "radical modification" of the legal standing of the slave, Davis stopped short of recommending the immediate enlistment of black southerners: "Until our white population shall prove insufficient for the armies we require and can afford to keep in the field, to employ as a soldier the negro...would scarcely be deemed wise or advantageous." If disaster struck, the president suggested that the 40,000 laborers with the army would be able to step quickly into the breach. Yet, Davis speculated that even this recourse might not be enough: "Should the alternative ever be presented of subjugation or of the employment of the slave as a soldier, there seems no reason to doubt what should then be our decision." The social and political implications of the step, Davis contended, caused him to hesitate: "If the subject involved no other consideration than the

[8] *Official Records*, Series 3, Vol. 4, 797–99.

mere right of property, the sacrifices heretofore made by our people have been such as to permit no doubt of their readiness to surrender every possession in order to secure their independence." The stability of republican institutions and white equality, the president believed, hung in the balance. Davis's proposal to free the slaves working for the army, along with his admission that arming all the slaves might eventually become necessary, began an unprecedented Confederate national debate on slavery. President Davis's final campaign would be an all-out political effort to save the Confederate nation through black military assistance.[9]

In early November, Secretary of War James Seddon also addressed the issue of arming slaves. In his annual report detailing the activities of the department, Seddon acknowledged the burgeoning public debate and argued that the idea had considerable merit: "Under the leadership of those whites to whom they have been habituated and in whom they have confidence, they would exhibit more steadfastness and courage than they will ever attain as soldiers of the enemy." Further, Seddon argued that the "assurance of emancipation" would provide enough incentive to fill the ranks with black men eager to fight for their southern homes. Despite this bold assertion of black loyalty, Seddon, unlike Davis, displayed little enthusiasm for arming the slaves: "My own judgment does not yet either perceive the necessity or approve the policy of employing slaves in the higher duties of soldiers. ... It will not do, in my opinion, to risk our liberties and safety on the negro, while the white man may be called to the sacred duty of defense." In these two statements of administration policy, both authors professed a firm belief that slaves would eagerly fight for the South in return for emancipation. Likewise, both Davis and Seddon suggested that white southerners would willingly sacrifice slavery for independence. Although both men were large slaveholders, Davis had come to identify himself with the Confederacy. If the new nation failed to achieve her independence, Davis had failed; therefore, the president was prepared to sacrifice everything for the cause. On the other hand, Seddon had been a loyal, hardworking Cabinet member, but he still considered himself a Virginian and a planter above all else. There were clear boundaries beyond which the secretary was not prepared to go. Davis and Seddon said the same basic things with different emphases and for dif-

[9] Ibid.

ferent purposes. Seddon hoped to inspire white enlistments by suggesting that black soldiers might eventually become necessary. In contrast, Davis raised the issue of freeing 40,000 black laborers with the army in order to spark discussion of the steps necessary to secure black loyalty to the southern cause. As Gorgas had confided to his diary, the bills to employ black laborers with the army provided the perfect opening wedge for both black Confederate soldiers and emancipation.[10]

In Richmond, the Union and Confederate artillery pieces could be heard as they hurled death at one another day after day. After five months of trench warfare, few southerners could hope that Grant would simply take his army and go home, as George McClellan had done in 1862. As the Union lines extended further south of Petersburg, daily the Confederate position became more precarious. All knew that once the last rail link with the Deep South was severed, the army must evacuate its positions and Richmond would fall into the hands of the enemy. Yet, many Virginians expressed an almost mystical faith in the ability of Robert E. Lee and the Army of Northern Virginia to salvage victory. They had always been outnumbered; the situation had always appeared desperate just before Lee saved the day. Unfortunately for the faithful, the Confederate army was a mere shadow of its former self, having lost key commanders and many veteran troops in the year since Gettysburg. Manpower shortfalls and a relentless foe restricted the Confederate armies to limited attacks. Lee could no longer hope to seize the initiative by a bold maneuver and turn the tables on his opponents, as he had done so often before. He simply lacked the men to make such daring plans possible. Although only partially understood by civilian leaders and the majority of Virginians, the stark reality of southern military weakness and northern military might shaped the debate over arming the slaves in Virginia.

The *Richmond Enquirer*, which had first raised the issue of arming the slaves, welcomed the president's message and his bold speculations. On 11 November the *Enquirer* affirmed that "dire necessity" and not preference justified the enlistment of black troops. Many outside observers, Nathaniel Tyler contended, had been deceived by northern propaganda and misunder-

---

[10] *Official Records*, Series 3, Vol. 4, 761–62; G.F.J. O'Brien, "James A. Seddon: Statesman of the Old South" (Ph.D. diss., University of Maryland, 1963) 475–77.

stood the purpose of the war: "The war has been slanderously called the slaveholders' war; undertaken for slavery, and maintained and supported solely for the perpetuation of negro slavery." Southerners, the *Enquirer* argued, knew that "negro slavery was the mere occasion and is not the object or end of this war." The sacrifice of slavery, the editor continued, would eloquently state this fact to the world. As he trumpeted the moral impact of the step, Tyler suggested that faithful slaves might be freed without renouncing slavery as a whole: "Cannot fidelity to the national cause, attested by endurance of hardship, by gallantry in action, and exposure to death, be rewarded with freedom without any compromise to the relation in which those are still held who have given no assurance of such fidelity?" Finally, the *Enquirer* ridiculed those who hinged their support for the measure on compensation to the owners: "We are wholly opposed to compensation for the negro. What! conscript a son, a husband, and a father, and pay for the slave!! The negro pays for himself when he fights for his former master." Clearly, even the most vocal proponent of black troops shied away from calling for full emancipation in November. Tyler enjoyed deriding greedy slave owners, but he still feared that many Virginians might not yet be ready for radical change. As with its opening remarks in October, the *Richmond Enquirer* continued to lead the proponents of black troops in Virginia.[11]

With the exception of the *Enquirer*, the Richmond papers had attempted to ignore the growing discussion until the publication of Davis's message to Congress. Each of the Richmond dailies printed the address in full and provided a wide variety of editorial comments. The *Richmond Sentinel*, considered by many as favorable to the administration, had called for reflection but no immediate action in an editorial just prior to the delivery of Davis's message: "If it shall ever be wise to act upon the policy, the necessity which alone could justify it, will have brought the popular mind to the appropriate conviction." Editor Richard M. Smith advised caution until the military situation demanded black troops, fearing that "mischief" would result from a premature canvas of the issue. In the paper's comments to accompany the address, the *Sentinel* supported the concept of arming slaves but continued to downplay the need for a practical effort to put it in motion: "The employment of slaves is a resource that we should not disown or forget,

[11] "The employment of slaves…," *Richmond Enquirer*, 11 November 1864, 2.

and which should be employed if necessity shall demand, and thus justify. But there is confessedly no such necessity now." Yet, after watching the measure to place 40,000 laborers with the army progress slowly through Congress, on 24 November the *Sentinel* savagely attacked those who begrudged Davis's promise of freedom to the faithful laborer: "We are told by some horrified individual that this is 'giving up the cause.' What cause? We thought that independence was, just now, the great question." Comparing the Confederacy to a ship chased by pirates, Smith asserted that by failing to discharge nonessential cargo—slavery—over the side, the ship of state risked capture by its enemies. Like the sea captain, Smith felt the Confederacy must sacrifice all to maintain independence: "If, to save our liberties, we find it necessary to emancipate, we shall have, therefore, lost nothing, while we shall have gained the supreme issue—our independence." Having thus proclaimed its understanding of the purpose of the war, the *Sentinel* chided those who resorted to constitutional defenses of slavery: "We look upon the whole subject of the employment of slaves...as a practical question for the judgment of military men rather than a theme for the closet speculations of scholars and theorists." Reflecting the administration's cautious moves toward arming slaves, the *Sentinel* had not taken the lead in early November, but the shallow arguments of many opponents forced the paper to take a firm stand for arming slaves in late November.[12]

On the other side of the issue, the *Richmond Whig* immediately chastised the president for his proposal to free the 40,000 noncombatant laborers. While approving the expansion of the size of the slave labor force with the army, the *Whig* declared, "We do not see that the purchase of the negroes by the Government, or the promise of their liberation, is at all necessary to the plan." Editor James McDonald noted two flawed assumptions in Davis's arguments: "The first is that the condition of freedom is so much better for the slave than that of servitude, that it may be bestowed on him as a reward. ... The second is that the Confederate Government has the right to acquire possession of slaves...and then emancipate them, without the consent of the States." While the *Sentinel* had compared freedom for the

[12] "The question of availing ourselves...," *Richmond Sentinel*, 2 November 1864, 2; "The President's Message," *Richmond Sentinel*, 8 November 1864, 2; "The Congress and the People...," *Richmond Sentinel*, 24 November 1864, 2.

black troops to the award of a medal, which made a soldier happy but no better off, the *Whig* contended that emancipation would permanently harm the black veterans: "We hold it to be an act of cruelty to deprive the slave of the care and guardianship of a master. If the slave must fight, he should fight for the blessings he enjoys as a slave, and not for the miseries that would attend him if freed." Clinging to the tenets of the traditional pro-slavery ideology, the *Whig* feared that the offer of freedom would force the surrender of the constitutional protections of slavery as well as require the painful admission of racial equality. Forty thousand laborers could not justify the step in McDonald's eyes. Beyond these editorials, the *Whig* selected its news items to reinforce its convictions against arming slaves. For instance, on 12 November the *Whig* chose to print the full remarks to Congress of Henry Chambers of Mississippi, who strongly assailed Davis's ideas. In contrast, the Congressional propositions of Williams Wickam of Virginia and Charles Villeré of Louisiana in support of black troops received only passing notice from McDonald. Even as the editor conceded that emancipation was preferable to subjugation, the *Richmond Whig* struggled mightily to prevent consideration of the president's radical notions.[13]

Davis's strongest critic, the *Richmond Examiner*, also seriously questioned the president's message. On 8 November the *Examiner* declared that Lincoln had enlisted black troops as a political rather than a military measure. After examining the French and Union armies' experiences with black soldiers, John Daniel argued that "the negro soldier costs far more than he is worth." Even if the slave proved more effective under southern commanders, the *Examiner* contended that the step would undermine the foundations of southern society: "If a negro is fit to be a soldier he is not fit to be a slave, and if any large portion of the race is fit for free labour…then the whole race is fit for it." The highest cost of arming and freeing the slaves, the editor believed, would be the admission that slavery was not the best condition for the black race, thus conceding that the institution was the moral evil that its opponents had long argued. Such an admission, he concluded, would de-

---

[13] "The Message," *Richmond Whig*, 8 November 1864, 1; "The President's Message," *Richmond Whig,* 9 November 1864, 1; "Speech of Hon. H.C. Chambers," *Richmond Whig,* 12 November 1864, 1; "House of Representatives," *Richmond Whig,* 12 November 1864, 2; Andrews, *The South Reports the Civil War,* 28.

moralize the people at home and open the South to ridicule from abroad. In the *Examiner*'s view, Davis's proposal to free the laborers for faithful service, as well as his suggestions that arming all the slaves might be necessary, must ultimately lead to "universal abolition" and new social relationships built upon equality of the races. On 16 November the *Examiner* again expressed surprise at Davis's ideas: "There was one branch of Northern policy which might have reasonably been regarded as wholly beyond the possibility of Southern imitation, namely, the employment of negro troops in our armies." Despite these powerful words against Davis's ideas, on 21 November Daniel confessed that the bill to provide the noncombatant laborers merited serious consideration: "A corps of forty thousand athletick [sic] negroes to dig the trench, drive the wagon, and cook the dinner of Lee's army, would immensely increase its efficiency." Ever cynical, Daniel and the *Examiner* strongly contested the recommendations of Davis along both theoretical and practical lines.[14]

Public officials also jumped into the debate that had arisen from Davis's bold speculations. On 8 November Henry Foote of Tennessee introduced a series of resolutions in the House of Representatives generally supporting Davis's comments, but Foote clearly feared the charge of hypocrisy and stressed the conservative nature of the resolutions: "A broad moral distinction exists between the use of slaves as soldiers in the defense of their homes and the incitement of the same persons [to insurrection] against their masters. The one is justifiable, if necessary, and the other is iniquitous." In response to Davis's ideas, William Swann of Tennessee, Charles Villeré of Louisiana, and Gustavus Henry of Tennessee all sponsored legislative actions concerning slave-soldiers. Although most of these resolutions sought to limit the use of slaves, their words appeared in the Richmond papers and were relayed throughout the Confederacy. Similarly, the remarks of Governor William Smith of Virginia flashed across the telegraph wires of the South announcing his strong endorsement of black Confederate troops. Smith resolutely stated that Virginians had few choices remaining: "Even if the result were to emancipate our slaves, there is not a man that would not

---

[14] "The writer of the message...," *Richmond Examiner*, 8 November 1864, 1; "One of the most curious...," *Richmond Examiner*, 16 November 1864, 1; "Publick opinion is decided...," *Richmond Examiner*, 21 November 1864, 1.

cheerfully put the negro into the Army rather than become a slave himself to our hated and vindictive foe." Contending that necessity forced the South to use all means available, Smith boldly proclaimed that the time had come to choose between independence and slavery: "Has the time arrived when this issue is…liberty and independence, or subjugation[?] …A man must be blind to current events; to the gigantic proportions of the war…who does not see that the issue above referred to is presented now." Acknowledging that many patriotic southerners still had reservations about arming their slaves, the Virginia governor called on his constituents to err by giving the army too much to fight with instead of too little: "I hold it to be clearly the duty of every citizen, however much he may doubt the wisdom and necessity of the policy, to cooperate in strengthening by every means our armies." Smith understood that he was treading on shaky political ground as he advocated the enlistment of slaves, but he could see the Confederate forces crumbling in the Shenandoah Valley and in the trenches around Petersburg and knew that half-measures would not meet the crisis.[15]

The dynamic debate that had developed in Richmond over arming the slaves sparked a thorough discussion of the issues in the Roanoke Valley of southwestern Virginia. Davis's message to Congress graced the pages of the *Lynchburg Virginian* in early November as the sound of Union General Philip Sheridan's cavalry echoed in the ears of the citizens of Southwestern Virginia. Although the blue cavalrymen had won a smashing victory against Jubal Early's Confederates at Cedar Creek on 19 October, active operations continued throughout November and December. The *Virginian* printed numerous accounts of barns burned, mills destroyed, and provisions lost. Such wanton destruction of property and the accompanying loss of life, the paper concluded, furnished "one of the foulest and blackest pages in human history." Culling items from Louisiana, Alabama, and New York papers, the

---

[15] *Journal of the Congress of the Confederate States of America, 1861–1865,* Vol. 7 (Washington: Government Printing Office, 1905) 260–65; "Confederate States Congress," *Richmond Whig*, 8 November 1864, 1; "Confederate States Congress," *Richmond Whig*, 11 November 1864, 1; "What Is to Be Done with Us?" *Richmond Whig*, 15 November 1864, 1; *Official Records*, Series 3, Vol. 4, 915–16.

Virginian presented a wide variety of views on how slaves should be used but favored pieces that accepted the need for some change.[16]

While differing with a column from the *Richmond Enquirer* that called for the immediate enlistment of 250,000 black troops, the Lynchburg paper praised the services of black units in the Revolution and suggested that the South had few viable options remaining: "We must, if this war continues, sacrifice the last able-bodied white man left and consent to have our negroes taken by force...or we must defeat the enemy at his own game, and make the negro fight for us and against the hated foe." Further, the *Virginian* questioned the patriotism of papers, like the *Raleigh Standard*, that rejected any expanded use of slaves in the army. The most influential news item to appear in Lynchburg during this opening phase of the debate came from Richmond. In his message to the Virginia House of Delegates, Governor William Smith affirmed, "Standing before God and my country, I do not hesitate to say that I would arm such portion of our able-bodied slave population as may be necessary and put them in the field, so as to have them ready for the spring campaign."[17] Clearly the ideas expressed by prominent politicians as well as the opinions of the capital's newspapers set the parameters for the local debate concerning arming the slaves.

From his editorial desk in Lynchburg, Charles Button eagerly joined the discussion of slave-soldiers. In response to Davis's message, Button stated that he had always seen black soldiers as a logical "dernier resort" that would provide freedom to some "who should vindicate their title to it by deeds of valor." Conceding that the situation might not yet demand the step, the Lynchburg editor argued that when the necessity was clearly established, slaves must be used: "We should be madmen not to avail ourselves of every means in our power to wage war against the unnatural foe who first seduced and then armed our domestics against us." On 6 December Button again warmed to the subject. Noting Sherman's collection of able-bodied slaves in Georgia, Button suggested that southerners might prefer to choose the best

[16] "The Battles of Cedar Creek," *Lynchburg Virginian*, 27 October 1864, 1; "Sheridan's Torch Everywhere Visible," *Lynchburg Virginian*, 20 October 1864, 2; "The Valley," *Lynchburg Virginian*, 28 November 1864, 1.

[17] "Employment of Negroes in Our Armies," *Lynchburg Virginian*, 20 October 1864, 1; "The Raleigh Standard...," *Lynchburg Virginian*, 25 October 1864, 1; "The Governor's Message," *Lynchburg Virginian*, 12 December 1864, 1.

slaves to enter the military rather than let the Union troops make the first selections: "Would we have them to earn their freedom in periling their lives to secure our liberties; or let them join the serried host of the enemy to assist in enslaving free white men?" Two weeks later, Button cited Lincoln's assertion that the North could not have continued the struggle without 200,000 black troops and questioned the intelligence of the Confederate policies that sacrificed "our sons rather than our slaves." After relating the success that the biblical patriarch Abraham had achieved with his armed slaves, the Lynchburg editor concluded, "believing that necessity is upon us, we should not hesitate to avail ourselves of this or any other means to affect our independence."[18] The thundering hooves of the Yankee horsemen no doubt added considerable emphasis to the news items and editorials appearing in Lynchburg.

In the Shenandoah Valley, the hoofbeats sounded much louder. Staunton, located on the junction of the railroad and Valley Pike, had grown significantly during the war as government shops and factories sprang up. Twenty miles to the north, Harrisonburg had suffered greater devastation in the early years of the war as both Union and Confederate armies had visited too often. Although impacted differently, both communities shared many wartime experiences. Harrisonburg and Staunton found themselves in the hands of David Hunter's army in June and both met Philip Sheridan's Union columns in September and October. These encounters provided a very real portrait of potential defeat and forced the citizens of Harrisonburg and Staunton cautiously to consider revolutionary measures to attain victory.

In the fall of 1864, the *Staunton Vindicator* focused squarely upon the rapidly deteriorating Confederate position in the region. On 28 October, the paper carried a detailed account of the Battle of Cedar Creek and General Early's address to his stricken army. Less than a month later, the loss from Sheridan's actions in neighboring Rockingham County was estimated at over $25,000,000, including the destruction of 450 barns and over 10,000 animals. Despite these grim tidings, the *Vindicator* found space to reprint an editorial from John Forsyth's *Mobile Register* calling for the consideration of

[18] Charles Button, "Negro Soldiers," *Lynchburg Virginian*, 11 November 1864, 1; Charles Button, "Sherman is laying…," *Lynchburg Virginian*, 6 December 1864, 1; Charles Button, "Negro Recruits," *Lynchburg Virginian*, 19 December 1864, 1.

black troops: "We advocated then [a year previously], as a last resort, and one to be used without hesitation, the arming of the negroes whenever it became necessary to secure our independence." Even as editor Sam Yost placed the idea before the people of Staunton, he included Forsyth's suggestion that the time had not yet come for the step. In addition to the president's message and brief notes on Congressional action, the *Vindicator* included two additional items to further the debate. On 4 November, the Staunton paper noted the speculations of the *New York News* on slaves in Confederate gray: "The slaves of the South can be made to supply an excellent material for infantary [sic]...under command of officers to whom they have rendered a life long unquestioning obediance [sic], and to whom they may be molded into an invincible machine." Such a scheme, the *News* hinted, would force the Union into a series of ruinous draft calls. Two weeks later, the Staunton paper demonstrated that it remained undecided on the issue as it published the *Savannah News*'s denunciation of the idea: "A measure so disorganizing, so unnecessary, unwise and impolitic, will, we feel confident, be rejected by our people and our Congress. Consistency, self-respect, Southern honor, and humanity demands [sic] it."[19] Appeals to consistency and honor must have rung a bit hollow in Staunton as Sheridan's raids continued throughout the Valley.

Calls for more troops and more supplies drew the attention of Yost, who struck out at the "barbarian" Union command: "Now Grant, wearied and sick of fighting the veterans of Lee with no avail, has turned his arms against the women and children of our land, hoping, doubtless, that he may gain a glorious victory (!) over them, a result already impossible to be attained over the former." Even as he decried Union actions, Yost complained bitterly about mismanagement in the Confederate quartermaster system that seemed to ignore some areas of the state while exacting large quantities of supplies from the Valley. Similarly, the treatment of newly enlisted troops also drew his ire. Despite these frustrations with Confederate policy, Yost approved the vast majority of Davis's suggestions in the annual message to

[19] "The Battle of Bell [sic] Grove," *Staunton Vindicator*, 28 October 1864, 2; "Gen'l Early's Address to His Army," *Staunton Vindicator*, 28 October 1864, 2; "Rockingham's Losses," *Staunton Vindicator*, 18 November 1864, 2; "Arming Negroes," *Staunton Vindicator*, 28 October 1864, 2; "Negroes to Fight for the South," *Staunton Vindicator*, 4 November 1864, 1; "Negroes in the Army," *Staunton Vindicator*, 18 November 1864, 1.

Congress. Although concerned by attempts to limit exemptions, he accepted the president's comments about changes in the slave's role without serious reflection: "The arming of slaves in defence [sic] of our liberties is not deemed essential at present."[20] Focused upon the prostrate condition of the surrounding area, editor Yost kept the issue of black troops before the public in the *Vindicator*'s news columns but did not attempt to use his editorial pulpit to advance the cause.

Down the valley, in Harrisonburg, the *Rockingham Register* devoted most of its attention to the "hard war" tactics shaping the fall campaign. In August, the *Register* had announced that while they regretted the necessity for retribution, "'forbearance instead of being a virtue' is a crime against ourselves." Developing the theme, the paper commended General John McCausland's burning of Chambersburg, Pennsylvania, as a fully justified action:

> They have burned whole towns; they have burned private residences; they have burned mills; they have burned churches; and even now they are doing their utmost to shell and to burn some of our chief towns. ... We hope and pray that the burning of Chambersburg may put a stop to burning elsewhere. If it does not, however, we hope the Confederates will again apply the torch.

As the fall campaign progressed, battle reports and lists of lost Confederate property figured prominently in the paper. Unlike the *Register*'s peers in Staunton and Lynchburg, no news items concerning black Confederate troops appeared in Harrisonburg. Rather, the editor affirmed his prerogative to print only those items he considered worthy: "We are the judges of what are proper subjects of discussions in our columns. ... We shall publish what we choose, and refuse to publish what we prefer to decline."[21]

The *Register*'s editor, John H. Wartmann, stoutly maintained his unwillingness to discuss the issue of slave-soldiers until the second week of December. Finally, with newspapers in Richmond, Charlottesville, and Lynch-

[20] S.M. Yost, "Retribution Will Come," *Staunton Vindicator*, 21 October 1864, 2; S.M. Yost, "A Word to the Wise," *Staunton Vindicator*, 2 December 1864, 2; S.M. Yost, "Upon the Revocation...," *Staunton Vindicator*, 4 November 1864, 2; S.M. Yost, "The President's Message," *Staunton Vindicator*, 18 November 1864, 2.

[21] "Burning of Chambersburg," *Rockingham Register*, 12 August 1864, 2; "We must repeat our protest...," *Rockingham Register*, 19 August 1864, 2.

burg all hotly discussing the role of slaves within the war effort, Wartmann entered the fray. He confessed himself humiliated "for our race," "for our consistency," "for the bending of the knee of that proud, chivalrous southern sentiment which has so brightly displayed itself...on hundreds of bloody battle fields." Slavery, he asserted, had been the "chief reason" for disunion. If the South could seriously consider a world without slavery, why had she left the Union? Beyond the problem of how to address the loss of laborers and the grave constitutional obstacles to manumission in return for faithful service, Wartmann argued that black troops simply would not be faithful: "It turns loose with arms in their hands a multitude of ignorant, unthinking creatures whose sympathies are open to the market of every itinerant Yankee." Having seen his own slaves leave him when Sheridan left the county only months before, the Harrisonburg editor felt betrayed and hoped to prevent his country from relying on people whom, he felt, would ultimately let them down. "Emancipation is Subjugation," he proclaimed. To him, the triumph of northern ideas would constitute just as damaging a result as battlefield annihilation.[22]

Clearly, Davis's message to Congress and related comments in the national press sparked considerable discussion in all three communities. With Sheridan devastating the Shenandoah Valley, Button challenged the citizens of the Roanoke Valley to address the dire choices facing the country. Leaping forward from a discussion of noncombatant laborers, the *Virginian*'s editor pushed forward a series of editorials and news items designed to promote a thorough debate of slavery. In contrast, the Shenandoah Valley journals tread more cautiously. Yost, in Staunton, provided news reports that would serve as a foundation for public comment, but public interest, as well as that of the editor, appeared to focus on more pressing issues. In Harrisonburg, Wartmann resolutely attempted to stifle all discussion of black troops by refusing to publish wire accounts about the issue and through his strong denunciation of the idea in his one editorial on the topic. Although far from reaching a consensus, the residents of the Roanoke and Shenandoah Valleys had begun to rethink the traditional role of slaves within southern society.

[22] John H. Wartmann, "Negro Soldiery...Abandonment of the Southern Idea," *Rockingham Register*, 12 December 1864, 1.

Occupied by the overwhelming requirements to meet Grant and Sherman in the field, many Confederate leaders willingly accepted the need to reconsider the role of slaves in the war effort. Following the lead of the *Richmond Enquirer*, the public as well as editors from all vantage points entered the discussions. In November, President Davis ignited a full-scale debate of the merits of slavery. Moving far beyond the idea of regularizing the impressment of slave labor, Davis challenged southerners to accept slaves as people with civic duties, as a person as well as their traditional role as property. The offer of freedom in return for faithful service struck at the heart of antebellum assertions that slavery was the best possible condition for the slave. Surprisingly, the fire of debate burned as brightly in the Roanoke and Shenandoah Valleys as it did in Richmond. All of these communities had experienced considerable growth due to the war, but the presence of the national and state governments clearly influenced the formation of public opinion in Richmond. Yet, with Sheridan marching unopposed through the Shenandoah Valley and Grant applying unremitting pressure at Petersburg, all three areas felt directly threatened by Union forces. The very real threat of Union victory led to virtually identical ideas expressed in each community.

Virginians expressed little wonder that Confederate leaders would consider arming slaves, and the overwhelming majority readily accepted the increase in the number of black laborers with the armies. In Richmond, Lynchburg, and the Shenandoah Valley many citizens wondered if the military situation now demanded the enlistment of slaves. With few exceptions, Virginians proclaimed their preference for black troops over military defeat, but most suggested that this ultimate crisis had not yet arrived. In November and December 1864, Virginians were prepared to seriously consider modifying slavery, but many hesitated when called upon to renounce the institution that had served them so well. The evolution of southern ideas about the importance of slavery in 1863 and 1864 highlighted the similarities in northern and southern views of race. Political considerations along with military necessity had forced Abraham Lincoln, and northerners in general, to reevaluate their views on the proper status of black men and women and to reconsider their objectives for the war. Similarly, military necessity forced Jefferson Davis to open an unprecedented discussion of the value of slavery to the South. In many ways, northern and southern attitudes as they considered the enlistment of former slaves demonstrated that differences in white opinion about race were matters of degree and not type. More importantly, the deliberate appraisal of the value of slavery underscores the sincerity of Confederate leaders and the common citizens of the South as they weighed southern independence against the preservation of slavery.

3

Radical Measures

In the military campaign of 1864, Confederate forces across the South suffered a series of military defeats that forced southern leaders to reassess the course of the revolution. Despite the best efforts of the southern armies, Sherman had taken the city of Atlanta, Grant had driven Lee across Virginia and into the trenches at Petersburg, and Lincoln's prospects for reelection improved daily. Without a significant shift in policy, the new Confederate nation's days appeared to be numbered. As the Confederate Government faced these mounting problems in Richmond, thoughtful Georgians examined their goals in the war, weighed the value of slavery, and attempted to define what sacrifices they were willing to make to gain independence.

The fall of Atlanta on 2 September left a distinct mark upon the Georgia mind and precipitated a period of intellectual ferment. On 29 September an anonymous correspondent wrote from Augusta to Secretary of War James Seddon and strongly recommended arming the slaves. "Native Georgian," as he identified himself, argued for nothing less than limited, compensated emancipation: "Promise them (those employed) freedom when the war is over. Compensate the owners, of course, with interest-bearing bonds." "All the able-bodied men," he continued, "might be used certainly as effectively as the Yankees use them against us." [1] Only through such innovative measures, "Native Georgian" contended, could the institution of slavery be maintained. While many Georgians doubtless agreed with Secretary Seddon's comment on the letter that this idea should wait until white men could not be found, the seeds of radical thought had clearly taken root in the Deep South. Davis opened his final campaign in the midst of this unsettled political climate in Georgia, and his speculations on the future of slavery sparked a fresh debate of southern war aims.

---

[1] United States War Department, *Official Records,* Series 4, Vol. 3, 693.

As one examines the slave-soldier issue in Georgia, three distinct regions emerge. First, the cities of Macon, Athens, and Milledgeville form a central region. These communities faced the threat of Sherman's columns in November and December but did not face a direct Union threat thereafter. Milledgeville entered the debate only in the second phase after Sherman exited the capital and the residents returned to their homes in December and January. Second, Augusta formed a separate eastern region because it faced the threat of Union assault not only during Sherman's march to Savannah but also as the Union columns marched through South Carolina in January and February 1865. The proximity to Union forces profoundly affected public attitudes in Augusta. Third, the cities of Columbus, Albany, and Blakely formed a distinct southwestern region. These communities relied heavily on largescale cotton production for their livelihood, contained a large number of refugees, both white and black, and never felt threatened by Union forces until near the end of the war. Although information flowed freely between the regions, the individual circumstances in each region, and particularly the proximity to the enemy, affected how Georgians framed the debate on arming the slaves.

In all three regions, newspapers provided the primary platform for the debate on the slave's role in the war effort. Contemporary news items, editorials, and letters to editors in each community reveal the intensity of the debate in Georgia. Diaries and private letters supplement the portrait provided by the newspapers. In the columns of the newspapers, individual men and women struggled with each other and within themselves to define what they were fighting to achieve. The first phase of this debate ran from Davis's speech in early November until the news of the defeats at Nashville and Savannah spread through Georgia during the last week of December. As soon as Davis's speech reached the world press, news reports poured into the newspaper offices of Central Georgia concerning arming slaves. While not indicative of local opinion, these stories established the context for the editors' and readers' interpretations of the debate.

In Central Georgia, the *Macon Telegraph and Confederate* set the tone of the debate as it published a series of news items, both for and against arming slaves. Only a week after Davis's speech, this paper ran an editorial from the *New York Times*, claiming that for the South to arm the slaves would be to concede the major issue of the war. Also, the New York editor saw little military value in Davis's proposal: "What the North has now between it and peace is an army of negro slaves, bought like cattle for service, and fighting under the lash… What the masters have tried in vain the slaves shall certainly not accomplish."[2] Similarly, a *London Times* editorial, appearing in the Macon newspaper on 29 December, saw an element of desperation in the proposal: "If Mr. Davis was also to summon the slaves to the field, it would be for the obvious reason that he was horribly in want of recruits."[3] Despite these negative appraisals from outside the state, the Macon paper closely followed the progress of the bill authorizing the 40,000 noncombatant laborers through Congress: "It now appears probable…that the measure recommended by President Davis…will be adopted by Congress, omitting the emancipation feature."[4] Among the southern supporters of the proposal was William Smith, Governor of Virginia, who boldly declared: "I do not hesitate to say that I approve the arming of such portion of our able-bodied slave population as may be necessary to put them in the field…for the spring campaign."[5] Although originating in Virginia, the Macon paper printed Smith's powerful endorsement on the front page of its 14 December issue. These news reports failed to produce a complete picture, but they formed a backdrop for the formation of public opinion in Macon.

Unwilling to sit idly by on such a major issue, editor Henry L. Flash of the *Macon Telegraph and Confederate* quickly jumped into the fray and denounced the bold words emanating from Richmond. Just prior to the president's speech, he proclaimed his opposition to arming the slaves: "If we decree such a policy, the old land-marks determining the relation between master and slave, are effectively swept away forever."[6] Upon reviewing the entire text of the president's message, Flash pointedly asked how the South could arm slaves without renouncing the entire Confederate ideology: "How does this dovetail with the position taken by the Southern people that slavery was the best possible condition for the negro? …It is an admission that

---

[2] "The Yankees on the Negro Soldier," *Macon Telegraph and Confederate*, 18 November 1864, 1.

[3] "Arming of the Negroes," *Macon Telegraph and Confederate*, 29 December 1864, 1.

[4] "The Negro Question," *Macon Telegraph and Confederate*, 17 December 1864, 1.

[5] "The Virginia Legislature," *Macon Telegraph and Confederate*, 14 December 1864, 2.

[6] "Negro Soldiers," *Macon Telegraph and Confederate*, 18 October 1864, 2.

slavery is a state, the release from which is a blessing and a boon."[7] Instead of emancipation, he recommended allowing the slaves who served faithfully as teamsters or pioneers with the army to choose their new state and master.[8] While opposing the arming of slaves on principle, the Macon editor recommended filling the southern ranks through a reduction in the number of professions exempt from conscription. Not keen to join the struggle himself, he claimed that good order required a few choice exceptions: "There are nevertheless certain pursuits which, if permitted to exist at all should be [exempt]. [One] of this number is the Press."[9] Noting the growing problems caused by roving bands of deserters in North Georgia, Flash, on 13 December, quickly retreated from tightening the conscription law: "These public disorders show conclusively the impolity and suicidal character of the practice of 'putting everybody who can carry a gun' into the army."[10] Having refused to arm the slaves on principle and to tighten the exemption law for practical reasons, the editor of the *Macon Telegraph and Confederate* failed to suggest any method for the Confederate army to fill its depleted ranks. By raising both the ideological problems caused by arming the slaves and the practical problems encountered by sending every white man to the front, Henry Flash set the stage for the local people to speak through their letters.

Another keen observer in Macon, editor Samuel Boykin of the *Christian Index*, also responded quickly to the president's speech. Although the small Baptist weekly carried few news items on the topic, the paper's editor spoke out forcefully against arming the slaves. On 11 November Boykin denounced the public debate of black soldiers: "Such a question ought never to have been agitated. Its discussion is fraught with infinite mischief."[11] Not only was the step not necessary, Boykin argued, but it simply would not work: "They would have no character to lose—no interest to protect—no

---

[7] Henry Flash, "The President's Message: Employment of Negroes," *Macon Telegraph and Confederate*, 15 November 1864, 2.

[8] Ibid.

[9] Ibid.

[10] Henry Flash, "Civil Disorders," *Macon Telegraph and Confederate*, 13 December 1864, 2.

[11] Samuel Boykin, "Arming the Negroes for Southern Defense," *Macon Christian Index*, 11 November 1864, 2.

inducement to fight."[12] Furthermore, Boykin argued that such a step would violate moral law: "Slaves are men, with reason, moral sense, and moral accountability. ... It is not just to constrain a slave to expose his life in...defense of the liberty of others."[13] A week later, on 18 November, the Baptist editor addressed the potential consequences of arming the slaves. Although noting the reduction in the agricultural labor force and the possibility of veteran units rejecting the slave-soldiers, Boykin focused on the long-term effects upon slavery. "The army," Boykin declared, "will be a propitious school wherein to teach the slaves many things inconsistent with...servitude—the use of firearms; a sense of self-reliance...[and] a vague perception of equality with the white race."[14] More importantly, Boykin wondered how the black veterans would fit into post-war southern society: "They would remain in our midst as freemen, entitled it is to be presumed with the rights of citizenship. ... To deny these after the promise of freedom, would be...an outrage upon truth and justice."[15] Despite the sound logic of the argument, the editor of the *Index* could not imagine southerners accepting black citizenship: "Yet, to grant to a negro such privileges would be abhorrent to every Southern sentiment and in conflict with all Southern opinion."[16] In the first phase of the debate, Boykin clearly defined the cost of black soldiers as the end of slavery and the acceptance of black citizenship. Without an overwhelming military necessity, Boykin refused to make the sacrifice.

Two types of letters appear consistently in the *Macon Telegraph and Confederate*: letters from the local area and letters to the paper from professional correspondents in the larger cities or with the army. The letters of Peter W. Alexander, the prolific Richmond correspondent of the *Savannah Republican*, were often published in the Georgia papers. On 11 November, "P.W.A.," as he signed his letters, opened the debate in Central Georgia by arguing that the issue had to be addressed before the spring campaign: "It will become necessary to send every white man in the Confederacy under

[12] Ibid.

[13] Ibid.

[14] Samuel Boykin, "Arming the Negroes for Southern Defense," *Macon Christian Index*, 18 November 1864, 2.

[15] Ibid.

[16] Ibid.

sixty years of age to the field, or enlist one or two hundred thousand negroes, or abandon the contest."[17] Declaring that General Robert E. Lee, General James Longstreet, and most of the rank and file of the army supported the idea of arming slaves, Alexander contended that the proposition deserved a cold, fair hearing: "It behooves us to discuss the great delicate question with perfect freedom from prejudice and passion."[18]

The local citizens who wrote to the *Telegraph and Confederate* often proved less detached than the professional journalist Alexander and more practical than the local editor, Henry Flash. Attempting to point out the shirkers who forced the country to consider arming the slaves, "Randolph" recommended that railroad conductors, the "regiments of men within the walls of these hospitals," and all doctors and lawyers "be stripped of their false colors and sent to the army."[19] Making the slave a soldier, he claimed, "would in the eyes of Christendom, heap deep and dire disgrace upon the South and put a final end to an institution, which the South is indebted for all that makes her superior."[20] Working from the assumption that the army would require 200,000 more men in the spring, "Sydney" offered a different approach: "If the exigency demands men to the extent above referred to, in God's name, do not sacrifice every white man in the Confederacy in preference to taking a few negroes from their fondling masters."[21] Arguing that the rich planter's love for his property produced a rich man's war and a poor man's fight, "Sydney" contended that displaced slaves should fill the depleted ranks: "There is [sic] in the Confederacy one or two hundred thousand able bodied negroes not engaged in agriculture. Many of them [are] refugees from the country overrun...and can be very well spared."[22] During this first phase of the debate, the Macon letter writers failed to agree on the proper policy, but their strong, passionate, and exceedingly practical letters show

---

[17] Peter W. Alexander, "Letter from Richmond," *Macon Telegraph and Confederate*, 11 November 1864, 1.

[18] Ibid.

[19] "Randolph," "Letter to the Editor—Negro Soldiers," *Macon Telegraph and Confederate*, 3 November 1864, 2.

[20] Ibid.

[21] "Sydney," "Letter to the Editor," *Macon Telegraph and Confederate*, 19 November 1864, 1.

[22] Ibid.

that many people not only cared deeply about the question but also held a wide spectrum of views on the proper course to be taken.

News items also arrived in the offices of the two Athens newspapers: the *Southern Watchman* and the *Southern Banner*. Both of these weekly journals printed copies of Davis's message in November and reported reaction from around the nation. On 23 November, after printing Davis's proposals on page 1, the *Watchman* ran a long editorial from the *Raleigh Confederate*, denouncing the debate that Davis's speculations had started: "The discussion which the President's Message will greatly encourage…is, in our judgment, much to be deprecated."[23] The idea of "negro troops," the Raleigh editor argued, involves "the utter subversion of the institution of slavery, if not the whole fabric of our State Governments, and the consequent destruction of civil liberty itself."[24] This news item, much as the one that appeared in the *Watchman* on 21 December, stressed the constitutional difficulties that the government would encounter in attempting to alter slavery in any manner: "Have we arrived at that point in Government ethics, when the Chief Magistrate…with his eye and hand on the Confederate Constitution…can cast that instrument to the winds upon the pleas of necessity?"[25]

While initial reports appearing in Athens opposed Davis's proposals, in December a few items supported the president. On 14 December, for example, the *Southern Banner* published a portion of Virginia Governor Smith's speech in favor of arming the slaves.[26] James A. Sledge, editor of the *Banner*, selected this item from the Press Association wire reports to print over similar speeches made by the governors of North Carolina and Alabama opposing black troops. Even the *Watchman*, the anti-administration paper in town, printed a resolution of the Alabama legislature that approved Davis's request for 40,000 noncombatants: "The policy of employing slaves as teamsters, cooks, hospital nurses, pioneers and sappers and miners, but not as soldiers in the army, is hereby approved and recommended."[27] Although the Athens papers printed opinions on both sides of the issue, the positions taken by

---

[23] "Slaves for the Army," *Southern Watchman*, 23 November 1864, 3.

[24] Ibid.

[25] Ibid.

[26] "From Richmond," *Southern Banner*, 14 December 1864, 2.

[27] "Alabama and the Confederate Government," *Southern Watchman*, 21 December 1864, 3.

each on the debate reflected their opinion of the administration's handling of the war.

While the choice of news items by the Athens papers reflected their approaches to Davis's proposals, only the *Southern Watchman* published a strong editorial on the subject. As the debate opened, editor John Christy attacked Confederate conscription policies and denounced the idea of black troops: "One hundred and forty thousand men are detailed to supervise the operations of their farms and plantations, an enviable lot in comparison with him who has neither, [and] is obliged to go to the field."[28] Even as he decried the rich man's war and the poor man's fight, Christy sought only to force all white men and not all men into the gray ranks. Although admitting that "radical measures" such as arming the slaves would greatly increase the army numbers, the *Watchman*'s editor would not consider the proposition: "We are of the opinion that such a thing as arming the negroes should not be countenanced for a moment."[29] In his view, southerners could not spare the food produced by slave labor. Instead, Christy argued that the South should use idle slaves as noncombatant laborers and that the Confederate government should round up all white "idlers" and send them off to the front.[30] During this first phase of the debate in Athens, the editor of the *Watchman* clearly stated his position against arming the slaves. In contrast, editor James Sledge's reticence at the *Banner* reflected the sensitive nature of the debate but left the proponents of these "radical measures" without a spokesman in Athens.

In support of its strong editorial position against arming the slaves, the *Southern Watchman* published two letters against the proposition during this first phase. On 23 November, "Nomen," who was serving with the Troup Artillery, wrote and denied the existence of a major manpower problem: "One third of the armies are not absent without leave nor are we needing any thick lip negroes at this time to handle the muskets."[31] In a similar spirit,

---

[28] "Confederate Resources—Another Statement," *Southern Watchman*, 2 November 1864, 1.

[29] John Christy, "Negro Soldiers," *Southern Watchman*, 2 November 1864, 2.

[30] "Confederate Resources—Another Statement," *Southern Watchman*, 2 November 1864, 1.

[31] "Nomen," "From the Troup Artillery," *Southern Watchman*, 23 November 1864, 3.

on 30 November the paper printed a letter from its Richmond correspondent, "Camillus," discussing the Congressional prospects for arming the slaves: "The proposition at first met with but little favor, but it seems to be gaining strength among members. Still, I do not think the measure will be adopted."[32] This correspondent could not imagine black troops in Confederate gray: "To enroll and put them in service," "Camillus" asserted, "and make them fight to perpetuate their own servitude is revolting…to Christianity and…to liberate them, strikes down at one blow the institution."[33] Although both letters in the *Watchman* strongly opposed arming the slaves, no letter writer appeared in either paper to advocate the measure. If local proponents existed, like the editor of the *Southern Banner*, they refrained from openly declaring their support for black troops during the first phase of the debate in Athens.

Although no advocate of arming the slaves stepped forward in the Athens newspapers, thoughtful men and women discussed the issue privately. After fleeing to Elberton to avoid Sherman, Warren Akin, a Confederate congressman from Northwest Georgia, gave the concept careful consideration. On 31 October, Akin wrote to an old friend, Judge Nathan Land, about the need for more men and discussed the idea of employing slaves: "As to calling out the negro men and placing them in the army, with the promise that they shall be free at the end of the war, I can only say it is a question of fearful magnitude."[34] Having broached the issue, Akin ticked off the possible problems: Can we still feed ourselves? Will the white soldiers accept it? Will it lead to a slave insurrection? Can the government afford to compensate the owners?[35] Despite these fearful contingencies, the Georgia congressman stoutly affirmed his willingness to risk all of these woes rather than face subjugation: "We may (if necessary) put our slaves in the army, win our independence, and have liberty and homes for ourselves and children. But subjugation will deprive us of our homes, houses, property, liberty, honor, and

---

[32] "Camillus," "From an Occasional Correspondent," *Southern Watchman*, 30 November 1864, 3.

[33] Ibid.

[34] Warren Akin, *Letters of Warren Akin: Confederate Congressman*, ed. Bell I. Wiley (Athens: University of Georgia Press, 1959) 32.

[35] Ibid.

everything worth living for."[36] Even with utter defeat staring the planters in the face, Akin saw little hope that the large slaveholders would support the use of black troops: "They give up their sons, husbands, brothers & friends, and often without murmuring, to the army; but let one of their negroes be taken, and what a howl you will hear."[37] Thoughtful men in North Georgia, like Warren Akin, carefully studied the proposition to arm slaves, but many feared that the public would not accept the idea in time.

Sherman's advancing columns threatened both Macon and Athens during this first phase of the debate, but no Union soldiers entered either city. In fact, after the Battle of Griswoldville on 22 November, Macon felt little threat from Sherman. In contrast, the arrival of General Henry Slocum's Union troops in Milledgeville on 22 November forced many citizens to flee, caused the state government to move to Macon, and totally disrupted community life. Throughout December, the citizens of Milledgeville straggled back into the city, struggled to reassert law and order, and attempted to rebuild their lives. Of course, the debate about arming the slaves, and many other things, had to wait until normal community life resumed.

Although newspapers ceased publication for brief periods, and most people focused strictly upon survival, many Georgians in Sherman's path understood that their government was considering arming the slaves. For example, on 19 November, Dolly Burge of Covington penned in her diary that the Union soldiers forced her male slaves to follow them, "saying that 'Jeff Davis wanted to put them in his army, but that they should not fight for him, but for the Union.'"[38] Although the proponents of black troops remained far from winning the measure's acceptance, the possibility appeared quite real to both Union and Confederate partisans. With the publication of Davis's address in Milledgeville on 6 December, few could doubt that the Confederate leadership must now contemplate "radical measures."[39] Sherman's passage brought a powerful sense of urgency to the debate about arming the slaves, but for the cities of Central Georgia, even those that had suffered occupation, the direct Union threat had passed by mid-December.

---

[36] Ibid., 33.

[37] Ibid.

[38] Dolly Burge, *A Woman's Wartime Journal: An Account of the Passage of Sherman's Army on the March to the Sea*, ed. Julian Street (Macon: J.W. Burke, 1927) 37.

[39] "Davis' November Message," *Confederate Union*, 6 December 1864, 2.

Although the debate began in earnest in Macon and Athens during November and December, much of Central Georgia was still suffering from Sherman's powerful blows and had little time to reflect upon such "radical" ideas. Only with the news of the military disasters of December and the return to normal community life in Milledgeville and other devastated areas would the debate about arming the slaves fully flower throughout Central Georgia.

Just as in Central Georgia, the first phase of the debate on arming the slaves opened in Augusta with numerous news reports arriving in the offices of the two main daily newspapers: the *Daily Constitutionalist* and the *Chronicle and Sentinel*. Unlike many of the items that appeared in the Macon newspapers, most of the stories on the issue in the Augusta papers originated in the South. Using reports from the Press Association of the Confederate States of America in Richmond, editor James Gardner of the *Daily Constitutionalist* provided his readers, on 11 and 16 November, with blow-by-blow accounts of the initial discussions in Congress on arming the slaves: "Mr. Swann [of Tennessee] thought an early declaration of opinion by Congress highly important. The country ought to be assured that Congress will not entertain the proposition."[40] Although far from inspiring, as the measure quickly went to committee, these reports showed where the congressmen stood and provided a fair idea of the bill's prospects.

Throughout this first phase, Gardner skillfully selected the news items for the *Constitutionalist* in order to highlight the importance of the discussion concerning black soldiers. Considering Alabama Governor Thomas Watts's comments concerning arming the slaves the most important, Gardner published this portion on 23 November, several days prior to running the entire address. While supporting Davis's request for 40,000 slaves in noncombatant roles, Watts appeared horrified by Davis's speculations: "The idea of using negroes in the army, except for teamsters, cooks, pioneer service, and for work on fortifications, and as nurses in hospitals, I think utterly indefensible in principle and policy."[41] On 27 November, Gardner quoted an address by Zebulon Vance, Governor of North Carolina, which flatly declared that any form of emancipation for black soldiers would make the war

[40] "Report of Congressional House Action," *Daily Constitutionalist*, 16 November 1864, 1.

[41] "Governor Watts' Message," *Daily Constitutionalist*, 23 November 1864, 1.

an "objectless waste of human life."[42] Further, Vance argued that independence was not the South's primary war aim: "Our independence I imagine is chiefly desirable for the preservation of our great institutions, the principal of which is slavery."[43] Although generally opposed to arming the slaves, news reports that appeared in the *Daily Constitutionalist* in November and December placed the issue squarely before the public and left room for further discussion.

In contrast to the extended coverage in the *Daily Constitutionalist*, editor Nathan S. Morse of the *Chronicle and Sentinel* attempted to ignore the efforts to arm the slaves. Although Morse published the president's address on 12 November, he made no editorial comments about Davis's remarks on the slave's role in the war effort.[44] Instead, he followed closely the comments of Georgia Governor Joseph E. Brown. In his November address to the Georgia legislature, Brown argued against arming slaves but recommended acceptance of the use of slaves in noncombatant roles: "I do, however, advocate the use of them as teamsters, cooks, hospital servants, and in every other menial capacity in which their services can be made useful."[45] Having dismissed the slave-soldier issue, Brown, and subsequently Morse, railed throughout November and December against the Davis administration for conscription, impressment, and a host of other "constitutional infringements." Morse did not publish another news item that mentioned arming the slaves until 28 December, when he noted the resolutions of the South Carolina legislature against freeing the noncombatant slave laborers who served faithfully with the army: "This State cannot consent to the proposition by which slaves so employed shall be purchased and declared free by the Confederate Government."[46] Hoping that the idea would wither and die, the editor of the *Chronicle and Sentinel* attempted to ignore the question of arming the slaves in his columns and thereby to stifle the debate.

In contrast to the strong editorial positions immediately taken in Macon by Henry Flash and in Athens by John Christy, James Gardner ap-

---

[42] "Governor Vance's Message," *Daily Constitutionalist*, 27 November 1864, 2.

[43] Ibid.

[44] "President Davis's Message," *Chronicle and Sentinel*, 12 November 1864, 2.

[45] "Governor Brown's Address," *Chronicle and Sentinel*, 6 November 1864, 2.

[46] "South Carolina and the Army Negro Question," *Chronicle and Sentinel*, 28 December 1864, 1.

proached the issue tentatively, feeling for the mood of the community. On 13 November, in an editorial concerning Davis's message, he endorsed the president's plan to employ 40,000 slaves with the army.[47] More importantly, Gardner accepted the possibility of arming the slaves and urged its serious consideration: "The employment of slaves is a grave question discussed, and will, as it should, meet the earnest and dispassionate attention of the Congress."[48] Although not endorsing the proposal immediately, Gardner, by not rejecting the idea out of hand, encouraged discussion, not only in Congress but also in the local community. Having called for serious discussion, Gardner waited impatiently for Congressional action until mid-December. Hearing nothing, he inveighed against the delay. Arguing that the exemption bill, currency regulation, and the role of the slave in the war were the only three issues of importance before Congress, the editor of the *Daily Constitutionalist* implored the members to take some action: "We do urge upon these gentlemen the necessity of attending the three important measures...and leave the quibbles...to the idle debaters of the street corners."[49] Lacking faith in Congress to act without pressure, he begged the people to demand action: "The whole land should speak out and demand of these men, men upon whom rest the safety of the republic, to make and attend to those laws which the times demand and those alone."[50] By moving slowly but refusing to rule out any option, James Gardner challenged the community to confront the issue as openly as possible.

Meanwhile, Nathan Morse at the *Chronicle and Sentinel* aimed his editorial arrows only indirectly at the debate about arming the slaves. Instead of addressing Davis's proposition for gradual, compensated emancipation, Morse argued against the president's challenges to civil liberties and to states' rights. On 13 November, he noted the centralization in the Union government and pleaded with the Confederate government not to follow the northern example: "Let us maintain our rights at home, and set the glorious example of upholding the laws of the country in the midst of the rudest

[47] James Gardner, "President Davis's Message," *Daily Constitutionalist*, 13 November 1864, 2.

[48] Ibid.

[49] James Gardner, "Details and Exemptions," *Daily Constitutionalist*, 22 December 1864, 2.

[50] Ibid.

shock of arms."[51] The Confederate Constitution's strong guarantee of property rights in slaves formed a key element in Morse's view of the law of the land. This was a subtle but effective way to frame his opposition to the use of black men in the gray ranks.

Despite the efforts of this Augusta editor, Georgians could not easily ignore the increasingly desperate state of the country. On 21 December, without directly mentioning Davis's proposals, the *Chronicle and Sentinel* decried the calls in other journals for such "rash and dangerous experiments" as arming the slaves: "One of the most alarming signs of the times is the growth of a lawless revolutionary spirit, that would obliterate the landmarks of the Constitution: that would engulph [sic]...the citizen in a centralized despotism."[52] Such appeals, Morse argued, lead only to "anarchy and despotism" rather than increased assistance for the army: "The plea of military necessity is the convenient pretext for the most flagrant violations of the constitution." [53] Although Yankee armies were marching triumphantly throughout Georgia, Morse still insisted that any discussion of altering the slave's position would destroy the state. "Let us not aggravate our troubles," Morse contended on 29 December, "by a repudiation of the established order of society. By such a course we shall nourish a foe in the camp." Despite Morse's efforts to smother the debate of Davis's proposals in Augusta, stunning military reverses at the end of December forced the issue of slave-soldiers onto the pages of all Georgia papers, even on those of the *Chronicle and Sentinel.*

While both Augusta editors initially took a cautious approach to arming the slaves, the professional correspondents of the *Daily Constitutionalist* exhibited far less reserve in their letters. For example, on 18 November, "Larkin," a Richmond correspondent, wrote glowingly of the chances of Congressional action to arm the slaves: "The question of extending the conscription act to the negro population of the Confederacy, is being extensively canvassed in private circles, and finds many supporters among the prominent men now here." "Larkin" astutely noted the key snag to passage: "The bounty of freedom for honorable discharge of their duties is the rock upon which

[51] N.S. Morse, "Civil Liberty," *Chronicle and Sentinel,* 13 November 1864, 2.
[52] N.S. Morse, "A Wild Suggestion," *Chronicle and Sentinel,* 21 December 1864, 2.
[53] Ibid.

the friends of the measure split."[54] Less than a week later, another Richmond correspondent, "Roundabout," argued that desperate times required desperate measures: "Whilst it is not considered necessary to arm the slaves at present, the ferocious war waged against us will be met with every resource and means of the Confederacy."[55] The question of necessity figured prominently in other letters from Richmond, including one from Peter Alexander on 24 November: "We must have every able-bodied man in the country, or a conscription of negroes. ... The truth is, we must have more men—if not white men, then black."[56] Although all of these letters came from professional correspondents and appeared only in the *Daily Constitutionalist*, these strong, clear expressions of opinion set an example that the common men and women of Augusta would follow as the war drew closer to home and as the necessity for action became patently obvious. In the news items he included and in his editorial columns, Morse stoutly refused to publish any letter touching upon arming the slaves in the *Chronicle and Sentinel*.[57] In Augusta, the correspondents of the *Daily Constitutionalist* took the lead in the debate and championed the necessity if not the principle of arming the slaves.

Unlike those in Eastern and Central Georgia, the residents of Southwest Georgia could discuss the value of slavery without the pounding hoof beats of Sherman's Union columns in their ears. As in Eastern and Central Georgia, Davis's message to Congress precipitated a deluge of news reports into the newspaper offices in Columbus, Blakely, and Albany. The two powerful Columbus dailies, the *Columbus Times* and the *Daily Sun*, set the tone for reporting in this southwestern region of the state. These Columbus papers covered the debate concerning arming the slaves fully by presenting numerous news items, editorials, and letters from several correspondents. Such a full discussion of the issue in Columbus eventually led to a similar

---

[54] "Larkin," "Letter from Richmond," *Daily Constitutionalist*, 18 November 1864, 2.

[55] "Roundabout," "Letter from Richmond," *Daily Constitutionalist*, 23 November 1864, 2.

[56] Peter W. Alexander, "Letter from Richmond," *Daily Constitutionalist*, 24 November 1864, 3.

[57] Although the evidence is only circumstantial for the first phase on 24 March 1865, Morse admitted to receiving a letter from "W.W." of the *Constitutionalist*. Morse attempted to refute "W.W."'s arguments but would not print his letter.

debate in Blakely's *Early County News* and in the *Albany Patriot*. Since Sherman did not venture into this region, the newspapers and not the Union army were in position to play the key role in shaping the debate in Southwest Georgia.

In the immediate aftermath of Davis's address, the *Columbus Times* printed news items about arming the slaves from outside the Confederacy, from Richmond, and from inside the state. On 22 November the *Times* reprinted an editorial from the *Chicago Times* that viewed the Confederate discussion of black troops as a demonstration of the remarkable resolve of the South: "It shows a vastly increased capacity for resistance on the part of the South, closes up one of the main sources from which we have been latterly drawing our recruits, and opens in the North a vista...along which we see interminable war."[58] Southern proponents of the measure could not have formed a stronger argument for the admission of black troops into the Confederate army. Less than two weeks later, on 3 December, the *Columbus Times* reprinted a similar item from the *St. Louis Republican*: "Does any one doubt the South can raise, equip, and put in the field three hundred thousand negro troops, who will prove as efficient to her in a military cause as our sable auxiliaries prove to us?"[59] Obviously, these northerners were struggling to understand the complex bond between masters and slaves. On 8 December the *Times* reprinted a column from a British abolitionist journal, the *English Church and State Review*, that grudgingly accepted the likelihood that southern slaves would indeed fight for the Confederacy: "The negroes...have tilled his fields and watched over his home and tended his wife and little ones while he was far away fighting against the friends who were to set him free."[60] Having received such faithful support, the *Times* wondered could not the South expect fidelity from its slaves on the battlefield? Although the discussion of black troops worried the adversaries of the South, people within the Confederacy expressed fears of a different nature.

While abolitionists feared that black troops might succeed in winning southern independence, many Georgians feared for the country's social

---

[58] "The *Chicago Times* on the Negro Question," *Columbus Times*, 22 November 1864, 2.

[59] "Yankee View of the Question," *Columbus Times*, 3 December 1864, 2.

[60] "Slavery in America," *Columbus Times*, 8 December 1864, 2.

structure. An expression of that concern appeared on 23 November when the *Columbus Times* reprinted a powerful editorial from the *Savannah Morning News*: "The proposition to put the negro in the army, strikes a fatal blow at the root of the institution of slavery, and if carried out, will effectually destroy…the whole super-structure."[61] By creating slave-soldiers, the *Morning News* feared, the South must admit that slavery was wrong and thereby concede the major issue of the war.[62] Furthermore, the editor of the Savannah paper argued, the proposition simply would not work: "The negro is destitute of the intellect, the patriotic emotions, the greatness of soul, so essential to make a soldier."[63] Similar editorials from the *Charleston Mercury* and *Richmond Dispatch* appeared in the *Columbus Times* during the first phase of the debate.[64] Despite the negative tone of these news items, the *Times* consistently reported the progress of the legislation in the Confederate Congress and kept the issue firmly before the public.

Meanwhile, the *Columbus Daily Sun* also printed numerous news items about arming the slaves. For example, on 9 November, the morning after a telegraphic transcript of the president's message appeared, the *Sun* cited the *Charlottesville Chronicle* as saying that General Lee strongly favored the use of black troops.[65] Although lacking a solid foundation, such reports lent credibility to Davis's speculations. While struggling for balance on the subject, on 20 November the *Sun* recorded the reservations of the governor of Alabama about freeing the faithful noncombatant laborers who served with the army: "To permit the Confederate Government to acquire property in them, and, ultimately, to emancipate such as faithfully perform service, would be as unconstitutional as it would be destructive."[66] Like the *Columbus Times*, the *Sun* relished the northern response to the idea. On 10 November the *Sun* reprinted an editorial from the *Chicago Times* that ridiculed the hypocrisy of the abolitionist movement. How can black troops be an "evidence of exhaustion" in the South and a "sound war measure" in the North?, the

[61] "A Most Ruinous Proposition," *Columbus Times*, 23 November 1864, 2.

[62] Ibid.

[63] Ibid.

[64] "The Richmond Dispatch," *Columbus Times*, 6 December 1864, 2.

[65] "Negroes for the Army," *Daily Sun*, 9 November 1864, 1.

[66] "Governor Watts's Message," *Daily Sun*, 20 November 1864, 2. The Confederate Constitution prohibited any limitation of slavery by the national government.

Chicago editor queried. "When abolitionism contemplates its own pictures of the dauntless heroism of negro soldiers, can it do less than tremble when it learns that the South is about to loose half a million of these ferocious fighters upon the North?"[67]

Thus, the *Daily Sun* regularly published news items both for and against arming the slaves and, therefore, significantly furthered the local debate.

Although both the *Columbus Times* and *Daily Sun* printed numerous news items about arming the slaves, neither newspaper took a strong editorial position on the issue during the first phase of the debate. Indeed, the editor of the *Times*, J.W. Warren, addressed the issue only once, when on 17 December he announced that Congress would soon approve Davis's request for 40,000 noncombatant laborers without the "emancipation feature": "This action of Congress will accord with the sentiment of the country and is all the sacrifices of principles demanded by the existing emergencies."[68] Clearly, during the initial phase of the debate, Warren did not feel directly threatened by Union forces and, therefore, could not see any necessity to arm the slaves.

In contrast, editor William Scruggs of the *Sun* quietly accepted the idea of black troops. On 11 November, at the end of a letter from a Richmond correspondent, Scruggs speculated that the South could form separate black units with white officers so that no one could claim equality of the races.[69] While far from a ringing endorsement, this comment from the *Sun*'s editor revealed a general acceptance of the concept of black men wearing Confederate gray. Although enraged by Davis's plans to curtail exemptions for doctors, ministers, and the press, Scruggs appeared unexcited by the president's plans to emancipate the slave laborers within the army.[70] After explaining the plan, he simply said, "No comments appear to be necessary."[71] Finally, on 31 December, in a highly suggestive statement, Scruggs argued that the South might need to alter the vision of 1861 to achieve its independence: "Our cause cannot be lost. … It will succeed, but perhaps not in the manner,

[67] "Arming Negroes in the South," *Daily Sun*, 10 November 1864, 1.
[68] J.W. Warren, "The Negro Question," *Columbus Times*, 17 December 1864, 2.
[69] William Scruggs, "The Army and Congress," *Daily Sun*, 11 November 1864, 2.
[70] William Scruggs, "President's Message," *Daily Sun*, 16 November 1864, 1.
[71] William Scruggs, "Arming the Negroes," *Daily Sun*, 11 November 1864, 1.

nor upon the precise basis marked out and erected by those who inaugurated it."[72] Did the *Sun*'s editor contemplate a new "cornerstone" for the Confederacy? In any event, the editors of the *Columbus Times* and *Daily Sun* approached the issue carefully, encouraged debate, and disclosed their own views subtly.

Soon after the publication of Davis's message to Congress, numerous correspondents addressed the notion of slave-soldiers in letters to the editor of the *Columbus Times*. In letters published on 18 and 19 November, "Jim," the paper's Richmond correspondent, expressed strong disapproval of any alteration in the slave's role in the war effort: "The discussion may be long and interesting, or sweetly brief. In either event Cuffee will not be permitted for the present to 'lay down the shovel and the hoe.'"[73] The publication of Congressional arguments against the measure, "Jim" argued, "would do good in many sections of the country, where weariness of the war is fast ripening into something worse."[74] To balance the picture, on 11 and 28 November, the *Times* reprinted Peter W. Alexander's letters to the *Savannah Republican* appraising the measure's Congressional prospects and recommending a full discussion of the issue. In the letter appearing on 11 November, Alexander suggested that most opponents of black troops had taken no active role in the war and, therefore, did not understand the depth of the crisis or the feasibility of the measure: "The men who favor it, on the contrary, are, for the most part, men of action, who have been actively engaged in our mighty struggle."[75] The conflicting views from the Richmond correspondents, printed in the *Times*, provided an excellent glimpse of the differing views in the capital.

The *Columbus Times* also printed letters on the subject from local citizens. For example, in a letter published on 18 November, "Dad Burnitt" described the powerful arguments for black troops that had appeared in Mobile's *Evening News*: "He [a Mobile editor] thinks the necessities of our

---

[72] William Scruggs, "The Prospect," *Daily Sun*, 31 December 1864, 2.

[73] "Jim," "From Our Richmond Correspondent," *Columbus Times*, 18 November 1864, 1.

[74] "Jim," "From Our Richmond Correspondent," *Columbus Times*, 19 November 1864, 1.

[75] Peter W. Alexander, "Army Correspondent of the *Savannah Republican*," *Columbus Times*, 11 November 1864, 1.

country demand that they enter the field. That it would be the salvation of the country, and save slavery itself."[76] In a more contemplative mood, on 5 December, part-time Columbus resident William Samford addressed Davis's proposals: "There is a deep substratum of public sentiment...that gradual emancipation may become the policy of the Confederacy—its war policy to secure independence."[77] This statement echoed many northern arguments for the Emancipation Proclamation as a just and necessary war measure. Such a pragmatic policy, Samford realized, came at a high price: "I say to put negroes in the army is to abolish slavery. ... When you make him a soldier he will never again be an [sic] humble, useful, and contented slave."[78] Even at such a sacrifice, Samford argued that the South had come too far to turn back to the Union: "We hear that it has become a war for Independence per se—that slavery or no slavery, we are to be a separate people. I think that this is the truth."[79] While not all men and women in Columbus held such radical views, the proponents of black soldiers had found a voice in the letter writers to the *Times*. Clearly, the correspondents of the *Columbus Times* took the idea of arming the slaves seriously and dared to express opinions contrary to traditional southern doctrine.

The *Daily Sun* also received many letters concerning the slave's role in the war. Another Richmond reporter, George W. Bagby, correctly reported that Davis's proposal for noncombatant laborers would not end the discussion of slaves in the army: "Mr. Davis inserts the entering wedge for the use of negro troops in our army. He talks of 40,000 pioneers—but his pioneers are to be drilled with the musket, and set free for good under it."[80] Despite doubting the president's sincerity, "Pan," as Bagby signed his letters, admitted that military necessity might force its acceptance: "Can the negro soldier ensure our independence? ...If the answer is in the affirmative, there should be no hesitation as to his employment."[81] Closer to Columbus, on 18 November, "Justitia" argued that "the white population of the country has been

[76] "Dad Burnitt," "Correspondence from Mobile," *Columbus Times*, 18 November 1864, 2.

[77] William Samford, "Letter from Samford," *Columbus Times*, 5 December 1864, 2.

[78] Ibid.

[79] Ibid.

[80] George W Bagby, "Letter from Richmond," *Daily Sun*, 16 November 1864, 1.

[81] Ibid.

so much exhausted that the Negroes' services must be invoked."[82] If the South freed the faithful black troops, "Justitia" declared, it would confess the injustice of slavery. On the other hand, he wondered whether it would be morally right not to free the slave-soldier: "If we were not to free him, would we not be regarded by the civilized world as...barbarous? For that we compel human beings to fight...to make perpetual their bondage."[83] While writers like "Justitia" struggled within themselves to find the right course, others affirmed that whatever should be done, it had to be done quickly. On 22 November the *Sun*'s Mobile correspondent, "Iter," looked out upon the Union fleet in Mobile Bay and declared, "If we intend to avail ourselves of this strength, we must act and act at once."[84] Unlike the editors of the Columbus papers, the correspondents of both the *Daily Sun* and *Columbus Times* openly discussed the pros and cons of arming the slaves and significantly advanced the debate in Southwest Georgia.

In contrast to the wide discussion of the issue in Columbus, the other cities in Southwest Georgia did not seriously enter the debate during November and December 1864. Although the *Albany Patriot* printed the president's message, editor J.W. Fears did not comment on Davis's proposals or print any news items or letters about arming the slaves. Similarly, E.H. Grouby, the editor of the *Early County News* in Blakely, published Davis's address but provided only limited space to the issue during the first phase of the debate. On 9 November Grouby endorsed the idea of slaves serving as noncombatant laborers, but he resolutely discouraged discussion of blacks serving as soldiers: "To put arms into the hands of our slaves and make soldiers of them, or to free them for the sake of making soldiers of them, should never be thought of."[85] While he offered these comments as though they were final, the Blakely editor began to retreat from them on 14 December when he argued that "peace and the arming of negroes" were the two great questions facing the nation.[86] Although initially hesitant to take a stand, the residents of Albany and Blakely observed the debate in Columbus and entered the fray in earnest in January and February 1865.

[82] "Justitia," "For the *Sun*—Tuskegee," *Daily Sun*, 18 November 1864, 2.
[83] Ibid.
[84] "Iter," "Letter from Iter," *Daily Sun*, 22 November 1864, 1.
[85] "Negroes to Be Used as Soldiers," *Early County News*, 9 November 1864, 1.
[86] "Lead Editorial," *Early County News*, 14 December 1864, 2.

Starting with President Davis's modest request for 40,000 slaves to serve with the army as noncombatants, the Confederacy moved quickly in November and December 1864 to a national debate about arming the slaves. The news reports, editorials, and letters to the editor of the Macon, Athens, Augusta, and Columbus papers show these small Georgia cities cautiously entering the national dialogue. The news reports served mainly to set the ideological parameters of the discussion and to provide a national context for the formation of local opinion. Henry Flash in Macon spoke out strongly against arming the slaves, but he was soon forced to admit that practical measures such as exemption reform provided little hope for filling the Confederate ranks. In contrast, James Gardner in Augusta proceeded cautiously, but by not rejecting the concept out of hand and by opening his columns to the community, he contributed mightily to get the local debate started. Of equal importance, the resolute steps of Sherman's columns defeated the efforts of Nathan Morse at Augusta's *Chronicle and Sentinel* and John Christy at the *Southern Watchmen* in Athens to stifle the debate in Georgia. In the letters to editors in Macon, Augusta, and Columbus, the common men and women of Georgia, as well as professional correspondents elsewhere, spoke out strongly about arming the slaves. Although many reflect the inner turmoil expressed by "Justitia" in Columbus, these average citizens of the Deep South appear amazingly open to the "radical measures" suggested in Richmond. The fire of debate concerning arming the slaves only smoldered in November and December, but the military reverses suffered by the Confederacy in late December 1864 fanned the embers into flames and furthered the transformation just begun in the Georgia mind.

4

A Shout in the Night

By the fall of 1864 many Texans had wearied of the war. Far as they were from Sherman's columns in Georgia and Grant's lines at Petersburg, the war was more a nuisance than a direct threat. Conscription, impressment, and taxes struck Texans as onerous measures imposed by Richmond officials. Like many North Carolinians and some Georgians, Texans wondered if the Confederate government had explored all options for peace. In Texas, unlike in the Shenandoah Valley of Virginia, no Union cavalrymen rode through the fields of friends and neighbors sending adrenaline and southern patriotism shooting through their veins. Virginians and Georgians found themselves decisively engaged with the war and could not ignore the reality of the Union armies. In contrast, Grant, Sherman, and even the revered General Lee appeared to many Texans as actors in a story that hardly involved them at all. True, wives missed their husbands, children missed their fathers, and parents longed for the return of their sons. Yet, the fundamental tenets of life in Texas continued as they had in the years preceding the war.

In November and December 1864 Texas planters had begun to process a record cotton harvest, and a discussion of modifying slavery seemed poorly timed to many of them. On 23 November a report appeared in Austin from an observer in Matamoros who spoke of 20,000 people crowded into the Mexican city and of 100 ships sitting off the bar waiting to load Texas products. The Union blockade did not extend below the Rio Grande River, and it was a simple matter to ship Texas cotton across the border and hence escape the Union noose that surrounded the coastal South. A correspondent to the Marshall paper, "Carlos," reported from Brownsville that "business is rapidly increasing, and you would be astonished to see the immense quantities of goods that are crossing the river." With cotton selling for approximately three times the pre-war price, Texans could afford to purchase not only essential military items from Europe but also luxury items unknown in the rest of the Confederacy. Many read with interest treasury agent Peter W. Gray's new regulations for the sale of cotton and tobacco across the border. Confederate tax collectors struggled to funnel the border traffic through four "open ports" and threatened to confiscate all cotton not taken through the correct channels. Many Texans, like Judge George W. Smith of Fayette County, resented the Confederate duties but had few choices. On 14 December one Texan reported seeing several hundred teams taking loads of cotton south and several hundred more returning with goods. Plantation slavery still functioned quite well in Texas, and with a market in Mexico, Texans set out to make as much money as they could.[1]

Jefferson Davis's speculations about the proper role for the slave in the war effort arrived in Texas as slaves began to harvest and to transport the 1864 cotton crop to markets in Mexico. While in Richmond the great men of the Confederacy discussed Davis's suggestions, an equally intense discussion on the proposition to arm slaves occurred among the citizens of the Trans-Mississippi South.[2] A number of public figures, from governors to military leaders to local dignitaries, used the newspaper columns to reaffirm their faith in slavery and the Confederacy. These journals allowed Texas leaders to reach a large audience across the vast expanses of the state and were intended to discourage the development of Unionist or separatist feelings in the immigrant and frontier communities. Although public sentiment is usually elusive, these newspapers provide considerable evidence that, by the spring of 1865, a number of Texans were willing to rethink the role of the slave in the Confederate South.

As in the East, President Davis's annual address to Congress, the southern defeats at Nashville and Savannah, and the failure of the Hampton Roads peace conference propelled the discussions of slavery. These crucial

---

[1] "From the Rio Grande," *Austin The Weekly State Gazette*, 23 November 1864, 2; "Brownsville, Oct. 11th, 1864," *Marshall Texas Republican*, 4 November 1864, 1; "Explanatory Instruction," *Austin The Weekly State Gazette*, 23 November 1864, 2; "General Orders," *Austin The Weekly State Gazette*, 21 December 1864, 2; "The LaGrange True Issue...," *Austin The Weekly State Gazette*, 7 December 1864, 2; "The Very Latest News," *Austin The Weekly State Gazette*, 14 December 1864, 2.

[2] The term "common" as used here is meant to denote people outside of government or important military position. Specifically, it means the average reader of a Texas newspaper.

events initiated three distinct phases in the Texas debate about arming slaves. With each phase, the opinions of many men and women evolved—and they adopted new opinions—as events approached a crisis. The public debate in Virginia followed almost immediately on the heels of the three precipitating events; the debate in Georgia followed the same pattern, but at a delay of two to five days because of the time required to transmit the news from Richmond; and the Texas debate lagged still further behind events in the East because of the even longer delays in receiving news from the capital. As the Union grasp on Richmond tightened in January and February, news accounts often arrived first in Texas from northern papers exchanged with the Union blockading squadron. Most Texans took such reports with a grain of salt and reserved judgment on events until southern papers made the two- to three-week passage across the Mississippi River. Despite the significant time lag, events that energized discussions of black Confederate troops in Virginia and Georgia also resonated in Texas. But because people in Texas were so differently affected by the war, their responses to the issue of slavery's future also differed.

Stretching over 150,000 square miles, Texas boasted a diverse Civil War population that included white settlers from across the Southeast, large numbers of Hispanic Tejanos, and a significant European immigrant community on the frontier. Commercial centers thrived along the coast, while staple-producing regions predominated near the Louisiana border. In the interior regions of the state, farmers balanced the raising of livestock with cotton production. Although Texas contained the lowest percentage of slaves of any of the Deep South states, it offered virgin soil to bold planters willing to make the move. In short, Civil War Texas was a dynamic state offering opportunity to a variety of groups, yet the political structure remained firmly tied to the slave economy.

As one examines the debate in Texas, three distinct geographical regions emerge. First, Houston and Galveston formed a Gulf Coast region of the state. Largescale production of cotton and sugar dominated economic activity and made the coastal area surrounding the two cities appear quite similar to commercial areas in the Deep South. Inundated with black and white refugees, Houston boasted a wartime population of nearly 8,000 and served as an important industrial center. While northern troops sat in New Orleans and occasionally threatened the coast, Houston experienced the war secondhand. In contrast, Galveston, which suffered Federal occupation for several months in the fall of 1862, lost population during the war due to the continued threat from the Union Navy. Confederate Troops closely monitored the movements of the Union blockading fleet from positions on Galveston Island throughout the war. Meanwhile, the closure of Confederate ports on the Atlantic brought a flurry of blockade-running activity to Galveston during the winter of 1864. The war had deeply impacted Galveston but it had not transformed it into a ghost town. Opinions expressed in the tri-weekly editions of the *Houston Telegraph* and the *Galveston News*, the papers with the largest circulations in Texas, carried considerable weight in the state but did not prevent the formation of distinct local ideas.

Representing a second region of the state, Dallas and Marshall reflected the views held in the staple producing regions of East Texas. Largely Anglo in composition, the citizens of East Texas depended upon cotton and slavery for their livelihood. Throughout the debate, the military headquarters of the Trans-Mississippi Department was located in Shreveport, Louisiana, only thirty miles from Marshall. Refugees from Louisiana, Missouri, and Arkansas arrived in East Texas early in the war and played key roles as the slave-soldier debate evolved there. The failure of the Union Red River campaign in the spring of 1864 and subsequent Union inactivity left the region rather complacent. They had met the enemy, and the blue-clad warriors had not come back. Sterling Price's foray into Arkansas and Missouri that fall worried a number of the citizens in Marshall, but no one expected an immediate threat to East Texas. Residents of Dallas and Marshall had not forgotten that a war existed, but it had no significant impact on their lives.

Finally, Austin, Bellville, and LaGrange represented a distinct central region of Texas. Planters and farmers in the area balanced largescale production of beef and corn with still profitable cotton. Austin remained the state capital, but most significant governmental decisions in this period were made at military headquarters in either Houston or Shreveport. In contrast to the Eastern and Gulf Coast regions of the state, Central Texas never saw the war. No Union forces ever threatened the region as they did Galveston throughout the war. Likewise, no defeated southern army ever returned to Austin as Sterling Price's columns did to Marshall in December 1864. Located 150 to 200 miles from the coast, Austin, Bellville, and LaGrange did not have direct rail and telegraph links with the other regions of Texas.

News reached this undisturbed area of the Confederacy by stagecoach, in letters, and in the columns of newspapers. Outside the mainstream of Texas's social and economic life, planters and German and Czech immigrants vied for local control and developed quite different views of what it meant to be a good Texan.

Each of the three regions of Texas entered the slave-soldier debate with a distinct view of the war based on local circumstances. Although the debate followed a different course in each area, Gulf Coast Texas, East Texas, and Central Texas all examined the issues carefully, weighed the value of slavery, and struggled to determine what price they were willing to pay to attain victory. In Texas, as in Virginia and Georgia, the initial phase of the debate began shortly after President Jefferson Davis first raised the issue in his address to the Confederate Congress. During these first two months, Texans from all three regions discussed their commitment to slavery and staked out the larger issues concerning the purpose of the war and the meaning of being a southerner.

President Davis's broaching of the subject of freedom for slaves laboring with the army brought a steady stream of news items into the offices of the *Houston Telegraph*. On 23 November the paper printed a synopsis of Davis's message. Although relegated to the telegraphic column, the *Telegraph*'s editor included the portion concerning the request for 40,000 slave laborers and even one of the president's radical concepts: "He also recommends acquiring for public service the right of property in the labor of slaves, the government engaging to liberate the negro on his discharge." In the same issue, the Houston paper reprinted an editorial from the *Chicago Times* that ridiculed the hypocrisy of the abolitionist movement. Similarly, on 3 December, in an editorial that first appeared in the *New York Times*, the Houston paper noted the fear that slave-soldiers inspired in the North: "We must have a new draft and a large one. This will not overmatch the negro recruits to Lee's and Hood's Armies. These negroes and all the whites that can be spared will swell the rebel forces." Unfortunately for President Davis and other advocates of arming the slaves, the measure inspired a similar fear in many southerners. After the full text of Davis's address appeared in Houston on 5 December, the *Telegraph* followed closely the debate in the Confederate Congress. On 19 December the powerful words of Senator Henry Foote of Tennessee boomed across the front page in Houston: "A general levy of the slaves for soldiers is unwise; their withdrawal from labor would be inexpedient so long as we can otherwise obtain as large an army as we can maintain." Echoing Foote's comments, on 30 December the *Telegraph* noted North Carolina Governor Zebulon Vance's opposition. Although Davis's proposals and speculations received a cool reception in Houston, the news items in the *Telegraph* provided a base for the formation of a local debate of the issue.[3]

Like many island residents, the *Galveston News* had moved inland to avoid Union threats and was publishing from offices in Houston when reports of the growing manpower crisis and President Davis's message arrived. An editorial reprinted from the *Richmond Enquirer* first raised the topic of slave-soldiers in the columns of the *News* on 9 November. The Richmond editor—fully aware of the threat of Union armies—contended that "every reflecting mind" must consider the slave option carefully and suggested the purchase, enlistment, and emancipation of 250,000 slaves: "We believe that the negroes, identified with us by interest, and fighting for their freedom would be faithful soldiers." In the same issue a Richmond correspondent mentioned a rumor of officer support for black troops, but quickly discounted it: "You need not attach much faith to it," he affirmed. Two weeks later, on 23 November, an editorial from Alabama appeared in the *Galveston News* opposite the synopsis of Davis's speech to Congress. The *Mobile News* editorial hailed the potential morale impact of black men in gray and asserted that the planters should decide the slave's course in the war: "If our slaves are to take part in this unhappy conflict, certainly we have a choice as to the side they shall take." Stopping short of total support, the Mobile paper declared that in the coming winter the South must consider the necessity of the matter. Yet, on 14 December, the Galveston paper reprinted an editorial from the *Richmond Whig* that stoutly decreed that slavery was not a matter open to debate.[4] Davis's proposal to free the slave engineers, cooks, and teamsters

---

[3] "Items of Interest," *Houston TriWeekly Telegraph*, 23 November 1864, 4; "Items of Interest," *Houston TriWeekly Telegraph*, 3 December 1864, 1; "President Davis's Message," *Houston TriWeekly Telegraph*, 5 December 1864, 1; "Confederate States Congress," *Houston TriWeekly Telegraph*, 19 December 1864, 1; "Items of Interest," *Houston TriWeekly Telegraph*, 30 December 1864, 1.

[4] "Opinion of the Press," *Galveston TriWeekly News*, 9 November 1864, 2; "A Richmond Correspondent Writes…," *Galveston TriWeekly News*, 9 November 1864, 2; "If the Yankees determine…," *Galveston TriWeekly News*, 25 November 1864, 2; "The

employed in the army in return for loyal service was, the *Whig* argued, not only unwise but also unconstitutional.[5] Items appearing in Galveston from northern papers also provided a mixed message. The *New York Herald* claimed to see a window of opportunity for the North in the slave-soldier debate: "The indications are that the South will soon be divided upon the question of freeing and arming the slaves. … The slaveholders will probably go against the plan, and the politicians will be in favor of it." On the other hand, two editorials from the *Chicago Times* also appeared in the *News* and took considerable delight in making fun of abolitionists who had repeatedly lauded the Union's use of black soldiers but decried the southern turn to black troops as a sign of weakness. While the editor of the *Galveston News* had firm opinions regarding the issue, he still was willing to open his paper to a variety of opinions. These conflicting opinions regarding slave-soldiers opened the discussion of the value of slavery and set the parameters of the local debate.[6]

Editor Edward H. Cushing of the *Houston Telegraph* did not possess a traditional southern pedigree. Raised in Vermont and schooled at Dartmouth, Cushing had journeyed to Texas in 1850 hoping to make a name for himself. Far from his New England roots, he became an outspoken proponent for states' rights and slavery. During the war, he championed the Confederate cause and led efforts in Texas in support of unpopular Richmond policies like conscription and the tax-in-kind. Yet, when Davis's message arrived in Houston suggesting new roles for slaves in the war, Cushing immediately proclaimed his opposition to any effort to employ slaves as soldiers. Reviewing the course of the war and the conduct of Texas slaves, on 23 November he claimed to see a divine sanction for slavery, an affirmation of the warm relationship between master and slave, and growing disillu-

---

President's Message, Synopsis," *Galveston TriWeekly News*, 25 November 1864, 1; "President Davis's Proposal for Manumitting Slaves," *Galveston TriWeekly News*, 14 December 1864, 1.

[5] The Confederate Constitution expressly forbade any action by Congress or the president concerning slavery. Confederate Constitution Article 1, Section 9, in Thomas, *The Confederate Nation*, 313.

[6] "Divide the South," *Galveston TriWeekly News*, 9 December 1864, 1; "News Items," *Galveston TriWeekly News*, 27 November 1864, 1; "*The Chicago Times…*," *Galveston TriWeekly News*, 9 December 1864, 2.

sionment among abolitionists in the North and in Europe. Based on these "results" of the war, he declared that the war had "vindicated the morality of slavery." After examining Davis's full message, Cushing embraced the president's proposal to use slaves in menial positions in the army but refused to seriously consider the implications of Davis's speculations: "The President reproves the proposition to arm the slaves, a step which we cannot but consider as unwise and unnecessary." Unable to see the manpower crisis, on 2 January Cushing emphasized the need for planters to produce large amounts of provisions and, more importantly, cotton: "If the war had only lasted a year or two, cotton might have been entirely omitted with prudence and advantage. But its long duration has given a tremendous impulse to its culture in every quarter." While the Union armies remained distant from Texas and the cotton trade with Mexico flourished, Cushing saw little need to adjust the slave's role in the war effort.[7]

Across town, Willard Richardson of the *Galveston News* was appalled at Davis's message. Although born in Massachusetts, Richardson had attended college in South Carolina and steeped himself in the states' rights doctrines of John C. Calhoun. Arriving in Texas in 1841, he achieved prominence as the editor of the state's largest circulation paper and spoke strongly for planter interests. On 12 December the Galveston editor fiercely attacked the idea of slave-soldiers and rebuked the president for considering even limited emancipation: "It is a matter of regret that any suggestion should have been made…that any emergency can arise to compel the South to an abandonment of the foundation principle upon which the institution of slavery rests: that is, the principle, that slavery is the best possible condition for the slave himself." Further, Richardson contended that if emancipation could be a boon to slaves, then the whole system must be morally wrong. "If they are capable of being safely entrusted with freedom," he declared, "they ought to be emancipated without conditions." Finally, the Galveston editor proclaimed that any Confederate effort to arm and free black troops would be the ultimate usurpation of local power: "If there can be a greater assump-

---

[7] Emory M. Thomas, "Rebel Nationalism: E.H. Cushing and the Confederate Experience," *Southwestern Historical Quarterly* 73 (January 1970): 343. E.H. Cushing, "The Present War," *Houston TriWeekly Telegraph*, 23 November 1864, 2; E.H. Cushing, "Lead Editorial," *Houston TriWeekly Telegraph*, 2 January 1865, 4.

tion of power or a more dangerous exercise of it, it is an act of the Confederate States Government by which it is declared that...the freedom of negroes is to be won by their fighting for it." In Richardson's view, the consequences of Davis's speculations had the potential for profound consequences: "The proposition which has been broached at Richmond to arm and drill...three hundred thousand slaves, will be very apt to finish the 'institution' and the 'Confederacy' before the spring campaign is opened." Ironically, the idea that the failure to fill the gray ranks might "finish" both institutions appears not to have occurred to him. Two weeks prior, Richardson had railed against all the "hale and robust young men" detailed from the army and estimated that 10,000 could be sent from Texas. While willing to send additional white men to the front, the editor of the *News* saw no need for black reinforcements and offered only limited recommendations on ways to supply the army's manpower needs. Far from the lines at Petersburg and Sherman's path through Georgia, Richardson failed to grasp the depth of the manpower crisis.[8]

Reflecting the opinion of the editor, the letters printed in the *Houston Telegraph* expressed considerable surprise that anyone would seriously consider black troops. On 20 December a letter from a soldier in Terry's Texas Rangers, a cavalry unit in Virginia, appeared in Houston. Citing an article from a Mississippi paper, the Ranger declared that many thought arming the slaves would increase the army by 200,000 and prevent the Union forces from enlisting the slaves to use against the Confederacy. Unwilling to concede freedom for faithful service as the Mississippi paper had suggested, this Texan trusted in divine intervention instead: "I feel confident that we will be able to gain our independence without the employment of negro troops. I believe a just God will give us victory if we will only hold out faithfully." In a similar vein, "T.A.," a frequent correspondent, accepted the use of slaves in menial roles with the armies but refused to consider their use as soldiers. The threat of internal unrest posed by armed blacks, in his view, overshadowed any assistance they might provide. Noting a discussion of the measure

---

[8] *Handbook of Texas Online,* Randolph Lewis, "Richardson, Willard," accessed October 26, 2016, http://www.tshaonlin.org/handbook/online/articles/fri13; Willard Richardson, "Mr. Davis's Recommendation of the Employment of Slaves in the Army," *Galveston TriWeekly News*, 12 December 1864, 2; Willard Richardson, "Some Time Ago...," *Galveston TriWeekly News*, 25 November 1864, 2.

in a Georgia paper, "T.A." argued that slaves could do more important work on the plantation: "Keep the remainder in [the] rear to fight famine, whilst our white men at the front hold in check an enemy not more formidable than the one that would overtake us in the rear, should the negro be foolishly transferred from the corn to the battle field."[9] Far removed from the Yankee columns, Houstonians remained focused on crop production, foreign trade, and the system that supported both.

None of the letters published in the *Galveston News* in November or December directly addressed black troops, but several touched on elements in the debate. Seeking the cause for God's wrath manifested against the South, "Jonah" on 7 November wrote concerning the sinfulness of southern slavery. Contending that Abraham had over 2,000 slaves and yet retained God's favor, "Jonah" concluded that although slavery was an "institution of God," the South had failed in its charge. Proclaiming slave marriages as unknown as marriage among cattle, "Jonah" argued that southern complicity in black adultery was the root problem. "So if we do not repent," "Jonah" prophesized, "He may take the slaves from us, and give them to others, who will use them without sinning and causing them to sin." The choice of the name "Jonah" suggests that the author was a slaveholder, a partaker in the sin. Further, like the biblical Jonah, the writer appeared to have wrestled mightily with the difficult message he felt compelled to tell. Confederate battlefield reverses caused many to question the path being followed in the South. For many like "Jonah," the issue was not slavery per se but how the South managed the institution.[10]

In a different vein, letters from "Traveler" and "J.T.M." pointed to divisions within white society as some planters resented having their slaves impressed, while at the same time soldiers were unable to find a place to spend the night. Clearly, the degree of sacrifice required of southern citizens was not symmetrical. Non-slaveholding whites served as the main element in the Confederate army, yet soldiers passing through Gulf Coast Texas often complained of poor treatment by merchants who refused to accept Confed-

---

[9] "Letter from the Rangers," *Houston TriWeekly Telegraph*, 20 December 1864, 1; "T.A.," "The *Macon Confederate*...," *Houston TriWeekly Telegraph*, 30 December 1864, 4.

[10] "Jonah," "When Will This War End?", *Galveston TriWeekly News*, 7 November 1864, 1.

erate script. Likewise, complaints about the impressment of slaves found little sympathy in the military camps and pointed to potential trouble between slave owners and the common soldiers. As important for the long-term debate in Galveston, "Item" reported large numbers of Union navy ships off the bar outside Galveston Bay. On 30 November, he wrote that firing in the night had caused many to race from their homes in the belief that another invasion of the island had begun. The persistent threat of U.S. Navy action provided a sense of urgency absent in other areas of Gulf Coast Texas. Although the letter writers in Galveston did not address the issue directly, their topics shed some light on local opinion about slavery and the war.[11]

In November and December 1864 President Davis's remarks concerning the slave's role in the war effort sparked considerable discussion in Gulf Coast Texas. Few citizens of Houston—a city booming with international trade and with essentially no Union threat—saw a need to modify slavery radically. As the U.S. Navy tightened its grip on other southern ports, blockade runners from Havana poured into Galveston Bay. Only in the letters from Galveston did the war appear to threaten. The separation of the Trans-Mississippi South from the rest of the Confederacy was reflected in the cool reception of Davis's proposals by the editors and the letter writers of Gulf Coast Texas.

In East Texas, Davis's remarks on slavery landed in a sea of debate about peace efforts and reconstruction. On 18 November the Marshall *Texas Republican* published a letter from Congressman William W. Boyce of South Carolina questioning Davis's willingness to listen to northern peace offers and blasting the administration's war measures: "Has not our Federal government done everything that a centralized military despotism could do? Indeed, if you [Davis] were appointed military dictator, what greater powers could you exercise than you now do?" Within the next two weeks the *Republican* printed similar letters from Vice President Alexander Stephens and Senator Herschel V. Johnson of Georgia urging renewed efforts to start negotiations with the northern states and broached the idea of separate state

[11] "J.T.M.," "Letter to the Editor," *Galveston TriWeekly News*, 9 November 1864, 1; "Traveler," "Observations of a Traveler," *Galveston TriWeekly News*, 21 November 1864, 1; "Item," "Letter to the Editor," *Galveston TriWeekly News*, 30 November 1864, 1.

action. The *Republican* balanced these letters with a series of resolutions passed by the Texas legislature concerning "peace, reconstruction, and independence." Refuting the idea of a convention of northern and southern states to end the war, the legislators assembled in Austin declared that the guarantee of slavery's existence was not the crucial point: "The Southern States did not secede from the Union upon any question such as the mere preservation of the slave property of their citizens. But...they were resolved to preserve their freedom and sovereignty." The antebellum status quo on slavery was not enough to achieve peace, they affirmed; "it must be coupled with our independence." Invoking the memory of "our murdered dead," the legislators in Austin had firmly denied the cry for a separate peace, but Davis's call in November for new sacrifices was heard by many East Texans who were frustrated with his administration and its conduct of the war. While the *Republican* endorsed the opinions of the legislature, the paper expressed sympathy with the complaints if not the solutions recommended by Boyce, Stephens, and Johnson.[12]

A telegraphic synopsis of Davis's remarks greeted a wary audience in Marshall on 2 December, but unlike many of its Texas peers, the *Republican* published the president's message in full on 16 December. Beyond the narrow terms of Davis's call for 40,000 laborers and his speculations on the military potential of the southern slave population, the citizens of Marshall were allowed to see the reasoning behind the step. Contending that southerners would willingly sacrifice their property for the cause, Davis focused on the social impact of the measure: "In its manifold phases it [arming slaves] embraces the stability of our republican form of institutions, resting on the actual political equality of all its citizens, and includes the fulfillment of the task...of Christianizing and improving the condition of the Africans." Clearly, the president had not borrowed the abolitionist ideas of Horace Greeley but, rather, proposed black troops as a way to maintain white society while conceding the humanity, if not the equality, of the South's black residents. As the citizens of Marshall contemplated Davis's ideas, the *Republican*

[12] "Letter from the Hon. W.W. Boyce," *Marshall Texas Republican*, 18 November 1864, 1; "Letter of Vice President Stephens," *Marshall Texas Republican*, 18 November 1864, 2; "Letter from the Hon. Herschel V. Johnson," *Marshall Texas Republican*, 2 December 1864, 1; "Joint Resolutions Concerning Peace, Reconstruction, and Independence," *Marshall Texas Republican*, 25 November 1864, 1.

provided brief accounts of Congressional action on black troops and conflicting reports of the war's progress. On 25 November the Marshall paper had reprinted an Alabama editorial which suggested that southern troops would soon be on the Ohio River, yet less than a month later, dreams of the Ohio were past. In late December Thomas C. Reynolds, the Confederate Governor of Missouri who was a refugee in Marshall, savaged the conduct of General Sterling Price in his unsuccessful fall campaign in Missouri. If the Confederacy hoped to mount another campaign to reclaim the southern states, much less cross the Ohio into the North, then a new source of soldiers had to be found. The combination of troubling war news along with Davis's challenges to traditional southern ideas about race must have made many in Marshall uncomfortable as they faced the new year.[13]

To the west, the *Dallas Herald* refused to be discouraged by southern reverses. On 19 November, the *Herald* printed a column from a New York paper praising Confederate strategy despite the loss of Atlanta: "While the rebel army has been defeated, Lee's strategy has won a signal victory in the postponement of the campaign." In the same light, the Dallas paper credited Price's raid into Missouri with relieving pressure that would otherwise have been applied upon Richmond or upon the army of Tennessee. On 3 December a brief summary of Davis's message appeared in the telegraphic column of the *Herald*: "The subject of employing negroes in the army is discussed at some length. The President dissents from those who advise a general levy and army [sic] of slaves for duty as soldiers." The president's call for 40,000 laborers was duly noted, but the depth of Davis's radical suggestions was not. In subsequent weeks, the *Herald* followed the debate as it developed in Congress and in the Deep South yet consistently highlighted the remarks of those opposed to slave-soldiers. For instance, on 24 December the Dallas paper printed an editorial from Georgia titled "The Negro Question in a Nutshell." "Congress has legislated enough…," the Georgian contended. "Send every white man to the field that belongs there. … Make teamsters, cooks, and hospital nurses of the negroes so far as they are needed…and

---

[13] "Synopsis of the President's Message," *Marshall Texas Republican*, 2 December 1864, 1; "Message of President Davis," *Marshall Texas Republican*, 16 December 1864, 2; "The Latest News," *Marshall Texas Republican*, 2 December 1864, 2; "The following extract…," *Marshall Texas Republican*, 25 November 1864, 2; "Governor Reynolds," *Marshall Texas Republican*, 23 December 1864, 1.

keep the remainder in the rear to fight famine." Such limited measures made perfect sense in the secure confines of Dallas. Two weeks later the *Herald* reported passage of a Senate bill authorizing 40,000 slave laborers to work with the army. Stripped of Davis's recommended emancipation feature, the Senate bill appeared acceptable if not ideal in East Texas.[14] Throughout the first phase of the debate, no voice of support for slave-soldiers was heard in the Dallas paper.

At his editorial desk in Marshall, Robert W. Loughery struggled to understand the desperate measures contemplated by Boyce, Stephens, and Davis. A strong states' rights Democrat, Loughery had championed the political ascendancy of his neighbor Louis T. Wigfall. Loughery, like Wigfall, saw the "cause" in stark terms. Men like Boyce and Stephens, he contended, had forgotten the principles of the revolution. "The people of the Southern States," Loughery affirmed, "should never lose sight of the issues involved in the contest. ... They are fighting for the principles of self government as announced in the memorable Declaration of Independence of 1776." The peace proposals, he asserted, were destined "to produce distraction and division at home, and to weaken public confidence in the success of our cause." Even as he published these letters, Loughery cautioned his fellow newspaper publishers not to promote southern divisions by the items they printed: "Every indiscreet editorial and communication which appears in their columns is seized upon by the enemy, and is used to the prejudice of our cause." Apparently, the Marshall editor considered any serious discussion of black troops a potential source of genuine division.[15]

---

[14] "The Washington correspondent...," *Dallas Herald*, 19 November 1864, 2; "The New York News...," *Dallas Herald*, 26 November 1864, 2; "By Sunday's Mail," *Dallas Herald*, 5 November 1864, 1; "Synopsis of the President's Message," *Dallas Herald*, 3 December 1864, 1; "By Wednesday's Mail," *Dallas Herald*, 26 November 1864, 1; "By Last Night's Mail," *Dallas Herald*, 3 December 1864, 2; "The Negro Question in a Nutshell," *Dallas Herald*, 24 December 1864, 2; "From Flake's Bulletin, Dec. 28," *Dallas Herald*, 12 January 1865, 2.

[15] Max S. Lale, "Robert W. Loughery: Rebel Editor," *East Texas Historical Journal* 21, no. 2 (October 1983): 4. "The Letters of Stephens and Boyce," *Marshall Texas Republican*, 18 November 1864, 2; "The Letters of Stephens and Boyce," *Marshall Texas Republican*, 25 November 1864, 2; "The People of the Southern States...," *Marshall Texas Republican*, 4 November 1864, 2.

Although the *Republican* provided Davis's complete message, Loughery strictly limited his coverage of the slave-soldier debate. Decrying impressment, conscription, and Davis's threat to slave property, Loughery applauded the South Carolina legislature for firmly denying the national government's right to legislate on slavery: "They affirm in our judgment, the true principles of government, and will we trust, exercise a salutatory influence on our public counsels." Sitting in Marshall, Loughery could not fathom the depths of despair that led Stephens to contemplate separate state action or the dire military circumstances that caused Davis to take the greatest political gamble of his life. Even as he later announced the fall of Savannah and the defeat of John B. Hood at Nashville, Loughery's world remained unshaken: "There are too many in the South ready to give up at every disaster which befalls our arms, not seeming to know the extent of our resources." Resources may have seemed abundant in East Texas, but few leaders in Virginia or Georgia found themselves oversupplied with anything but faith in the cause.[16]

In Dallas, John W. Swindells echoed the confidence of his East Texas comrade. In the *Herald*, Swindells refused to acknowledge any effort to modify slavery. In the same issue in which the synopsis of Davis's message appeared, Swindells ridiculed Republican efforts to work a constitutional amendment through the U.S. House of Representatives to ban slavery. "Lincoln, in his next message," the Dallas editor proclaimed, "will recommend the abolition of slavery. Of course slavery will be abolished on paper in much the same way that most of the Yankee victories are obtained." The Dallas editor appeared unable to believe that Lincoln might genuinely intend to end slavery, much less that the President of the Confederacy had seriously questioned the role assigned to the black population of the South. During the next six weeks, Swindells ignored all discussions of slavery. On 12 January he announced the fall of Savannah and the destruction of Hood's army but made no immediate call for new sources of manpower for the army. Instead, Swindells downplayed the importance of Savannah and admonished

[16] "The People of the Southern States…," *Marshall Texas Republican*, 4 November 1864, 2; "We had the pleasure…," *Marshall Texas Republican*, 11 November 1864, 2; "South Carolina," *Marshall Texas Republican*, 6 January 1865, 2; "We republish in this issue…," *Marshall Texas Republican*, 6 January 1865, 2.

Davis that he could commission but could not create generals. Far from the battlefields in Virginia and Georgia, Swindells refused to seriously consider any effort to modify slavery. The Dallas *Herald*'s editorial indifference and consistent disregard of all news items favorable to arming slaves significantly retarded the development of the debate in Dallas.[17] Remote as they were from the developments on the battlefields, readers in Dallas simply could not comprehend the urgency of the slavery issue.

Like the editors of the Marshall *Republican* and the Dallas *Herald*, East Texans did not respond to Davis's call for discussion about the slave's role in the war effort during November and December. Although no letters directly addressed the topic, several relevant items did appear. On 19 November, "Beta Omega" wrote from Shreveport calling for new sacrifices and unity: "Our final success depends upon a united, determined resistance. Life is not so dear or peace so sweet as to be purchased at the price of chains and slavery." In Dallas two public meetings were held to discourage those tempted by discussions of peace negotiations. Nathaniel Burford, the local enrolling officer, addressed a large gathering of men and women on 16 November concerning the dire consequences of reconstruction. Similarly, on 7 January, in another public meeting, the citizens of Dallas reaffirmed their resolve to stay the course: "Our often repeated purpose never to submit to Yankee abolition rule and power, remains inflexible and unshaken." Further, the citizens declared, "We desire peace with all its accompanying blessings, but...we can only accept the same upon honorable terms, and upon a basis of a full recognition of our Independence." Clearly, the citizens of East Texas sought to reassure themselves of their common resolve to see the war through to its conclusion. The failure to address the slave-soldier issue in any of these meetings demonstrated the dramatic differences between the situation in Texas and the situation east of the Mississippi River. In Texas, circumstances had not reached a point where leaders, newspaper editors, or common citizens felt the need to confront the difficult issue of arming slaves. Whatever their prior opinion, Virginians and Georgians were compelled by events

---

[17] "Later," *Dallas Herald*, 3 December 1864, 2; "From the tenor of the dispatches...," *Dallas Herald*, 12 January 1865, 2; "The Houston Telegraph...," *Dallas Herald*, 12 January 1865, 2.

unfolding about them to at least consider the idea of black men in gray uniforms.[18]

In Central Texas slaveholders approached Davis's suggestions about modifying slavery with considerable trepidation. Recognizing it as a serious threat to divide their already splintered community, planters attempted to stifle the debate over arming slaves. In the opening months of the war, large numbers of German and Czech immigrants from Central Texas had eagerly joined the state militia, but few men rallied to the Confederate standard. This lack of Confederate patriotism caused political leaders to question the region's loyalty. While Unionist ringleaders were rounded up and some hung, Unionist sentiment remained strong in Central Texas. Confederate authorities found themselves unable to attain results from local officials and resorted to martial law, sending troops into Bellville and LaGrange in January 1863. Organized resistance to the Confederacy subsided in the face of overwhelming force, but tensions remained high as conflicting Confederate and Unionist sentiments stayed just beneath the surface. Therefore, in the fall of 1864, slaveholders grappled with the idea of arming slaves with one eye upon its impact on their slave society and the other firmly fixed on the non-slaveholding immigrants in their midst.[19]

A synopsis of Davis's message appeared in Austin on 30 November, but few people immediately responded to the president's bold speculations about slaves in the army. Most Texans paid more attention to Davis's ideas about curtailing exemptions from the army and to discussions of foreign affairs. Although unheralded, a steady stream of news items concerning the arming of slaves began to arrive in the Austin offices of *The Weekly State Gazette*. In response to Davis's address, the paper published numerous accounts of congressional efforts to repeal the military exemptions for editors and for slave owners supervising more than fifteen slaves. Yet, in the discussion of the proposed changes to the conscription laws, the Austin paper provided brief notices of the discussions of new roles for slaves. On 30 November and 7 December news items appeared discussing the use of slaves "in all positions

[18] "Our Shreveport Correspondence," *Dallas Herald*, 19 December 1864, 2; "According to previous announcement...," *Dallas Herald*, 19 November 1864, 2; "Proceedings of a Public Meeting," *Dallas Herald*, 12 January 1865, 2.

[19] Claude Elliot, "Union Sentiment in Texas, 1861–1865," *Southwestern Historical Quarterly* 50 (April 1947): 449–77.

in the army except as soldiers." Unlike the longer accounts of the battles over exemptions, few names of congressmen were given in either support or opposition to the measure. The only item that directly discussed Davis's proposition to free all the slave laborers who faithfully served with the army came from South Carolina and appeared in Austin on 4 January. Noting that Robert Barnwell Rhett sponsored the resolutions, the *Gazette* reported the South Carolina legislature's unwillingness to consider any modification of slavery and cited their assertion that any congressional act that might lead to emancipation was strictly unconstitutional. Many in Austin did not immediately grasp the importance of the slave-soldier debate or possibly did not believe that southerners would seriously consider such a radical step.[20] This cool response to the president's suggestions for modifying slavery stood in sharp contrast to southerners in Virginia and Georgia who had witnessed the devastation of the war firsthand and realized that desperate measures were called for.

The words of Jefferson Davis rang out in *The Bellville Countryman* on 6 December and resonated in a community already discussing the value of slavery. An editorial from the *Huntsville* [TX] *Item* appeared in the Bellville paper on 22 November and sparked considerable interest as the East Texas editor commended a discussion of arming the slaves "as much more to the point than railing against croakers." Arguing that national independence was the South's true war aim, the Huntsville paper boldly declared that "neither negroes nor slavery will be permitted to stand in the way of the success of our cause." In a different vein, on 6 December the Bellville paper gleefully reprinted an editorial from the *Chicago Times* that ridiculed the hypocrisy of the abolitionist movement. Finally, on 20 December *The Countryman* detailed President Abraham Lincoln's efforts to attain congressional approval for the Thirteenth Amendment. This wide-ranging discussion of slavery in Bellville took place against the backdrop of planters hauling their 1864 cotton crop toward San Antonio and on to Mexico. The news items that ap-

---

[20] "Synopsis of the President's Message," *Austin The Weekly State Gazette*, 30 November 1864, 2; "Joint Resolutions Concerning Peace, Reconstruction, and Independence," *Austin The Weekly State Gazette*, 9 November 1864, 1; "Congressional News, Southern Dispatches," *Austin The Weekly State Gazette*, 30 November 1864, 2; "Congressional News," *Austin The Weekly State Gazette*, 7 December 1864, 2; "The following are resolutions...," *Austin The Weekly State Gazette*, 4 January 1865, 2.

peared and recommended a modification of slavery must have seemed quite uncalled for to many readers as they started for Matamoros with their loads of cotton and anticipations of great profits.[21]

President Davis's speculations on slavery drew immediate and impassioned comment in LaGrange. As in Austin, the local weekly, *The LaGrange Patriot,* elected to print only a telegraphic synopsis of Davis's remarks. Ironically, the paper suggested the speech was too long to print but in the same issue copied two full columns of a speech by Union General Benjamin Butler. Despite the *Patriot*'s apparent lack of interest, on 10 December it noted the opposition of the *Memphis Appeal* and the support of the *Huntsville* [TX] *Item* for the president's recommendation that the slaves laboring with the army should be freed. In both instances, the LaGrange paper printed only a snippet from the other journals. On Christmas Eve, the *Patriot* broke the pattern and reprinted a long piece from the *Galveston News.* In it, Willard Richardson of the *News* chided the president for suggesting that slavery might not be the best condition for the slave: "If it be admitted that the negro can enjoy freedom, without injury to their own condition or to those around them, but that, having the physical power, we will compel their servitude, the declaration would be ignoble; for it would assert the maintenance of injustice by force." Unlike the items that appeared earlier, which had advocated black troops, the *LaGrange Patriot* copied the Galveston editorial in full and the paper endorsed Richardson's conclusions. Two additional items touching on modifications of slavery appeared on 7 January but neither received extensive space. Clearly, the *Patriot* attempted to lead public opinion on the issue by quite carefully choosing the news items to be printed on this issue.[22]

---

[21] "The President's Message, Synopsis," *Bellville Countryman*, 6 December 1864, 1; "There Has Been a 'Shaking of the Knees,'" *Bellville Countryman*, 22 November 1864, 2; "The Discussion in the South…," *Bellville Countryman*, 6 December 1864, 2; "News Items," *Bellville Countryman*, 20 December 1864, 1.

[22] "Since the publication…," *The LaGrange Patriot*, 10 December 1864, 2; "The Memphis Appeal…," *The LaGrange Patriot*, 10 December 1864, 1; "The Huntsville Item…," *The LaGrange Patriot*, 10 December 1864, 2; "Mr. Davis' Recommendation of the Employment of Slaves in the Army," *The LaGrange Patriot*, 24 December 1864, 2; "The following are resolutions…," *The LaGrange Patriot*, 7 January 1865, 1; "The Slavery Question," *The LaGrange Patriot*, 7 January 1865, 2.

At the *Austin State Gazette* David Robinson attempted to ignore the unsettling portions of the president's address. A resolutely Democratic Party paper, the *Gazette* had a lengthy heritage of challenging elected officials. In 1861 the *Gazette*, then edited by John Marshall, had led the campaign to force Sam Houston from the governor's chair. A week after printing the telegraphic synopsis of President Davis's message, Robinson acknowledged receiving the full text, but while calling it an "interesting document," said he could not publish it in its entirety "on account of its length." The editor's reticence on slavery fit well with his often-expressed conviction of the South's ultimate victory on the battlefield. On 7 December he recounted a meeting with a commander whose regiment had just gone into winter quarters near Washington, Texas: "His regiment...will remain there while the severe winter weather lasts, unless disturbed by the Yankees, of which there is not much probability." As late as his New Year's Day editorial, Robinson praised Hood's movement into Tennessee and declared that the capture of Nashville "may be expected with reasonable certainty." In the same piece, the editor described Lincoln's efforts as "'a war to the knife' upon southerners and their 'peculiar institutions,'" yet called for unity but not additional sacrifices for the cause. In this first phase of the debate he instead aimed his editorial arrows at speculators. In particular, he decried those who dealt with Yankee merchants in Mexico and returned with cognac and fine wine rather than more useful goods. Many Texans, he contended, had resumed their pre-war business relations with little thought of the soldier in camp or the widow at home. Confident of military success and reassured by adequate provisions, David Robinson saw little need to address Davis's speculations on slavery.[23] A thousand miles distant from the eastern armies, the Austin editor did not perceive the situation as a crisis that called for extraordinary measures.

---

[23] *Handbook of Texas Online,* Patrick Cox, "Austin State Gazette," accessed October 26, 2016, http://www.tshaonline.org/handbook/online/articles/eeayy; David Robinson, "The President's Message," *Austin The Weekly State Gazette*, 7 December 1864, 2; David Robinson, "We were pleased to meet...," *Austin The Weekly State Gazette*, 7 December 1864, 2; David Robinson, "The Prospect," *Austin The Weekly State Gazette*, 4 January 1865, 2; David Robinson, "Notwithstanding the Dispatches," *Austin The Weekly State Gazette*, 14 December 1864, 2; David Robinson, "Fifty thousand bushels...," *Austin The Weekly State Gazette*, 21 December 1864, 2.

At his editorial desk in Bellville, John P. Osterhout read Davis's comments with more of an open mind than many of his Central Texas counterparts. At age twenty-five, Osterhout had left the Pennsylvania Dutch community of his birth and immigrated to Texas in 1851. Plying his skills as a lawyer and editor, he found favor with the large German population in Bellville and slowly won acceptance from the planters. As his tenure in Texas lengthened and sectional tensions rose, Osterhout purchased several slaves, thus confirming his credentials as a real southerner and true Texan. Yet, he found himself in 1864 straddling a fine line between the views of the non-slaveholding German community in Bellville and the planters. "The result of the present contest," he proclaimed on 6 December, "seems in part to depend upon *carrying Africa into the war*!" Immediately after this startling observation, Osterhout asserted that slave-soldiers did not have to be the immediate answer: "While there can be no objection to sending Cuffee to the front, it appears that the government is still blind to its interests in not conscribing, without mercy, and without regard to age or anything else...every man who has ever been heard to declare his ability to whip from two to ten Yankees single handed."

Ridding the Confederacy of arm-chair generals, the *Countryman*'s editor suggested, would accomplish "more toward clearing the country of the 'hated invaders' than by taking Africa bodily into the conflict." The men at home who could avoid the conscription officer, he argued, laughed and had fun and made money. "What do they know or care of the horrors of war?" he asked. Osterhout's suggestion that slaves might need to assume a new role in the war stands in stark contrast to the tone of the rest of his editorials. When and on what terms Osterhout expected to see black troops playing a crucial role in the southern war effort, he never said. Even as he ridiculed the stay-at-home heroes, Osterhout demonstrated more thought than his Central Texas peers who simply ignored the need for more soldiers and restated the old pro-slavery ideology.[24]

---

[24] Randy J. Sparks, "John P. Osterhout, Yankee, Rebel, Republican," *Southwestern Historical Quarterly* 40/2 (October 1986): 112–13; J.P. Osterhout, "Something Over Two Thousand...," *Bellville Countryman*, 6 December 1864, 1; J.P. Osterhout, "For Several Days...," *Bellville Countryman*, 20 December 1864, 1. The italics do appear in the original.

Editor William McClellan at the *LaGrange Patriot* did not ignore Davis's comments on slavery as Robinson in Austin had tried, nor did he venture radical ideas of his own as Osterhout in Bellville had done. With twenty-five years' experience as a southern newspaper editor, McClellan treated this contentious issue gingerly. Hesitant to choose sides, he expressed his views by carefully selecting the editorials for inclusion in the paper and by responding to the ideas put forward in them. For instance, on 10 December McClellan noted the radical tenor of an editorial that first appeared in Huntsville, Texas, but chose to comment on the ideas without printing it. "The Huntsville Item," he declared, "in imitation of the Yankees, goes in for putting our slaves in the army to fight the battles of the country." Suggesting that one could not always learn from one's enemies, McClellan proclaimed, "The highest dictates of policy in our judgement, and not a mawkish sentimentality, forbid it." In contrast, after reprinting the long editorial from Galveston, the LaGrange editor affirmed his total agreement. "In our opinion," McClellan asserted, "his [Willard Richardson's] views are sound and just, and the measure recommended by the President, is not only in conflict with the spirit and genius of our institutions; but as a matter of policy is unwise and will prove fatal and disastrous, both to the institution, and to our existence as a government." No original editorial directly addressed slave-soldiers, but McClellan's epistle protesting the suspension of the writ of habeus corpus, the suppression of the press, and the emergence of Richmond as an "enslaver" of southern liberties fit nicely with his opinions on the employment of slaves in the army.[25]

Only one letter addressing the manpower shortage appeared in the *State Gazette* during the first phase of the debate. On 11 January the Austin paper copied an anonymous letter first published in Galveston that suggested women must fill the needs of the army: "In view of the present disastrous news, and the urgent need for filling up immediately the depleted ranks of the army, the patriotic ladies of Texas...should step forward at once

[25] *Handbook of Texas Online,* A.L. McClellan, Jr., "McClellan, William Brownlow," accessed October 26, 2016, http://www.tshaonline.org/handbook/articles/fmc10; William McClellan, "The Huntsville Item...," *The LaGrange Patriot*, 10 December 1864, 2; William McClellan, "We copy from the *Galveston News*...," *The LaGrange Patriot*, 17 December 1864, 2; William McClellan, "It is encouraging...," *The LaGrange Patriot*, 7 January 1865, 2.

and...supply the place of those clerks, whose employment is such as they could undertake." The use of unmarried ladies, the author claimed, would shame all able-bodied men remaining at home into the ranks and release a significant number of soldiers from non-combat roles. Such a move, he or she averred, would produce a better effect than additional congressional legislation: "Let the ladies, who have ever been foremost in aiding their country's cause, but make this effort, and it would accomplish more than all the conscript laws put together can now do."[26] Unfortunately, the *Bellville Countryman* and the *LaGrange Patriot* published few letters during this phase of the debate, and none related to arming the slaves. The absence of letters on the topic suggests that the reading public also did not understand the gravity of the Confederacy's situation. By contrast, the papers of Virginia, Georgia, and even Gulf Coast Texas presented a number of letters that discussed the topic fully and reveal a lively interest in the issue.

In November and December 1864 Davis's remarks concerning the slave's role in the war effort sparked considerable discussion in Texas. Few citizens of Austin—a city dominated by legislative action and not Union military action—saw a need to modify slavery radically. As the U.S. Navy tightened its grip on southern ports, foreign trade boomed across the Texas-Mexico border. Foreign consumer items, unknown in much of the Confederacy, graced the streets of Texas cities, and obscured the picture of impending crisis. Discussing plans for the holidays, one Central Texas observer confessed, "All sorts of good things can be had on the streets, for Christmas, at very reasonable rates; far more than we had anticipated."[27] Advertisements in Austin, Marshall, and Houston mirrored the Bellville editor's assessment. The difference in conditions of the Trans-Mississippi South from the rest of the Confederacy was stark. Without an immediate Union threat or proximity to an active theater of war, local opinion in Texas was slow to change during the first phase of the larger Confederate debate about slavery. The men and women of Texas had seen little of the hard war that Grant and Sherman were practicing in the East. The continuation of the cotton trade in Texas

---

[26] "A Correspondent of the News," *Austin The Weekly State Gazette*, 11 January 1865, 2.

[27] J.P. Osterhout, "For Several Days...," *Bellville Countryman*, 20 December 1864, 1.

through Mexico provided a powerful incentive to maintain slavery at all costs. The idleness of the Union troops in the Trans-Mississippi region provided a strong sense of security in Texas. The vast distances to the key battlefields and consistent, strong economic forces in large part explain why the citizens of Texas differed so drastically from their brothers and sisters in Virginia and Georgia on the potent issue of slavery's future.

Phase II

Savannah to the Hampton Roads Conference

5

With Us or Against Us

On a bitterly cold, rainy afternoon, Union General George Thomas smashed into the flanks of John Bell Hood's weary Confederate veterans south of Nashville. Outnumbered two to one, the southerners stood valiantly until just before twilight on 16 December. First single men quit firing, and then small units began to run. Sam Watkins, a Confederate soldier from Tennessee, eloquently described the destruction of the army in which he had served for almost four years: "Soon the whole army had caught the infection, had broken, and were running in every direction. … The army was panic stricken. … General Frank Cheatham and General Loring tried to form a line at Brentwood, but the line they formed was like trying to stop the current of the Duck River with a fish net." Most of Hood's army, which had been closely pursued for two weeks, either surrendered or decided that they had seen enough of the war and went home. Thomas's victory was complete. Not only had Hood's plan to retake Tennessee failed, but he also had needlessly destroyed his command.[1]

Six days later, William T. Sherman presented the city of Savannah as a Christmas present to Abraham Lincoln. Although Confederate patriots attempted to diminish his accomplishments, Sherman had brought the war home to Georgians as never before, slicing a sixty-mile swath through the center of the state. As Sherman's columns burned barns, killed livestock, and rounded up slaves, Confederate morale fell before the Union soldiers' blades. Georgia and the Deep South as a whole lay open to the enemy. At the same time, Ulysses S. Grant's Union army maintained resolute pressure against Robert E. Lee's gray-clad veterans outside Petersburg, thus preventing Davis from shifting forces from Virginia to meet the emergency in the Deep

---

[1] Sam R. Watkins, *"Co. Aytch": A Side Show of the Big Show* (Columbia, TN: *Columbia Herald*, 1882; reprint, New York: Touchstone, 1997) 240–41 (page references are to the reprint edition).

South. Suddenly, Confederate military leaders found that they had no viable force to face the victorious armies of Sherman and Thomas. These devastating Confederate losses in December 1864 sent doubt and despair racing through the countryside and lent a new sense of urgency to Jefferson Davis's final campaign.

As the Confederate military situation crumbled in December 1864, President Davis and Secretary of State Judah P. Benjamin attempted to propel the idea of a "radical modification" of slavery onto the front pages of southern newspapers. The president's message to Congress in November had sparked an exchange of ideas, but much of the debate had remained on a theoretical level. Most Virginians bold enough to discuss black troops during the first phase of the debate prefaced their remarks with "if it ever becomes necessary" or "if calamity every strikes." News arrived in Richmond on 19 December of Hood's defeat and the appearance of Sherman along the Atlantic coast. The president and the Cabinet immediately recognized that a "calamity" had struck and that the strategic situation had changed dramatically. New Confederate troops had to be found to meet Sherman as he marched north and to confront Thomas in Mississippi. In the emergency, President Davis, Secretary of State Judah Benjamin, and Secretary of War James Seddon sought to advance the public debate over the role of slaves in the war effort by contacting prominent men in each of the states and asking them to use their influence to ignite popular support for black troops.[2]

On 21 December, Benjamin wrote Frederick A. Porcher of Charleston asking him to awaken the people of South Carolina to the depth of the crisis and to the potential advantages of arming the slaves: "Can you not yourself write a series of articles in your papers, always urging this point as the true issue, viz, is it better for the negroes to fight for us or against us?" Undergirding the secretary's argument was the conviction that slavery had been so badly wounded by the war that it could not survive the contest. Benjamin contended, "If you could get your newspapers, or any one of them, to commence a discussion of this point, the people would rapidly become educated to the lesson which experience is sternly teaching us." Benjamin believed that the war had clearly demonstrated, and southerners were finally ac-

[2] "The News from Savannah—Movements of Sherman—Fall of Fort McAllister &c." and "The account from Nashville…," *Richmond Examiner*, 19 December 1864, 1.

knowledging, that the slave population understood the issues at stake and could and would fight for their own best interests. In this regard, Benjamin described the flow of southern black men away from the plantation and into the Union army as "steady, fatal, and irreversible." Further, he argued that a radical modification of slavery provided the only means to stem the tide of laborers leaving the South.[3]

Ever the pragmatist, Benjamin suggested that "cautious legislation" for the emancipation of the soldiers' families could be orchestrated without fully renouncing the pro-slavery ideology:

> We might then be able, while vindicating our faith in the doctrine that the negro is an inferior race and unfitted for social and political equality with the white man, yet so modify and ameliorate the existing condition of that inferior race by providing for it certain rights of property, a certain degree of personal liberty, and legal protection for the marital and parental relations.

Even as Benjamin made these revealing admissions to Porcher, the crafty secretary recommended stressing necessity and avoiding the subject of general emancipation in order to gain popular and congressional support for the measure. "It is enough for the moment," Benjamin declared, "that the Confederacy should become the owner of as many negroes as are required for the public service and should emancipate them as a reward for good services."[4]

Following the approach outlined in his letter, Benjamin believed, would produce the support needed to arm the slaves in time for the spring campaign: "Public opinion is fast ripening on the subject, and ere the close of the winter the conviction on this point will become so widespread that the Government will have no difficulty in inaugurating the policy foreshadowed in the President's message [arming slaves to prevent defeat]." Although Benjamin wrote in response to a letter from Porcher, the timing of his letter and the detailed instructions about techniques to be used to raise public support for black troops place it in a pattern of communications employed by the Davis administration to spur acceptance of arming slaves. This coordinated effort to prompt friends of the administration to come out publicly in sup-

---

[3] *Official Records*, Series 4, Vol. 3, 959–60.
[4] *Official Records*, Series 4, Vol. 3, 959–60.

port of black southern troops lay at the heart of Davis's campaign to reshape the Confederacy. As Benjamin's letter demonstrates, this new strategy was not based on a newfound belief in black equality but, rather, in a cold-blooded appraisal of the might of the Union army and the South's inability to counter it without significant black assistance.

Longstanding allies of the administration rallied to the president's standard in the moment of despair. John Forsyth, the editor of the *Mobile Advertiser and Register*, had a relationship with Jefferson Davis that went back many years. Prior to the opening of hostilities, Davis had sent Forsyth to Washington as part of a peace commission, and they continued to correspond during the war. For instance, in July 1864, Davis instructed General Braxton Bragg to meet with Forsyth and several other editors in order to drum up support for the replacement of popular General Joseph E. Johnston as commander of the Army of Tennessee by the brash Texan John B. Hood. As the president attempted to foster the newspaper debate over arming slaves, he again turned to the Mobile editor for aid. On 31 December, Forsyth wrote the president and described in detail the despondency produced by Sherman's march through Georgia. Astutely pointing to the precarious position of Lee's army after Hood's defeat, Forsyth announced that he believed that the time had come to place slaves in the Confederate army "to the extent needed to make our army a match for the enemy…with a promise of freedom to such of them as serve faithfully." Couched in a similar manner to Davis's speculations in November, the Mobile editor argued that the South could no longer afford dual war aims: "We cannot carry on our shoulders our freedom & the institution of slavery." Accompanying his arguments, Forsyth enclosed an editorial he had written to that effect for the president to peruse.[5]

In response, on 21 February, Davis wrote Forsyth and praised the piece the editor had forwarded and the general editorial policy of the *Mobile Advertiser and Register*: "The article inclosed…is a substantial expression of my own views on the subject of employing for the defense of our country all able-bodied men we have, without distinction of color. … The influence of your journal in the line which you propose to take would be a valuable assis-

[5] Andrews, *The South Reports the Civil War,* 454; Dealer's catalog—Carnegie Book Shop, #251, item 167. AAS search 1975.

tance." In a manner similar to Benjamin's letter to Porcher, Davis strongly advocated stressing the theme that the South must choose whether the slaves "will fight for or against us": "All arguments as to the positive advantages or disadvantages of employing them are beside the question, which is simply one of relative advantage between having their fighting element in our ranks or in those of the enemy." In contrast to the popular image of an aloof, stone-like president, Davis was actively campaigning to win congressional and popular support for black Confederate soldiers. In similar fashion, James Seddon wrote to militia General Howell Cobb of Georgia and to the Conscription Bureau Chief, James S. Preston, then visiting his home state of South Carolina. Seddon drew the difficult task of trying to change the minds of state leaders in states generally unfriendly to the administration and its wartime policies. These administration efforts to win allies—along with the startling Union victories of December—ignited a new discussion in Confederate newspapers about the necessity to arm the slaves.[6]

The Richmond papers, considered the cream of southern journalism, played leading roles in framing the debate. Often their editorials not only were intended for their local readers but also were designed to impact the development of public opinion across the South. Their editors well knew that Richmond editorials would be reprinted in local papers throughout the region. In the wake of the twin defeats at Nashville and Savannah, the Richmond press provided a variety of ways to address the military crisis. On 19 December the *Richmond Examiner* provided clear, accurate accounts of the Confederate defeats at Nashville and at Fort McAllister near Savannah. Reflecting on the dismal reports the following day, John Daniel expressed a new willingness to consider a larger role for slaves in the war effort:

> The Bill for impressment of slaves...might be very properly enlarged and amended...by placing at the disposal of the military authorities, not forty thousand negroes, but eighty or one hundred thousand; and by leaving it to General Lee, at his discretion, and according to the exigencies of the service, to use them in *any* way he may think needful. [emphasis in context]

These were brave words for a journal that spent most of its space attempting to protect the people from the government. Slave owners, Daniel

[6] *Official Records*, Series 4, Vol. 3, 979, 981, 1009, 1110.

contended, should be compensated, with the slave becoming "the property of the Confederate Government, as impressed mules and horses do." Such a policy, the *Examiner* argued, would not have troubled anyone if Davis had not, "with his usual judgment, introduced the topick [sic]...accompanied by speculative suggestions which were eminently fit not to be made." The tenor of Davis's radical ideas, and not the long-term employment of slaves with the army, disturbed Daniel.[7]

As to the timing of the call for black troops to enter the field as soldiers, the *Examiner* contended that General Lee and not the Congress or president should make the decision: "No person out of the army, and very few in it are capable of deciding at what precise moment the necessity of our affairs demands that we shall use the tremendous reserve force in our hands; and 'the time' might chance to be put off too late." The December defeats had severely shaken the *Richmond Examiner*'s faith in military success, but the paper continued to question the viability of radical measures to modify slavery.[8]

In contrast to the *Examiner*'s reflections, on 17 December the *Richmond Whig* responded to the first partial reports from Nashville and Savannah by boldly asserting that the Confederate defeats meant nothing. Noting the failure of Sherman to liberate the Union prisoner-of-war camp at Andersonville or to disturb the Confederate manufacturing centers at Augusta and Macon, Nathaniel Tyler pronounced the march to the sea "comparatively pointless." "Savannah is not the Confederacy," Tyler contended, "nor yet Georgia, nor yet anything more than simply Savannah; its capture would count about as much to the conquest of the South as the capture of Chicago towards the conquest of the North." Sherman's movement from Atlanta to Savannah, the *Whig* argued, had significantly improved the southern strategic position: "The Yankees have, during the campaign, lost between three and four hundred thousand men—that they have only gained Savannah, while they have given up all the country between Tennessee and the Gulf." Although technically true, as northern garrisons had not remained in the

---

[7] "The News from Savannah—Movements of Sherman—Fall of Fort McAllister &c." and "The account from Nashville...," *Richmond Examiner*, 19 December 1864, 1, 2; "The Bill for the impressment...," *Richmond Examiner*, 20 December 1864, 1. Italics appear in the original.

[8] "The Bill for the impressment...," *Richmond Examiner*, 20 December 1864, 1.

wake of Sherman's columns, Tyler failed utterly to comprehend the dramatic impact of the Union march through Georgia. Crops bound for Lee's army had been destroyed; wives wrote their soldier husbands asking them to come home; and the inability of southern forces to meet the Yankee units undermined the faith of many in the southern cause.[9]

On 22 December the *Richmond Whig* finally conceded the gravity of the situation and declared that "this is undoubtedly the darkest hour we have ever seen." Yet, even with this admission, the *Whig* set out to dispute northern claims that the "resources of the Confederate States, as to arms bearing men, are on the point of exhaustion." The paper's editor took the returns from the 1860 census from the eleven primary Confederate states and estimated that 2,799,818 white males lived in the South in 1860. Next, editor Nathaniel Tyler added an estimate of the number of men who had reached the age of seventeen since the beginning of the war. Finally, Tyler projected deductions for normal mortality, the number lost to camp diseases and battlefield deaths, and a percentage for those caught behind Union lines in Arkansas, Louisiana, Tennessee, and Virginia. These calculations left a potential white soldier population of 729,257. Of this number, Tyler suggested, just over one third would be needed to serve in positions considered essential to a republican society, such as ministers, doctors, and newspaper editors. These men would be technically conscripted and then immediately given a "detail" so that they could resume their civilian occupations until the nation needed their services in the field more than their professional services at home. Even with this liberal reduction, Tyler found 461,864 white men available to continue the struggle: "It is much larger than any force we have ever had under arms, and is amply competent not only to defend the country, but to turn back the tide of invasion across the border, and to redeem those States which have already been overrun."[10]

---

[9] Tyler made a correct geographic argument but a faulty manpower argument. His assessment of 300,000 Union losses was totally unfounded. While he was probably referring to the combined Union losses in all theaters in 1864, he gave the impression in the article that Sherman's march had been a costly one for the Union. Quite simply, it was as inexpensive as any campaign in the war. "Sherman at Savannah," *Richmond Whig*, 17 December 1864, 1; "Yesterday was the first day…," *Richmond Whig*, 2 January 1865, 1.

[10] "Patience and Hope" and "Physical Resources of the Confederacy," *Richmond Whig*, 22 December 1864, 1.

Tyler hoped his estimate would demonstrate two things: first, that there was no reason to despair of the southern cause, and secondly, that the South did not need to call on slaves to take the field as soldiers. Based on seemingly objective figures, this study proved to be quite influential as newspapers across the South reprinted it and built arguments based on its conclusions. If Tyler's numbers were correct, the South did not have to choose between the preservation of slavery and independence. In January 1865, this one item raced across the telegraph wires of the Confederacy and reassured many southerners even as it muddied the picture that Davis needed all to see. As Jefferson Davis tried to shore up southern morale in the wake of defeat, he could not allow Tyler's wishful thinking to prevent serious consideration of new sources for soldiers.

In yet another vein, in late December the *Richmond Enquirer* had learned of a diplomatic initiative proposed by Louisiana Congressman Duncan Kenner and approved by President Davis. On 29 December the *Enquirer* examined and endorsed Kenner's scheme to offer the abolition of slavery in the Confederacy in return for British or French recognition and aid. If this concession to European sensibilities proved ineffective, the *Enquirer* suggested that Kenner might offer for the Confederacy to revert to a colonial status as well as abolition in return for aid. Becoming a colony of Britain or France would offend all republican sensibilities, but either European power had the potential to prevent a northern triumph. Unable to leave Wilmington prior to the fall of Fort Fisher, Kenner found his mission thoroughly discussed and often ridiculed in Virginia and across the South prior to his departure. As in October, the *Enquirer* had raised a controversial issue, which set the stage for a wider debate.[11]

Editor John Daniel at the *Richmond Examiner* was astounded by the *Enquirer*'s endorsement of the diplomatic scheme. To fly back to the colonial bosom of mother England, Daniel argued, southerners would have to "recant all those high words we have had in our mouths for two or three generations, about liberty, rights of man and democracy." Unreasoned fear, he

[11] The *Enquirer* often floated trial balloons for the administration. It is unclear if the Kenner mission originated in the Cabinet or with the President. It is likely that Cabinet members saw this as an undesirable alternative if they failed to win popular support in the slave-soldier campaign. *Richmond Enquirer*, 29 December 1864, in Andrews, *The South Reports the Civil War*, 482–83.

believed, had hatched the idea: "One is ashamed even to refute and rebuke this mean suggestion begotten of terror upon ignorance." In a second piece on the topic on 2 January, the *Examiner* asserted that southerners must remember the pursuit of independence required the discussion of practical means and not mere theories: "If we are asked whether we would, or would not purchase the material aid of England and France in our present struggle by abandoning slavery instantly and on the spot, we again say yes. ... But it happens...the alternative is not present to us; we are not asked to choose between the two—except by some essayists." In fact, the *Examiner* attributed noble motives to the proponents of the abolition-for-recognition scheme, but the paper resolutely advised its readers that nothing could or would come of it.[12]

The controversial ideas discussed in the Richmond papers during this most sobering Christmas season brought forth a number of responses from individual citizens. On 28 December, John H. Gilmer, a local legislator of some note, wrote an open letter to a member of the Virginia Senate concerning the ongoing discussions of slavery. Gilmer took exception to the messages of Davis and Seddon presented to Congress in November: "The President, the Secretary-at-War, and Congress, have nothing more to do with it—than their rivals—in the United States." Such "unconstitutional interference" with slavery, Gilmer argued, called for "state interposition" to block the ideas current in the capital, just as U.S. congressional interference with slavery had required secession. The specter of northern abolitionism had been replaced by a new threat from within the South: "When Congress so far forgets its constitutional restrictions, and the inherent rights of the States, as to legislate on this subject, the death knell of the Confederacy will have been sounded." Gilmer concluded his argument by declaring, "No slave must be elevated to the equal of the soldier, and no soldier degraded to the equal of the slave." If soldiers rejected black assistance, opponents of the measure knew, it would form a powerful supporting argument for the traditional pro-slavery ideology.[13]

[12] "Lead Editorial," *Richmond Examiner*, 30 December 1864, 1; "Let us not...," *Richmond Examiner*, 2 January 1865, 1.

[13] "Letter from John H. Gilmer, to a Member of the Virginia Senate," *Richmond Whig*, 2 January 1864, 1.

Two letters from soldiers appeared in the *Richmond Examiner* in response to the December defeats. On 31 December "A Virginian Officer" wrote to the *Examiner* and bitterly complained of Congressional efforts to reorganize the army. In closing, though, the officer made a startling request: "Give us General Lee as commander in chief of the forces, and put 50,000 African muskets in the field before next spring." This writer did not elaborate on his ideas behind the use of the "African muskets," but clearly he considered arming slaves a key component in raising the morale and efficiency of the army. A week later, the *Examiner* printed a series of resolutions from an artillery battery serving in Virginia. After reaffirming their resolve to see the war through to victory, the artillerymen denounced all discussions of peace on dishonorable terms: "We view with the utmost abhorrence the idea of arriving at a settlement of our difficulties by sacrificing slavery or by yielding dishonorably in any way, thereby inviting the aid of any foreign power." Eighty Confederate veterans signed this repudiation of the idea of trading abolition for recognition. These letters expressed the opinions of a few individuals in the army, but people increasingly called on the army's commander, Robert E. Lee, to hear his assessment of the situation.[14]

With discussions of military reverses, the arming of slaves, and European protectorates filling the air, Virginia legislator Andrew Hunter on 7 January wrote to Lee and requested his view of "the wisdom and sound policy…of converting such portion of this [negro] population as may be required into soldiers, to aid in maintaining our great struggle for independence." Hunter acknowledged that his own prejudices against the idea had lessened over time: "I have given it much earnest and anxious reflection, and…the general objections to the proposition itself, as well as the practical difficulties in the way of carrying it out have been greatly lessened as I have more thoroughly examined them." Having stated his purpose, Hunter reminded Lee that George Washington during the revolution had often provided advice to the Continental Congress and indirectly to the people. Hunter realized that Lee's opinions would be decisive on the issue and intimated to the general that it was his duty to provide direction to the nation. Beyond a basic request for information, Hunter asked three specific questions. First, the legislator

---

[14] "A Virginia Officer," "To the Editor of the Examiner," *Richmond Examiner*, 30 December 1864, 1.

queried, "Do you think that by a wisely devised plan and judicious selection negro soldiers can be made effective and reliable in maintaining this war in behalf of the Southern States?" Second, Hunter asked if the arming of a portion of the slaves would significantly injure the overarching institution of slavery. Third, Hunter asked if the introduction of black combat troops would allow some of the white soldiers to be returned to civilian positions in support of the war effort. Finally, Hunter requested an overall assessment of the impact of black soldiers on the army and the nation.[15]

As soon as the newspaper debate began in October, partisans on both sides of the issue had invoked the name of the commander of the Army of Northern Virginia in support of their own ideas. William Miles had received a letter announcing the general's frank assessment of black troops in October, but since Lee's ideas did not coincide with the congressman's opposition, Miles had not published the letter. Government insiders occasionally mentioned Lee's support for arming the slaves, but since the words did not come from Lee's mouth directly, his position remained unclear. Lee apparently feared overstepping the bounds prescribed for military leaders concerning political affairs. As a young officer, he had noted and condemned the political wranglings of Zachary Taylor and Winfield Scott, his commanders in the Mexican War. Although still reticent on the issue in public, on 11 January he replied to Hunter's request and produced a powerful argument for black troops in Confederate gray.[16]

Pointing to Union numbers, Lee declared his preference for white troops but quickly noted the inability of the white population to meet the manpower requirements: "In view of the preparations of our enemies, it is our duty to provide for continued war and not for a battle or a campaign, and I fear that we cannot accomplish this without overtaxing the capacity of our white population." Weighing the effects of black troops, he noted that each slave that escaped to the Union army added combat power to the enemy and in equal measure subtracted labor from the South. "We must decide," Lee proclaimed, "whether slavery shall be extinguished by our enemies and the slaves used against us, or use them ourselves at the risk of the effects which may be produced upon our social institutions." The impact of Con-

---

[15] *Official Records*, Series 4, Vol. 3, 1007–1009.
[16] Ibid., 1012–13.

federate emancipation and enlistment of the slave, the general contended, could be no more pernicious than the Union model.[17]

To ensure the new soldiers' fidelity, the general recommended a program of "gradual and general emancipation" for all slaves, designed to provide the new soldier with a powerful incentive to work for Confederate success: "Such an interest we can give our negroes by giving immediate freedom to all who enlist, and freedom at the end of the war to the families of those who discharge their duties faithfully (whether they survive or not)." Mere promises of potential freedom, Lee argued, would not be enough: "We should not expect slaves to fight for prospective freedom when they can secure it at once by going to the enemy, in whose service they will incur no greater risk than in ours." Such a course, Lee asserted, would produce efficient Confederate soldiers, cut off a major source of Union recruits, and force the North to reassess the costs of the war. Despite the strong convictions contained in his reply to Hunter, Lee still did not speak out publicly on the subject of arming the slaves. Lee's views became better known within the government but did not become widely known for several crucial weeks.[18]

In contrast to the bold ideas of Lee, Generals Joseph E. Johnston and Howell Cobb clung to old concepts even as they attempted to meet Sherman's columns. After suppressing General Patrick Cleburne's original memorial in January 1864, Johnston had written Davis recommending the use of slaves in non-combatant roles to free white men for battle: "A ready mode of doing this would be by substituting negroes for all the soldiers on detached or daily duty—As well as company cooks, pioneers & labourers [sic] for engineer service." Despite the misfortunes of 1864, Johnston on 3 February 1865 restated his previous position without modification in a letter to Senator Louis T. Wigfall. Johnston strongly espoused the use of slaves in the army as laborers but not as soldiers. In spite of the thrashing administered by Sherman, Howell Cobb, commander of all Georgia state troops, also resolutely refused to consider arming the slaves. On 8 January Cobb wrote to Secretary of War James Seddon and denounced the idea of slave-soldiers: "The day you make soldiers of them is the beginning of the end of the revolution. If slaves will make good soldiers, our whole theory of slavery is

[17] Ibid.

[18] Ibid.

wrong." Instead, to fill the ranks, Cobb argued that conscription must be stopped and a system of volunteer units established: "For heaven's sake try it before you fill with gloom and despondency the hearts of many of our truest and most devoted men by resorting to the suicidal policy of arming our slaves." Cobb could not envision a southern world without slavery.[19] Lee's opinions outweighed those expressed by less influential leaders, but the administration must have wondered how well the new commander-in-chief represented his command.

After the immediate shock of the December defeats passed, the Confederacy settled down to a thorough debate of the options remaining to them. On 28 December, the *Richmond Sentinel* declared, "Our late reverses have done much towards preparing the minds of our people for the most extreme sacrifices." Richard M. Smith, the editor of the *Sentinel*, challenged Virginians to face the hard fact that all they had would be consumed by the war: "It would be far more glorious to devote our means to our success than to lose them as spoils to the enemy. Our situation, too, stripped of our property, but master of the government, would be infinitely better than if despoiled by the enemy and wearing his bonds." Southerners had long professed such views, Smith noted, but now they needed to prove the strength of their convictions by resolute action.[20]

Common sense and common humanity, the *Sentinel* editor argued, demanded the adoption of black Confederate troops: "Shall we send our sons, and deny our negroes? Shall we spend our blood, and deny our money? Shall we withhold anything from our country when we should be saving it for the foe?" Selfish efforts to cling to slaves or money or constitutional dogmas could only hasten the nation's destruction. In Smith's view, there was no rational argument for holding anything in reserve in the crisis: "It would be adding disgrace to our misery, if we were overcome without having first exhausted every resource of defense." Richard Smith at the *Sentinel* did not project radical proposals to end the war but, rather, called on Virginians—and southerners in general—to live up to their bold assertions that they would sacrifice all for independence.[21]

---

[19] Ibid., 1009.

[20] "It becomes us coolly…," *Richmond Sentinel*, 28 December 1864, 2.

[21] Ibid.

Echoing the concerns of the *Sentinel*, on 21 January the *Richmond Enquirer* questioned the causes behind the delay in getting military reform legislation through Congress. With the winter passing quickly, the *Enquirer* suggested that a great opportunity to retrain and reorganize the army was slipping away: "If the conscription of negroes had been promptly passed at the opening of the session these troops would now be in camp and under drill." Reviewing the string of Confederate disasters from Nashville to Savannah to the fall of Fort Fisher, the paper marveled that Congress had failed to act: "It was expected that Congress would have, ere this, taken measures for the next campaign. But instead of war measures, time has been wasted in pursuing the *ignis faturae* of peace."[22]

A week later, the *Enquirer* assailed Confederate congressmen representing large slaveholding constituencies who appeared unwilling to discuss arming and freeing the slaves. The true cant of such men, the *Enquirer* reported, demonstrated great demoralization: "We shall throw ourselves upon the protection of the enemy. They will grant us, at least, the temporary use of our slaves." Yet, in Congress these same men said only that they did not need to sacrifice slavery because "we do not believe emancipation will ensure independence and we do not, therefore, make the experiment." In answer to these slave owners, the *Enquirer* pointed out the Lincoln administration's success in Congress with a constitutional amendment to prohibit slavery, and asked them how long a Union promise to protect slavery would last.[23]

The idea of congressmen arranging peace to protect slave property appalled editor Nathaniel Tyler: "Then we should have a premature peace to secure to a comparative few the temporary use of their property? These [congress] men would have given life, limb, property, and a great cause for the special gain of a few." Tyler contended, "These reconstructionists...would sell their own liberty and the liberty of the disinterested gallant slaveholding and non-slaveholding soldier for the contemptible privilege of working their negroes some five or ten more years." These views expressed behind the closed doors of Congress, Tyler argued, did not accurately reflect the sentiments of the South's slaveholding class but, rather, depicted the ideas of old Unionists and a selfish few without public spirit: "We know

---

[22] "The month of January...," *Richmond Enquirer*, 21 January 1865, 2.
[23] "Slaveholding Reconstructionists," *Richmond Enquirer*, 28 January 1865, 2.

hundreds that would be willing—if any guarantee of freedom could be given—to subscribe every slave they possess to the success of the cause." Yet the treachery and selfishness of a few, the *Enquirer* concluded, was delaying the passage of measures to arm the slaves and thus placing the liberty of all southerners at risk.[24]

After the fog of battle lifted and the full scope of the December defeats could be seen, the *Richmond Whig* agreed with its peers that affairs had reached a crisis. In a series of year-end reviews, the *Whig* stoutly maintained its argument that the Confederacy had the resources necessary for success, but the paper questioned the resolve of the people. On 24 December, editor James McDonald dramatically recounted the heroic efforts of the Greeks at Thermopylae and of Frederick the Great during the Seven Years War, but he then suggested that southerners were not ready to make equal sacrifices. "While everybody knows these things, everybody may not be ready to imitate what he is so very willing to admire." Several days later, McDonald again questioned the morale of the people: "No calamity is without remedy to people determined not to be cast down by misfortune. ... But, after all, everything depends upon the people. ... If they are determined to submit, there is nothing more to be said."[25]

Two weeks later, the *Whig* aimed its editorial arrows at government mismanagement rather than the people: "It would be easy to defeat these combinations [Sherman and Grant]; but General Lee must have more men. The enemy...has taken measures to recruit. Why will not our Congress do the same? Why are they wasting the precious hours in talk, talk, talk—everlasting talk—that results in nothing?" On 12 January the *Whig* chided Edmund Kirby Smith, Confederate commander in the Trans-Mississippi Department, for selfishly retaining 60,000 idle troops when they were needed in the East: "The transient immunity from the chances and perils of war thus gained by a portion of the country, would be dearly purchased by the final destruction of the whole." Four days later, the *Whig* blasted the president for allowing so many to escape conscription. In all of these editorials,

---

[24] Ibid.

[25] "The Price of Independence," *Richmond Whig*, 24 December 1864, 1; "Present Aspects," *Richmond Whig*, 24 December 1864, 1.

the need for more men dominated, yet not until 19 January did McDonald discuss black troops.[26]

The *Richmond Whig* shifted its position on arming slaves on 19 January. Contending that the South had not utilized slavery enough, the *Whig* proclaimed, "As soon as the Federal Government indicated its purpose to introduce the negro into the ranks, and especially the Southern negro, it should not have been a serious question with us whether we should employ our slaves in some kind of military service." Prompt action to expand the slave's role in 1862, McDonald suggested, might have changed the course of the war: "We might have defeated their policy of recruiting amongst our negroes by placing [slaves] in our own service, if not as soldiers, at least as accessories." Clearly, McDonald reached this conclusion not in 1862 but in the bleak winter of 1865. The *Whig* saw the light only when McDonald realized that the Confederacy could not attain the men required for the spring campaign by tightening conscription laws or from some mythical army in Texas.[27]

The military necessity argument had finally won over the editor of the *Richmond Whig*, but an editorial on 30 January demonstrated that he remained far from willing to abandon slavery. Repeating an idea proposed by "an influential congressman," probably John Atkins of Tennessee, the *Whig* endorsed the idea of the government purchasing slaves for the army and then giving ownership of the new slave-soldiers to individual white soldiers already in service. "This plan," the *Whig* affirmed, "would serve, first, to transform the negro into a soldier by the readiest and most efficient process, and thereby at once double the number of our troops." Second, the editor believed that the act of issuing a slave to each soldier would increase the army's commitment to slavery and, at the same time, discredit the idea of a slaveholder's war fought primarily by non-slaveholders. Finally, the presentation

---

[26] Edmund Kirby Smith would have been delighted to look out upon 60,000 men. Unfortunately for the Confederacy, he had no such large force. Confederate operations during Sterling Price's Missouri campaign in late 1864 had largely depleted the limited resources he had. Speculations and accusations often flew between the theaters with very limited real knowledge of military conditions in either area. "The last accounts...," *Richmond Whig*, 11 January 1865, 1; "The 60,000 men...," *Richmond Whig*, 12 January 1865, 1; "The House of Representatives...," *Richmond Whig*, 16 January 1865, 1.

[27] "In war the greatest wisdom...," *Richmond Whig*, 19 January 1865, 1.

of the new soldier as a slave would disprove the idea of racial equality in the ranks. At the bottom of the piece in which he discussed this scheme, McDonald stepped back and asserted that the time for such steps might not yet have come. Although firmly opposed to administration policy, the *Whig*'s editor could not deny the need for more men. The *Richmond Whig*'s acceptance of the concept of black military assistance remained shaky in January, but the paper found it had few alternatives except reconstruction.[28]

In addition to the reports of military movements and efforts to arm slaves, Virginia, but particularly Richmond, was transfixed by the visits of Francis P. Blair, an old political friend of Davis's from Maryland, to the Confederate capital in January. Blair first met with Davis on 12 January and began an exchange of ideas and letters with Lincoln that led to the Hampton Roads peace conference in early February. Although the course of the negotiations remained secret, the newspapers and the citizens of Richmond speculated on the significance of the events. On 13 January the *Richmond Examiner* savagely attacked the president for meeting with Blair. Suggestions of peace, the *Examiner* admonished the president, could not bear fruit: "We know beforehand that Lincoln and his party will never recognize the independence of these States; and UNDER NO CIRCUMSTANCES, ON NO CONDITIONS, can these States return to the Union." By raising the hopes of the people, the *Examiner* feared that Blair's visit would produce divisions and a "vacillation of purpose." Editor John Daniel cynically suggested that Lincoln's purpose behind allowing Blair to come to Richmond was to provide a stimulus for northern recruiting. "Talk about it," Daniel argued, "serves only to unsettle weak minds, and to lead the thoughtless, the ignorant, and worse than all, the cowardly, into errours [sic] which will only prolong the duration of this struggle." Although derisive concerning the peace negotiations, the *Examiner* offered few proposals of its own to aid the southern cause.[29]

On 9 January, Daniel decried the course of the war and called for a convention of the states to consider drastic revisions of the Confederate gov-

---

[28] "The *New York Times*...," *Richmond Whig*, 30 January 1865, 1.

[29] "If the Messrs. Blair...," *Richmond Examiner*, 13 January 1865, 1; "It may be hoped...," *Richmond Examiner*, 18 January 1865, 1; Charles W. Sanders, Jr., "Jefferson Davis and the Hampton Roads Peace Conference: 'To secure peace to the two countries,'" *Journal of Southern History* 63 (November 1997): 809–17.

ernment. In particular, the *Examiner* resented the centralizing measures adopted by the Davis administration in the name of military necessity: "Have we enclosed ourselves in an iron circle of necessity, out of which egress is none?" Many southerners had come to resent the repeated pleas of military necessity, but in all likelihood, the removal of Davis and his entire Cabinet would have failed to satisfy Daniel. Davis and other advocates of arming slaves found themselves confronting an influential editor determined to restrict the power of the central government. Yet, as the bill designed to provide 40,000 slave laborers to the army moved through Congress, the *Examiner* cautioned the legislators not to cross the will of the people: "Whatever comments or objections the policy of the bill may call forth, the country in its present temper, will not sustain any hesitation or resistance to this measure, founded on cupidity, or reluctance to sacrifice property—any amount of property—in the common cause." Doubtless, Daniel was trying to warn the congressmen that public sentiment had turned decidedly against limiting slave roles in the name of preserving property. Such reasoning would have clearly affirmed what a number of soldiers and their families felt—that the war had become a rich man's war and a poor man's fight. Daniel had not shifted from his opposition to black troops but, rather, hoped to derail the measure without aggravating the tensions between slaveholders in Congress and the non-slaveholders who composed the vast majority of the Confederate army. In this second phase of the slavery debate, the *Examiner* attempted to limit internal Confederate divisions, whether arising from peace movements or measures to employ black troops.[30]

Controversial issues like arming slaves, peace negotiations, the purchase of European recognition, and revisions of the conscription laws challenged the leadership of the Confederacy to determine new priorities in the face of military defeat. In late December and early January, these complex issues merited the attention of not only generals and Cabinet secretaries but also widely dispersed Confederates who sought to ensure their views were heard in Richmond. On 21 January, Confederate diplomat James Mason wrote to Secretary of State Benjamin from London and expressed surprise at the debate in the South concerning the role of slaves in the war effort. European

[30] "Men are asking…," *Richmond Examiner*, 9 January 1865, 1; "The 'cold fit' of depression…," *Richmond Examiner*, 3 February 1865, 1.

friends of the Confederacy, Mason reported, had responded quite positively to the idea of black Confederate troops: "It is considered by them with much favor as a measure carrying large auxiliaries to our armies, whilst in their opinion it would be a first step toward emancipation." In contrast, Mason conceded to Benjamin that he regretted the loss of agricultural labor and the obligation that would devolve upon the nation to free the faithful veterans, thus greatly expanding the free black population. Far from the seat of government, Mason had difficulty understanding the factors that had led the administration to seriously consider the step. Feeling a direct threat from the Union army, Governor Charles Clark of Mississippi had written Davis asking if slaves needed to be enrolled into the service immediately. Although Clark's original message did not survive the war, the president's response suggests the urgency of the governor's communication. On 25 January Davis informed Clark that "there is no necessity for an actual enrollment of male slaves as described." The president did urge Governor Clark to meet the state's quota for slaves to be used as teamsters and laborers with the army. Although it remains unclear exactly what Clark had proposed, Davis's comment that Confederate enrolling officers did not need to get involved suggests that the governor had contemplated a process verging on regular enlistment of black slaves. With the president pressing resolutely for congressional action, the Mississippian must have suggested immediate state action. Even if Clark did not envision their manumission, his preparation to put male slaves through the process undergone by whites intimates a willingness to arm slaves as soldiers that few Confederate leaders at that point had matched.[31]

Individual citizens of the Confederacy also weighed in on the great issues facing the nation. On 7 January a letter from "An East Tennessean" appeared in the *Richmond Whig*, addressing the idea of a colonial protectorate purchased by the southern abolition of slavery. The "East Tennessean" demonstrated a flawed understanding of European politics as he declared, "The Government of Great Britain and France will be controlled, not by the exploded dogmas of fanaticism, but by wise considerations of material interest." True, national interest did set the tone of British and French policies, but like many Confederate diplomats, the "Tennessean" continued to under-

[31] *Official Records*, Series 2, Vol. 3, 1258–59; *Official Records*, Series 4, Vol. 3, 1039.

estimate anti-slavery opinion in Europe. On 18 January, "X" penned a letter to the *Richmond Examiner* in which he reported to have had a conversation with Union General Benjamin Butler during a recent visit within the Union lines. Butler, "X" reported, "hoped that President Davis would carry out the policy of arming the slaves on his side. … He would like them to come into contact with black soldiers on the other side." "X" further claimed that Butler had questioned Davis's submission of the decision to arm slaves to Congress rather than simply instituting black troops as a military policy.[32]

While the remarks on black troops encompass only a small portion of a larger letter, the comments of "X" appear quite suspect. First, Benjamin Butler had been one of the first Union generals to arm blacks and had thus drawn considerable anger in the South. He was seen by many Confederates as a man without integrity. It would have been difficult to find a Union general that southerners would have been less willing to listen to on the subject of race. Second, although present in Virginia during part of December, Butler was fully engaged planning and executing an operation against Fort Fisher, thus leaving him little time to talk to anyone, much less a southerner. Third, "Butler's" recommendation that the Confederacy should arm slaves through military fiat rather than the path chosen of winning congressional approval fit too nicely with the *Examiner*'s conception of how the Davis administration operated. Although it cannot be proven that the conversation did not occur, this piece has the distinct mark of a John Daniel attempt to embarrass his opponents.

Of greater merit, on 29 January J.W. Ellis wrote from Raleigh to President Davis, advocating a plan that would offer a slave and fifty acres of land to every non-slaveholding Confederate veteran as a form of pension. "Thus," Ellis argued, "you spread the institution. You make every family in the Government interested in it [slavery]." Beyond limiting class divisions in the ranks, the North Carolinian speculated that the measure would bring northern deserters and European men into the Confederate ranks if offered the same incentives: "We can command thousands of men from Ireland, Germany, Poland, Austria, England, and France by offering them a home in sunny South and a servant." These incentives to white enlistment, Ellis

[32] "An East Tennessean," "For the Whig," *Richmond Whig*, 7 January 1865, 2; "To the Editor of the Examiner," *Richmond Examiner*, 18 January 1865, 1.

hoped, would bring a multitude of blessings to the Confederacy: "We will thus avoid the trouble of arming slaves. We will remove the prejudices against the institution and bring all the world up to its support from interested motives." In comparison to other sacrifices being discussed in the Confederacy, Ellis believed the cost exacted by his proposal quite small: "The slave-owners can well afford to give up to the soldiers who have and will fight to maintain the institution 1,000,000 of slaves to secure forever the other 2,500,000." Although utterly unrealistic, Ellis's ideas addressed the problems under consideration in Richmond. Clearly, Ellis remained firmly tied to slavery even as he suggested sacrificing a part to save the whole.[33]

In a different vein, John H. Stringfellow wrote the president just prior to the return of the peace commissioners. Stringfellow stated that he believed Davis had already realized that black troops must be used but feared that political considerations constrained his actions. "It is held by us," the author declared, "that slaves will not make soldiers, therefore we refuse to put them in the service. ... Escaped slaves fight and fight bravely for our enemies; therefore a freed slave will fight." As a veteran of Bloody Kansas and current resident of Henrico County, Virginia, Stringfellow had seen the war up close, thus convincing him that radical steps were required: "I think that this contest has proven that in a military sense it [slavery] is an element of weakness, and the teachings of Providence as exhibited in this war dictate conclusively and imperatively that to secure and perpetuate our independence we must emancipate the negro." Emancipation, Stringfellow contended, would benefit the Confederacy in several ways. "If our slaves were freed would the Yankees be able to raise another recruit amongst them?" the author asked. Further, by removing the incentive for slaves to flee, the South could retain the nation's labor force and thereby cause the Union armies to search for new sources of laborers and soldiers. In addition, Stringfellow suggested that emancipation enacted by the Confederacy would allow southerners to set favorable terms for white landowners: "The white man only will have any and all political rights, retain all his real and personal property, exclusive of his property in his slave; make the laws to control the freed negro,

[33] *Official Records*, Series 4, Vol. 3, 1041–42.

who having no land, must labor for the landowner, and…on terms about as economical as though owned by him."[34]

In this analysis, Stringfellow demonstrated considerable insight into the advantages that whites would retain and the disadvantages that would plague blacks for years to come. Finally, the author attempted to address the legalistic defenses of slavery that so troubled many southerners as they contemplated freeing the slaves: "We burn an individual's cotton, corn, or meat to keep it from the enemy, so we can take his negro man and set him free to keep him from recruiting the enemy's Army." This powerful letter in support of arming and freeing the slaves arrived on Davis's desk as the Confederacy teetered on the edge of agreeing to arm the slaves. The scheme outlined by Stringfellow suggests that many in Virginia were coming to understand that the employment of black troops was not enough, but that freeing all the slaves would also be necessary.[35]

Shifting attitudes in Southwestern Virginia mirrored the shifting attitudes seen in the capital. If possible, the threat of Union cavalry provided an even more pronounced sense of urgency than that produced by Grant's men at Petersburg. Reports from refugees fleeing General Philip H. Sheridan's continuing campaign in the Shenandoah Valley added significantly to the sense of urgency produced by news items describing the failures at Savannah and Nashville. The capture of the state's salt works in Saltville, Virginia, just prior to Christmas brought home the immediate necessity to reinforce the southern armies. In the wake of the disasters at Nashville and Savannah, the *Virginian* sought to find a ray of hope on the horizon: "We are not as badly off as we were this time last year. The enemy has tried his best and he can never make such another exertion." Black soldiers provided one of the few alternatives to simply hoping that the Union forces could not match their campaign of 1864. On 12 January the *Virginian* printed an item from the *London Times* suggesting that southerners were too worried about how others would perceive the step and not worried enough about how well it would work. Surprised the South had not taken the step before, the London editor

---

[34] Ibid., 1067–71.

[35] Ibid.

contended that black men in gray would be as loyal as the men of Baltimore in blue.[36]

Several days later, the words of Kentuckian George D. Prentice appeared in Lynchburg and expressed the earnestness of the southern debate: "The Jeff Davis Government has conclusively resolved to free and arm the slaves—that two hundred thousand of them would soon be equipped and put into the field to fight us, under the stimulus of the promise of their own liberty and that of their wives and children, and of a proprietary interest in the soil." Unlike accounts of the less controversial bill to use slaves as laborers with the army, the *Virginian* produced a series of reports detailing the Congressional debates over arming black troops. For example, on 4 February the comments of John Atkins of Tennessee burned across the pages in Lynchburg: "Between subjugation and using our slaves in our defense every principle of nature and self-preservation requires the latter; therefore, we should at once put one hundred thousand slaves…in the field." In Congress in early February many echoed Atkins's sentiments, but most stopped short of saying that the action must be taken immediately.[37]

The December defeats found Charles Button at the *Lynchburg Virginian* struggling with the demon of despair. Comparing the situation to that of Frederick the Great as he stood alone against all the powers of Europe, Button prepared to make any sacrifice to stave off defeat: "Give up slavery; everything but our freedom, to save ourselves from the domination of the beastly Yankee." Despite these brave words, on 3 January the Lynchburg editor stopped short of agreeing with the editor of the *Richmond Enquirer*, who had recommended immediate abolition and acceptance of a colonial protectorate from a European power. The *Virginian*'s editor feared that widespread emancipation would harm the ex-slave as well as the South. "No matter how

---

[36] "Stoneman-Burbridge Raid," *Lynchburg Virginian*, 30 December 1864, 2; "Stoneman's Raid—A List of Munchausens," *Lynchburg Virginian*, 6 January 1865, 1; "The Situation," *Lynchburg Virginian*, 3 January 1865, 2; "Arming the Negroes of the South," *Lynchburg Virginian*, 12 January 1865, 1; "The Arming of Slaves," *Lynchburg Virginian*, 16 January 1865, 2; "Congressional," *Lynchburg Virginian*, 28 January and 2, 4 February 1865, 2.

[37] "Arming the Negroes of the South," *Lynchburg Virginian*, 12 January 1865, 1; "The Arming of Slaves," *Lynchburg Virginian*, 16 January 1865, 2; "Congressional," *Lynchburg Virginian*, 28 January and 2, 4 February 1865, 2.

this struggle may eventuate," Button asserted, "slavery in some form or other; in effect, if not in name, will exist in these Southern States...for generations to come." Three days later, Button attempted to drive home the point by examining the financial demise of Haiti after the black masses received their freedom. While many considered him a radical on racial issues as he championed black troops, the editor of the *Virginian* displayed significant racial prejudice even as he called for black assistance on the battlefield.[38]

First rumors and then northern newspaper articles arrived in Staunton broadcasting the most unwelcome news about the capture of Savannah and the defeat of Hood. On 23 December, the *Vindicator* attempted to brush off the reports as propaganda, but slowly the depth of the calamity began to sink in. Closer to home, the raid on Saltville reinforced the idea that no place in western Virginia was safe from the blue troopers. Even Lynchburg had spent several sleepless nights in anticipation of a visit from Sheridan. While her contemporaries in Richmond fought over the slave-soldier question, the Staunton paper provided only a few snippets on slavery. On 20 January a report appeared in the *Vindicator* claiming to represent Sherman's views of slavery: "He says slavery will exist in the South after the conclusion of peace, let the war terminate as it may...and that he [Sherman] expects to own a thousand slaves in the South one of these days." The failure of many slaves who had followed the Union column into Savannah to permanently join the blue ranks may have provided some cheer, but Valley residents well knew that once slaves tasted freedom, they rarely returned to their former masters.[39] While some in the Shenandoah Valley may have wanted to believe that emancipation was simply a war measure that could not stand up in court, few could have doubted the Union general's grim resolve as they read about his advance into South Carolina.

At his editorial desk, Samuel Yost attempted to place the best possible face on the December defeats: "Sherman has advanced through the state of Georgia and now holds the city of Savannah, but the country thro' which he

---

[38] Charles Button, "It was considered a Roman virtue...," *Lynchburg Virginian*, 31 December 1864, 1; Charles Button, "A Republic to Let," *Lynchburg Virginian*, 3 January 1865, 1; Charles Button, "We have heretofore said...," *Lynchburg Virginian*, 6 January 1865, 1.

[39] "Gen'l Sherman on Slavery," *Staunton Vindicator*, 20 January 1865, 1; "War News," *Staunton Vindicator*, 20 January 1865, 2.

passed is still as much unconquered as it was before his onward movement commenced." In many ways, these comments might have applied equally well to the Shenandoah Valley. Strong Union forces had driven through all opposition and laid waste to large sections of the heartland of Virginia, as Sherman had in Georgia. The editor of the *Vindicator* was doubtless speaking to himself as well as to his readers when he enjoined them to "let each and all of us resolve to do our whole duty, and never, for one moment give way to despondency." On 27 January, despite receiving word of the fall of Fort Fisher, Yost trumpeted the state's allegiance to the Confederate cause: "She [Virginia] was now willing to give her means as freely as she had given her sons."[40] Even as Yost remained on the sidelines, as black troops were being discussed in Congress, he was struggling mightily to maintain public faith in the southern war effort.

In Harrisonburg, the *Rockingham Register* greeted the new year with the "hope that the tide of our disasters and misfortunes has turned." In subsequent weeks, Wartmann selected the news items carefully to stem despair, but also to discourage calls for new manpower policies. On 20 January, the *Register* reprinted the statistical study produced by the *Richmond Whig*, which argued that, despite battle losses, the South possessed only 12,000 fewer men than at the beginning of the war. In a similar vein, the Harrisonburg paper copied a piece from an Augusta, Georgia, paper, which acknowledged the darkness of the hour but compared it to the trying moments of 1778 during the American Revolution.[41] Clearly, the *Register*'s editor hoped to rekindle the revolutionary spark even as he called on the Southern people to resist any change of principle.

Wartmann's editorials also reflected this policy as he ridiculed the Richmond press for exposing their "foolish fears in the face of the world." As talk of emancipation in return for faithful service on the battlefield animated the Confederate capital, the Harrisonburg editor questioned his comrades' grasp of the situation: "We are far, very far, from being reduced to the painful alternatives discussed with so much zeal by our intelligent friends of the

---

[40] S.M. Yost, "With this our first…," *Staunton Vindicator*, 6 January 1865, 2; S.M. Yost, "Cotton and Tobacco," *Staunton Vindicator*, 27 January 1865, 2.

[41] "We have had but little news…," *Rockingham Register*, 6 January 1865, 1; "Physical Resources of the Confederacy," *Rockingham Register*, 27 January 1865, 1; "A Contrast—1778 and 1864," *Rockingham Register*, 20 January 1865, 1.

Richmond press." The following week, on 27 January, Wartmann continued to develop the argument by contending that small steps taken in crisis could have long-lasting implications: "The loss of property may be repaired and the injury done to a country made right again; but a people who are dishonored and humiliated by Submission can never lift up their heads again." Wartmann printed long lists of those who had lost property, such as barns and cattle, and glorified their sacrifice, but he understood the slavery question to be one of principle and, therefore, not open to negotiation. If the Confederacy would only show its resolve to stay the course, he asserted, Union efforts would quickly collapse: "We steadfastly believe that our independence will soon be an admitted fact. Certain it is, it will speedily come when our 'calculating' antagonists discover that there is no such thing as a mean and cowardly and dishonorable 'back down' to be proposed or submitted to by the South."[42] Although eager to continue the fight for his principled stand, Wartmann offered no solution to the South's pressing manpower needs.

The defeats at Nashville and Savannah served as catalysts in the Roanoke and the Shenandoah Valleys. In Lynchburg, Charles Button struggled with the implications of his decision that slaves must be armed. Union military activity ensured that these Virginians could not forget the urgency of the issue. In contrast, the two Shenandoah communities had already felt Sheridan's wrath. Further, Union cavalry operations continued in the valley throughout the period, providing incentive for change but also preventing the development of a dispassionate dialogue on the topic. Did these Shenandoah residents see black troops as a viable Confederate alternative? Had they seen so much northern military might that they considered all new sacrifices wasted?

In the second phase of Davis's campaign, Virginians found themselves confronted by a series of complex, yet interrelated issues. The Confederate defeats at Nashville and Savannah had made immediate reinforcement of the southern armies the number-one priority of all leaders. Despite the impres-

---

[42] John H. Wartmann, "We hope our brethren," *Rockingham Register*, 20 January 1865, 2; John H. Wartmann, "Peace and Submission—War and Independence," *Rockingham Register*, 27 January 1865, 2; John H. Wartmann, "Destruction of Property by the Enemy in Rockingham," *Rockingham Register*, 27 January 1865, 2.

sive statistical study produced by the *Richmond Whig*, no civilian or military official could seriously accept the argument that the South did not need more men. Behind the scenes, Davis and the Cabinet conducted a well-designed, political operation to ignite the slave-soldier debate in each of the southern states. Relatively reticent in public on the issue, the president missed no opportunity to advocate arming the slaves in private. In his memoirs, Davis remembered repeatedly telling groups of congressmen how he had armed and led his slaves against a body of lawless white men.[43] Similarly, Robert E. Lee unequivocally expressed his support for black troops in private but continued to refuse to enter the public debate. In contrast, the Richmond papers published bold ideas like the *Richmond Enquirer*'s proposition to trade emancipation in return for recognition. The resulting discussion in the other Virginia journals demonstrated the depth of southern commitment to sacrifice everything for the cause, but also their lingering commitment to slavery.

With both the *Richmond Sentinel* and *Enquirer* questioning the loyalty of the slave owners, a clearer image of the divisions within Virginia society emerges. Most Virginians were willing to promise to give all for the cause, but when the necessity arose to arm the slaves after the December defeats, many Virginians hesitated. The variety of options to fill the ranks, presented in the press, failed to create a clear consensus in January. From initial public discussions of arming slaves in November, the debate had shifted in late December and January from a theoretical question to a practical matter. In Virginia the debate now revolved around the question of Benjamin, Lee, and Stringfellow: Will the slaves fight for us or against us?

---

[43] Jefferson Davis, *The Rise and Fall of the Confederate Government,* Vol. 1 (New York: D. Appleton and Co., 1881) 518.

6

A Matter of Necessity

On 21 December the city fathers of Savannah rode out to meet General Sherman and his victorious blue columns. The long, destructive march through the state had indeed made Georgia howl. The previous week Union General George Thomas had destroyed the army of Tennessee at Nashville. News of the two great defeats arrived in most Georgia communities at approximately the same time and produced a most sobering Christmas season. Suddenly no area of the Deep South appeared safe as both Sherman and Thomas stood unopposed. From these reverses, the debate entered a second phase caused by the military necessity to place a new army in the field.

As the Confederate military situation crumbled in December 1864, President Jefferson Davis attempted to propel the idea of a "radical modification" of slavery onto the front pages of southern newspapers. Considering the administration's shaky standing with Georgia Governor Joseph E. Brown and Vice President Alexander Stephens, who was at home in Crawfordville, Davis did not dare to take the direct approach used by Judah Benjamin in South Carolina. Instead he had Secretary of War James Seddon broach the idea of black troops with militia General Howell Cobb. "I should be pleased to have your views as to the prospects from this quarter [stricter enforcement of conscription], as likewise…your opinion as to the practicability and policy of employing negroes as soldiers."[1] As one of the largest slave owners in Georgia, Cobb had often trumpeted the pro-slavery position, but he was considered by leaders in the Davis administration as the best hope to lead the debate in the state. As importantly, Seddon questioned Cobb on what reward the Confederacy should offer the black recruits: "If [it is] to be resorted to, should they be held as slaves, be promised emancipation, or be at once freed?"[2] Unlike other states to which administration lead-

---

[1] *Official Records*, Series 4, Vol. 3, 981.

[2] Ibid.

ers wrote, the Davis administration had no prominent allies in Georgia. Therefore, Seddon did not attempt to direct how the debate of slavery should be conducted as he and Davis had done with others. Arguments to arm slaves would come from the people of Georgia rather than their leaders.

After the loss of Savannah and the disaster at Nashville, the news reports that arrived in Central Georgia reflected less fear of the nation's losing its ideological foundations and more interest in avoiding total military defeat. The newspapers in Macon, Athens, and Milledgeville mirrored this desperate tenor in their news items, editorials, and letters. Although continuing its editorial opposition to arming slaves, the *Macon Telegraph and Confederate* printed numerous editorials from other papers as news items, even though these exchange editorials strongly favored the policy. On 5 January 1865, this Macon paper reprinted an editorial written by John Forsyth of the *Mobile Register* that argued strongly that the time had come when the South must sacrifice all for honor and freedom: "In the foreground of this picture of national military disaster, we shall not fail to discover, torn up root and branch, the institution of domestic slavery."[3] Necessity and common sense, the Mobile editor contended, demand nothing less than arming the slaves: "With such reserves and pressed as we are, is it not folly to hesitate to avail of it and fill our depleted army?"[4]

The reports from John Thrasher's Press Association of the Confederate States also reflected a bolder mood in Congress. On 31 January and 6 February, accounts of Congressional action appeared on the front page, with national leaders emerging to lead the fight to arm the slaves: "Senator Burnett declared he preferred independence to negro slavery and if the time ever arrived when it became necessary to use negroes in aid of accomplishing that end, he would employ them."[5] Henry Flash, the editor of the *Telegraph and Confederate*, and many individual citizens accepted this shift to necessity as an obvious reflection of the deteriorating military situation around them.

The *Southern Confederacy*, originally an Atlanta paper, printed numerous news items about arming the slaves from its new offices in Macon. On

---

[3] John Forsyth, "The Crisis—The Remedy," *Macon Telegraph and Confederate*, 5 January 1865, 2.

[4] Ibid.

[5] "Confederate Congress," *Macon Telegraph and Confederate*, 6 February 1865, 2.

20 January the *Confederacy* published a report from the *Richmond Whig* that denied any necessity to arm the slaves and attempted to show that enough white men yet remained to win the war.[6] In an editorial from the *Memphis Appeal*, which appeared in the Macon paper on 22 January, an opponent of arming the slaves argued that too many white men wanted the benefits of slavery without paying the price. This Memphis editor decried the large number of able-bodied men trading slaves in Montgomery: "Has everybody thus engaged reflected that...the institutions of the South are in such imminent danger that the services of all interested in their preservation are needed to protect...them?"[7] Other news items focused not upon the number of white men but upon the advisability of using black men. On 26 January the *Confederacy* cited a report of the *Charleston Mercury* that declared General Robert E. Lee's support for the use of black troops.[8] On 5 February, in a report of the Congressional debate on slave-soldiers, the paper noted Tennessee Congressman John Atkins's opposition to emancipation but acknowledged his recommendation of the enlistment of 100,000 slaves to prevent subjugation.[9] The news reports from both the *Confederacy* and the *Telegraph and Confederate* clearly show that the national debate had shifted after the Christmas defeats from a theoretical discussion of whether the slaves should ever be armed to a very practical debate about whether the recent military reverses now made the step necessary.

A new, urgent tone entered the editorials of the *Macon Telegraph and Confederate* after Sherman's march through Georgia and the disaster at Nashville. Although the direct threat of Union soldiers striking Macon passed before the first of December, Henry Flash, the editor, could not deny the critical situation of the Confederacy. On 2 January he argued that congressional attempts to tighten the exemption bill resembled an old woman trying to fill a bottomless pit with a ladle.[10] In his view, desertion rather than holes in the conscription law caused the problem as the troops deserted faster than the new conscripts arrived. Unable to ignore the chorus calling for

---

[6] "Encouraging," *Southern Confederacy*, 20 January 1865, 1.

[7] "Plenty of Men Left," *Southern Confederacy*, 22 January 1865, 1.

[8] "What Lee Thinks," *Southern Confederacy*, 26 January 1865, 2.

[9] "Confederate Congress," *Southern Confederacy*, 5 February 1865, 1.

[10] Henry Flash, "The Congressional Dipper," *Macon Telegraph and Confederate*, 2 January 1865, 2.

employing black troops, Flash pleaded with his readers on 5 January to keep the faith in the Confederate cause and in slavery: "A doubting and hesitating spirit seems to have seized upon a portion of our press and people...To doubt and to hesitate is to invite assault and court defeat."[11] Although continuing to consider arming the slaves the first, ominous step toward general emancipation, this Macon editor recognized the critical nature of the manpower crisis and pleaded for immediate action: "Whatever policy is to be adopted, must be adopted without delay."[12] Despite the military disasters at Nashville and Savannah, the editor of the *Telegraph and Confederate* remained anchored in traditional southern ideology and rejected the idea that necessity demanded black troops.

At the editorial desk of the *Southern Confederacy*, W.H. Barnes resolutely refused to consider any modification of the slave's role in the war effort. Arming the slaves, Barnes argued on 20 January, would only produce large bands of armed, desperate slaves hiding in the southern countryside.[13] Noting the high rate of white desertion, Barnes questioned the idea that a promise of freedom would keep black men in the gray ranks: "With the enemy they know they would get freedom at once. With us, they would get freedom after the war...There would exist an immediate certainty of freedom on one side; an uncertainty on the other."[14] Holding fast to the old proslavery ideology, Barnes argued that slavery provided the best possible life for the slave, but he doubted that the slaves would fight for such a life: "We have no idea he can be convinced of the fact sufficiently to take up arms and fight bravely for our cause as his cause, for our country as his country."[15] Seeing little hope for winning the fidelity of the black troops if slavery remained untouched, Barnes concluded, "Let us put the negro to work, but not to fight."[16] The military disasters at Savannah and Nashville and the resulting cries of necessity had little effect upon this editor's views of arming the slaves.

---

[11] Henry Flash, "Straws," *Macon Telegraph and Confederate*, 5 January 1865, 2.

[12] Henry Flash, "No News," *Macon Telegraph and Confederate*, 6 January 1865, 2.

[13] W.H. Barnes, "Negroes in the Army," *Southern Confederacy*, 20 January 1865, 2.

[14] Ibid.

[15] Ibid.

[16] Ibid.

In the *Christian Index*, the Baptist weekly published in Macon, longtime editor Samuel Boykin produced a series of introspective commentaries on the southern reverses. Having realistically examined the disasters of December, the Baptist editor attempted to find a ray of hope: "The whole field presents to our mind a gloomy aspect. Although we cannot penetrate the darkness which hovers over our prospects, yet we do not yield our faith in our final success."[17] On 26 January, as he again announced a southern defeat with the fall of Fort Fisher, Boykin struggled to find the cause of Confederate failure: "While God has punished us terribly for our wickedness, and for the abuse of the institution which He has committed to us, we do not believe that He purposes...the destruction of that institution."[18] Such comments reflected collective guilt over the abuses of slavery, like the disregard of slave marriages, rather than a deep-seated guilt over slavery itself, which continued to be seen as a divinely ordained institution. Although taxed sorely by the military reverses, Boykin maintained his opposition to arming the slaves. On 2 February the editor of the *Christian Index* called for new and greater sacrifices but never mentioned slave-soldiers: "The independence of our country deserves every sacrifice we can make: upon its altars let us lay ourselves, our property, our comfort, our all."[19] Although rigid on the idea of black troops, Boykin's editorials, like those of Henry Flash at the *Telegraph and Confederate*, reflected the growing desperation felt in Macon.

Upon the reports of the enormous army losses of December, a large number of letters arrived in the office of the *Macon Telegraph and Confederate*. While "necessity" was the watchword, the letter writers fully understood the radical nature of the debate. Asking what necessity could justify dumping one's principles, "Q" argued on 6 January that "every life that has been lost in this struggle was an offering upon the altar of African Slavery."[20] Few correspondents agreed so firmly with the paper's editor. On 11 January "Solon" claimed that the South could not avoid arming the slaves because necessity demanded it: "We should...promptly take hold of all the means that

[17] Samuel Boykin, "Notes on the Times," *Christian Index*, 5 January 1865, 3.
[18] Samuel Boykin, "Notes on the Times," *Christian Index*, 26 January 1865, 3.
[19] Samuel Boykin, "Endure! Endure! Endure!", *Christian Index*, 2 February 1865, 2.
[20] "Q," "Letter to the Editor," *Macon Telegraph and Confederate*, 6 January 1865, 2.

God has placed within our reach to help us through the struggle."[21] In a letter published on 13 January the fear of subjugation appears as the principal motivation for arming the slaves: "We are ready, and it is necessary that we do those, or worse things, rather than be subjugated by the Yankees."[22]

Many who wrote the *Telegraph and Confederate*, like "Janus" and "John Hampden," contended that southern "apathy and indifference" had made it necessary to arm the slaves.[23] On 23 January "John Hampden" firmly declared that slaves must be enlisted because no amount of conscript laws would ever fill the armies: "At least a half million of the lazy, cowardly rascals, contrive to stay, inspite [sic] of you, so long as money is more powerful than patriotism."[24] To complement these local proponents of arming the slaves, the minutes from different group meetings began to arrive. On 19 January, the minutes of a county meeting in Upson County showed the majority of citizens in favor of arming the slaves as they called for a state convention to approve the measure.[25] Clearly, many men and women in Macon now felt that only by arming the slaves could they overcome the reverses suffered at Nashville and Savannah. The howls of necessity drowned out the ideological calls from the measure's opponents in the ears of Macon's citizens.

Unlike the letters in the *Telegraph and Confederate*, the letters concerning arming the slaves that appeared in the *Southern Confederacy* originated outside the local community. For example, on 20 January "Mobilia" wrote that the Mobile newspapers had sparked a great debate in the city: "I am anti-negro as regards the war question, though the papers are for it with one voice—indeed one journal openly advocates abolition."[26] Other letters also reflected a new openness to radical ideas. Thus, on 24 January a Mississippi correspondent provided anecdotal evidence that arming the slaves might

---

[21] "Solon," "Letter to the Editor," *Macon Telegraph and Confederate*, 11 January 1865, 1.

[22] "Letter to the Editor," *Macon Telegraph and Confederate*, 13 January 1865, 1.

[23] "Janus," "Letter to the Editor," *Macon Telegraph and Confederate*, 19 January 1865, 1.

[24] John Hampden, "Letter to the Editor," *Macon Telegraph and Confederate*, 23 January 1865, 2.

[25] "County Meeting," *Macon Telegraph and Confederate*, 19 January 1865, 1.

[26] "Mobilia," "Letter from Mobile," *Southern Confederacy*, 20 January 1865, 1.

work: "There was a negro in our party, who pitched in, and...killed a Yankee negro. ... This faithful Confederate negro, though a slave, has been in our army all the time, and has made many a Yankee bite the dust."[27] Such an account fit well with the Davis administration's admonition to stress arming the slaves but not emancipation. From such accounts in the *Confederacy*, the citizens of Macon saw that the debate was engulfing the whole South, not simply Central Georgia.

The letters that appeared in the *Christian Index* echoed the soul-searching of the paper's editor. On 5 January the *Index* published a letter from "J.L.D." arguing that the South must repent to achieve victory: "The war which afflicts us, has a manifest connection to slavery, and it ought to be our first inquiry, whether in relation to this subject we have committed any sin which has offended God."[28] As with many reformers, "J.L.D." condemned the failure to protect slave marriages. "We may," he asserted, "have failed greatly in our duty to the slaves that God has placed under our authority."[29] To regain favor with God and success on the battlefield, "J.L.D." believed, the South had to correct the abuses of slavery: "The rod of God is upon us—disaster staring us in the face. ... Let God's chastisement have its proper affect [sic] on our hearts."[30] The staggering defeats of December forced grave soul-searching in the correspondents of the *Index* and led many Central Georgians to rethink their own ideological foundations and question whether they were living up to their own ideals as supposedly Christian masters.

Meanwhile, in Athens, the *Southern Watchman* announced the stunning southern defeats at Nashville and Savannah on 28 December. In January most news reports focused upon different peace proposals and the idea of holding a convention of delegates from areas of the state. Such ideas, pet projects of Governor Joe Brown and other Davis opponents, reflected the despondency that resulted from the military disasters. Telegraphic reports of congressional debates composed the only news items to appear in this Athens paper concerning arming the slaves. On 1 February editor John Christy

---

[27] "Cuffee vs. Cuffee," *Southern Confederacy*, 24 January 1865, 1.
[28] "J.L.D.," "Our Chastisement," *Christian Index*, 5 January 1865, 1.
[29] Ibid.
[30] Ibid.

of the *Watchman* printed a summary of the debate about black troops in the Confederate House of Representatives, highlighting the opposition of William Miles of South Carolina and James Ramsey of North Carolina.[31] In a similar vein, on 8 February, the *Watchman* cited Congressman Thomas Gholson's assertion that the South's best hope for peace rested in getting the deserters back to the army and "by ceasing to agitate the policy of employing negro troops—a measure which has already divided public sentiment and produced much despondency."[32] Only on 15 February, as House passage of the measure approached, did the *Watchman* finally report the views of a congressman who supported arming the slaves. The news items that appeared in the *Southern Watchman* in the second phase of the debate reflected the despondency from the military reverses and the continuing opposition of the paper's editor to the idea of arming the slaves.

The other weekly in Athens, the *Southern Banner*, also closely followed the debate in Richmond. On 1 February the *Banner* reported that General Lee had met with an unidentified Congressman and had vehemently urged arming the slaves: "The member of Congress was opposed to the use of slaves as soldiers, but General Lee's arguments induced him to withdraw all opposition."[33] Unlike the *Watchman*, the *Banner* did not stress the views of the opponents of the measure; instead, it printed the comments of leaders from both sides.[34] On 15 February the *Banner* published a transcript of the Senate debate of 6 February in which Albert Brown of Mississippi emerged as a strong proponent of arming the slaves. Brown recommended "that the committee on military affairs be instructed to report a bill...to take within the military service...a number of negro soldiers, not to exceed 200,000."[35] As justification, Senator Brown trumpeted the necessity of the measure: "Now if ever was the time, we were in the very crisis of our fate."[36] The news items published in the *Banner* provided a far clearer reflection of the congressional debate over the use of black troops than did the partisan reports that appeared in the *Watchman*.

---

[31] "Congressional," *Southern Watchman*, 1 February 1865, 3.
[32] "Congressional," *Southern Watchman*, 8 February 1865, 3.
[33] "Richmond Gossip," *Southern Banner*, 1 February 1865, 2.
[34] "Congressional," *Southern Banner*, 1 February 1865, 2.
[35] "From Richmond," *Southern Banner*, 15 February 1865, 3.
[36] Ibid.

Despite the military disasters at Nashville and Savannah, John Christy at the *Watchman* stoutly refused to consider any modification of slavery. On 4 January he declared any scheme to trade emancipation for foreign recognition as "unmanly" and "foolish."[37] In his view, the slavery question had not changed since the election of 1860: "Should we yield to our enemies more than they claimed? Shall we voluntarily surrender, not only our right to extend slavery in the Territories, but relinquish all claim to it in the States?"[38] A week later, Christy decried the radical ideas discussed in Athens and in the exchange papers: "Wild schemes are daily urged—such as conditional abolition of slavery, putting slaves in the army, going back to a colonial state."[39] These ideas, if discussed at all, the editor argued, should be discussed in a convention of the states. The bold editorials and letters appearing in Augusta's *Daily Constitutionalist* also drew the wrath of the *Watchman* editor. After comparing the *Constitutionalist* to William Lloyd Garrison's *Liberator*, Christy argued that political leaders could not convince the people that the primary purpose of the war was independence: "They will never make the people believe it. They know they were urged to secede immediately...to save the institution of slavery."[40] The open discussion in Augusta of the freed blacks' role in an independent Confederacy appalled the *Watchman's* editor. Such ideas, Christy declared on 8 February, had no place in the South.[41] As Central Georgia started to recover from Sherman's march, Christy sought refuge in traditional southern ideology to bolster his faith in eventual victory.

While Christy refused to consider new ideas, his local rival at the *Southern Banner*, James Sledge, tentatively accepted the idea of a "radical modification" of slavery. On 8 February Sledge strongly endorsed a modification of the slave codes in order to protect slave marriages. Without a purification of slavery's abuses, he suggested, God will not bless our arms: "The Southern Confederacy will never thrive unless it thrives upon morality and

---

[37] John Christy, "Abolition—Foreign Protection," *Southern Watchman*, 4 January 1865, 2.

[38] Ibid.

[39] John Christy, "State Convention," *Southern Watchman*, 11 January 1865, 2.

[40] John Christy, "Abolitionism," *Southern Watchman*, 8 February 1865, 3.

[41] Ibid.

order."[42] In a more radical tone, on 15 February Sledge applauded the House vote to allow the 40,000 slaves detailed for the service to bear arms: "From the vote…we presume that Congress is getting right on the subject of arming the negroes and will cackle less and act more."[43] Unlike the *Watchman*, Sledge published the names of the congressmen voting for each side. In the Georgia delegation, Warren Akin of Northwest Georgia; Hiram Bell of Northeast Georgia; Mark Blandford, representing Columbus; George Lester, representing Atlanta; and John Shewmake, representing Augusta, supported the idea of slave-soldiers. Joseph Echols, the congressman representing Athens; Clifford Anderson, representing Macon; and James M. Smith, representing LaGrange, opposed the measure. Julian Hartridge of Savannah and William E. Smith of Albany did not participate in this vote.[44] The division in the Georgia delegation illustrated the growing support in Georgia for the idea of arming the slaves. Although hesitant at first, James Sledge gradually accepted the necessity of modifying slavery during the second phase of the debate.

Although no letters concerning black troops appeared in the Athens papers during January and February, individual citizens discussed the issue in their private correspondence. General Howell Cobb, the commander of state troops in Georgia and a longtime Athens resident, figured prominently in the debate. On 3 January an anonymous Georgian wrote to Cobb to advocate the use of slaves in the army. This writer, who signed the letter as "E," astutely noted that attempts to limit details and exemptions would cut production and lead to disorder: "It will not do to take all the [white] male population out of the country. … I see but one alternative left us and that [is] to fill up our army with negroes."[45] "E" contended, "They have done some very good fighting for the Yanks, and I cannot see why they will not do as well for us if we give them their freedom."[46] Citing growing support for the idea,

---

[42] James Sledge, "Religious Duties of Masters to Slaves," *Southern Banner*, 8 February 1865, 2.

[43] James Sledge, "The Negro Question in Congress," *Southern Banner*, 15 February 1865, 1.

[44] Ibid.

[45] Ulrich Phillips, ed., *The Correspondence of Robert Toombs, Alexander Stephens, and Howell Cobb* (New York: Da Capo Press, 1970) 656.

[46] Ibid., 657.

the letter writer pleaded with Cobb to use his influence as a statesman and a slave owner to lead the Confederacy to put slaves in the army in order to prevent subjugation: "Now Gen[eral], if you think as I do, and as a large majority of the people of Georgia, you are the man to lead off in this thing."[47] Finally, "E" stressed the necessity of the measure to prevent utter ruin: "Anything but reconstruction or subjugation. I feel as confident as I can that if we levy a sufficient force of our black population that it will save us from either."[48]

Unknown to "E," Cobb also discussed the subject in a letter written the same week. On 8 January Cobb wrote to Secretary of War James Seddon and denounced the idea of slave-soldiers: "The day you make soldiers of them is the beginning of the end of the revolution. If slaves will make good soldiers our whole theory of slavery is wrong."[49] Instead, to fill the ranks, Cobb argued that conscription must be stopped and a system of volunteer units established: "For heaven's sake try it before you fill with gloom and despondency the hearts of many of our truest and most devoted men by resorting to the suicidal policy of arming our slaves."[50] Thus, while both "E" and Cobb recognized the necessity of filling the depleted ranks, they developed radically different plans.

Northwest Georgia Congressman Warren Akin also discussed the issue with his wife, who had moved to Elberton after Sherman had burned their home in Cass County. Although he had been reluctant in October to radically change the country's social structure, Akin changed his mind after the news arrived from Nashville and Savannah. Recognizing the critical nature of the crisis confronting the Confederacy, he declared, "We are in a deplorable condition—standing on the verge of an abyss. ... The fate of the Confederacy will be settled in six months, one way or another, and I very much fear the worst."[51] Despite his understanding of the grave issues at stake, Akin did not anticipate the groundswell of support for black troops. "I am surprised," Akin wrote to his wife on 26 December, "to find so many officers

[47] Ibid. The brackets in this quotation appear in Phillips's text.

[48] Ibid.

[49] Ainsworth, ed., *The War of the Rebellion*, 1009. *Official Records,* Series 4, Vol. 3 Serial 129, 1009.

[50] Ibid.

[51] Akin, *Letters of Warren Akin,* 74–75.

and men in favor of putting negroes in the army. This feeling is increasing rapidly...among the soldiers."[52] On 8 January Mary Frances Akin, the Congressman's wife, reported a similar rise in the measure's popularity in Elberton: "Everyone I talk to is in favor of putting negroes in the army and that immediately."[53] Furthermore, she argued that the fighting had already reshaped the South's social structure: "I think slavery is now gone and what little is left of it should be rendered as serviceable as possible. ... The negro men ought to be put to fighting."[54] In response, on 23 January, Akin told his wife that he supported the measure: "A great change is going in the public mind about putting negroes in the army. I have heard from different portions of Georgia, and the People are for it."[55] From congressmen in Richmond to refugees in Elberton to common people like "E," many Georgians found themselves reassessing the value of slavery in light of the necessity to stem the Union tide.

In Milledgeville, the news of the disasters of Savannah and Nashville reinforced the feelings of necessity born during Sherman's occupation of the city in November. Despite the need to field an army to face Sherman, the *Confederate Union* published only news items that condemned the idea of black troops during the second phase of the debate. On 17 January this Milledgeville paper reprinted an editorial from Macon's *Southern Confederacy* that argued that the South could not feed itself without slave labor: "It is impossible for the women and children to support themselves and our army, if the able-bodied men, white and black, have all to be taken from the fields of production."[56] In a similar editorial reprinted in Milledgeville on 7 February, the editor of the *Brandon* [MS] *Republican* railed against the "one hundred thousand able-bodied men now holding little appointments in the various departments."[57] Such bureaucrats, the Brandon editor believed, forced the South to consider radical measures: "These are the men who are now clamorous for arming the negroes or for agreeing to gradual emancipation...

[52] Ibid., 54.

[53] Mary Frances Akin, *Letters of Warren Akin: Confederate Congressman*, ed. Bell I. Wiley (Athens: University of Georgia Press, 1959) 117.

[54] Ibid.

[55] Akin, *Letters of Warren Akin,* 94.

[56] "Making Soldiers of Negroes," *Confederate Union*, 17 January 1865, 2.

[57] "From the Brandon *Republican*," *Confederate Union*, 7 February 1865, 1.

We are opposed to arming or setting free the negroes as long as we have this hundred thousand fat, sleek, lazy, 'last ditch' men to recruit."[58] Preoccupied with printing these editorials against the measure, the *Confederate Union* did not comment upon the debate in Congress until 14 February, when it grudgingly admitted that passage looked likely: "From the late action of Congress, there is no doubt that the negroes will be put in the army. Both houses are in favor of the proposition."[59]

The *Confederate Union*'s rival in Milledgeville, the *Southern Recorder*, provided only a few more news items that proposed ways to fill the gray ranks. On 10 January the *Recorder* reprinted an article from the *Macon Telegraph and Confederate* that termed any modification of slavery a sign of weakness and condemned the arming of the slaves as "a preliminary step—an entering wedge—towards general emancipation."[60] On 7 February the *Recorder* announced that the Confederate House had repealed all exemptions and now all white men between eighteen and forty-five owed service.[61] Finally, on 14 February this Milledgeville paper carried a synopsis of the arguments in Congress for black troops.[62] Although far from a comprehensive discussion of the issue, the news items that appeared in the *Southern Recorder* reflected a much broader spectrum of opinion than those printed in the *Union*.

At the editorial desk of the *Confederate Union*, Joseph Nisbet consistently refused to consider any change in the slave's role in the war effort. On 17 January Nisbet asserted that the idea, bandied about by the Richmond papers, of the South asking to return to a colonial status in return for European intervention would only highlight the young nation's weakness: "It would turn out to be an act of gratuitous and unavailing humiliation."[63] In such a scheme, as proposed in the *Richmond Enquirer*, the South would agree to gradual emancipation. Nisbet's editorial, titled "Let Us Not Cherish Delusions," argued that emancipation would only make the South a less at-

---

[58] Ibid.

[59] "News Summary," *Confederate Union*, 14 February 1865, 2.

[60] "Straws," *Southern Recorder*, 10 January 1865, 2.

[61] "Exemption Bill Repealed," *Southern Recorder*, 7 February 1865, 2.

[62] "The Proceedings in Congress," *Southern Recorder*, 14 February 1865, 2.

[63] Joseph Nisbet, "Let Us Not Cherish Delusions," *Confederate Union*, 17 January 1865, 2.

tractive possession: "By abolishing slavery we would destroy the element which would make us desirable either as allies or as colonies, for without the products of slave labor we could not be profitable to our friends or masters."[64] Finally, Nisbet asserted that Georgians should not delude themselves with thoughts of reconstruction, because the North wanted "unconditional submission" rather than a return to the old Union: "Our only hope of an honorable peace is in our power to injure our enemies. Submission now means death."[65] Although he astutely pointed out the flaws in others' schemes, Nisbet never seriously considered the idea of white and black southerners fighting together in order to achieve independence for the South.

In contrast, R.M. Orme at the *Southern Recorder* remained open to new ideas. Upon receiving news of the defeats at Nashville and Savannah, Orme declared that enough men remained in the South to stop Sherman, if they were properly led: "It is no time for small and minor points to be looked after. We must have an army that can meet Sherman in his future movements."[66] The *Recorder*'s editor initially objected to a discussion of trading slavery for European intervention, but on 17 January Orme yielded to the calls of necessity and recommended considering the idea: "If the Confederate government is, in the opinion of our authorities, so far exhausted in men and means…then it is wise to take into consideration the proposition of emancipation."[67] Accepting European conditions for intervention, he suggested, might be the lesser of two evils: "It is true, the entertaining of such a proposition is humiliating; but better do that, than reconstruct with our hated enemy."[68] While far from a true disciple of emancipation, Orme understood the grave situation and accepted that radical measures provided the best hope to avoid utter defeat.

During January and February, only one letter appeared in either Milledgeville paper concerning arming the slaves. On 17 January the *Confederate Union* published a letter from "Ozina" that advocated the idea of black

[64] Ibid.

[65] Ibid.

[66] R.M. Orme, "The Times," *Southern Recorder*, 3 January 1865, 2.

[67] R.M. Orme, "Selling Out," *Southern Recorder*, 10 January 1865, 2; and R.M. Orme, "Emancipation," *Southern Recorder*, 17 January 1865, 2.

[68] R.M. Orme, "Emancipation," *Southern Recorder*, 17 January 1865, 2.

troops but strongly opposed freeing the faithful soldiers: "While we freely surrender our slaves to fight, we think the preservation of our future liberty and the happiness of the slaves, demand that we retain possession of them."[69] In response to those who considered such a policy immoral, "Ozina" cited the biblical precedent of Abraham using his slaves as soldiers without granting their freedom. Finally, "Ozina" argued that if the slaves must be freed, then the South should simply rejoin the Union and end the bloodshed: "If we are to free them thus gradually, we might as well do as Abraham Lincoln says and free them at once; and stop this horrible war."[70] This letter from Milledgeville clearly showed the internal turmoil that radical ideas like emancipation engendered in southern communities.

The second phase of the debate in Central Georgia revolved around the necessity to field an army to meet the Union threat. Without a direct military threat to Macon, Athens, and Milledgeville, news items from South Carolina and Virginia provided the sense of necessity. Moderate editors like Henry Flash of Macon and James Sledge of Athens understood the need to field a new army, but struggled to adapt their old pro-slavery ideas to the new situation. In contrast, several editors, like W.H. Barnes of the *Southern Confederacy*, John Christy of the *Southern Watchman*, and Joseph Nisbet of the *Confederate Union*, attempted to ignore the crisis. The bold comments that appeared in the *Macon Telegraph and Confederate* and in the Cobb and Akin letters show that many Central Georgians would not follow the head-in-the-sand approach advanced by the advocates of traditional southern ideology. In short, though a few editors ignored the calls of necessity, the common men and women of this central region, as seen in their letters, heard the howls of necessity and explored radical solutions to the manpower problem.

Sherman's capture of Savannah did not end the direct military threat to Augusta as it did to the cities of Central Georgia. As articles arrived from other papers debating the necessity of arming slaves, Sherman's methodical progress through South Carolina continued to threaten Augusta and left little doubt about the need for immediate action. On 7 January Augusta's *Daily Constitutionalist* reprinted an editorial from the *North Carolinian* argu-

---

[69] "Ozina," "Letter from Ozina," *Confederate Union*, 17 January 1865, 2.
[70] Ibid.

ing that only slaves could fill the gray ranks depleted by desertion: "If the fighting men will not go, we must make something else go to fight, it matters not what that something is, be it black, white, or gray."[71] The Carolina editor further suggested that by arming the slaves, a few key white men, like mechanics, could be released from service. Others also looked for benefits outside the direct military value of arming the slaves. An editorial from the *Richmond Enquirer* that appeared in the *Constitutionalist* on 7 January argued that by emancipating the faithful soldiers, the South could show the world that it fought not "merely for negro slavery" but also for the "self-government of whites."[72] Others, like the editor of the *Mobile Register*, whose comments appeared in Augusta on 8 January, focused strictly upon the theme of necessity and common sense: "It is not a question of taste and preference, but one of dire necessity—a choice of fearful evils. ... Men differ as to this policy; but who can deny that if we do not use our servants to fight for their masters, with a guarantee of their freedom, our enemies will so use them against us?"[73] The *Constitutionalist*'s editor, James Gardner, highlighted these editorials, rather than the debate in Congress, to demonstrate that other southern communities also were considering radical changes. As Sherman's army pressed forward into South Carolina, these calls for arming the slaves struck a highly responsive chord among the citizens of Augusta.

In contrast to the news items that appeared in the *Constitutionalist*, Augusta's *Chronicle and Sentinel* focused its coverage upon the debate in Congress. In particular, the editor sought out voices of congressional opposition to drown out the calls for radical change, in effect, misrepresenting the tenor of the debate in Richmond. On 14 February the *Chronicle and Sentinel* printed a long transcript of the Senate debate of 3 February about arming the slaves. In this account, the opposition of Senator James Orr and Senator Augustus Maxwell received great emphasis.[74] "It involved," Maxwell argued, "abolition of slavery. He could scarcely realize that he had heard such a proposition discussed in the Confederate Senate."[75] At the very end of the

[71] "Conscription of Negroes," *Daily Constitutionalist*, 7 January 1865, 2.

[72] "The Foreign Protectorate," *Daily Constitutionalist*, 7 January 1865, 1.

[73] "The Spirit of the Press," *Daily Constitutionalist*, 8 January 1865, 3.

[74] "Employment of Negroes in the Army," *Chronicle and Sentinel*, 14 February 1865, 2.

[75] Ibid.

account, the paper published a statement by Senator Henry Burnett that advocated the use of slaves in the army and trumpeted Lee's support of the measure. "If he was convinced that there was white material enough in the country," Burnett declared, "he would vote against negro soldiers, but he was not convinced of it, and, if called an abolitionist, he was in good company."[76] Among the Georgia newspapers, only in the *Chronicle and Sentinel* did the comments of Orr and Maxwell overshadow the strong statements of Burnett.[77]

On 17 February the *Chronicle and Sentinel* again manipulated the coverage of the congressional debate in order to emphasize the opposition view. To introduce the Senate debate of 4 February, the paper's editor, Nathan S. Morse, printed a portion of the debate of 2 February. Morse quickly noted that Senator Albert Brown had supported the idea of black troops and then quoted a long passage from a speech of Louis Wigfall against the measure.[78] Below the Wigfall speech, Morse printed the Senate debate of 4 February in which Senators John Watson, George Vest, and William Simms declared their support for black troops. "When it was found necessary," Watson declared, "to arm them to whip back the Yankee horde, he would…favor that proposition, even to the conscription of the last able-bodied negro."[79] If the editor of the *Chronicle and Sentinel* had not placed the Wigfall comments of 2 February above the account of the Senate debate, no voice of opposition would have appeared.

Although he had been cautious in the first phase of the debate, after the staggering military reverses of Nashville and Savannah, editor James Gardner took a strong stand in the *Daily Constitutionalist*. Immediately upon receiving the news of the disasters, he argued that the proposition to arm the slaves had "derived irresistible force to our minds from Gen. Sherman's march…through the very heart of Georgia."[80] Sherman's recruitment of

---

[76] Ibid.

[77] See *Macon Telegraph and Confederate*, 6 February 1865; Columbus *Daily Sun*, 5 February 1865; and *Columbus Times*, 6 February 1865.

[78] "Senate Debate on the Negro Soldier Bill," *Chronicle and Sentinel*, 17 February 1865, 2.

[79] Ibid.

[80] James Gardner, "We Must Use the Negro, or the Enemy Will Use Him Against Us," *Daily Constitutionalist*, 5 January 1865, 2.

slaves into his army as he moved through Georgia also merited Gardner's notice and helped to justify his new position: "The whole question reverts and resolves itself into the terse and startling sentence of General Lee that, 'we must use the negro or the enemy will use him against us.'"[81] Having accepted the concept of arming the slaves, this Augusta editor foresaw great potential in the new policy: "We have, then, in our negro population an element of stupendous power, and the material for an army at once disciplined and, in time, courageous."[82]

Despite this ringing endorsement of the slave-soldier, Gardner still considered emancipation to be "unwise and injudicious" and clung to the old pro-slavery argument that slavery provided the best life for the African race: "We favor the using of slaves in every possible way...aimed at by the Confederate Government and these Southern people; but let them be used as slaves."[83] Although still unwilling to give up slavery, he confessed on 14 January that future military reverses might force even that final sacrifice: "As between reunion or any character of submission to the Yankee, and the entire obliteration of negro slavery; individually we should say slavery must go."[84] The shattering defeats of December forced the editor of the *Daily Constitutionalist* to accept the arming of the slaves, but his shift represented only a fraction of the transformation that had occurred in the minds of the people in Augusta.

In contrast, at the *Chronicle and Sentinel* editorial desk, Nathan Morse condemned all efforts to alter slavery. On 8 January, for example, he strongly argued that foreign intervention secured by the sacrifice of slavery would "be bought at too great a price." To him, "a surrender of slavery is a surrender of everything. It is subjugation by the Yankee idea. ... If we are Yankees, why not be in the Union?"[85] Morse not only defended the institution of slavery,

---

[81] Ibid.

[82] James Gardner, "Slaves for the Army," *Daily Constitutionalist*, 31 December 1864, 2.

[83] James Gardner, "Slaves for War Purposes," *Daily Constitutionalist*, 29 December 1864, 2.

[84] James Gardner, "Shall Slavery Be Abolished For Foreign Recognition and Independence?" *Daily Constitutionalist*, 14 January 1865, 2.

[85] N.S. Morse, "Richmond Gossip," *Chronicle and Sentinel*, 8 January 1865, 1; and "Emancipation and Foreign Intervention," *Chronicle and Sentinel*, 10 January 1865, 2.

but also on 1 February defended the privileged position of large slave owners at home. He lamented, "It is a sad fact that 'the rich men at home' have been the supporters of the war, with little reward beyond suffering, loss, and taxation."[86] Furthermore, Morse strongly objected to the idea of taking the planters' most valuable property—slaves. He argued that once the slaves entered the army, the planters would lose their greatest resource and yet still be expected to feed the army, care for the families of the black troops, and pay exorbitant taxes.[87] Obviously, Morse did not understand the poor whites' complaint of a rich man's war and a poor man's fight. The fundamental transformation of the public mind in Augusta had not touched the editor of the *Chronicle and Sentinel.*

Sherman's relentless push into South Carolina brought forth a series of bold, thoughtful letters to the editor of the *Daily Constitutionalist*. On 31 December, in the first of several letters, "Harry South" wrote the paper to argue that the times demanded the abandonment of the old slave ideology: "In times of all great revolutions…it often becomes necessary to change long established customs, however tenaciously they may have been adhered to."[88] Arguing that the army must have men before the spring campaign, he found only one source to fill the ranks: "The only plan that suggests itself to our mind, is the employment of one or two hundred thousand slaves in our armies."[89] Finally, "Harry South" claimed that the slave must receive his freedom in return for faithful service: "We believe it is the best policy of the government to make them a voluntary offer of freedom, if they will serve the cause of the South until independence is achieved."[90]

In a similar vein, "W.W." wrote to the *Daily Constitutionalist* and contended that immediate help in the field was more important than hanging onto empty principles. The "services [of the negro] in the field of war are worth more in our present emergencies than the indefinite and uncertain

[86] N.S. Morse, "Demagogues," *Chronicle and Sentinel*, 1 February 1865, 2.

[87] Ibid.

[88] Harry South, "Letter to the Editor—Negroes for the Army," *Daily Constitutionalist*, 6 January 1865, 2.

[89] Harry South, "Letter to the Editor—Negroes for the Army," *Daily Constitutionalist*, 31 December 1864, 2.

[90] Harry South, "Letter to the Editor—Negroes for the Army," *Daily Constitutionalist*, 6 January 1865, 2.

perpetuation of slavery."[91] The overriding necessity to meet the Yankee armies led "W.W." to call for the ultimate sacrifice from the slave owner: "The opinion is daily gaining ground that we shall never succeed against the power of the North and the negro combined. ... Victory will ultimately crown the arms of that side whose banner is borne by the emancipated slave."[92] Similar calls for the South to surrender her old prejudices echoed in the letter of "Mentor," which appeared in the *Constitutionalist* on 2 February: "If we expect to achieve anything worthy of renown, we must ourselves be men of new ideas."[93] These letters to the editor of the *Daily Constitutionalist* typified the striking transformation of the public mind from a worldview focused on slavery to one embracing independence at any cost.

The *Chronicle and Sentinel* printed only one letter in support of the paper's pro-slavery position, however. In that lone epistle, published on 5 January, "Madison" decried government attempts to suspend the writ of habeas corpus, cut exemptions for ministers and editors, and "to impress slaves as soldiers, and to reward their fidelity with freedom."[94] "Madison" did not elaborate on the virtues of slavery or the problems caused by arming the slaves, but merely listed it as one of several government "usurpations." No correspondent rose in the *Chronicle and Sentinel* to challenge the powerful, radical arguments of "Harry South," "W.W.," or "Mentor." The bold letter writers of the *Daily Constitutionalist* thus stood in stark contrast to the empty columns of the *Chronicle and Sentinel.*

Unlike the people in Central and Eastern Georgia who had felt the wrath of Sherman directly, the defeats of December surprised many in Southwestern Georgia—and the news struck them particularly hard. Many refugees from Central Georgia and even as far away as Savannah fled to the relative safety of Columbus, Albany, and Thomasville. For the first time, many Southwest Georgians contemplated the idea of utter defeat. Joseph LeConte, a Confederate official traveling through Southwest Georgia to reach his plantation in Eastern Georgia, noted the tremendous despair of the citizens in his diary on 31 December: "The whole of south-west Georgia,

[91] "W.W.," "Letter to the Editor," *Daily Constitutionalist*, 24 January 1865, 2.

[92] Ibid.

[93] "Mentor," "Letter to the Editor," *Daily Constitutionalist*, 2 February 1865, 2.

[94] "Madison," "Is It Treason to Advocate Secession?" *Chronicle and Sentinel*, 5 January 1865, 2.

both soldiers and citizens, seems in despair. … News of the fall of Savannah received this week renders the gloom still deeper."[95] As LeConte waited at Doctortown for an opportunity to rescue his daughter near Savannah, he found himself struggling to keep faith in the Confederacy: "I have wrestled in agony with this demon of despair. My anxiety for the safety of my friends and of my daughter, the certain loss of everything I own…is swallowed up in the dread of this one great all-including calamity [loss of the 'cause']."[96] Although Sherman affected Southwest Georgia only indirectly, reports from the refugees and news items appearing in the papers quickly brought home the necessity to significantly reinforce the southern armies.

In the wake of the Confederate disasters at Nashville and Savannah, numerous news items in the *Columbus Times* addressed the manpower shortage. At first, the *Times* attempted to deny the problem. On 5 January the paper reprinted the popular but misleading statistical study produced by the *Richmond Whig* arguing that the South had sufficient numbers to meet the Union threat.[97] Even as late as 24 January the *Times* copied an editorial from the *Memphis Appeal* contending that "we cannot yet see the necessity" to recommend drastic measures like arming the slaves.[98] As the full magnitude of the twin defeats sank in, however, the items in the *Times* increasingly reflected the necessity for some action. On 19 January the paper printed the comments of Congressman James Pugh of Alabama recommending that slaves replace all white men at home: "The idea is, to make every able-bodied white man…between the ages of eighteen and forty-five, an arms-bearing soldier."[99] In Georgia, many white women believed there were already too few white men at home and too many slaves to manage for their own safety and comfort. On 24 January the bold voice of the Jackson *Mississippian* rang out in Columbus and declared independence the South's primary war aim: "The people of the South, we have no doubt, are prepared to give up slavery for the sake of their independence."[100] Finally, as the debate

---

[95] Joseph LeConte, *'Ware Sherman: A Journal of Three Months' Personal Experience in the Last Days of the Confederacy* (Berkeley: University of California Press, 1937) 22.

[96] Ibid., 23.

[97] "Physical Resources of the Confederacy," *Columbus Times*, 5 January 1865, 2.

[98] "Arming the Negroes," *Columbus Times*, 24 January 1865, 1.

[99] "Views of the Military Committee," *Columbus Times*, 19 January 1865, 2.

[100] "More Important Rumors," *Columbus Times*, 24 January 1865, 1.

heated up in Congress, the *Times* quoted the strong endorsements of Senators Henry Burnett and Albert Brown for arming the slaves. He had seen, Brown boomed on 12 February, "with pleasure, a revival of the war spirit, but...still feared our armies were not strong enough to withstand the enemy without the employment of negro troops."[101] Despite early attempts at denial, the overwhelming necessity to fill the gray ranks in order to meet Sherman's columns forced the *Columbus Times* to confront the issue.

Unlike the *Times*, the Columbus *Daily Sun* readily accepted the theme of necessity after the December disasters. Thus, on 6 January the *Sun* quoted Virginia Governor William Smith, who demanded that the South use all its resources, even the slaves, to avoid defeat. "We should not," Smith asserted, "from any mawkish sensibility refuse any means within our reach which will tend to enable us to work out our deliverance."[102] The northern papers, the *Sun* noted, took the possibility of southern deliverance by black troops quite seriously. In an editorial reprinted from the *New York World* on 15 January, the New York editor argued that passage of the Thirteenth Amendment would prolong, not shorten, the war: "The passage of the constitutional amendment would cause the South to offer up the doomed institution on the altar of independence, and [thus]...enable them to prolong the struggle."[103] The *Sun* also cited the *New York Tribune*'s assertion that the South would soon "decree some sort of emancipation," which would ensure their recognition if blessed again by military success.[104] On 2 February a report from Grenada, Mississippi, claimed that many Mississippi planters favored arming the slaves: "Every planter with whom he [the Grenada editor] has conversed, favors the plan in the heartiest manner, even men who own large numbers of negroes."[105] Recognizing that many still disliked the idea of black troops, the *Sun* strongly condemned the only alternative: sending every white man to the front. On 8 February the paper denounced the closing of a shoe factory in Augusta that produced 300 pairs of shoes a day so that the white men working there could join the army: "Their absence from the shop renders about three hundred good soldiers unfit for service because they are

---

[101] "Richmond, Feb. 7," *Columbus Times*, 12 February 1865, 2.

[102] "Arming Negroes," *Daily Sun*, 6 January 1865, 2.

[103] "The Employment of Slaves in the Confederacy," *Daily Sun*, 15 January 1865, 1.

[104] "Slavery the Ban to Recognition," *Daily Sun*, 20 January 1865, 2.

[105] "The Sentiment of Mississippians," *Daily Sun*, 2 February 1865, 1.

barefooted...This is saving at the spigot and losing at the bunghole."[106] The immediate necessity to arm the slaves shone through the news items that appeared in the *Daily Sun*.

At the editorial desk of the *Columbus Times*, J.W. Warren contemplated the significance of the December defeats and called for greater unity among Georgians rather than the adoption of radical measures. As the Union army approached Savannah, Warren claimed that Sherman's harsh treatment had forged unity in the state: "The march of Sherman has hushed the voice of complaint, called the people together for common defense, and taught them that they cannot afford the luxury of dissensions."[107] On 18 January, estimating that the South needed 160,000 men to stem the Yankee tide, Warren counted over that number if all state troops were committed and all small commands consolidated.[108] Although he had claimed to see greater unity emerging from the defeats, the editor of the *Times* questioned the willingness of the state troops to fight indefinitely and the southern people's devotion to the cause: "Unhappily, the masses of mankind are made of common clay, and selfish love of money and of ease corrupt and quench the nobility of spirit with which God animated it."[109] On 11 February Warren again affirmed his opposition to slave-soldiers and his inability to see any necessity to radically alter slavery: "Our affairs have not reached and, if we do our duty, will never reach that desperate condition when we should be ready and willing to sacrifice everything to secure our independence."[110] Such editorial comments reflected Warren's conviction throughout the second phase that a lack of spirit among the people and not a lack of soldiers posed the major threat to the Confederacy.

In contrast, after news of the defeats at Nashville and Savannah arrived, editor William Scruggs of the *Daily Sun* immediately called for the adoption of the most radical measures. Thus, on 5 January he proclaimed slavery a hindrance rather than an aid to the southern cause: "There is a settled con-

---

[106] "Doubtful Policy," *Daily Sun*, 8 February 1865, 2.

[107] J.W. Warren, "But What of Confederate Unity?" *Columbus Times*, 17 December 1864, 2.

[108] J.W. Warren, "The Yankee Plan of Campaign—The Confederate Power to Defeat It," *Columbus Times*, 18 January 1865, 2.

[109] Ibid.

[110] J.W. Warren, "Lead Editorial," *Columbus Times*, 11 February 1865, 2.

viction in the minds of many people that slavery...is the hindering cause...and that a scheme of gradual emancipation would excite the sympathy and secure the aid of the Christian world."[111] In the same editorial, Scruggs termed Vice President Alexander Stephens's declaration of slavery as the "chief cornerstone" of the Confederacy a "short-sighted policy."[112] In addition, on 7 January the *Sun*'s editor argued that slavery was not the "CAUSE," but merely the "occasion of our war for Independence."[113] Instead of slavery, Scruggs recommended that the right of self-government form the nation's "CAUSE."[114] On 13 January Scruggs predicted that many opponents of arming the slaves would soon shift to support the measure and that the bill would receive approval from Congress: "Parties at Richmond appear to be impressed with the magnitude of the crisis, and the great responsibility resting upon those whose duty it is to provide means for a further prosecution of the war."[115] On 14 January, citing General Lee's statements that the South "must use the negroes, on our side, or the enemy will use them against us," the *Sun*'s editor called for an immediate trial: "The necessity being thus stated, the policy might be left to rest as a matter of experiment—and surely the experiment is worthy of a trial."[116] Although he tread softly upon the subject during November and December, after the disasters at Nashville and Savannah, William Scruggs boldly questioned the central role of slavery in Confederate identity and strongly advocated the immediate introduction of black troops into the army.

As J.W. Warren struggled with the concept of necessity at the *Times* editorial desk, the letters to the paper reflected a broad spectrum of opinion in Columbus. On 10 January, for example, in a letter first printed in the *Charleston Courier*, "A Bonded Man" recommended arming slaves with shotguns and shovels and issuing two slaves per white soldier: "Such a corps would...effectually demonstrate the practicability of using our slaves in war, and in the only way in which they can be advantageously employed, under

[111] William Scruggs, "Lead Editorial," *Daily Sun*, 5 January 1865, 2.
[112] Ibid.
[113] William Scruggs, "The Issue," *Daily Sun*, 7 January 1865, 2.
[114] Ibid.
[115] William Scruggs, "It Is Not Improbable," *Daily Sun*, 13 January 1865, 2.
[116] William Scruggs, "Gen. Lee in Favor of Arming Negroes," *Daily Sun*, 14 January 1865, 2.

the eyes of their masters."[117] In contrast, in the *Times* on 19 January a private soldier argued against black troops: "It is not to the generals of the army…that we are to look for public sentiment. Go to the privates of the army…You will not find one in a thousand that will advocate it."[118] Although soldier opinion actually remained divided, on 14 February "Virginius," the *Times*' correspondent in Richmond, reported growing support for using "the great reserve element of our strength."[119] "The negro," "Virginius" declared, "is an element of strength to us in various ways, and the sentiment is almost unanimous that, in preference to subjugation, his qualities as a soldier should be tested."[120] Rather than advocating full-scale conscription of slaves, this Richmond correspondent suggested an experiment with the 40,000 laborers being recruited for the army: "Let Gen. Lee take the responsibility of arming, drilling, and fighting a portion of those placed at his disposal. … The experiment can be made in a way harmless to the cause…and to the full satisfaction of Gen. Lee and all who agree with him."[121] Despite its strong editorial position against arming the slaves, the *Columbus Times* printed several letters advocating innovative modifications of slavery.

While the letters in the *Times* recommended experiments, the citizens of Columbus writing to the *Daily Sun* advocated immediate, radical changes to the slave's role in the war effort. On 3 January George Bagby wrote from Richmond that the December defeats now pushed necessity to the fore: "As the worst seems to have come to the worst, there is an evident increase of the feeling in favor of arming the negroes, and I think it will be done."[122] Although he expected acceptance of the measure, Bagby announced his personal opposition on 8 January: "Without slavery…this war will have been a wicked rebellion and a failure. Therefore, we must cling to slavery and sink

---

[117] "A Bonded Man," "How to Use Negroes in the Army," *Columbus Times*, 10 January 1865, 2.

[118] "SPENCE," "Communicated," *Columbus Times*, 19 January 1865, 1.

[119] "Virginius," "From Our Richmond Correspondent," *Columbus Times*, 14 February 1865, 1.

[120] Ibid.

[121] Ibid.

[122] George Bagby, "Letter from Richmond," *Daily Sun*, 3 January 1865, 2.

or swim with it."[123] The traditionalist views of this Richmond correspondent stood in stark contrast to the letters from the local area published in the *Sun*.

On 5 January a local physician, Dr. S. Annan, wrote to the paper to advocate a policy of limited emancipation in return for European intervention. Recognizing the devastating effects of such a policy upon agriculture, Annan recommended holding all blacks in servitude until age thirty: "As it is plain we cannot cultivate our lands without black laborers, I would suggest that we agree to the emancipation of all over thirty years of age."[124] Although Annan never addressed the question of black troops directly, other writers soon did. On 26 January "Iter" argued that the people would support black soldiers if General Lee would ask for them, and suggested enlisting the slaves from the most threatened areas first.[125] In a bold appeal, on 28 January, W.A. Mallory, an army surgeon recently returned from a northern prison, informed the *Sun* that the idea of black southern troops upset the Yankees greatly and, therefore, was solidly supported in the Army of Northern Virginia: "I have talked with a number of efficient officers of General Lee's army, [and] almost to a man they favor it."[126] In addition, Mallory offered his slaves to the government and volunteered to lead them: "All, and the highest honors I ask at the hands of my Government, [is] that I be assigned to duty in the first Confederate Negro Regiment."[127]

These bold letters, the strong editorial stand taken by the *Sun*, and the overwhelming necessity to put men in the field brought forth a series of four thought-provoking letters by T.J. Cox. In these letters Cox addressed all the major arguments against arming the slaves and produced a powerful argument for black soldiers. In his first letter on 25 January, Cox avowed that necessity, not choice, demanded the use of the slaves: "It is only as a *dernier resort* that we favor the policy of arming a portion of our slaves; but if…we are not sufficiently strong to repel…the foe…then we advocate it as a *mili-*

123 George Bagby, "Letter from Richmond," *Daily Sun*, 8 January 1865, 2.

124 S. Annan, "Important Subject," *Daily Sun*, 5 January 1865, 2.

125 "Iter," "Letter from Iter," *Daily Sun*, 26 January 1865, 1.

126 W.A. Mallory, "Letter from a Soldier in Richmond," *Daily Sun*, 28 January 1865, 1.

127 Ibid.

tary necessity."[128] In the same letter, Cox argued that southerners must use all their resources and not worry about the cost: "If citizens were as free to yield their title to property in negroes, as they appear to be in giving up their children…there would not be so much ado about nothing."[129] If the people would support the idea fully, Cox argued, it would produce quality troops: "If judiciously officered by White men and sufficient inducements given them—such as kind, but firm treatment, personal freedom, pecuniary compensation, and homes among us after the close of the war—there can be but little doubt that they may be made efficient."[130] Having sounded the trumpet for emancipated black troops, Cox prepared to face the wrath of the measure's opponents.

Over the next three days, Cox attempted to answer all the standard arguments put forward against arming the slaves. On 26 January he contended that the white veterans would accept the black soldiers because, "during the excitement of battle, [they] would neither know nor care, whether the skin of their comrades was white or black."[131] Admitting that the loss of food produced by the slaves provided the strongest argument against the idea, Cox declared on 27 January that agriculture must become more efficient, and that men, not foodstuffs, were the resource needed immediately: "The meagerness of provisions is by no means, our greatest strait—*we need more men.*"[132] Finally, on 28 January Cox contended that the South could accept slave-soldiers without the dishonor of renouncing its traditional ideology: "Emancipation would not be tendered as a right, nor as proof of [the]…sinfulness of the institution, but only as a medium to ensure the fidelity and good conduct of those to whom it is administered."[133] In this series of letters, Cox employed sound reason and a thorough understanding of the Confederate mind in order to argue that the South could and should

---

[128] T.J. Cox, "For the *Sun*," *Daily Sun*, 25 January 1865, 2. The italics appear in the original article.

[129] Ibid.

[130] Ibid.

[131] T.J. Cox, "For the *Daily Sun*," *Daily Sun*, 26 January 1865, 2.

[132] T.J. Cox, "For the *Daily Sun*," *Daily Sun*, 27 January 1865, 2. The italics appear in the original article.

[133] T.J. Cox, "For the *Sun*," *Daily Sun*, 28 January 1865, 2.

accept black troops. Altogether, the bold letter writers of the *Sun* produced an overwhelming argument for the necessity to arm the slaves.

As in the first phase, the newspapers in Blakely and Albany hesitantly followed the lead of the Columbus dailies. On 1 February Blakely's *Early County News* cited an editorial from the Jackson *Mississippian* declaring its preference for "gradual emancipation to any connection with the hated Northman."[134] Arguing that gradual emancipation was "the true policy of the South," the Mississippi editor contended, "If the adoption of such a policy [gradual emancipation] guarantees our recognition and intervention...it would be an act of supreme folly for us to turn our backs on it."[135] Although nothing came of the idea of trading emancipation for intervention, this discussion planted a seed that grew as more and more men went to the front. On 8 February the *News* decried the use of women to replace men in the conscript offices in Raleigh, North Carolina: "We are truly sorry to see some of the women of the South are getting so forward and losing their self-respect almost entirely."[136] Without black men in the ranks, the Blakely editor contended, there was no alternative to women working outside the home. Finally, on 15 February the *News* reprinted an editorial from the Goldsboro *North Carolina State Journal* trumpeting Lee's support for black troops: "If Gen. Lee can trust to the fidelity of the negro, we might safely do so. If he thinks there is a necessity which demands the negroes as soldiers, with what grace can we tell him there is not?"[137] Although slow to acknowledge the debate, the *Early County News* reprinted a series of bold editorials during the final weeks of the second phase.

The new emphasis on arming the slaves in Blakely came partly from a growing realization of the necessity of the measure, and partly from a change in editors of the *News*. Until 25 January, E.H. Grouby edited the *News* and strongly opposed radical adjustments to slavery. For instance, on 18 January Grouby denounced the editor of the *Richmond Enquirer* as an abolitionist: "If you ever do, Mr. *Enquirer* attempt to preach abolitionism to your readers, may a gang of them club together and hang you as high as Hayman."[138] On

[134] "More Important Rumors," *Early County News*, 1 February 1865, 1.
[135] Ibid.
[136] "Lead Editorial," *Early County News*, 8 February 1865, 2.
[137] "Negroes for the Army," *Early County News*, 15 February 1865, 1.
[138] E.H. Grouby, "Arming Negroes," *Early County News*, 18 January 1865, 3.

25 January T.E. Speight took over for Grouby at the *News*, and editorials favoring arming the slaves began to appear. Although not commenting on slave-soldiers directly, Speight cautioned his readers on 8 February that the South did not want to be remembered as the country too greedy to make the sacrifices required to achieve independence: "Remember that life and property, at best, are of but short duration, but that history endures forever."[139] The change in editors of the *Early County News* significantly changed the tone of the paper, but the necessity to put men in the field to meet the Union armies also forced the issue.

Although the *Albany Patriot* did not run any major news items concerning arming the slaves, the position of the paper's editor, J.W. Fears, shifted considerably during the second phase of the debate. On 26 January Fears grudgingly endorsed the idea of arming the slave laborers recruited for the army: "We are not prepared to say that the idea is a good one, as our negroes are needed to make provisions; yet 40,000 might be spared to experiment with."[140] Although willing to experiment, Fears strongly opposed any promise of freedom for faithful service: "Only put them there as slaves, and after the war let them remain as slaves."[141] As the second phase progressed and as Sherman marched victoriously through South Carolina, Fears reassessed his position. Thus, on 16 February he announced that Congress was still considering arming the slaves, and he expressed his support for the measure: "We hope they will side with the great Lee and put the last one of them in the trenches."[142] Although not reflected in the news reports in the *Albany Patriot*, Fears had clearly shifted his editorial position in light of the necessity to meet and defeat the enemy.

Although neither the *Early County News* nor the *Albany Patriot* printed any letters on the subject of arming the slaves, a few local citizens discussed it in their correspondence. For example, on 10 January Samuel Clayton, a resident of Cuthbert, near both Blakely and Albany, wrote to President Davis to urge the enlistment of black troops. Clayton argued that no hope could be expected from abroad and that the South must rely on its own re-

---

139 T.E. Speight, "Editorial," *Early County News*, 18 January 1865, 3.

140 J.W. Fears, "Pay the Soldiers," *Albany Patriot*, 26 January 1865, 2.

141 Ibid.

142 J.W. Fears, "Congress," *Albany Patriot*, 16 February 1865, 2.

sources: "The recruits must come from our negroes, nowhere else. We should…promptly take hold of all the means that God has placed within our reach to help us through this struggle."[143] Furthermore, Clayton stoutly denied that the sacrifice of slavery gave up the question of the war: "Put the sword and the musket in his hand, and make him hew down and shoot down those who come to destroy the institution. … Would this be giving up the question? I opine not."[144] Having lost two sons in the war, Clayton called the measure's opponents "gold worshippers" and "slaves in spirit." In his opinion, "He who values his property higher than his life and independence is a poor, sordid wretch."[145] Finally, Clayton pleaded with the president to lead the fight to obtain congressional approval for arming the slaves: "Our Congress should make haste and put as many negro soldiers in the field as you and General R.E. Lee may think necessary."[146] Clearly, in many circles, the pleas of necessity heard in Columbus also resounded in the ears of those in the smaller communities of Southwest Georgia.

The shattering defeat at Nashville and Sherman's march to the sea introduced an urgency to the debate about arming the slaves not present in the first phase. In January and early February 1865 southerners weighed the value of slavery and attempted to determine what sacrifices they must make in order to achieve independence. News reports in Central Georgia underscored the gravity of the situation, but no immediate threat to these cities emerged. In contrast, Sherman's march through South Carolina, at one point coming within fifteen miles of Augusta, contributed significantly in Eastern Georgia to the feelings of necessity to arm the slaves. While Macon's W.H. Barnes and Milledgeville's Joseph Nisbet clung tightly to the old pro-slavery ideology, bolder Central Georgians realized something had to be done quickly. The Cobb and Akin letters clearly show that many Central Georgians remained open to new, radical ideas. In Augusta, James Gardner threw caution to the wind and advocated arming the slaves, but without the offer of freedom. In Columbus, William Scruggs at the *Daily Sun* openly advocated not only black troops but also their emancipation. In Macon, Au-

143 *Official Records,* Series 4, Volume 3, 1010.
144 Ibid., 1011.
145 Ibid.
146 Ibid.

gusta, and Columbus, the editors surrendered the initiative to local citizens writing to the papers to suggest the bold ideas that could meet the emergency. The votes taken in the Confederate Congress reflected the depth of the divisions in the state. Representatives from overrun and threatened areas did tend to vote for arming slaves, but so did the representative from unthreatened Columbus. The views expressed in the local Georgia papers could not have been lost on their leaders in Richmond. If the letters published in Georgia did not cause the congressmen to accept black troops, the discussions at home and the strong voices calling for assistance from the slave population certainly made the decision to vote for black soldiers easier. In Cuthbert as well as other Georgia communities, the idea of black soldiers appealed to many who felt that the large slave owners had not sacrificed as much as the average man. The depth of the slavery debate allowed long-obscured divisions in white society to surface. The poor men who were fighting and dying wanted the rich men to aid them, and slave-soldiers provided a severe test of slave-owner unity with the soldiers in the army. In the Georgia letters, one can clearly see the peculiar institution beginning to slip from its preeminent position in favor of southern independence.

Patrick Cleburne.

Courtesy the Library of Congress.

Confederate President Jefferson Davis Jefferson Davis fought to the very end for an independent Confederate nation defined by the war.

Courtesy the Library of Congress.

Governor William Smith of Virginia

Courtesy the National Archives.

Robert E. Lee's support of black troops proved pivotal in the slave soldier debate.

Courtesy the Library of Congress.

Judah Benjamin

Courtesy the Library of Congress.

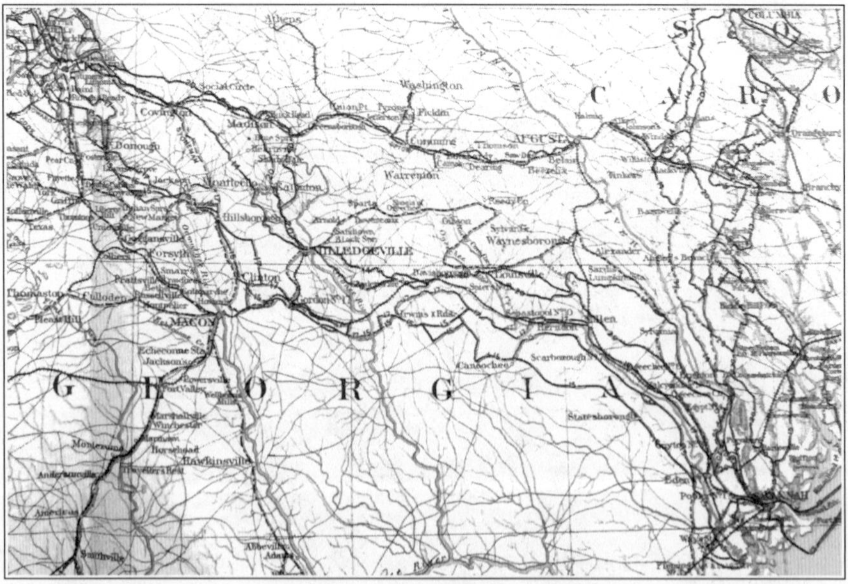

Sherman's route through Georgia.

"War of the Rebellion: Atlas to Accompany the Official Record," plate 117.

Sherman's men attempted to destroy the will and the ability of Georgians to continue to help the Confederate war effort during their march to the sea.

Courtesy the Library of Congress.

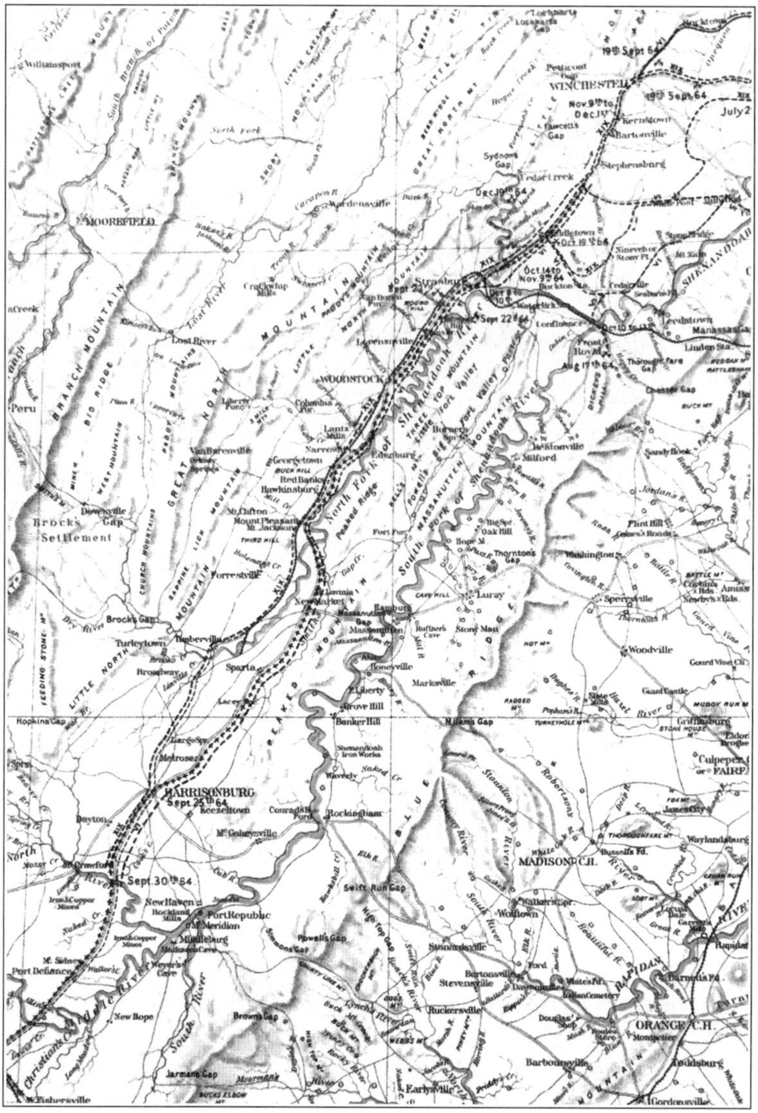

Sheridan destroyed Early's army and then destroyed all supplies that might have been used to help the Confederate cause.

"War of the Rebellion: Atlas to Accompany the Official Record," plate 74.

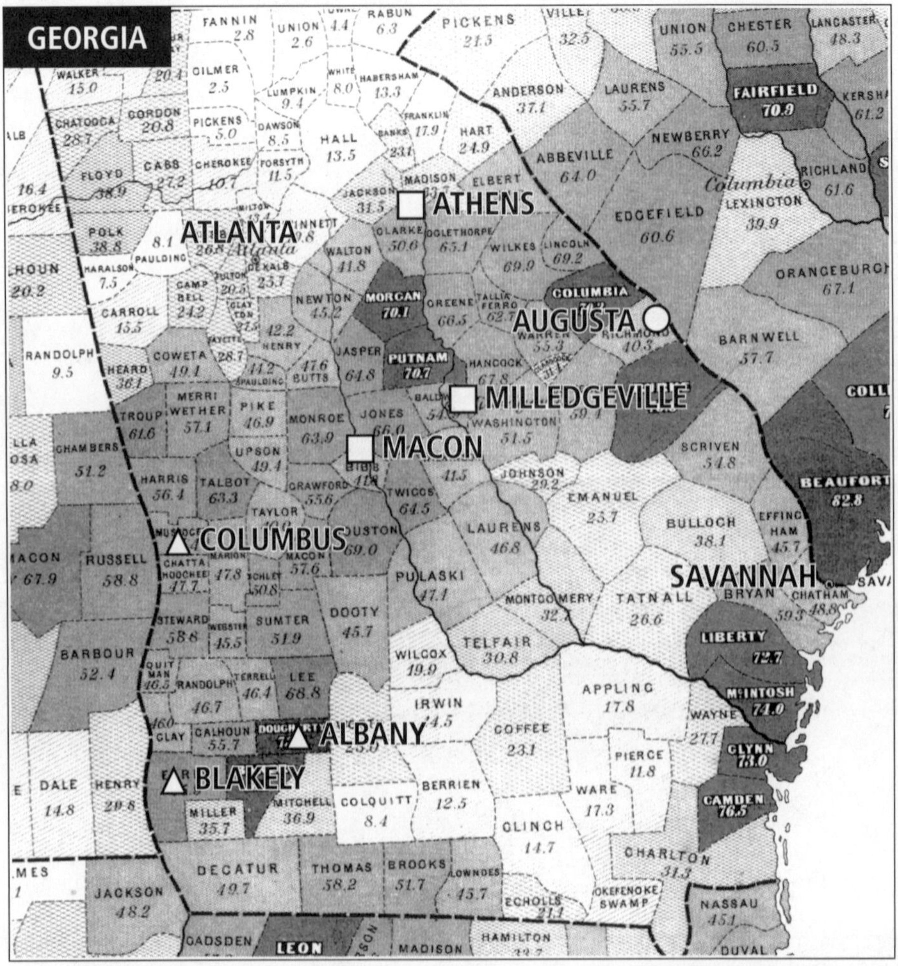

The numbers in each county report the percentage of the population who were slaves in 1860. Proximity to the Union army would ultimately prove more important in determining white attitudes to black troops than the prevalence of slavery.

Courtesy the Library of Congress.

GEORGIA	VIRGINIA	TEXAS
□ Central	□ Richmond Area	□ East
○ Eastern	○ Roanoke Valley	○ Central
△ Southwestern	△ Sheneandoah Valley	△ Gulf Coast

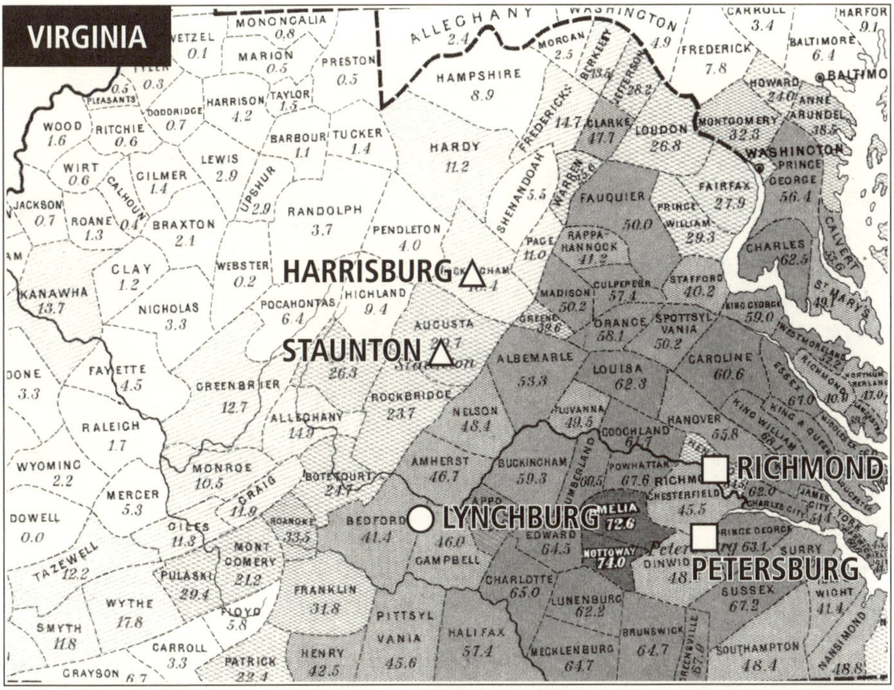
VIRGINIA
HARRISBURG
STAUNTON
RICHMOND
LYNCHBURG
PETERSBURG

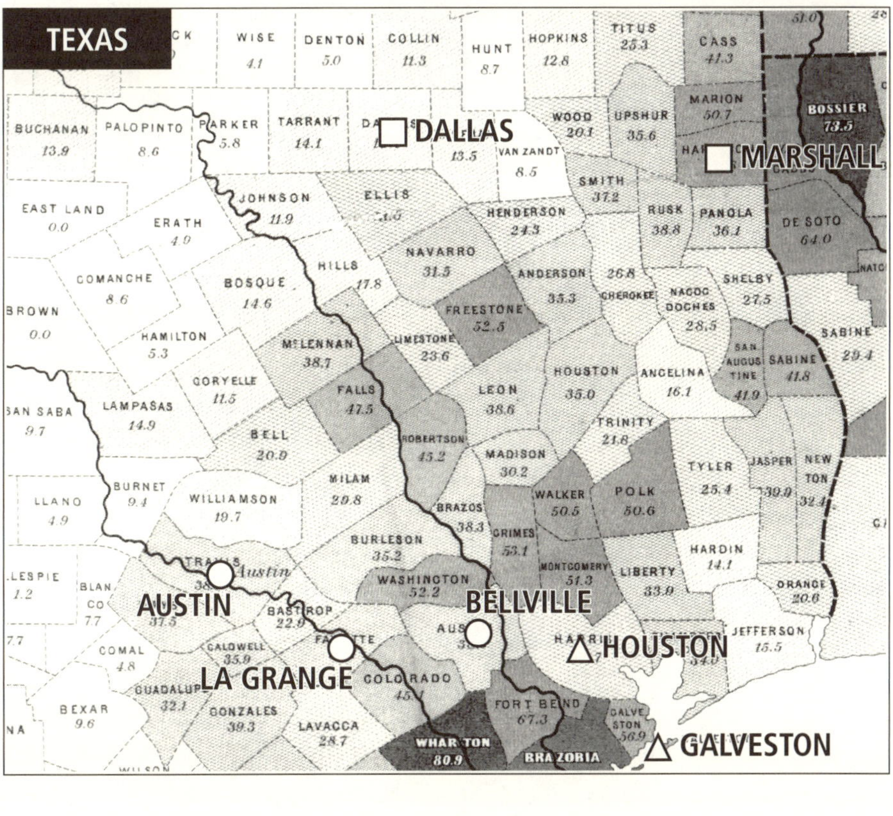
TEXAS
DALLAS
MARSHALL
AUSTIN
BELLVILLE
HOUSTON
LA GRANGE
GALVESTON

The Dunlop home in Petersburg: Union artillery constantly reminded Confederate leaders and citizens of the need to strengthen the army.
Courtesy the Library of Congress.

7

No Need to Choose

As the dawn of a new year broke, the Confederacy awoke to the startling prospect of southern defeat. Confederate leaders in the Trans-Mississippi Department had seen the fall of 1864 as a period of considerable promise. After the Union army's retreat from northern Louisiana at the end of the Red River campaign, General Nathaniel Banks's blue troops remained idle near New Orleans. Seizing the opportunity, in September, Confederate Department commander Edmund Kirby Smith sent General Sterling Price with 12,000 cavalrymen to raid Missouri. Intrigued by the success of guerrilla groups like those commanded by Bill Anderson and William Quantrill, Price hoped to disrupt Union operations in his home state, divert attention from William T. Sherman's army in Georgia, and find new recruits in Arkansas and Missouri. Price's movements as he threatened Kansas City and exaggerated reports of thousands of fresh recruits cheered southerners, and particularly Texans, in October and November. After six weeks of dodging Union forces in Missouri, the disappointing reality set in as the remnants of Price's column trudged back to East Texas with fewer than 6,000 men. Missourians had not risen to the Confederate standard as many Texans had hoped. Members of the irregular guerrilla outfits who had joined Price melted away as the opportunities for blood and plunder disappeared with the gray-clad veterans. Price's abortive campaign did not cause panic in Texas because the Union commanders did not attempt to exploit their advantage. As the depth of Price's failure became known in early January, thoughtful residents in the Trans-Mississippi began to understand the size of the looming Union threat so apparent east of the Mississippi.[1]

News of these twin misfortunes at Nashville and Savannah arrived in Texas during the first ten days of the new year, shaking some Texans from

[1] James McPherson, *Battle Cry of Freedom: The Civil War Era* (New York: Ballantine, 1988) 786–88.

their complacency. Yet the continued inactivity of the Union forces in Louisiana allowed many Texans to ignore the sense of urgency that struck Virginia and Georgia in January 1865. Edmund Kirby Smith's forces in Shreveport, guarding the gates to Texas, felt no pressure from the Union army, but they could offer little aid to the Confederate armies east of the Mississippi. Ashbel Smith, commanding troops on Galveston Island, battled a poor logistical system rather than blue hordes. Even so, the staggering reverses in the East, along with Price's failure in Missouri, sparked the slave-soldier debate in Texas. Yet, without the large influx of refugees or wounded soldiers that occurred in Georgia and Alabama, the magnitude of the twin defeats in the East did not become immediately apparent. Cotton prices remained high as trade boomed across the Mexican border and through the porous blockade of Galveston. Blockade runners that previously anchored in Atlantic ports now shifted their trade to Galveston. In this bull economy, the lack of hard currency rather than the war caused the most concern. The absence of offensive Union efforts west of the Mississippi helped shape popular opinion and caused many to continue to question the necessity of radical modifications of slavery.

On 14 January Governor Pendleton Murrah addressed the state from his offices in Austin. The deteriorating military situation, he argued, could not be denied: "The hand of adversity, in the concluding weeks of the memorable year just ended, has been laid heavily upon our compatriots East of the Mississippi, and partially so on this side." The state, Murrah asserted, must not expect assistance from the East but, rather, must draw on its own resources to meet the northern threat. "It is therefore necessary," the Governor affirmed, "that as much cotton should be grown as possible, after planting sufficient bread-stuffs to sustain the army and the country." Cotton exported through Mexico, he realized, provided the only sure means to gain the military items needed to continue the war. Nevertheless, the governor noted and decried the importation of luxuries that, he suggested, exhibited the "want of harmonious concert, energetic action, and patriotic self-denial of our own people." Without mentioning Davis's call for 40,000 black laborers, Murrah urged slave owners to respond promptly to military requests for assistance by willingly supplying slaves for work with the army. Above all other things, unity of effort within the state and the nation, the Governor believed, was the key to improving Confederate fortunes: "Let all from this time forward, so act in all the various relations of life, as to demonstrate to our soldiers that not they alone but every heart in the land is engrossed in the cause for which they fight and die."[2] Murrah's call for renewed sacrifices laid the groundwork for continuing the debate over arming slaves.

The *Houston Telegraph* presented a variety of news items from both sides during the second phase of the debate. On 9 January the *Telegraph* reprinted a letter written by Peter W. Alexander, the Richmond correspondent of the *Savannah Republican*. "It may be stated positively," Alexander declared, "that Gen. Lee and the army of Northern Virginia generally are in favor of using the negro as a soldier." Similarly, on 16 January an editorial from the *London Times*, reprinted in Houston, questioned why the South had not fielded black troops previously: "The South has no reason to doubt that the negro will fight just as bravely in support of the cause of slavery which is the cause of his master, as he will in the cause of liberty." Against these positive portrayals of black soldier potential, the *Telegraph* reprinted the *Richmond Whig* study that used 1860 census figures in an attempt to prove that the Confederacy had enough white men to fill the depleted ranks. The inclusion of Tennessee, Kentucky, and other overrun areas made the number of potential recruits appear more than adequate and doubtless encouraged those opposed to radical steps. Hence, despite a new willingness to print articles in favor of arming the slaves, the *Telegraph* continued to dispute the need for such radical steps.[3]

In late January, as the depth of the Confederate military reverses sank in, it became harder to ignore the necessity argument, even in Texas. On 30 January, as word arrived that the Union Navy had closed the port of Wilmington, North Carolina—the final Atlantic port—the *Telegraph* noted an article from Richmond that reported that Lee had proposed a plan to draft black soldiers and to free them and their families. The present crisis, the *Richmond Examiner* affirmed, "demands that every possible sacrifice of life and property should be made to secure our national independence." Even as the new nation crumbled militarily, Confederate leaders attempted to rede-

---

[2] Pendleton Murrah, "To The People of Texas," *Marshall Texas Republican*, 3 February 1865, 1.

[3] Peter W. Alexander, "Items of Interest," *Houston TriWeekly Telegraph*, 9 January 1865, 3; "Items of Interest," *Houston TriWeekly Telegraph*, 13 January 1865, 3; "Physical Resources of the Confederacy," *Houston TriWeekly Telegraph*, 22 February 1865, 2.

fine what it meant to be a southerner. Confederate nationalists hoped to define themselves not by their racial hierarchy but by shared ideals of self-government and individual liberty. With an eye to the revolution of 1776, Confederate leaders attempted to use the common experience of the war as a means to cement a regional coalition into a nation. Hatred of colonial policy had not been enough in the first revolution to form a unified government, and as the war developed, Davis and others had come to understand that slavery and its defense were not a strong enough bond to build a sound country. Four days later, the words of Governor Henry W. Allen of Louisiana expressed these sentiments as his words thundered across the pages in Houston: "Our willingness to fight armed negroes against them…may be taken by them as the sign and measure of our inexhaustible hatred, while it will prove conclusively to the nations of the world that we intend to maintain our independence at any and every possible cost." Even as Allen asserted the primacy of independence over the preservation of slavery, the *Telegraph*'s editor called special attention to the resolutions of the South Carolina legislature that strongly opposed any change in slave status. While printing a few news items in favor of arming the slaves, the *Houston Telegraph* continued to tailor its news coverage to reflect its continued opposition.[4]

Unlike Sherman in the Carolinas and Philip Sheridan in the Shenandoah Valley, the inactivity of the Union forces in Louisiana allowed many Texans to ignore the crisis. Upon confirmation of the fall of Savannah, the *Galveston News* contended that Sherman had gained little: "As this place was of no military purpose to us, its loss will weaken the enemy more than ourselves, as they will have to garrison the city." Further reports from Tennessee caused some fear that Hood's defeat might lead to a movement toward Texas. On 13 January the *News* reacted in alarm to reports of Union landings near Brownsville: "We believe we are liable to an invasion by water at any moment. … The enemy may come down upon any point on our coast with a formidable fleet, without our having any previous warning." During this unsettling week, editorials from the *Liverpool Courier*, Paris's *La France*, and

[4] "By Telegraph," *Houston TriWeekly Telegraph*, 30 January 1865, 4; "Message of Gov. Allen," *Houston TriWeekly Telegraph*, 3 February 1865, 1; "Report of the South Carolina Committee," *Houston TriWeekly Telegraph*, 10 February 1865, 1.

the *Chicago Times* appeared in Galveston and laid out the potential benefits to the South of emancipating and enlisting the slave population.[5]

While these editorials and wire service reports of Congressional action intrigued many, the most influential news item to appear in Galveston concerning black troops originated in Texas. On 20 January Judge John T. Mills addressed a letter to the *Galveston News* concerning the role of the slave in the war effort. Prefacing his remarks by noting his vote for secession in the Texas Secession Convention and his longstanding ownership of slaves, Mills stated that there were only two roads to peace: submission and reunion or emancipation and continuing the struggle. Slavery, he argued, was not worth the cost that southerners were paying. "In fact," Mills proclaimed, "more of that [southern blood] has already been shed than every slave in the Confederacy is worth." Acknowledging that the idea of arming slaves required "meditation" and "reflection" on the part of slave owners, he argued the institution was doomed because "not only the Yankees, but the world, is against us on the slavery question." In his opinion, the reverses of 1864 proved that the South could not win their independence alone: "The North will never recognize our independence until she is compelled by a greater power than we alone can bring to bear upon her." By freeing the slaves and offering themselves as a colony to England or France, the Confederate states, Mills believed, could thwart northern aims and secure the right of self-government. "The blood of our brave soldiers," Mills concluded, "will not have been shed in vain, should we gain our independence and lose our slaves."[6]

A prominent slave owner willing to arm slaves was big news in Texas even in January 1865. Born in Ireland and raised in South Carolina, Mills in

---

[5] "The Dispatches of Friday…," *Galveston TriWeekly News*, 8 January 1865, 2; "He had heard…," *Galveston TriWeekly News*, 8 January 1865, 2; "Letter from Brownsville" and "We have heard…," *Galveston TriWeekly News*, 13 January 1865, 1; "New York, Dec. 28," *Galveston TriWeekly News*, 15 January 1865, 1; "The 'poor whites' who form…," *Galveston TriWeekly News*, 13 January 1865, 2; "The *Chicago Times*…," *Galveston TriWeekly News*, 11 January 1865, 1.

[6] John T. Mills, "Judge Mills's Letter," *Marshall Texas Republican*, 24 February 1865, 1. The letter first appeared in the *Galveston News* on 8 February 1865. This issue of the *News* did not survive the war, but the letter was reprinted in several other papers across the state. *Handbook of Texas Online*, J.C. Conradt, "Mills, John T.," accessed October 26, 2016, http://www.tshaonline.org/handbook/online/articles/fmi38.

1837 had come to Texas where he used his legal skills for the Republic as a district judge. Although unsuccessful in his bid for governor in 1849, Mills was a well-known political leader and widely respected throughout Texas. Judge Mills probably selected the Galveston paper because of its wide circulation and influence in the state. Publishing in the *News* ensured that prominent politicians and editors would encounter his letter. The strongly supported idea of emancipation in return for European protection makes this an intriguing proposal. In December President Davis had sanctioned Congressman Duncan Kenner's mission to England and France to offer a similar proposition. Intended as a top-secret venture, word of Kenner's efforts surfaced in the Richmond press in early January. Mills put forward his ideas at the exact time that Kenner was to embark for Europe and the idea was first broached in Richmond. Although no document survives to prove the connection, it is quite possible that a letter—like the December letters of Judah Benjamin to Frederick Porcher, or that of Jefferson Davis to John Forsyth, or that of James Seddon to Howell Cobb—arrived at Mills's door requesting that he ignite the debate over employing black troops with the army. Whether inspired by his own adept reading of events or conceived in coordination with friends in Richmond, Mills's letter served as potent fuel for the smoldering debate in Texas.[7]

At his editorial desk, Edward Cushing of the *Houston Telegraph* saw no "extremity" that required radical measures like arming the slaves: "For ourselves, we do not believe that any military necessity exists for laws which violate the constitution." Rather, as he announced the loss of Savannah and the defeat of Hood, Cushing declared, "We believe the morning, though still far off, will surely dawn, and this belief enables us to view lightly the misfortunes of war." Yet in contrast to these bold assertions, by late January he penned a soul-searching critique of the war effort titled "Ultimate Success," which betrayed many doubts. Even in his darkest mood, he stoutly refused to consider arming the slaves or even freeing the laborers working

[7] *Official Records,* Series 4, Vol. 3, 959-60; Benjamin to Porcher, 959–60; and Davis to Forsyth, 1110. The original Forsyth to Davis (31 December 1864) letter on the topic is in private hands. Dealer's catalogue—Carnegie Book Shop. #251 item 167. While the case for a letter from Davis is circumstantial, the timing and content of Mills's letter suggests strong coordination with the Davis administration. Mills and Benjamin had known each other before the war and had worked closely on several legal matters.

with the army. In the final analysis, Cushing blamed poor generalship rather than manpower shortages for the bleak Confederate position. While conceding that he would prefer emancipation to subjugation, the Houston editor flatly stated that he did not yet have to choose: "We believe we can save our country and all its institutions."[8] Far from Grant's ever-tightening lines at Petersburg and Sherman's vengeful columns in South Carolina, the choice did not seem imperative.

At the *Galveston News*, Willard Richardson opened the new year with a stirring call for planters to aid the country: "There was a time it was patriotic to plant more corn and less cotton. It is patriotic now to plant a large crop of cotton, because...it is the only available product that can support our army." Cut off from all Confederate sources east of the Mississippi, Richardson begged the planters to make the state independent with their cotton. Military reverses had forced this step, and the continuing stream of discouraging news that reached Galveston in January led Richardson to admit discussions of slave-soldiers into his columns. On 5 February the editor affirmed that a wise man must consider all contingencies: "By some it is believed that emancipation may be made instrumental in securing our independence." Although willing to discuss the matter, Richardson did not consider the issue imperative: "We believe our people are prepared for any sacrifice rather than ever be compelled to fraternize with Yankees again, but we do not believe yet that this sacrifice is necessary." As prominent southerners publicly stepped forward in support of black troops, the Galveston editor defended his publication of their radical ideas. Commenting on an address of Louisiana Governor Henry Allen, Richardson restated his opposition to black Confederates even as his newspaper became the principal arena for the debate in Texas:

> However much we differ with those who think it necessary to arm our negroes to aid us in this desperate struggle and to offer them freedom as a reward for faithful services...still we cannot deny that the opinions

[8] E.H. Cushing, "Our Neighbor the News...," *Houston TriWeekly Telegraph*, 25 January 1865, 4; E.H. Cushing, "Lead Editorial," *Houston TriWeekly Telegraph*, 4 January 1865, 2; E.H. Cushing, "Ultimate Success," *Houston TriWeekly Telegraph*, 27 January 1865, 2; E.H. Cushing, "We Have Always...," *Houston TriWeekly Telegraph*, 1 February 1865, 2.

of such men as President Davis, Gov. Allen, and many others of our truest and best citizens are entitled to respectful consideration.

Although he penned a rebuttal to the revolutionary proposals of Davis and Mills, Richardson allowed letter writers to the *News* to challenge the bold arguments for slave-soldiers in detail. In February and March, Richardson made the debate over arming and freeing slaves the focus of the *Galveston News* and, thus, significantly advanced the debate in Texas.[9]

Prior to the publication of Judge Mills's ideas, a number of correspondents submitted letters to the *Houston Telegraph* and demonstrated a new willingness to consider alternatives to the status quo. On 20 January a powerful letter from William Sledge of Chappell Hill, Texas, appeared in Houston. Noting Lincoln's success with black soldiers, Sledge suggested the Confederate leaders should consider forming a force of 100,000 black troops to take the war to the North. Necessity, he argued, and not a preference for black assistance required the change in policy. Stopping short of advocating emancipation, Sledge called on his countrymen to speak out and for the public to hold meetings to debate the new course. In response, several thoughtful letters appeared in the *Telegraph* over the next two weeks. On 27 January, a letter from "Freestone," a sixty-year-old slave owner from Fairfield, declared that the Confederacy must act on the measure quickly before the majority of able-bodied slaves entered Union service: "It is high time for us to look at our condition as practical men, it is high time to call forth all our reserves." Comparing the use of slave-soldiers to the northern use of Irish and German immigrants, "Freestone" blasted southern squeamishness: "We are too chivalric, too high minded and lofty in our notions to use the means that God and circumstances have placed at our disposal." Although this was intended as the first of several submissions, Cushing refused to publish—and discarded—"Freestone's" subsequent letters. Taking a different tack, on 29 January "A Soldier" responded to Sledge and "Freestone" by questioning the motivation of the proposed black regiments: "He [the advo-

[9] Willard Richardson, "Cotton Our Main Dependence During This War—The Duty of Cotton Planters," *Galveston TriWeekly News*, 1 January 1865, 2; Willard Richardson, "We have admitted...," *Galveston TriWeekly News*, 5 February 1865, 2; Willard Richardson, "Our readers will find...," *Galveston TriWeekly News*, 8 February 1865, 2; Willard Richardson, "The communication of Judge Mills...," *Galveston TriWeekly News*, 24 February 1865, 4.

cate of slave-soldiers] will have to locate in him [the black soldier] that feeling of patriotism and pride of character and of country, which I regret to say, I see lacking in even a vast number of our white men." Continuing along the same line, the letter writer suggested that rather than conferring in public meetings, Texans should form regiments and move to the field. Despite editor Cushing's strong opposition to the measure, the *Telegraph* received a series of thoughtful responses to Sledge's letter, clearly demonstrating that many Texans considered the debate over the slave's role in the war effort a critical issue.[10]

On 8 February, Cushing decried the discussion of abolitionism burning across the pages of the *Houston Telegraph* and the *Galveston News*. The principal source of the discussion, he argued, was not the poor whites but, rather, the discouraged slaveholders. Judge Mills' letter had attracted far more attention than the Houston editor cared to acknowledge. Astounded at the tone of the debate about the measure in other Texas newspapers, the *Telegraph*'s editor refused to further the give-and-take about the importance of slavery by allowing the issue into his columns: "We have received a score of such letters ourself [sic], which have all been incontinently cast aside as a disgrace to their authors." Such people, he believed, were not good Confederates attempting to help the cause but, rather, demoralized wretches: "When they consider that we are so near that last resort [armed slaves] as to make it worthwhile now to talk about it, they are...exhibiting a weakness which the circumstances are very far from justifying." Two days later, Cushing renewed his assault by suggesting that the property of all southern proponents of abolition should be confiscated. Even as the Confederacy crumbled during the second phase of the debate, Cushing continued to trumpet "the righteousness, the justice, and the utility of the institution of slavery." Unlike in Virginia and Georgia, where residents had experienced the war firsthand, in Gulf Coast Texas slavery remained the ultimate test of southern loyalty.[11]

---

[10] "Freestone," "Employment of Negroes in the Army, No. 1," *Houston TriWeekly Telegraph*, 27 January 1865, 2; "A Soldier," "Letter to the Editor," *Houston TriWeekly Telegraph*, 29 January 1865, 2.

[11] E.H. Cushing, "Lead Editorial," *Houston TriWeekly Telegraph*, 8 February 1865, 2; E.H. Cushing, "Lead Editorial," *Houston TriWeekly Telegraph*, 10 February 1865, 2.

In the wake of the December defeats and Sledge's bold letter to the *Telegraph*, two Gulf Coast Texans wrote the *Galveston News* to discuss the idea of black troops. On 29 January "Porcupine" called for the Confederacy to rethink the parameters of the war effort: "The lesson taught us by Sherman's march through Georgia, and by Hood's defeat in Tennessee, should not be lost to the Government. … In self-defense we are compelled to invade the North and inflict upon them every wrong they have heaped upon us." Espousing the Old Testament concept of "an eye for an eye," "Porcupine" argued that the Confederate armies must meet Union black troops with Confederate black troops. Further, the author recommended that the gray ranks, reinforced with the new black troops, abandon conventional tactics and adopt a campaign directed against the northern people. Armed with turpentine and matches, "Porcupine" suggested, the slave-soldier would make a valuable contribution to the cause. In a more measured note, Caleb G. Forshey wrote and described a series of private meetings held by community leaders interested in military affairs in which the arming of slaves had been discussed. Sledge read a paper at the first meeting and, a week later, Forshey presented a statistical analysis that detailed the potential impact of black service on the war effort. As a former West Point cadet and the founder of the Texas Military Institute, Forshey spoke with some authority on military affairs. While Sledge and Forshey received a respectful hearing, the meeting of civic leaders (principally planters) did not endorse the immediate enlistment of their slaves: "All were of the opinion that a large negro force should be used, but considerable difference of views was expressed as to the manner of using them." Military necessity caused by the December defeats had opened the door to discussion of arming slaves, and as the measure began to draw support, the smoldering slave-soldier debate caught flame in Galveston in January.[12]

In February, fifteen Texans responded to Mills by writing the *Galveston News* to counter his arguments. While many of these writers covered similar ground, the letters demonstrated that Texans were weighing the value of

[12] "Porcupine," "What Shall We Do to Be Saved?", *Galveston TriWeekly News*, 29 January 1865, 1; C.G. Forshey, "Negro Force for C.S. Army," *Galveston TriWeekly News*, 29 January 1865, 2; *Handbook of Texas Online,* Donald W. Olson, "Forshey, Caleb Goldsmith," accessed October 26, 2016, http://www.tshaonline.org/handbook/online/ articles/ffo16.

slavery carefully as they reassessed the purpose of the war. On 12 February "H" wrote from Grimes County and suggested that the discussion of black troops was premature: "It were much better the question had not presented itself to the people, until an actual necessity arose for it. … I do not think the time is now, or ever will be when it will become necessary to enlist the slave in our defense." In the same issue, "Soldier" described the debate as a subject bound to inspire divisions and "fraught with evil." Three days later, "Fort Bend" savagely attacked Mills's proposition to trade emancipation for a European protectorate. Such a policy, "Fort Bend" declared, would lead the South down the path traveled by Haiti and the British Caribbean:

> Emancipation having already, in some of the most fertile and beautiful portions of the New World, worked out evils so stupendous as to be almost beyond the powers of computation to measure them, building up a mighty barbarism, and a huge heathenism in the center of America, now threatened to inflict upon this Confederacy still greater evils.

Confederate planters recoiled in horror from the fate of the sugar islands, but failed to realize that the decline of the Caribbean plantations was more complex than simply the loss of the slave labor force. In the next two issues, "Southern" and "Caleb Cutwell" again raised the specter of Haitian and Jamaican emancipation. Independence achieved by accepting the fate of the Caribbean, "Fort Bend" affirmed, would not be worth the cost:

> Without stopping to doubt…the probability of our thus ignominiously gaining our independence by the perpetration of so foul a crime against ourselves and our posterity, and even against the poor negro himself, let us calmly reflect and consider whether the peace and independence which we might thus obtain would be worth the sacrifice.

Unlike the president and many of the Texas editors, some defiant Texas planters were prepared to accept defeat before the loss of slavery.[13]

While many focused on the ramifications of arming slaves, other correspondents to the *News* addressed the purpose of the revolution. On 15 Feb-

[13] "H," "Eureka, Grimes County, Feb. 4th, 1865," *Galveston TriWeekly News*, 12 February 1865, 2; "Soldier," "Emancipation," *Galveston TriWeekly News*, 12 February 1865, 1; "Fort Bend," "ED News," *Galveston TriWeekly News*, 15 February 1865, 1; "Southern," "The Destiny of African Slavery," *Galveston TriWeekly News*, 15 February 1865, 1; "Caleb Cutwell," "Emancipation—Its Impolicy," *Galveston TriWeekly News*, 17 February 1865, 1.

ruary "Woodside" from Matagorda County asserted that Mills had erred in his contention that self-government, and not slavery, had always been the primary Confederate war aim. "It was the trampling of our rights," "Woodside" argued, "in this institution which determined the Southern States to establish a government of their own choice in which they could frame laws for its preservation." In his view, slavery had been, currently was, and must continue to be the cornerstone of the Confederacy. Further, he considered the discussion of black troops an unjustified admission of Confederate failure: "We have the same great and noble Generals, numberless men left, and our prospects are brighter than they have been at other times." True, Lee still commanded at the defenses of Richmond, but the men were easier to count than in 1862. Apparently, "Woodside" did not consider the need to meet Sherman or replace Hood's losses as imperative as the residents of Virginia and Georgia did. Yet, in Texas a significant number of citizens agreed with the writer. Resolutions adopted at a public meeting in Goliad on 15 February echoed the arguments of the letters in the *News,* as the committee termed the debate over arming slaves "premature, unwise, and unnecessary." In Goliad the preservation of slavery remained the primary war aim: "The prosperity and happiness of our country depends upon our system of slavery; and whether this doctrine be true or not, it is the institution of our choice, not to be wrested from us by any power on earth." Texans like "Woodside" and the citizens of Goliad considered the institution of slavery untouchable and the only cause that justified continuing the war.[14]

Finally, two correspondents addressed the implications of Judge Mills's proposals on the relationship between planters and non-slaveholding whites. In his second submission on the topic to the *News*, "Caleb Cutwell" proclaimed, and editor Richardson highlighted, that "THE EMANCIPATION OF THE SLAVES OF THE SOUTH WILL BE THE DESTRUCTION OF THE POOR WHITES." Drawing on the experiences of the working classes in Europe, the author predicted that white equality and republican institutions would quickly disappear in the wake of black liberty: "In most free States, the ownership of more property than the poor

[14] "Woodside," "Another Reply to Judge Mills," *Galveston TriWeekly News*, 15 February 1865, 2; F. Fauntleroy, "Public Meeting," *Galveston TriWeekly News*, 15 February 1865, 3.

can acquire, is a necessary qualification to the right to vote, and in those free States where they are allowed this right, they must cast their votes at the beck and nod of their rich employers." The equality of all white men (based on race, not class), so essential to white southern cohesion, "Caleb Cutwell" warned, was in jeopardy. Therefore, the enlistment of black troops, in the correspondent's opinion, offered a far greater threat to the non-slaveholders than continuing to fight the "slaveholders' war." On 17 February, "J.L.G.," an owner of fifty slaves, approached the same problem from a different angle. To cement the relationship between the non-slaveholding whites and the planters, the author proposed a revolutionary shift in property: "The slave owners of the South, [should] agree voluntarily or if not be forced by some mode of State legislation to divide their slaves among the white families of the South." Although he proposed limited compensation to the present owners, few of his slaveholding peers could have welcomed the plan for the redistribution of their wealth. Even so, "J.L.G." predicted that the benefits would outweigh the sacrifice: "We believe the mode suggested, by which they (the negroes) would be disseminated among us would give us greater strength and unanimity than any possible measure whatever." Not surprisingly, "J.L.G." also offered to arm his slaves if the president deemed it necessary. In January and February, the correspondents of the *News* addressed all the elements in the slave-soldier debate. Far from the wild panic some opponents professed to see, the letter writers took the issue seriously, examined the long-term implications of the steps involved, and struggled to decide what sacrifices they were willing to make to achieve victory.[15]

During the second phase of the debate, the unsuccessful return of Price as well as the defeats at Nashville and Savannah served as catalysts for the discussion of black troops in Gulf Coast Texas. Still, Cushing at the *Telegraph* and many others in Houston discounted the recent defeats and held firm to the old arguments against modifying slavery. These Texans understood that Lee's army faced a powerful Union army at the gates of Richmond, but they could see little difference in this situation and the military circumstances of 1862. Hood had lost a major battle, but the Army of Ten-

[15] "Caleb Cutwell," "Emancipation—Its Consequences," *Galveston TriWeekly News*, 22 February 1865, 2; "J.L.G.," "Important Hints for Consideration," *Galveston TriWeekly News*, 15 February 1865, 1.

nessee had lost battles before. To Cushing and Richardson, the dire position of affairs east of the Mississippi River appeared not only far away but almost irrelevant to the state of affairs in Texas. In contrast, the quite varied letters that appeared in the *Telegraph* and the *News* painted the picture of a community beginning to reassess its war aims. Many of the letter writers more accurately understood the situation than did the editors. While most citizens of Gulf Coast Texas remained rooted in the Cotton South, John Mills, William Sledge, and others challenged the community to look beyond their relative prosperity and see the Confederacy as a whole. Judging by the letters written in response to Mills and Sledge, most Texans could not perceive the immediate necessity for arming slaves. Nevertheless, the issue could no longer be swept under the rug by editors unprepared to address the issue. The idea of arming slaves in Confederate gray and marching them off to fight the country's battles was seriously discussed in Gulf Coast Texas during the second phase of the national debate. The old taboo against ever questioning the merits of slavery had been broken. The impossible to contemplate had become possible to consider.

The return of Price's veterans through the streets of Marshall troubled many in the East Texas community, but the city's leaders saw no direct threat to the region and, therefore, steadfastly clung to slavery. Planters noted with considerable trepidation the publication of new treasury regulations intended to tighten Confederate control of the cross-border trade. In 1864 the state and Confederate governments had competed for cotton contracts, leading to conflicting orders and charges of corruption. From his headquarters in Marshall, Treasury agent Peter W. Gray issued detailed instructions for the shipment and sale of cotton, tobacco, sugar, molasses, and rice as he attempted to straighten out the conflicting customs regulations. In spite of the December reverses, slaves continued to sell for up to $4,000 each. Buyers seemed not to question the long-term viability of the institution. Editor Robert Loughery of the *Marshall Republican* advertised for the return of a fourteen-year-old runaway slave in January. Despite some slight disruptions caused by the war, slaves worked the cotton fields and a few ran away, but the institution of slavery remained alive and well in East Texas.[16]

[16] "Additional Instructions Under the Regulations of Overland Commerce With Mexico," *Marshall Texas Republican*, 20 January 1865, 2; "To the People of the Trans-

The southern reverses at Savannah and Nashville brought a steady stream of news items to Marshall advancing various options to fill the gray ranks. For example, the *Marshall Texas Republican* reprinted an editorial from the *Richmond Sentinel* that called on southerners to commit "ourselves to the diligent devotion of all our resources" to the cause. As reprinted in Texas, the *Sentinel*'s call for planters to commit their slaves to the army was omitted. The Marshall paper laughed at a Virginia paper's assertion that Texas had retained 500,000 men in reserve. The editor noted that the state had only 8,000 men in the state militia and these were engaged on the frontier fighting Indians. Both Virginians and Texans had grand misconceptions of the others' manpower resources. On 3 February the *Republican* printed a synopsis of a Richmond article that described Robert E. Lee's ideas on arming slaves. The *Enquirer* had based the piece on unofficial sources, which significantly lessened the impact of "Lee's sentiments" in Marshall. Refusing to joust with Lee directly, the *Republican* endorsed an editorial from the *Houston Telegraph* that firmly denied the need for black troops: "Those who favor the idea of arming the slaves argue that we are in extremity and must put a gun into the hand of every man that can carry one. We do not believe that." Responding to the calls for emancipation in return for a colonial protectorate, the Houston editor affirmed the health of slavery: "It is said by some of the weakest kneed that the institution is in a manner gone, that it only stands in the way of recognition, and we better lose that than existence. It hasn't yet by far come to this alternative [slavery or independence]." Despite the battlefield reverses, the *Marshall Republican* continued to tailor its news items in accordance with its opposition to arming slaves.[17]

The military failures of December led the *Dallas Herald* to follow the debate over arming slaves with considerable care. On 26 January and 23 February the *Herald* presented details of legislative efforts to provide the

---

Mississippi Department," *Marshall Texas Republican*, 27 January 1865, 1; "We publish in another column…," *Marshall Texas Republican*, 17 February 1865, 2; "The Latest News," *Marshall Texas Republican*, 3 February 1865, 2; "It was once the uniform rule…" and "Runaway," *Marshall Texas Republican*, 27 January 1865, 1.

[17] "Reconstruction in Congress," *Marshall Texas Republican*, 13 January 1865, 1; "The Texas reserves…," *Marshall Texas Republican*, 20 January 1865, 1; "The Latest News," *Marshall Texas Republican*, 3 February 1865, 2; "Sound Views," *Marshall Texas Republican*, 17 February 1865, 1.

40,000 laborers President Davis had requested for the army. In between these legislative accounts, the Dallas paper chronicled the shifting views toward black troops presented in Richmond. On 9 February a bold editorial from the *Richmond Sentinel* appeared in the Dallas paper: "All our servants and all our property yielded up to assist in the defense of our country would mean no more but it would be far more glorious to devote our means to our success than to lose them as spoils to the enemy." A week later the *Dallas Herald* summarized a piece from another Richmond paper: "It brings forward Gen. Lee's proposition to conscript negroes and to liberate them and the wives of those who are made soldiers. It demands that every possible sacrifice of life and property should be made." As the slave-soldier bill moved through the Confederate Congress, the Dallas paper often printed portions of the debate but rarely chose to quote the most vocal proponents of slave-soldiers. For instance, on 9 March the words of John Atkins of Tennessee rang out in Dallas: "Between subjugation and arming our slaves in our defense every principle of nature and self preservation requires the latter, therefore, we should at once put a hundred thousand slaves…in the field." Pointing to the time-honored principle of the South, the congressman did not envision black troops fighting for their own freedom: "To render them effective, an immediate interest in the institution of slavery should be guaranteed to all our soldiers in the army. … The government should purchase all the slaves thus put in and give to each white soldier a slave, with all the rights of property &c." Atkins's proposal for their employment without a promise of emancipation made his ideas acceptable in Dallas. Atkins, like many in Texas, simply assumed the slaves would fight for the interests of their owners without looking for a benefit to themselves. Few of the men in the trenches would have agreed.[18]

---

[18] "Confederate Congress," *Dallas Herald*, 26 January 1865, 1; "Richmond, Jan. 29," *Dallas Herald*, 23 February 1865, 2; "The following article…," *Dallas Herald*, 9 February 1865, 1; "A Late *Richmond Enquirer*…," *Dallas Herald*, 16 February 1865, 1; "By Friday Nights Mail," *Dallas Herald*, 9 March 1865, 1. In this report of the House debate of 8 February, the Dallas editor quoted briefly from James Orr and August Maxwell, who opposed arming slaves, but simply paraphrased the remarks of Henry Burnett in support of the measure. Atkins' call to arm slaves without granting freedom fit Loughery's purpose best.

At his editorial desk in Marshall, Robert Loughery received the news of the defeat of Hood with grave concern: "If that report be true; it is indeed a calamity, and joined to the successful termination of Sherman's march to the Atlantic, is the severest blow of the war." Even in the gloom of defeat, however, Loughery resolutely denounced Davis's plan to free the laborers with the army: "If the Confederate Government has the right to free forty thousand negroes, under any pretext, it possesses an equal right to set them all free. The old Washington Government never contemplated an act more odious or alarming." On 20 January the editor examined the 1860 census returns, estimated the South's manpower potential at 500,000 white men, and thus denied the need for black troops. "The enemy can spare no formidable force," Loughery contended, "to invade the trans-Mississippi Department. We are safe from the horrors of war until the campaigns are ended in the East, and the Yankees can raise more troops." Responding to those who advocated attempting to gain recognition though emancipation, the Marshall editor announced that only evil would come of the idea: "The declaration that we are willing to give up African slavery, can have no other tendency, as we conceive, than to create distrust and despondency at home and to lead foreign nations to believe our rulers…desperate." Looking out from his offices in Marshall, Loughery could still see no military cause for alarm.[19]

In Dallas, John Swindells did not commit a full editorial in the *Herald* to the idea of arming slaves. Rather, he provided his views on the topic in the selection of items to be included in the paper and in his introductions of editorials from other papers. For instance, on 9 February a long editorial from the *Richmond Sentinel* advocating arming slaves took up most of the front page in Dallas. Swindells apologized for the radical views so prominently displayed, contending that the credence given the piece in other parts of the Confederacy made it worthwhile to print: "The following article…has attracted no little attention in Richmond, it having been attributed at least in substance, if not in language to the President. We doubt if he had anything

[19] Robert Loughery, "The News," *Marshall Texas Republican*, 13 January 1865, 2; Robert Loughery, "The Macon Telegraph…," *Marshall Texas Republican*, 13 January 1865, 2; Robert Loughery, "Confederate Resources," *Marshall Texas Republican*, 20 January 1865, 1; Robert Loughery, "News and Rumors," *Marshall Texas Republican*, 13 February 1865, 2; Robert Loughery, "No visitations of fortune…," *Marshall Texas Republican*, 10 February 1865, 2.

to do with it." Despite the closing caveat, Swindells did not shorten the editorial as he did on many occasions but printed the full text of the original; therefore, the haunting words from Richmond rang out in Dallas: "Shall we withhold our sons and thus reserve them as servants for the Yankees? Shall we send our sons and deny our negroes? Shall we send our blood and refuse our money?" In a similar manner, Swindells endorsed the stinging assessment of Davis first found in the *Tyler* [TX] *Confederate Journal*: "The cold, icy, independent character of the President has almost isolated him. … His next in power has not given him the aid of his counsel. … The people have misunderstood him. He without design on either part, has for nearly two years, stood alone." Only such isolation and a necessity that the people of Texas did not yet see could explain Davis's suggestion that the South must arm and free its slaves.

On 16 February Swindells included a news item from Georgia that at first glance looked like simply a humorous story, but underneath packed a strong message. In the story, Mrs. Roby of Eatonton, Georgia, had her farm attacked by Union deserters. Roby turned to her slave named Anderson for aid: "He mounted a mule, called his dogs, and with a double barrel [sic] shotgun in hand, he made for the fugitives. … The Yankees refused to give up and fought the dogs; whereupon the *colored gentleman* fired on the party." The story continued with a modest "Captain Roby" turning his prisoners over to "the proper authorities." "Captain Roby [Anderson]," the Georgian continued, "simply remarked that he would fight to the last in suspense [sic] of his country… We have no doubt that hundreds, nay thousands, of our colored population are ready to give the same proofs of their fidelity." This account from Georgia received considerable space in the *Herald* and suggests much more than that a motivated slave could capture Yankee deserters. First, it demonstrated that slaves could be trusted with firearms as they went to meet the foe. Second, the direction of the act by a woman and the transfer of the prisoners to "proper authorities" illustrated that armed black men would remain under control and not immediately act like savages; therefore, southern women and civil authorities could trust black troops in the field. Finally, the piece suggested that the southern slave population saw the Confederacy as their country and identified with southerners, not their northern "liberators." Swindells could not make these statements openly in East Texas even if he had wanted to. Yet, this astute, longtime editor could not have been unaware of the radical implications of the story. John Swindells did not write any editorials about arming the slaves, but he kept the idea clearly before the public by the items he included in the *Herald*.[20]

John Mills's letter to the *Galveston News* had caught his neighbors in East Texas off guard. Although well known throughout the state, Mills had lived in East Texas since 1837 and in Marshall since 1854. He was one of "them." On 24 February the editor of the *Marshall Republican* relented and printed Mills's letter. In the piece, Mills challenged much of the southern orthodoxy still accepted in East Texas. First, he asserted, "We did not begin, nor have we carried out this war in defence [sic] of slavery." Second, he stated a harsh truth that many in Virginia and Georgia had been forced to accept in the fall: "There certainly can be at this time no thinking man but that looks upon the institution as doomed." Invading armies, refugee planters, and runaway slaves had so disrupted the plantation system of the Deep South and Upper South that only a few could still hope for its revival. Emancipation, Mills believed, must be accepted, but the South yet had the chance to dictate the terms of slavery's demise: "They have attempted to humble us and subjugate us by a threat of the emancipation of our slaves. We will make our separation from them eternal, by voluntarily doing it ourselves." Finally, Mills scolded the president for not going far enough on modifying slavery in his November address: "Were I he, I would not hesitate at once to make the proposition of the gradual emancipation of slavery to England, France, and the other great powers upon their recognition of our independence." Clearly, Mills forced the citizens of Marshall to examine all of their assumptions about slavery, the purpose of the war, and the meaning of being a southerner.[21]

Robert Loughery waited to publish John Mills's letter in the *Marshall Republican* until he had received two forceful epistles countering the judge's radical ideas. In his introduction to the letters, Loughery attempted to discredit Mills's ideas: "The letter of Judge Mills, it seems to us, is a very silly and ill-timed production, and is receiving much more attention than it mer-

---

[20] "The following article...," *Dallas Herald*, 9 February 1865, 1; "The South Carolina Resolutions," *Dallas Herald*, 2 February 1865, 1; "Yankees Captured by a Negro," *Dallas Herald*, 16 February 1865, 2.

[21] John T. Mills, "Judge Mills's Letter," *Marshall Texas Republican*, 24 February 1865, 1.

its." Unlike the *Galveston News,* which relied on quantity to overwhelm Mills's contentions, the *Marshall Republican* carefully selected the responses. On 24 February, Colonel Clayton C. Gillespie, commander of the 26th Texas Cavalry, penned a lengthy reply that firmly denied any necessity existed that would justify such a step. While approving of the use of slaves in the army as laborers, Gillespie asserted that the army was "not yet ready to fight for a free negro Confederacy or to allow one to exist on this southern land." The colonel indignantly proclaimed Mills's letter to be "the fruit of panic, the pitiful panic that is now upon the country, and of which every man who participated in it ought to be ashamed." In the same issue, "Randolph" directly countered Mills's assessment of the nation's war aims: "Lincoln is fighting first for abolitionism and equality, second, for the overthrow of states' rights or Union. We fight first for slavery and to resist equality, second for state sovereignty." Independence without slavery had little appeal for this Marshall letter writer. Further, "Randolph" proclaimed that southerners would dishonor their fallen soldiers as well as revered slave owners of the past if they continued the fight without maintaining slavery: "We must vindicate the characters of Abraham, Moses, Socrates, and Washington. This is our first and highest duty, to defend and vindicate our institutions." Many in Marshall agreed with the responses to Mills and predicted dire consequences if the South armed slaves. Even so, the citizens of East Texas had clearly begun to discuss the issue in detail.[22]

The *Dallas Herald* did not print a copy of Judge Mills's letter and published only a snippet from one of the many who rose to dispute his claims. In the one partial letter on the topic that appeared in Dallas, a reader would not have known what it was talking about unless he had read another newspaper: "If we continue loyal and true to the principles on which we defined the mighty conflict, that sympathy and those good wishes will go on increasing till we shall come forth triumphant." To many, this assertion that the Confederacy needed only to stay the current course to attain the world's assistance must have seemed odd and out of place. On 9 March the editor ad-

[22] Robert Loughery, "The Communication of Col. Gillespie," *Marshall Texas Republican*, 24 February 1865, 2; Clayton C. Gillespie, "The Confederate Motto—No Compromise," *Marshall Texas Republican*, 24 February 1865, 1; "Randolph," "What Are We Fighting For? Fiat Justicia," *Marshall Texas Republican*, 24 February 1865, 1.

mitted receiving a number of unsigned letters that he refused to print. To another, he said the letters' content was unacceptable: "We would say to our correspondent 'Shelbyite' that we can see no good results to be gained by the publication of his communication, and beg respectfully to decline it." The *Herald* did mention that public meetings were held in Davis, Marion, and Harrison Counties, during which peace, reconstruction, and the state of the country were discussed. The resolutions of the Harrison County meeting were published, but they simply restated the legislature's ideas from November. The *Herald* clearly received far more communications concerning arming slaves than it was willing to publish.[23]

In contrast to its earlier coverage, the *Austin State Gazette* presented a variety of news items about the military situation during the second phase of the debate. On 11 January the Austin paper announced the arrival of Sherman in Savannah and the defeat of Hood's army. Unwilling to accept the reports of the disasters at face value, the *Gazette* declared, "All the news we have is direct from Yankeedom, therefore the reports we have yet received...must be taken with the usual discounts for exaggerations and misstatements." As late as mid-February the *Gazette* printed items designed to minimize the impact of the December defeats: "In a struggle that has been in progress for nearly four years, and that may be protracted for years to come, they are of small *relative* importance and effect." In light of the *Gazette*'s effort to lessen the impact of the defeats on southern morale, it appears ironic that the account went ahead to compare the December defeats to the pivotal losses at Fort Donelson and Vicksburg. On 22 February the charge of a Houston judge to a grand jury appeared in Austin. The case before the court involved treason, and the judge took the opportunity to define treason in the broadest possible sense. The ideas were expressed not only for the jury but also for the wider community, which had begun to question the old social boundaries. In his charge, the judge warned that there was no room for compromise with the North and of the vile consequences of submission: "Our lands are to be divided among our conquerors. Our slaves are to be emancipated and we are to be slaughtered, or if we survive are to be-

[23] "Col. Ashbel Smith concludes...," *Dallas Herald*, 9 March 1865, 1; "We would say...," *Dallas Herald*, 9 March 1865, 2; "Capt. Adam Hope...," *Dallas Herald*, 23 February 1865, 1; "The Marshall Republican...," *Dallas Herald*, 9 March 1865, 2.

come slaves to cruel taskmasters." Despite such bleak appraisals, only one news item in Austin directly discussed black troops. In this article, the *State Gazette* cited a London report noting that the European powers would accept Confederate emancipation as a basis for recognition. During the second phase of the debate, the Austin editor tailored the news items in the paper to minimize the threats to the Confederacy and to keep local attention away from radical measures.[24]

In the immediate aftermath of the defeats at Savannah and Nashville, news items in the *Bellville Countryman* describing fluctuations in the price of cotton outnumbered reports of the debate over arming slaves. On 24 January an editorial from Boston grudgingly conceded the lasting strength of slavery: "Sambo doesn't move notwithstanding that Gen. Sherman is ready to help him. ... We have been waiting for three years for an insurrection, and it seems that we might as well have looked for a rising in a graveyard." While this undoubtedly reassured some planters, other items must have caused concern. On 14 February *The Countryman* noted Earl Russell's comments in England: "I cannot but believe that the civil war in America whichever way it may end...that out of these events the African race are to receive their freedom." In the same issue, a letter from a Richmond correspondent appeared arguing that arming the slaves would be the ultimate proof that the South would never surrender. Clinging to the illusion of blacks as a "feeble, unwarlike, and submissive race," the author declared, "It will be a strange corollary to this war if the campaign of 1865 finds 200,000 armed negroes from the North trying conclusions with 200,000 armed negroes from the South." The news items that appeared in *The Countryman* emphasized the distance between the war and Bellville, but nevertheless kept the community's attention focused on the manpower crisis.[25]

---

[24] "By Friday's Mail" and "By Sunday's Mail," *Austin The Weekly State Gazette*, 11 January 1865, 1; "The Very Latest News," *Austin The Weekly State Gazette*, 11 January 1865, 2; "Extracts from Judge Hill's Charge...," *Austin The Weekly State Gazette*, 22 February 1865, 1; "The Very Latest News," *Austin The Weekly State Gazette*, 22 February 1865, 2.

[25] "The Sonora Times...," *Bellville Countryman*, 17 January 1865, 1; "Since the Publication...," *Bellville Countryman*, 14 February 1865, 1; "The Boston Traveler...," *Bellville Countryman*, 24 February 1865, 1; "Earl Russell," *Bellville Countryman*, 14 February 1865, 1; "I Have Reasons...," *Bellville Countryman*, 14 February 1865, 1.

The "most saddening and depressing" reports of Sherman's arrival at Savannah and of Thomas's victory at Nashville appeared in LaGrange on 7 January. In the wake of defeat, the *LaGrange Patriot* elected on 21 January to print the radical notions of the *Huntsville* [TX] *Item* concerning the need to fill the gray ranks: "While the Yankees are constantly replenishing in that element [men], a blind man on a galloping horse could not fail to perceive that our seed is running out." Calling on planters to "lay aside the sin of selfishness," the Huntsville paper proclaimed that the South must avail herself of the "reserve force" God had given them or "we shall ere his [Lincoln's] new term expires, have no negroes at all." "Though we can't get all we expected to get at the start," the Huntsville editor soberly concluded, "war is such a monstrous lever, we must be thankful for what we get, and praise the gods we got off so well." No other news item expressed such a willingness to abandon slavery, but the inclusion of this piece suggests that the editor of the *LaGrange Patriot* considered it much less impossible than he had two months before. In the same issue, a message from Governor Pendleton Murrah called on Texans to make new sacrifices for independence: "If the people will but count life and property nothing worth; and will sacrifice the one, and give up the other, for the pearls of inestimable price[:] liberty and independence." While never mentioning slavery, the governor suggested that Texans must choose between greater sacrifices and defeat. A month later, on 25 February, the *Patriot* reprinted an editorial from San Antonio questioning efforts to win foreign recognition by emancipating the slaves. "However it might aid our struggle to abandon the system of domestic slavery, the several States each within itself, can alone determine and enact the measure." Forced to confront fearful choices in January and February, the editor of the *LaGrange Patriot* selected a wider variety of news items and presented a more balanced assessment of the situation during the second phase of the debate.[26]

---

[26] "From Northern accounts…," *The LaGrange Patriot*, 7 January 1865, 2; "Sherman seems to have knocked…," *The LaGrange Patriot*, 21 January 1865, 1; "Governor Murrah publishes…," *The LaGrange Patriot*, 21 January 1865, 2; "We copy the article…," *The LaGrange Patriot*, 25 February 1865, 1. Duncan Kenner, with the blessing of the Confederate government, left for France and Britain with an emancipation for recognition proposal in December 1864. Although approached as a secret mission, a number of

At his editorial desk in Austin, David Robinson acknowledged that Sherman's march to the sea and Hood's defeat at Nashville had changed the military landscape, but he consistently opposed all radical steps advanced in the name of military necessity. Announcing the capture of Savannah, Robinson made a small concession to the gravity of the situation: "The place is represented [in southern accounts] as unimportant, but we cannot regard that as distracting from Sherman's success for he has gained and accomplished all he expected to do." On 25 January, Robinson declared it the duty of the state to develop all her resources and to exploit her access to markets. "With the cotton under her control…it can well be imagined," he asserted, "that…she might have maintained…not only the States of the Trans-Mississippi Department, but to a great degree, have contributed to her sisters east of the river." More efficient use of the state's resources, he contended, was crucial to reversing the current troubles: "The State can export all the cotton it can command. … The vast resources of Texas, now dormant, could be developed, and thereby the citizens supplied with the necessary articles of common use." Despite such pleas, Robinson strongly opposed radical measures such as arming the slaves: "There is nothing in our federative system which can be had by the plea of 'military necessity' orders, which cannot be equally well, and equally promptly obtained by pursuing a conservative policy, in harmony with the political theory of the rights of the several States." Even after the December defeats, the *Austin Gazette*'s editor failed to see the need to modify the nation's military policies, his traditional states' rights doctrine, or the central place afforded to slave-produced cotton.[27]

In Bellville, John P. Osterhout announced the loss of Savannah, the defeat of Hood, and the fall of Fort Fisher without panic—they all seemed so far away. In an editorial concerning Vice President Alexander Stephens and the southern peace movement, Osterhout refused to be discouraged: "Thro' all the gloom and misery of the war, we think we see in the future the Confederate States recognized among the powers of the earth." A month later,

---

Confederate newspapers discussed the idea in January 1865. Almost all gave up on the idea after the Union's strong stance at the Hampton Roads Conference came to light.

[27] David Robinson, "The Very Latest News," *Austin The Weekly State Gazette*, 11 January 1865, 2; David Robinson, "Texas—Her Duty," *Austin The Weekly State Gazette*, 25 January 1865, 2; David Robinson, "Texas—Her Duty," *Austin The Weekly State Gazette*, 22 February 1865, 2.

on 21 February, the editor of *The Countryman* berated the *Galveston News* for printing John Mills's letter in favor of freeing and arming the slaves: "Such a communication appearing in some journals at this or any previous time, would ensure its [the paper's] immediate destruction." With tensions remaining high between the non-slaveholding immigrants and the planters in the Bellville community, Osterhout addressed Mills's ideas without quoting from the letter or even mentioning the author's name. In an accompanying editorial, Osterhout clarified his position on black troops: "We have been, and are…well satisfied that slaves must ultimately be placed in the army as soldiers to help do the fighting." Opposition from civilians and soldiers, he believed, was fruitless: "They might as well be opposed to the use of artillery, or any of the mechanical arts now used." Holding such views, how could he bicker with the *News*? "They must fight," the Bellville editor proclaimed, "fight not as freemen, or freedmen, but fight as slaves; and if they survive the contest they are to remain slaves." Osterhout was prepared to arm the slaves to aid the war effort but not ready to sacrifice slavery in the process.[28] Unlike military and civilian leaders in the east, he saw no difficulty with slave-soldiers remaining slaves even as they fought for the liberty of their masters. Few soldiers in the Petersburg trenches expressed similar hopes that black men could be driven into battle with the whip. By February 1865 Lee and his generals were struggling to keep white men who fought for their own freedom in the ranks. Only someone far from the scene of battle and supported by the appearance of still compliant slaves could hope to send black men as slaves to fight Grant's legions. As importantly, black soldiers fighting as slaves provided the only acceptable solution in Bellville, where the German and Czech farmers continued to look for other sources to fill the gray ranks while their planter neighbors jealously guarded their valuable slave property. Even in the dire military straits of January 1865, Osterhout felt compelled to walk a fine line between the factions in Bellville.

Despite a new willingness to publish a wide range of news items in the *LaGrange Patriot* concerning slavery, William McClellan clung to his states' rights principles during the second phase of the debate. Known as an oppo-

[28] J.P. Osterhout, "The Vice President," *Bellville Countryman*, 24 January 1865, 1; J.P. Osterhout, "Abolitionism," *Bellville Countryman*, 21 February 1865, 1; J.P. Osterhout, "Slave-soldiers," *Bellville Countryman*, 21 February 1865, 1.

nent of secession in 1861, the *Patriot*'s editor was careful to avoid the appearance of breaking faith with the Confederate cause. On 14 January McClellan lauded Governor Joseph E. Brown of Georgia for his faithfulness to the "integrity of the original purposes of our revolutionary movement." "We would to God," he asserted, "we had thousands of such men in the Southern Confederacy as Gov. Brown." Like Brown, McClellan displayed a very tenuous loyalty to the president: "If President Davis adopts, or urges the adoption of, any harsh, improper, or dangerous measures of policy, it is legitimate enough…that the public press…bring the force of public reason to bear against them." Upon announcing Congressional approval of the 40,000 laborers for the army, McClellan bitterly declared that the Confederacy "has engulphed [sic] all the municipal powers of the States, and centralization and consolidation are no longer odious theories, but 'fixed facts.'" If the government could do this, he rhetorically asked, why could it not adopt Lincoln's policy of compensated emancipation? On 18 February McClellan made his clearest statement on the concept of slave-soldiers when he lauded the December resolutions of the South Carolina legislature against black troops. Proclaiming military necessity the "plea of the tyrant," he cautioned Texans to reject those who called for radical measures: "They rush precipitately, and without due caution, into other extremes; and while escaping an imagined danger; they fall into the gins and snare of infinitely more fatal consequences." Yet, McClellan argued that the Carolinians had not gone far enough, because they admitted that some future occasion might demand the sacrifice of slavery. Abolitionist doctrines, he contended, "ought to have been fully met, plumply denied, in the present and in the future, actually, or contingently. Wherever such a contingency shall arise, the real controversy is at an end; and its continuance would be but…the *mad play of passion*." William McClellan could not imagine a Confederacy without slavery and could not see any purpose in the war if it was not meant to uphold the rights of slave owners.[29]

[29] William McClellan, "Gov. Brown, of Georgia…," *The LaGrange Patriot*, 14 January 1865, 2; William McClellan, "It is said…," *The LaGrange Patriot*, 21 January 1865, 2; William McClellan, "A bill has passed…," *The LaGrange Patriot*, 18 February 1865, 2; William McClellan, "Lead Editorial," *The LaGrange Patriot*, 18 February 1865, 2. The italics appear in the original.

In contrast to the intransigence of many in Central Texas, two letter writers emerged in the wake of the December defeats to address forcefully the issue of arming the slaves. On 20 January a powerful letter from William Sledge, a slave owner from Chappell Hill, near Bellville, appeared in the *Houston Telegraph*. Noting Lincoln's success with black soldiers, Sledge suggested the Confederates follow the Yankee example: "May it not be proper for our Government to give authority by act of Congress, to the slave owners of the South to raise an invading force of one hundred thousand blacks to be officered by their owners?" Unwilling to champion abolition, Sledge argued that events forced such a course: "The late successful march of Sherman's army through Georgia...proves one of two things—we have not the men to have successfully opposed him or they are where they should not be." Further, Sledge proclaimed that common sense required the enlistment of black troops: "We risk the lives of our children to disease in camp, and destruction of life by musket shot, reserving the negro as a dernier resort. Why wait until our manhood is gone?"[30] The writer called for black troops but did not offer a firm suggestion on the new soldiers' reward for faithful service. Arguing that black troops must be had, Sledge called for others to speak out and for the public to hold meetings to debate the new course and, in particular, the steps needed to secure black soldiers' fidelity.

Sledge drew considerable interest from the readers of the *Telegraph*, but no one responded to his ideas in the Central Texas papers. The choice of a Houston paper rather than *The State Gazette* or *The Countryman* appears significant. The triweekly format of the *Telegraph* provided more room for letters, but the editor, Edward Cushing, also had taken a much more favorable stance toward the Confederate government, if not to black troops, than any of the Central Texas editors. Possibly, Sledge believed his ideas would reach a broader audience as well as receive more favorable treatment in Houston. Although these reasons appear persuasive, other factors might have figured in the equation. Many potential proponents of arming slaves from Central Texas may have been too intimidated by their slaveholding peers to speak out. The troops sent to LaGrange and Bellville in January 1863 had attempted to snuff out Unionist feelings in the area with their bayonets. Key

---

[30] William M. Sledge, "Letter to the Editor," *Houston TriWeekly Telegraph*, 20 January 1865, 2.

Unionist leaders had either left the area or been silenced, but no rush to the Confederate enrolling officer ensued. In fact, in early January 1865 a letter to the *Galveston News* bitterly complained of Germans fleeing the state to avoid military service. The Central Texas editors also had reason to feel uneasy. Osterhout as a Pennsylvania native and McClellan as a former opponent of secession had to worry about the security of their own positions should they appear unsound on the slavery issue. Unlike Sledge, the German and Czech farmers owned few slaves and could not point to longstanding ties with the community. Plantation slavery and immigrant farmers had coexisted for years, but during this debate their interests were quite different. The immigrants hoped to keep their sons out of the ranks while the planters hoped to keep their slaves in the cotton fields rather than leading them onto the battlefields. By stepping forward to champion arming and freeing slaves, an editor or a letter writer would have risked a terrific backlash from the powerful planting interests.[31]

On 24 February, A.S. Broaddus of Burleson County spoke for Central Texas planters in a letter to the *Galveston News.* Broaddus compared Judge Mills's letter to the peace proposals of Alexander Stephens and suggested that discussions of emancipation had the potential to seriously divide the state: "Just such letters and views as those expressed by Judge Mills, have done us more harm in the last six months than Yankee General[s] and Yankee armies could do to us in ten years." Emancipation—whether as an offer to win recognition or as a means to fill the ranks—he contended, violated a sacred charge passed down to southerners from their fathers: "I do not regard the abolition of slavery as a question of time. I believe that God has ordained it, and that he does not intend the slaves shall be given up to the Yankees who are their worst enemies; or that they shall be cursed with freedom." Speaking for many Central Texas slave owners, Broaddus insisted that he could see no military necessity to enroll black troops. He solemnly concluded that he would rather leave his home and all he had than live in a South with three million free blacks. As with Sledge, Broaddus elected to enter the slave-soldier debate through the columns of the Gulf Coast papers. His letter would have fit much better with the editorial positions of the

---

[31] "Parrhesia," "Leaving the Country to Avoid the War," *Galveston TriWeekly News*, 1 January 1865, 1.

Central Texas papers, but he may have feared that its publication in Bellville or LaGrange might have ignited a local debate regarding black troops that would have been difficult for planters to control. In Central Texas, far more letters were written concerning new Confederate cotton regulations governing the overland trade with Mexico than the issue of arming the slaves. Fourteen hundred miles from the trenches at Petersburg and the ravaging columns of Sherman, many Texans could not yet sanction revolutionary change. In some combination, small weekly newspapers, timid editors, and ethnic divisions with class overtones limited the voices heard in Central Texas concerning arming the slaves.[32]

During the second phase of the debate, the defeats at Nashville and Savannah as well as Price's ragged return to Texas served as catalysts for renewed discussion. The dire state of affairs east of the Mississippi River forced Texans to take the idea of arming slaves seriously for the first time. To some, the Union armies appeared far away and almost irrelevant, but to many more, the threat to the Confederacy—if not immediately to Texas—seemed quite real. In contrast to intransigent editors like Cushing in Houston and Robinson in Austin, intrepid Texans emerged in each region who began to discuss the steps the South must take to stave off defeat. The bold letters of William Sledge and John Mills and the correspondents who responded to them brought the debate to life in Texas. The letters that were printed in the *Houston Telegraph*, the *Galveston News*, and the *Marshall Republican* pulled Texas into the larger Confederate debate of war aims. These letters paint the picture of a community beginning to examine and reconsider the fundamental tenets of its society.

For the moment, Jefferson Davis's campaign had failed in Texas. Most Texans remained unwilling to take the steps Mills suggested, but the resulting discourse demonstrated just how far these Texans who had not felt the impact of hard war were willing to go. Editor Osterhout of the *Bellville Countryman* expressed the views of many when he openly supported black soldiers after the fall of Fort Fisher. Even so, his consistent unwillingness to discuss emancipation fit well with the world of cotton and slaves that still existed in Texas. Most Texans could not see the need to go any farther. Few

---

[32] A.S. Broaddus, "Burleson Co., Texas, Feb'y 20th, 1865," *Galveston TriWeekly News*, 19 February 1865, 3.

Texans lost sight of the fact that steps taken to meet the manpower crisis would permanently change the social fabric of the South. While many in Virginia and Georgia began in January to question seriously the centrality of slavery in the South, "King Cotton" and the labor institution that supported the throne continued to rule in Texas.

Phase III

Hampton Roads to Appomattox

8

A Reasonable Sacrifice

In the fall of 1864, Jefferson Davis had undertaken several innovative measures to reverse the fading southern fortunes. First, the president in his message to Congress had recommended new roles for slaves. After initial discussions in Congress in November, the measure totaled 40,000 slave laborers had become stalled in committee. Second, Davis in December had dispatched Duncan Kenner to Europe to propose emancipation of the slaves in return for formal recognition of the Confederacy as a nation and military assistance. Although Kenner had not yet presented the idea in London or Paris, word of the mission had leaked to the southern press, and little hope remained that the states would ratify any treaty that the diplomat might secure. Third, Davis had entered into peace discussions with Union emissary Francis P. Blair in January. Despite considerable misgivings, the Confederate president agreed to send representatives to meet with Abraham Lincoln. Within minutes of reaching Hampton Roads, Alexander Stephens's visions of ending the war through diplomacy vanished, because Lincoln flatly refused to consider any terms that allowed for southern independence. None of the three initiatives had borne fruit. Yet, one of the three remained if the president could reenergize the discussions concerning arming slaves.

The final phase of the debate to arm the slaves opened with the return of the unsuccessful Confederate peace commissioners from Hampton Roads on 3 February. If peace was to come, southerners came to realize they must "conquer a peace" on the battlefield. "We have been fairly pressed against the wall," the *Richmond Sentinel* proclaimed on 6 February, "and told plainly that there is no escape from utter ruin, save such as we shall hew out with manful swords. … There are no peace men among us now!" In light of the failures of the peace conference and the unsuccessful efforts to gain foreign recognition, black soldiers appeared the only viable option left to fill the thin gray ranks and thus preserve the Confederate nation. Administration efforts to force resolution of the issue began in earnest on 9 February with Secretary of State Judah P. Benjamin's speech in Richmond demanding passage of the bill to arm the slaves. With the armies desperately in need of men, Benjamin declared that the Confederacy must employ every means available to prevent defeat: "War is a game that cannot be played without men. … Is it not a shame that men who have sacrificed all in our defense should not be reinforced by all the means in our power? Is it any time now for antiquated patriotism to argue a refusal to send them aid, be it white or black?" Benjamin tried to show the short-sightedness of the opponents of arming the slaves who feared Confederate emancipation but took little notice of the threat of Federal reconstruction: "It looks to me very much like a man rushing forth from his burning house, and begging his neighbors, for heaven's sake, not to throw water on the blazing roof, because it might spoil his furniture." The Confederate house might be on fire, but the secretary professed to have the remedy: "Let us say to every negro who wishes to go into the ranks on condition of being made free—'Go and fight, you are free.'"[1] From Benjamin's speech to final passage of the act to arm the slaves on 13 March, the debate raged fiercely as Congress and the people attempted to determine the sacrifices necessary to meet the crisis.

On the same day that Benjamin spoke in Richmond, two Confederate senators came out strongly for arming the slaves. In January both houses of the Confederate Congress had debated bills both to place slave laborers with the army and to form black combat units. All of these efforts had come to nothing as opponents obscured the central issue by tying the measures to Davis's speculations about liberating the slaves for faithful service. Thus, the enemies of black troops kept the proposals from coming to a final vote. In early February, Senator Albert G. Brown of Mississippi had introduced in the Senate a bill to arm and free 200,000 slaves. On 9 February Brown forced a vote on the measure while the Senate was in secret session. John B. Jones, a clerk to the Secretary of War, noted the consequences of the bill's failure: "Senator Brown's resolution to put 200,000 slaves in the army was voted down in secret session. Now the slave owners must go in themselves, or all is lost." With Sherman on the loose in the Carolinas, many southern veterans deserted and went home to protect their families. Robert E. Lee

[1] "Speech of Hon. J.P. Benjamin," *Lynchburg Virginian*, 13 February 1865, 1.

needed dramatic numbers of new recruits to compensate for the up to eight percent of his troops that deserted each month. The few slave owners that Jones had mentioned might have filled a battalion, but Lee needed new brigades, divisions, and corps.[2]

Gustavus Henry of Tennessee, the other senator to enter the fray on 9 February, spoke at the conclusion of Benjamin's speech. The military crisis, Henry asserted, demanded the use of black troops: "When we have a population that can be used in our defense, I, for one, will call forward that population to ward off tyranny and oppression. If the negro can be used to secure independence, I shall not hesitate about bringing him forward." A Confederate offer of freedom along with the shared southern heritage, the senator argued, would cement the relationship between black and white Confederate troops: "If freedom is offered to the negro he will fight for us with more alacrity than he now does under the persuasions, threats, and punishments inflicted by unfeeling Yankee soldiers." Even as he conceded that the slave desired his freedom, Henry reached a fantastic conclusion about the remainder of the slave population: "I would not free their families; for what sort of freedom would that be which would entail upon the negro the care of his wife and three or four children without the means by which to support them?... In fact he would beg you to take back his wife and children and support them for him." If Henry was speaking of caring for the soldiers' families during the war, then the statement makes some sense. Many white soldiers expected their wealthy neighbors to provide aid to their families while they were in the army. If, as it appears, Henry believed that slaves would fight for the enslavement of their wives and children, he understood very little about the reasons southern soldiers fought. To many whites in the Army of Northern Virginia, maintaining their own liberty and that of their families was their primary reason for enduring the hardships of the trenches. Lee suffered from desertion in early 1865 not because the men could not stand the trenches, but because Sherman was threatening the things they held most dear.[3] Any thoughtful observers would have recognized that black

---

[2] John B. Jones, *A Rebel War Clerk's Diary,* ed. Early S. Miers (Baton Rouge: Louisiana State University Press, 1958) 495; McPherson, *Battle Cry of Freedom,* 821.

[3] "Mass Meeting at the African Church—Additional Details," *Richmond Enquirer,* 13 February 1865, 2.

soldiers would have had similar attitudes. Although seriously flawed in its conception of why men fought, Henry's public expression of support for arming the slaves fit well with the administration's desire to bring the issue to a decision.

As a response to the failure in the Senate of Brown's proposal to arm slaves, Benjamin wrote Lee outlining his strategy to gain approval for black soldiers: "At the public meeting on Thursday...I proposed that those slaves only who might volunteer to fight for their freedom should be at once sent to the trenches." Despite a warm reception at the meeting, the secretary acknowledged that many hesitated to agree to such a step because they feared the reaction of the troops in the field: "Some of the opponents of the measure are producing a strong impression against it by asserting that it would disband the army by reason of the violent aversion of the troops to have negroes in the field with them." A clear statement of support from the army, the secretary suggested, would disarm the congressional opponents of black troops: "If we could get from the army an expression of its desire to be re-enforced [sic] by such negroes as for the boon of freedom will volunteer to go to the front, the measure will pass without further delay, and we may yet be able to give you such a force as will enable you to assume the offensive." Benjamin perceived that congressmen would find it increasingly difficult to turn down requests from not only general officers but also the individual white soldiers in the ranks. Appeals from non-slaveholding soldiers had the potential to make the politically powerful slaveholders in Congress appear quite selfish and unpatriotic. Interestingly, the secretary did not request for Lee to make a public statement. Further, Benjamin's plan demonstrated the centrality of the army in the formation of Confederate identity. To many southerners, the Confederate army was a far better reflection of the new nation than its elected government. Only with the army speaking strongly for the measure could the administration hope to gain a congressional majority for a bill to arm the slaves.[4]

Benjamin and Lee need not have worried about spurring the soldiers to call for black reinforcements. The failure of the peace conference and the daunting campaign ahead led many soldiers to hold unit meetings and express their views in resolutions that were then submitted to Congress and

---

[4] *Official Records*, Series 1, Vol. 46, Part 2, 1229.

the newspapers. Unlike former communications sent by individuals, the letters published in February often were signed by numerous soldiers. Three days prior to Benjamin's letter to Lee, a letter from a unit stationed at Petersburg appeared in the *Richmond Enquirer*. "A small experiment," the soldiers argued, "with three thousand negroes will help us more than all the acts of Congress combined, and…if the thing be properly done, we will soon hear no more about the negro being unfit for a soldier." Further, the writers chastised Congressman Thomas Gholson for saying that arming slaves would add little to the army's strength since only 300,000 slaves fell within the age parameters. "If we bring out 100,000," they astutely noted, "it will make the work of recruiting in the North still more difficult, and will accomplish our success." These soldiers understood that if even one third of the military-age male slaves could be placed in the Confederate army, it would significantly reduce the South's manpower deficit. Unlike the congressman, these veterans had come to accept the idea that the slaves would fight for one side or the other. Disheartened by planters who appeared more interested in maintaining slavery than the cause of independence, the soldiers called on the members of Congress to demonstrate their commitment to the cause: "Let us see that the cause is more precious than the negroes or their wealth; that everything will be given to support it, and we will fight with the assurance that if we fall it will be in the discharge of the loftiest social duty." On the other hand, a war that did not involve the quest for national existence, the soldiers declared, "is not worth the life of any mule that has perished in the war."[5]

A week later the enlisted men of an Alabama unit met in Petersburg and called for black assistance: "We the undersigned, soldiers of the 15th regiment, Alabama volunteers…believe the time has come for the arming and putting into the Confederate States service two hundred thousand…negroes." The resolutions forwarded to the *Enquirer* contained the signatures of 143 of the 200 men in the unit. Officers had not attended the meeting and, therefore, could not have influenced the ideas of the rank and file, as some opponents of the use of black soldiers had previously asserted. In an accompanying cover letter, the unit's commander noted the strong convictions of his men: "Some of the Congressmen seem to be very tender-

[5] "The following letter…," *Richmond Enquirer*, 8 February 1865, 2.

footed on this point, but I think here is evidence that at least one regiment means political independence at any price." The *Enquirer* endorsed the sincerity of the Alabamians in a closing comment: "Here is a regiment in earnest, and which means 'independence,' and which will not permit any question of taste or *smell* either to stand between them and freedom." Worn down by years of service, many Confederate soldiers saw the black reinforcements as their best hope for a successful conclusion of the contest.[6]

Resolutions from similar meetings appeared in the other Richmond papers, but on occasion, the editors tailored the letters to fit their own purposes. For instance, on 11 February, the *Richmond Examiner* printed portions of resolutions submitted by two units. Interestingly, in neither set of resolutions as printed in the *Examiner* does the idea of arming slaves appear. In his introduction, the editor acknowledged that he had omitted some resolutions: "We have had to abridge the proceedings of all the meetings, but give below the principal resolutions." Even as the paper abridged the resolutions, it managed to find the space to give the name and regiment of the committee members and the exact location of the unit. The appearance of a letter from a lone soldier in Wise's Brigade also suggested that the *Examiner* was "pruning" unacceptable ideas rather than conserving space. This Virginian wanted to ensure that his oppositional stance toward black troops had been noted: "I voted against the adoption of the negro clause altogether, and voted with others against making it unanimous." The author closed his note by proclaiming the "RIGHT OF PROPERTY THE BASIS OF INDEPENDENCE." On 18 February, the *Examiner* allowed the full text of resolutions approved by Thomas's Brigade to appear. The final statement of the Georgians must have chilled the paper's editor: "When, in the opinion of President Davis and General R.E. Lee, it shall become necessary to arm a portion or all of the slaves capable of bearing arms, and make soldiers of them, we will accept it as a necessity and cheerfully acquiesce, preferring, as we do, any and all sacrifices to subjugation." As resolutions from military units continued to pour into the paper's office, the *Examiner* had difficulty finding units that supported the paper's opposition to black troops.[7]

---

[6] "The opinion of the soldiers…," *Richmond Enquirer*, 21 February 1865, 2.

[7] "Spirit of the Army," *Richmond Examiner*, 11 February 1865, 2; "Camp Wise's Brigade," *Richmond Examiner*, 11 February 1865, 2; "Thomas' Brigade," *Richmond Examiner*, 18 February 1865, 2.

The *Richmond Sentinel* also published numerous letters from soldiers in the field. For instance, on 21 February the *Sentinel* printed the resolutions of Davis's Brigade, which spoke almost exclusively to the slave-soldier issue. First, the Mississippians declared their support for congressional efforts to arm the slaves. Second, the troops stressed the necessity to arm negroes and reassured the nation that the army would approve the radical step: "It will create no dissatisfaction in our ranks, but will be hailed as an evidence that everything will be subordinated to the interest of the cause." Finally, the soldiers challenged their state government to prepare to field black troops just in case the measure failed in Congress: "We respectfully request the Legislature of our State to raise, arm and equip, one or more negro brigades, and place them in active service." Noting the receipt of letters from units originating in Texas, Mississippi, Kentucky, Georgia, South Carolina, and Virginia, the *Sentinel* admitted some surprise at the depth of commitment expressed in the letters from the trenches: "The gallant men who are bearing the...burden of the day in the trenches, and who are confronted by long lines of dusky soldiers, are calling upon Congress to send them similar material to oppose that which the enemy is employing against them." In the crush of meetings, Second Corps commander John B. Gordon wrote to Lee to inform the general of his command's view of slave-soldiers: "The officers and men of this corps are decidedly in favor of the voluntary enlistment of the negroes as soldiers...The opposition to it is now confined to a very few, and I am satisfied will soon cease to exist in any regiment of the corps." Clearly, Confederate units were undergoing patriotic revivals in response to the failure of the peace conference and, therefore, produced a series of calls for the introduction of black men into the Confederate army.[8]

As units met and espoused arming the slaves in February, southerners again turned to military leaders like Lee and Joseph E. Johnston, not only for military deliverance but also for guidance on the role of the slave in the war effort. Although unwilling to arm the slaves prior to the Hampton Roads Conference, Joe Johnston changed his mind as he prepared once again to take the field against Sherman. On 12 February, only nine days af-

[8] "Negro Troops—A Voice from Mississippi Soldiers," *Richmond Sentinel*, 21 February 1865, 2; "Voice of the Army and of the People," *Richmond Sentinel*, 23 February 1865, 2; *Official Records*, Series 1, Vol. 51, Part 2, 1063.

ter denouncing the idea of slave-soldiers, Johnston again wrote Senator Louis T. Wigfall and betrayed his change of heart: "But don't let us be subjugated. Even should emancipation be necessary to prevent it." Of greater popular interest, on 23 February the *Richmond Sentinel* published a letter from the new General-in-Chief strongly advocating arming the slaves. "I think the measure," Lee affirmed, "not only expedient, but necessary...I do not think that our white population can supply the necessities of a long war without overtaxing its capacity and imposing great suffering." The release of his letter to Ethelbert Barksdale confirmed the views attributed to Lee after his exchange of letters with Hunter and stressed the importance of freedom to attain effective soldiers: "Those who are employed should be freed. It would be neither just nor wise, in my opinion, to require them to remain slaves." Under good officers, Lee argued, they will become efficient soldiers: "They possess all the physical qualifications, and their habits of obedience constitute a good foundation for discipline." The Virginia papers also published portions of a letter from Lee to William P. Miles. The commander ignored the theoretical issues and echoed the standard administration argument: "We must use the negroes on our side, or the enemy will use them against us." Each slave that joined the Union army, Lee reasoned, was a double loss to the Confederacy because the South lost a laborer, but, at the same time, the North added to its numerical advantage on the battlefield. This process of removing labor as they filled the blue ranks, the general contended, had been used "with great help to our adversaries and to our great disadvantage." With Johnston renouncing his previous conservative stance and the publication of the powerful letters from Lee on the subject, few could question the support for black troops in the Confederate army.[9]

As military units bombarded Congress with resolutions of support for arming slaves, the bill to provide 40,000 slave laborers for the army remained stuck in committee. If the congressmen chose to omit the emancipation feature, the bill in question would have sparked little controversy as it simply raised the manning levels from the act of February 1864. Yet, upon assum-

---

[9] Gilbert E. Govan and James W. Livingood, *A Different Valor* (New York: Konecky and Konecky, 1956) 339–40; "Employment of Negro Soldiers," *Richmond Sentinel*, 23 February 1865, 2; "General Lee on Arming the Negroes," *Lynchburg Virginian*, 24 February 1865, 2.

ing the position of Secretary of War in February 1865, John C. Breckinridge was informed by Jeremy F. Gilmer, the Confederacy's chief engineer and, thus, de facto head of the slave labor units, that the year-old slave laborer act had never fully gone into effect. "Up to this time the number of slaves impressed by conscript officers and delivered for organization is small. ... A better and more permanent organization of negro labor is demanded for military and civil engineer service." Subsequently, Gilmer devised a structure for the black labor battalions that closely resembled an infantry battalion of eight companies. Despite considerable potential, the measures passed by Congress to provide permanent laborers never met expectations. Planters preferred the old system of short-term impressments to the semi-permanent slave laborer envisioned by Congress.[10]

Although the bill providing for 20,000 laborers had not worked well, Congress again enacted legislation to conscript free black males and to impress slaves to perform duties as engineers, cooks, teamsters, and other menial tasks. The bill as approved did not provide for the purchase or manumission of the laborers, as the president had requested. Yet, the bill for 40,000 laborers was not signed by Davis until 28 February 1865. A number of factors probably slowed the bill's transit through Congress. Primarily, it was shoved aside as the legislators discussed the more provocative measures that envisioned the same men, but carrying rifles rather than shovels. This act was a triumph for neither side. The proponents of arming slaves believed the slave laborer bill without importance, and the opponents of black troops considered the measure an entering wedge for the larger scheme. Despite the apathy shown toward the measure in Congress, on 14 March Governor William Smith of Virginia called for ten percent of all the state's slaves in order to fill the state's quota. The "sternest necessity," Smith affirmed, demanded the sacrifice.[11]

On 15 February, Ethelbert Barksdale reported the more controversial bill to employ slaves as soldiers to the House and formally recommended passage. Military Committee Chair William Miles asked and received per-

---

[10] *Official Records*, Series 4, Vol. 3, 1084–86; James H. Brewer, *The Confederate Negro: Virginia's Craftsmen and Military Laborers, 1861–1865* (Durham, NC: Duke University Press, 1969) 163.

[11] *Official Records*, Series 4, Vol. 3, 1114–17, 1138–39.

mission to print a minority report from the committee. Over the next several days, proponents and opponents of arming slaves jousted in secret session. Finally, on 20 February the Confederate House passed a bill authorizing the president to call on the states for a "quota of three hundred thousand troops...to be raised from such classes of the population, irrespective of color, in each State as the proper authorities thereof may determine." Although far less than Davis and his comrades would have liked, they had won a narrow victory by a vote of forty to thirty-seven. In the Senate, the bill's prospects appeared much slimmer. On 15 February, Williamson Oldham of Texas introduced a bill to arm 200,000 slaves, inaugurating ten days of intense debate. Albert G. Brown of Mississippi, Henry Burnett of Kentucky, and Oldham tried to rally support for the bill, while Augustus Maxwell of Florida, James Orr of South Carolina, and Louis T. Wigfall of Texas attempted to derail the proposal. After considerable sparring, the Senate voted the measure down by a vote of eleven to ten on 24 February. The *Lynchburg Virginian* decried the negative votes of the two Virginia senators: "Messrs. Hunter and Caperton, voted against the negro bill—against giving Gen. Lee more soldiers! These gentlemen will find ere long that they mis-represented [sic] Virginia upon the subject." While opponents of black troops trumpeted the bill's defeat, the friends of the measure regrouped.[12]

In the final stages of the Senate debate, the *Richmond Sentinel* pronounced Virginia unified on the need to arm slaves: "We believe that never before has there been, in favor of any important measure, so united and so anxious a state of the public mind as that which we are now witnessing. This clear unmistakable and emphatic popular will, the Senate is disappointing." Pointing to Lee's clarion call for black troops, the *Sentinel* argued strongly that no one should contest the general's assessment of the needs of the country. Military necessity and the firm conviction that the Union army would enlist all those that the South did not, undergirded the paper's position: "The Yankees have determined that the negro play a part in the great drama

---

[12] "Congressional," *Lynchburg Virginian*, 14 February 1865, 2; "Congressional," *Lynchburg Virginian*, 15 February 1865, 2; "A Bill to Provide for Raising 200,000 Negro Troops," *Lynchburg Virginian*, 15 February 1865, 2; "Defeat of the Negro Bill," *Lynchburg Virginian*, 25 February 1865, 2; "Our Virginia Senator...," *Lynchburg Virginian*, 25 February 1865, 1.

on one side or the other, and it will be the consummation of folly if we permit him to play it against us."[13]

On the other side of the issue, the *Richmond Examiner* sought desperately to nullify the influence of Lee and the army in the congressional debate. On 16 February the *Examiner* acknowledged the impact of Lincoln's ultimatum demanding reunion on slave-soldier discussions: "The idea of employing negroes to help in the defence [sic] of their homes, has greatly ripened in the publick [sic] mind." Editor John Daniel stuck to the logic behind pro-slavery thought even as he conceded that no one could deny Lee's request. The offer of freedom in return for faithful service, Daniel believed, placed southerners in a morally reprehensible position: "They [slaves] think it a boon and a blessing; they will deem it a reward, and will give more zealous and faithful service in the hope of it...This...is also abolition;...because it would be abandonment of the negro race in this country to misery and eventual extirpation." Even as the *Examiner* washed its hands of the emancipated slave, the paper admitted that the needs of the spring campaign and the calls of Lee could be met in no other way. On 25 February, the *Examiner* argued that while Lee might have a privileged position concerning questions of military necessity, he held no such place in reference to the moral, political, and social issues raised by arming slaves. "Those Senators," Daniel contended, "who hold that it would be a cruel injury, both to white and black, to sever their present relation of master and slave...and is at war with the first principles of this relation...those Senators are undoubtedly right." Based on Lee's advocacy of freedom for the black veterans, Daniel placed the general's character into question and confessed having some "doubt whether he is what used to be called a 'good Southerner.'" Forced by military circumstances and overwhelming popular support for black troops to come to grips with the idea, the *Examiner*'s editor accepted the practical considerations that demanded arming slaves, but steadfastly resisted all arguments that contended that the step was morally acceptable.[14]

With the bill to arm the slaves hanging in the balance, the Virginia legislature intervened and tipped the balance. In a series of resolutions adopted

[13] "Voice of the Army and of the People," *Richmond Sentinel*, 23 February 1865, 1; "The question of employing negroes...," *Richmond Examiner*, 25 February 1865, 1.

[14] "The idea of employing negroes...," *Richmond Examiner*, 16 February 1865, 2.

on 4 March, the House of Delegates authorized the Confederate government to call upon Virginia for all of her free blacks and up to twenty-five percent of her slave population. Further, the legislators instructed the state's two senators to change their votes: "Our senators are hereby instructed and our representatives requested to vote for the passage of a law to place at the disposal of the Confederate authorities as many of the male slaves…as he [Lee] shall deem best." To make their meaning completely beyond doubt, the legislators continued, "Nothing in the foregoing shall be construed into a restriction…or a prohibition to the employment of the slaves…as soldiers or otherwise, as the General-in-Chief may deem most expedient." Even before the Senate could again address the issue, on 6 March the House of Delegates passed a bill making it lawful for blacks in the army to bear arms and carry ammunition in all areas of Virginia. Unlike the state's senators, the Virginia legislature vigorously pursued the enrollment of black troops into the Confederate army. With every constituency in the state either overrun or under severe threat, these bold and desperate Virginians were seizing the only means they had remaining.[15]

The citizens of Southwest Virginia became fully engaged in the debate over arming the slaves during the last phase. Two men running for election to the House of Delegates wrote letters to the paper voicing their support for black troops. Ironically, in light of public opinion in Virginia and Texas, Williamson Oldham of Texas and not one of the Virginia representatives introduced the bill to arm the slaves in the Senate. After the measure failed in the Senate on 25 February, the *Lynchburg Virginian* highlighted the efforts in the House of Delegates to force R.M.T. Hunter and Allen Caperton to change their votes. After the Senate reversed itself on 8 March, the Lynchburg paper chronicled the efforts of J.W. Pegram and Thomas Turner to enlist black troops in Central Virginia.[16]

---

[15] *Official Records*, Series 1, Vol. 51, Part 2, 1068; *Official Records*, Series 1, Vol. 46, Part 3, 1315.

[16] "Employment of Negro Soldiers," *Lynchburg Virginian*, 25 February 1865, 1; "To the Voters of Campbell and Lynchburg," *Lynchburg Virginian*, 18 March 1865, 2; "To the Voters of Campbell and Lynchburg," *Lynchburg Virginian*, 21 March 1865, 2; "A Bill to Provide for Raising 200,000 Negro Troops," *Lynchburg Virginian*, 15 February 1865, 2; "Instructions to Our Senators," *Lynchburg Virginian*, 1 March 1865, 2; "Putting Negroes in the Army," *Lynchburg Virginian*, 2 March 1865, 1; "A Generous Offer," *Lynch-*

From his editorial desk, Charles Button lamented the slow pace of congressional action: "We cannot but regret, and regret deeply, that the measure was not adopted months ago, so that the army might by this time be enjoying the benefit of the recruits." Congress's omission of the emancipation feature also troubled the editor: "It will devolve upon the patriotic slave-holders themselves to supply…an undoubted evidence of their freedom, conditioned upon their rendering faithful service." Looking over some old clippings, Button suggested that southern trepidation about placing men in the ranks resembled that expressed in northern journals as the first black units entered the Union army.[17] A strong proponent of black soldiers, Button lamented the lack of courage expressed in the Congressional act but must have taken considerable pride in how Lynchburg and Southwest Virginia as a whole responded to the idea of black assistance.

The citizens of Roanoke, Campbell, and Bedford Counties and the city of Lynchburg held public meetings to discuss the situation of the nation after the Hampton Roads Conference. Each gathering noted the support of Lee for black troops and passed a resolution calling for the measure's immediate adoption. The wording of the resolutions adopted in Roanoke County demonstrated well the sincerity of these men and women as well as the sharp differences that remained:

> While there have been differences of opinion amongst us as to the necessity and policy of enlisting a portion of our slaves in the army…and whether with or without changing the social status of the slaves, yet holding our independence to be paramount…we compromise all differences of opinion and urge…the immediate adoption of some plan to put as many slaves in the army as the Commander-in-Chief may deem necessary.

Obviously, the citizens of the Roanoke Valley had struggled with the issue of arming but, particularly, freeing the slaves. While military necessity must have played a key role in the debate in southwestern Virginia, the Union threat had not caused them to unthinkingly accept radical steps. In the

---

burg Virginian, 23 March 1865, 2; "Colored Troops," *Lynchburg Virginian*, 18 March 1865, 1.

[17] Charles Button, "The Negro Bill," *Lynchburg Virginian*, 8 March 1865, 1; Charles Button, "The important message…," *Lynchburg Virginian*, 20 February 1865, 1; Charles Button, "In looking over…," *Lynchburg Virginian*, 16 March 1865, 1.

wake of Congressional approval, on 23 and 24 March the *Virginian* published the names of thirty slave owners offering to free their slaves to give them to the cause.[18] After considerable soul-searching in January, the citizens of Lynchburg embraced the idea of black troops during the third phase of the debate and attempted to put it into practice in the waning days of the Confederacy.

A similar transformation occurred in the Shenandoah Valley. Although the editor had warned his readers against "building castles in the air," the *Staunton Vindicator* lashed out at Abraham Lincoln when he learned of the failure of the Hampton Roads peace conference: "In the name of God, Liberty, and the heritage of our children, let us put our foot upon croakers and meet the emergency like men…Mr. Lincoln has made his ultimatum—utter submission or extinction…we will die or be free." In response to the crisis, on 27 February the citizens of Augusta County met in a public meeting in Staunton. After some discussion, the gathering adopted a series of patriotic resolutions in which they proclaimed their willingness "to lay our all if need be upon the altar of our country." The ninth and final resolution proved the most difficult:

> That whilst some of our fellow citizens opposed the arming of our negroes, we are content with the knowledge that we have the sanction of God for using all the means in our power…and if this means of resistance be deemed necessary and available by such men as President Davis and by Gen. Robt. E. Lee, we shall not stop to discuss abstract questions, but will cheerfully give our servants, as we have our sons to our country.

Surely, this difficult decision demonstrated the resolve of the citizens of the upper Shenandoah Valley to continue to resist. Patriotic words are often hollow, but the meeting also collected over 7,000 pounds of meat, 135 bar-

---

[18] "G.W.D.," "Campbell County," *Lynchburg Virginian*, 21 February 1865, 2; P.H. Huff, "At a meeting of the citizens of Roanoke County…," *Lynchburg Virginian*, 25 February 1865, 2; Jno. Speed, "War Meeting in Lynchburg," *Lynchburg Virginian*, 2 March 1865, 2; "G.W.D.," "At a meeting of the citizens of Bedford county…," *Lynchburg Virginian*, 8 March 1865, 2; "The Right Spirit," *Lynchburg Virginian*, 21 March 1865, 1; "The People of Roanoke…," *Lynchburg Virginian*, 23 March 1865, 1; "The Right Spirit," *Lynchburg Virginian*, 24 March 1865, 1.

rels of flour, and $115,000 in Confederate securities.[19] In a time of great scarcity, this appears an eloquent demonstration of Confederate unity.

In Harrisonburg, John Wartmann found himself caught up in the euphoria of the peace conference, declaring that "glad tidings of great joy" would soon ring out. The following week, on 10 February, he could not hide his disappointment: "God only knows how anxious our people were for Peace; he alone knows how resolute and determined they are to secure their independence, or to perish in the attempt." "One more supreme effort," he assured his readers, would be all it would take to finish the race. The Harrisonburg editor, if not his readers, was at the point of his final efforts. On 20 February, Colonel Peter Roller took the chair at a public meeting in Rockingham County. After an endorsement of the "States' Rights" principles that precipitated secession, the meeting addressed the difficult issue of filling the gray ranks. Predictably, they called on all able-bodied white men to enter the military immediately. Then, they approved a highly equivocal resolution:

> Whilst, we do not endorse the policy or believe in the efficacy of putting negroes in the armies of the Confederate States as soldiers with guns in their hands, we will cheerfully acquiesce with any policy in regard to the disposition of these negroes which the Confederate Congress shall see fit to adopt—agreeing to take any and all chances in preference to bending the knee to the iron will of Yankee despotism.

There was considerable reservation in the Rockingham County resolution about arming slaves absent in the meetings in the Roanoke Valley and in Staunton. Had the residents of Harrisonburg seen more of Sheridan and of the Union army and, therefore, considered the contest over? Possibly the frequent occupations of Harrisonburg by the Federal soldiers led the residents to fear disorder more than the citizens living near Lynchburg. After the evacuation of Petersburg and Richmond, Wartmann pleaded with his readers to maintain order: "Above all, it becomes us to frown down and repress all efforts to create social disorder. Let us show to the world that we can bear disasters and sad misfortunes with a noble and cheerful grace."[20]

---

[19] S.M. Yost, "Commissioners to Washington," *Staunton Vindicator*, 3 February 1865, 2; S.M. Yost, "Our readers may remember…," *Staunton Vindicator*, 24 February 1865, 2; S.M. Yost, "Public Meeting," *Staunton Vindicator*, 24 March 1865, 1.

[20] John H. Wartmann, "Good News," *Rockingham Register*, 3 February 1865, 2; John H. Wartmann, "No Peace!", *Rockingham Register*, 10 February 1865, 2; John H.

Public meetings like those in Rockingham, Augusta, Campbell, Roanoke, and Bedford Counties provide one of the clearest reflections of mass sentiment concerning the slave-soldier debate in Virginia. Local officials chaired such meetings, but common citizens participated in the discussions and were called upon to make monetary and other donations to prove their resolve. The meat and flour offered to the Nation by the citizens of Augusta County had significant value in the 1865 marketplace and potentially might have served as an insurance policy against approaching Confederate defeat. The provisions offered were clear proof of continued commitment to the southern cause in a time of tremendous scarcity in the Valley. While postwar chroniclers may dismiss these sacrifices, no one who had felt Sheridan's wrath and known the hard winter of 1865 would have made such a judgment.[21]

On 13 March, Jefferson Davis signed into law "An Act to Increase the Military Force of the Confederate States," marking a radical shift in the Confederate revolution. The bill authorized the president "to ask for and accept from the owners of slaves, the services of such number of able-bodied negro men as he may deem expedient...to perform military service in whatever capacity he may direct." The measure further stipulated that the new soldier was to receive equal clothing, rations, and pay with the white soldiers in the same branch of service. The final section of the act struck a powerful blow at the effort to fill the Confederate army with black recruits: "Nothing in this act shall be construed to authorize a change in the relation which the said slave shall bear toward their owners, except by the consent of the owners and of the States in which they may reside and in pursuance of the laws thereof." The Confederate Congress had agreed to arm the slaves but refused to take the step all who discussed the issue seriously considered essential. With white men deserting at a rate of one hundred per night in February and March 1865, who could have expected slaves to be driven into battle with the whip? In short, the Confederate Congress had adopted a compromise that pleased no one. Opponents of the measure had been forced by

Wartmann, "Meeting in Rockingham," *Rockingham Register*, 24 February 1865, 2; John H. Wartmann, "Richmond and Petersburg Evacuated," *Rockingham Register*, 7 April 1865, 2.

[21] William Blair, *Virginia's Private War* (New York: Oxford University Press, 1998) 132.

popular sentiment to allow black men into the gray ranks. Even with the final provision, thoughtful men understood that the institution could never be the same. Warfare taught too many skills and ideas that were incompatible with servitude. On the other hand, advocates of black Confederate troops had been unable to gain a majority in either house of Congress to approve emancipation. They knew that no intelligent man would fight to continue his own servitude and that of his family, if by simply changing sides he could run the same risks but gain freedom for both himself and his family. As soon as the measure was approved, Davis, Benjamin, Lee, and others began looking for ways to work around the emancipation issue.

After signing the bill to arm the slaves, Davis immediately wrote General Lee asking for suggestions on ways to make the law, as passed, effective. Acting quickly, on 15 March, Lee selected J.W. Pegram and Thomas P. Turner to raise the first unit and issued orders for them to begin recruiting. Unprepared for large numbers of new recruits, the Confederate army scrambled to open camps of instruction. A month prior, J.T.L. Preston, acting superintendent at the Virginia Military Institute, had offered the services of the cadets to assist in the fielding of black troops: "In the event of the troops being raised you might command the services of our corps of cadets with their officers to perform the work of organization and drilling in the shortest time and with the greatest efficiency." The cadets had trained the initial southern armies in 1861 and now stood poised to repeat the process. Finally, on 23 March the Secretary of War published regulations governing the enlistment of slaves. In the middle of mundane policies on where the new troops should assemble and what types of units should be formed, Davis and Lee inserted their own limited emancipation regulation: "No slave will be accepted as a recruit unless with his own consent and with the approbation of his master by a written instrument conferring as far as he may, the rights of a freedman, and which will be filed with the superintendent." In this manner the army would create a contract between the black soldier and the government that offered freedom to one and loyal soldiers to the other. If the Confederate effort to arm slaves were to have any chance of success, this emancipation regulation was essential.[22]

[22] *Official Records*, Series 4, Vol. 3, 1093, 1144, 1161, 1308.

In the final six months of the Civil War, Virginians grappled with racial issues that had lain dormant for decades as they struggled to define a new role for the slave in the war effort. While military circumstances served as catalysts, army leaders and common soldiers played key roles in the larger debate over the course of civilian society. Letters from the soldiers in the trenches at Petersburg and those deployed in the Shenandoah Valley illustrated the deep commitment of those still in the ranks and painted a clear picture of the problems faced. Their powerful appeals for black reinforcements underscored the transition within Confederate society itself from slavery and independence as war aims to independence alone. Immediately after the failure of the peace conference, Davis, Benjamin, and Lee took bold steps to energize the debate over arming slaves. Confederate leaders repeatedly told Virginians that the slaves would enter the war on one side or the other and challenged them to risk letting go of slavery so they could hold onto independence.

The citizens of Virginia observed the destruction all about them and over time their attitudes on a number of topics, including slavery, shifted. Even John Daniel at the *Richmond Examiner* grudgingly accepted the fact that black men would wear Confederate gray. After the Hampton Roads Conference, Virginians readily accepted the need to arm slaves, but many differences remained concerning the role of the black veteran in the post-war South. Lee's public support for black soldiers proved essential as he reassured many whites that one could support radical modifications of slavery and still be a good southerner. Unfortunately for the advocates of black troops, Lee's ideas, the appeals of the soldiers, and the brave comments of the slave owners in Lynchburg were unable to move the Confederate Congress sufficiently so that a clear emancipation promise could be made to the prospective soldiers. Yet, based on the letters from military units, the public meetings in the Roanoke and Shenandoah Valleys, and the actions of individual slave owners who offered their slaves to the cause, the vast majority of Virginians had seen their values transformed by the war. These Virginians had felt the full force of the war and discovered that slavery had become much easier to sacrifice than independence.

9

All for Independence

On 3 February 1865 the three Confederate commissioners, Vice President Alexander Stephens, Judge John A. Campbell, and Senator Robert M.T. Hunter, rode slowly back from the failed peace conference at Hampton Roads and into the southern lines at Petersburg. With the commissioners' return, all realistic hope for a negotiated settlement to the war ended. With Lincoln offering no terms except submission and reunion, the unsuccessful peace initiative quieted many of the Davis administration's critics and reenergized the efforts to fill the gray ranks. Black soldiers provided the only viable option remaining for the Confederacy. Without hope for foreign intervention or a negotiated peace, southerners had to choose between slavery and independence.

The final phase of the debate to arm the slaves began on 9 February with the publication of Secretary of State Judah P. Benjamin's speech that demanded passage of the bill to arm the slaves.[1] Meanwhile, in Georgia, Governor Joseph E. Brown addressed a special session of the legislature in Macon on 17 February and stoutly declared that black soldiers would not fight for the South: "We cannot expect them if they remain with us, to perform deeds of heroic valor when they are fighting to continue the enslavement of their wives and children."[2] Although Brown realized that partial emancipation would not work, he could not imagine the South abandoning the institution of slavery altogether: "It is said we should give them their freedom in case of their fidelity;...that we should give up slavery, as well as our personal liberty and State sovereignty, for independence. ... If we are ready to give up slavery, I am satisfied we can make...a better trade."[3] Many

[1] "Secretary of State Benjamin's Message," *Macon Telegraph and Confederate*, 21 February 1865, 2.

[2] "Governor's Message," *Macon Telegraph and Confederate*, 18 February 1865, 1.

[3] Ibid.

in the audience strongly disagreed with Brown. As one soldier in the hall confided to his diary: "Governor Brown's message…was a tirade of abuse and personalities unworthy of a statesman. … My opinion is that the Governor is an ambitious demagogue who is willing to destroy his country in order to accomplish his wicked and seditious purposes."[4] Even Henry Flash, the editor of the *Macon Telegraph and Confederate*, decried the bitterness of the governor's message and his unwillingness to make additional sacrifices for the cause. Brown's comments stood nearly alone in Georgia in their dogged defense of slavery. From Benjamin's and Brown's speeches to final passage of the act to arm the slaves on 13 March, the debate raged ferociously as Congress and the people attempted to determine the sacrifices necessary to preserve the southern way of life.

Benjamin's speech, Brown's message, and the failure of the Hampton Roads Conference forced many in the Confederacy, including the citizens of Central Georgia, to take sides on this most divisive issue. On 15 February the *Macon Telegraph and Confederate* published part of a letter from the new General-in-Chief, Robert E. Lee, strongly advocating arming the slaves. "I am," Lee affirmed, "favorable to the use of our servants in the army. … I would hold out to them the certainty of freedom and a home, when they shall have rendered efficient service."[5] Other news items from the army also advocated the enlistment of black soldiers. On 1 March the *Telegraph and Confederate* noted initial efforts in Virginia to organize black volunteer companies from the slaves working for the army.[6] Although ignoring this development editorially, this Macon paper again mentioned these black units in Virginia later in the month.[7] In addition, several news items expressed impatience with congressional wrangling on the issue. For example, on 2 March the *Telegraph and Confederate* reprinted a powerful editorial from Mobile decrying Congressional hesitation: "If but Congress had the manhood of the army—if it faithfully reflected the fearless patriotism of the country—it

---

[4] Thomas Key and Robert Campbell, *Two Soldiers: The Campaign Diaries of Thomas J. Key, C.S.A. and Robert J. Campbell, U.S.A.*, ed. Wirt A. Cate (Chapel Hill: University of North Carolina Press, 1938) 193–94.

[5] "Conversation with Confederate Leaders," *Macon Telegraph and Confederate*, 15 February 1865, 1.

[6] "From Richmond," *Macon Telegraph and Confederate*, 1 March 1865, 2.

[7] "From Richmond," *Macon Telegraph and Confederate*, 29 March 1865, 1.

would authorize a negro army of 200,000 men."[8] The news items appearing in the *Telegraph and Confederate* in February and March reflected growing support for radical measures.

Although the *Telegraph and Confederate*'s chief rival, the *Southern Confederacy*, ceased publication in early February, the *Christian Index* provided extended coverage of the slavery debate in Macon. On 16 February the *Index* reprinted an editorial from the *Confederate Baptist* arguing that all must be sacrificed for independence: "Suppose that the crisis may demand emancipation. Let it come. Anything short of submission...may be tolerated; and we had better give up slavery than submit to reconstruction."[9] As support for black troops continued to rise, on 9 March the *Index*'s editor, Samuel Boykin, noted the Virginia legislature's adoption of measures to arm the slaves and called for similar measures in Georgia: "We want independence. We want freedom from Yankee rule. ... To accomplish these objects, we are ready for any sacrifice."[10] Finally, on 16 March the *Index* reported General Lee's support for black troops and his recommendation of the promise of freedom and land for faithful service.[11] As the prominent leaders of the South addressed the issue, Brown's opposition appeared less relevant and a wave of support for slave-soldiers confronted the Macon editors.

Despite the tide of news reports and letters to the editor supporting the proposition, Henry Flash, the editor of the *Macon Telegraph and Confederate*, continued to refuse to accept the idea of arming the slaves and tried to ignore it. Attempting to show alternatives to black troops, Flash highly praised the replacement of white teamsters with slaves to drive the wagon trains of the rebuilt Army of Tennessee: "It places in active service in the field, a brigade of men who make better soldiers than teamsters, and furnishes the army with a large available material that is very effective."[12] Similarly, he lauded a speech of Senator Benjamin Hill of Georgia, who argued that deserters

---

[8] "Letter to the Editor—*Mobile Register*," *Macon Telegraph and Confederate*, 2 March 1865, 2.

[9] "Clippings from Our Exchanges," *Macon Christian Index*, 16 February 1865, 3.

[10] Samuel Boykin, "Notes on the Times," *Macon Christian Index*, 9 March 1865, 3.

[11] "Notes on the Times," *Macon Christian Index*, 16 March 1865, 3.

[12] Henry Flash, "The Wagon Train of the Army...," *Macon Telegraph and Confederate*, 15 February 1865, 2.

returning under Lee's amnesty order and 200,000 men who would soon lose their exemptions would fill the gray ranks.[13]

While eager to print wishful thinking that supported his position, Flash attempted to ignore the government's efforts to enlist slave-soldiers. On 15 March, the day word reached Macon that the bill placing slaves in the Confederate army had passed both houses of Congress, Flash printed only the barest note in the "Telegraphic" column and refused to editorially acknowledge its passage.[14] On 21 March, in a major editorial inappropriately titled "All Hands to the Pump," he called for all Georgians to exert themselves to the maximum: "Let every man put his shoulder to the wheel and go to work as though the fate of the contest depended upon his own individual exertions. ... Everyone, male and female, can do something in whatever sphere they may be placed, to help along the cause."[15] Neither in this editorial nor in any other instance up to the surrender of Lee's army did the editor of the *Macon Telegraph and Confederate* ever acknowledge the employment of black soldiers in the southern armies. Despite the stubborn opposition of Henry Flash, the citizens of Macon showed through their letters that he had lost touch with popular sentiment long before.

In contrast to the adamant opposition of Flash, editor Samuel Boykin of the *Christian Index* reflected the shift in local opinion toward arming the slaves. Upon learning of the failure of the peace conference, on 16 February, Boykin declared that victory would come only on the battlefield and that all talk of negotiations and conventions must end: "We have no alternative left us but to unite and fight on as long as there is a man left."[16] Continuing in this radical vein the following week, on 23 February, Boykin announced that he had changed his mind and now favored arming the slaves: "If this measure is really necessary to our success...we say, put the slaves into the army, but make them free men at the same time and give them an interest in the

[13] "Senator Hill's Message," *Macon Telegraph and Confederate*, 20 February 1865, 2.

[14] "Congressional," *Macon Telegraph and Confederate*, 15 March 1865, 2.

[15] Henry Flash, "All Hands to the Pumps," *Macon Telegraph and Confederate*, 21 March 1865, 2.

[16] Samuel Boykin, "Notes on the Times," *Macon Christian Index*, 16 February 1865, 3.

soil which they are called to defend."[17] By granting immediate freedom and land, Boykin argued, "You furnish them with a substantial motive to faithfulness."[18] Although astutely realizing that emancipated soldiers would deserve "all the rights and privileges of citizenship," Boykin declared that slavery and white supremacy must bow to the cause of independence: "Independence from their [northern] hated domination is the one great end of this revolution. Let that end be accomplished at all hazards."[19] From a forceful defense of slavery in November, Boykin had moved in January to curbing abuses of slavery, in particular, the disregard for slave marriages. Finally, as the situation deteriorated in February and March, Boykin had to choose between slavery and independence and shifted his position to advocate emancipation and citizenship for Georgia's black population.

After reading the text of Benjamin's speech, hearing Brown's remarks, and seeing the views of Lee, the citizens of Macon deluged the newspaper offices with letters to the editors strongly supporting arming the slaves. In a letter published in the *Telegraph and Confederate* on 24 February, a South Georgia planter argued that 150,000 armed slaves could prevent Yankee victory.[20] Discrediting those who accused the planters of creating a rich man's war and a poor man's fight, he offered his slaves to the cause: "I have three sons in the army, all under twenty years of age; and I have a few negroes within military age. The latter can go as freely and cheerfully as did the former, if the government will...open the way for their service."[21] Other letters appearing in the *Telegraph and Confederate*, like the one signed "Volunteer of '61," called for all men—both black and white—to rise up together and "make the enemy feel the horrors of war on his own soil."[22] In the only letter on the subject published in the *Christian Index*, "Vidette" echoed the letter writers of the *Telegraph and Confederate* and argued for black troops but against emancipation: "If there is a military necessity for our servants to help

[17] Samuel Boykin, "Notes on the Times," *Macon Christian Index*, 23 February 1865, 3.

[18] Ibid.

[19] Ibid.

[20] "Sire and Son," *Macon Telegraph and Confederate*, 24 February 1865, 2.

[21] Ibid.

[22] "Volunteer of '61," "Letter to the Editor," *Macon Telegraph and Confederate*, 27 February 1865, 1.

us by bearing arms…it might be well to act on the plan of old Abraham, that is make no big promise to free them."[23] Although a few still hoped to cling to some form of slavery, the vast majority in Macon favored arming the slaves and understood that the soldiers and their families must be freed in return. Proponents and opponents alike believed that this step meant the abandonment of the institution of slavery.

Along with the letters of individual support, many local groups held meetings and sent resolutions advocating arming the slaves to the *Macon Telegraph and Confederate*.[24] While the citizens of Troup County offered their slaves to the cause on 21 February, the meeting at Fort Valley produced a powerful argument for their support of the measure: "We are prepared whenever they shall ask it of us, to devote our slaves to the maintenance of a cause which is already rendered doubly dear by the blood of our kindred. Having freely given the white men, a decent self respect if nothing more, should induce us to as promptly offer the slave."[25] Finally, complementing the individual and group letters, on 22 February and 1 March the paper published letters from two Georgia brigades in the army of Northern Virginia stoutly calling for black recruits to join them.[26] These soldiers mirrored the determination and devotion evident in the resolutions from Fort Valley: "We call upon Congress to take the necessary steps for immediately placing…two hundred thousand negroes in the ranks. … We care not for the color of the arm that strikes the invader of our homes."[27] Judging from the letters written to the *Macon Telegraph and Confederate*, individual planters, local citizens groups, and Georgia soldiers all strongly supported arming the slaves. Despite the resolute opposition of Henry Flash, the citizens of Macon willingly accepted the black soldier, opting for southern independence rather than the institution of slavery.

Benjamin's address and the failure of the peace conference sparked renewed interest in Athens in the debate concerning arming the slaves. On 8

---

[23] "Vidette," "For the *Christian Index*," *Macon Christian Index*, 16 March 1865, 1.

[24] "Troup Meeting," *Macon Telegraph and Confederate*, 21 February 1865, 1.

[25] "Meeting at Fort Valley," *Macon Telegraph and Confederate*, 13 March 1865, 2.

[26] "Meeting of Thomas' Brigade," *Macon Telegraph and Confederate*, 22 February 1865, 2.

[27] "Meeting of Anderson's Brigade," *Macon Telegraph and Confederate*, 1 March 1865, 2.

March the *Southern Watchman* printed a speech given by Howell Cobb calling for all white men to come forward and do their duty: "What do we need?... We need an army, and food and clothing for them... We have still enough men left to win our independence; and when I speak of men, I mean white men."[28] Cobb claimed that slaves should provide the food and clothing while the white men fought on the battlefield. Yet, the steady tread of the Union columns drowned out Cobb's traditional arguments as reports of new southern defeats in the Carolinas continued to arrive in Athens. On 8 March the *Watchman* reported that the Confederate House and the Virginia House of Delegates had approved the enlistment of black troops.[29] These developments received scant attention, appearing on pages two and three and warranting no comment from the editor. In contrast, on 15 March the *Watchman* trumpeted the defeat of the bill to arm the slaves in the Confederate Senate by one vote: "We look upon the defeat of this bill as a fortunate escape from a great evil."[30] The news reports in the *Southern Watchman* consistently reflected the paper's opposition to arming the slaves.

In contrast to the *Watchman*'s negative reports, the *Southern Banner* provided a thorough record of the debate in the Confederate Congress. On 22 February the *Banner* noted the measure's progress: "In the Senate the bill for raising 200,000 negro troops was reported back from the Committee on Military Affairs with amendments."[31] On 15 March the *Banner* reported with regret the defeat of the measure: "It appears that the bill was lost in the Senate on Tuesday, 21st [February], by eleven to ten."[32] As in the reports of the House debates, this Athens paper printed the names of the Senators voting for each side, including the opposition of Georgia Senator Herschel V. Johnson. Senator Hill was in Georgia attempting to drum up support for the government and did not vote. Having announced the bill's passage on 22 March, the *Banner* printed the text of the bill the following week.[33] Unlike the reports in the *Watchman*, the *Southern Banner*'s coverage provided the

---

[28] "Speech of Howell Cobb," *Southern Watchman*, 8 March 1865, 1.

[29] "Congress" and "Dispatch News," *Southern Watchman*, 8 March 1865, 2, 3.

[30] "Congress—The Negro Bill," *Southern Watchman*, 15 March 1865, 3.

[31] "Congressional," *Southern Banner*, 22 February 1865, 3.

[32] "From Richmond—Negro Bill Defeated," *Southern Banner*, 15 March 1865, 2.

[33] "President's Message," *Southern Banner*, 22 March 1865, 2; "Negro Soldier Bill," *Southern Banner*, 29 March 1865, 2.

men and women of Athens with a fair account of the final acceptance of black troops by Congress.

At the *Southern Watchman*'s editorial desk, John Christy stoutly maintained his opposition to any modification of slavery. On 22 February and again on 15 March, Christy denounced the idea of southern emancipation and its proponents, particularly the letter writers who appeared in Augusta's *Daily Constitutionalist*: "The proposition to abolish slavery now, we look upon as a base surrender—the most abject submission to the enemy. … What apology can be made for Southern abolitionists?"[34] Unable to imagine any good coming from freeing the slaves, Christy described all such ideas as "infinitely worse than the wildest dreams of the reconstructionists."[35] Although unwilling to sacrifice the institution of slavery, Christy suggested that many were not doing their duty and called for new sacrifices: "Have you given your property? Ah! 'there's the rub!' Many who have sent their sons to the field will not give a peck of corn."[36] Despite this call for new sacrifices, on 15 March Christy reaffirmed his opposition to arming slaves: "The adoption of this policy would be a complete surrender to the enemy of the original cause of quarrel; for whatever it may now be it certainly commenced about slavery."[37] Although realizing that "the cause" had changed for many, Christy had not modified his own personal war aims. When word arrived of the measure's final passage, on 22 March, the *Watchman*'s editor only grudgingly accepted the news: "It is too late now to discuss the merits of this scheme. … If, however, it turns out, upon experiment, that we are mistaken in our views, no one will be better pleased than we."[38]

Unlike Christy at the *Watchman*, James Sledge at the *Southern Banner* weighed the value of slavery and found that it could be sacrificed. On 15 February, just prior to the arrival of the reports of the peace commissioners and Benjamin's speech, Sledge announced his support for arming the

[34] John Christy, "Abolition," *Southern Watchman*, 15 March 1865, 2.

[35] Ibid.

[36] John Christy, "Have We Done Our Whole Duty?", *Southern Watchman*, 8 March 1865, 2.

[37] John Christy, "Congress—The Negro Bill," *Southern Watchman*, 15 March 1865, 3.

[38] John Christy, "The Negro Bill," *Southern Watchman*, 22 March 1865, 2.

slaves.[39] As the final phase of the debate unfolded, Sledge never responded to Christy's arguments but simply highlighted the news items that discussed the formation of black units. Less strident than his rival, Sledge avoided direct calls for emancipation and let the reports of congressional action and rampaging Union armies argue the case for black troops. With no immediate threat to the city, the citizens of Athens, like Sledge, appeared willing to wait to see what happened as no letters on the subject appeared in either paper. Although the *Southern Watchman* and *Southern Banner* discussed the issue thoroughly, the local debate in Athens never flowered.

After the return of the peace commissioners and the fiery speeches of Benjamin and Brown, the debate concerning the arming of the slaves flourished in Milledgeville. Although still strongly pro-slavery, the *Confederate Union* could not ignore the debate raging in Congress. On 7 March the *Union* noted the shift of Tennessee Senator Landon Haynes from opposing black troops to supporting the measure: "The institution of slavery could only be maintained," Haynes contended, "by the achievement of… independence… To achieve that independence he would vote to arm the negroes."[40] As support for black soldiers grew in Richmond, the *Union* shifted its focus to the discussion of the issue in the Georgia legislature. On 14 March the paper reported that the few state legislators assembled in Macon had disapproved the idea of arming the slaves: "The tenor of these resolutions does not object to slaves being employed as laborers, teamsters, cooks, etc., but opposed their use in the capacity of soldiers. Adopted."[41] Joseph Nisbet, the *Union*'s editor, highlighted the legislature's vote under the title "Georgia Has Spoken," but relegated the news of Congressional approval of black troops to the telegraphic column: "The Confederate Congress has passed a bill authorizing the employment of negro troops. … The President is to ask for and accept from the owners the services of such number as he may think expedient."[42] Even in this final phase, the *Confederate Union* clung to the ideas of states' rights and slavery.

---

[39] James A. Sledge, "The Negro Question in Congress," *Southern Banner*, 15 February 1865, 1.

[40] "Confederate States' Congress," *Milledgeville Confederate Union*, 7 March 1865, 1.

[41] "Georgia Legislature," *Milledgeville Confederate Union*, 14 March 1865, 2.

[42] "What's the News?" *Milledgeville Confederate Union*, 14 March 1865, 2.

In contrast, the *Southern Recorder* promoted the rising tide of support for arming the slaves in a series of favorable news items. On 21 February the *Recorder* reprinted an endorsement of black troops by former Virginia Governor Henry A. Wise: "Give up slavery…but never yield with it the right of self-government. … Let us make the sacrifice of giving up our pride and self indulgence and…let the African go free…to save our own freedom."[43] In contrast to the *Union*, the *Recorder* closely followed the debate in Congress. On 14 March the *Recorder* not only published the snippet from the telegraph announcing the measure's passage in the House, but also provided a synopsis of the bill.[44] In the same issue, R.M. Orme, the paper's editor, noted General Lee's letter to Congressman Ethelbert Barksdale, which declared that "negroes under proper circumstances will make efficient soldiers."[45] Two weeks later, as Lee's lines crumbled at Petersburg, the *Recorder* printed the text of the "Negro Soldier Bill" and noted the provisions for black soldiers to receive the same clothing and pay as white troops and the lack of a promise of freedom.[46] Unlike the *Confederate Union*, the *Southern Recorder* focused upon the major debate in Congress and presented a realistic picture of the crisis facing the Confederacy.

Despite the failure of negotiations and the desperate need for men, Joseph Nisbet at the *Confederate Union*'s editorial desk refused to consider arming the slaves. On 7 March, Nisbet declared that black soldiers would destroy southern society: "There is no stronger blow that can be struck against the very structure of our political institutions than…to put the negro in the army as a soldier."[47] Slavery, Nisbet argued, could not survive if slaves helped to secure southern independence: "If it is done, Slavery is virtually abolished…and no power under heaven can resurrect it… Put them in as soldiers and the relation of master and slave ceases."[48] In a similar vein, on 14 March Nisbet called for all the white men to do their duty and remove the necessity for arming the slaves: "The free white men of the Confederacy

[43] "Henry A. Wise," *Milledgeville Southern Recorder*, 21 February 1865, 2.

[44] "Confederate Congress," *Milledgeville Southern Recorder*, 14 March 1865, 2.

[45] Ibid.

[46] "Latest News," *Milledgeville Southern Recorder*, 28 March 1865, 2.

[47] Joseph Nisbet, "Negroes for the Army," *Milledgeville Confederate Union*, 7 March 1865, 2.

[48] Ibid.

ought to fight for their liberties and independence… If they will not, the negro will never win the inestimable boon for them."[49] Although he professed a strong desire for independence, Nisbet could not bring himself to sacrifice the peculiar institution to achieve it.

The failure of the Hampton Roads Conference induced R.M. Orme, the editor of the *Southern Recorder*, to reconsider his opposition to arming the slaves. On 21 February, Orme noted a sharp rise in local support for black soldiers: "Since the failure of our peace commissioners, many…are for putting 200,000 negroes in the field to help on the cause of Confederate independence."[50] Orme cautiously announced his acceptance of the measure: "We have been opposed to putting negroes in the army…but far be it from us to throw the slightest impediment in the way of our Government when it is struggling for its existence as a nation."[51] Rather than advocating the enlistment of large numbers, the *Recorder*'s editor called for an experiment first: "Let us try 10,000 negroes as soldiers and if they prove true [and] can stand fire…then those of us who thought differently will be encouraged and willing to put in the 200,000 without reserve."[52] Furthermore, Orme argued that the Confederacy must free its black soldiers: "The promise of liberty to our negroes might be of advantage, but to put them in the army without the promise, would be rather a dangerous experiment."[53] Finally, when the measure passed in Congress, Orme called for all Georgians to support the new law: "Whatever difference of opinion may have hitherto existed in reference to the expediency of this step, should now be dispelled, as the Government, in its wisdom, has found it necessary to take it."[54] R.M. Orme thus weighed the value of slavery and found that he could sacrifice it.

As Central Georgia learned of the failure of the Hampton Roads Conference and congressional efforts to arm the slaves, the citizens of Milledgeville entered the debate and some selected independence over slavery. De-

---

[49] Joseph Nisbet, "Georgia Has Spoken," *Milledgeville Confederate Union*, 14 March 1865, 2.

[50] R.M. Orme, "Negroes As Soldiers," *Milledgeville Southern Recorder*, 21 February 1865, 2.

[51] Ibid.

[52] Ibid.

[53] Ibid.

[54] R.M. Orme, "Latest News," *Milledgeville Southern Recorder*, 28 March 1865, 2.

spite Nisbet's strong opposition to the measure, no letters appeared in the *Confederate Union* on the subject. In contrast, the *Southern Recorder* received and printed three letters supporting black troops. Miss Augusta J. Evans, a citizen of Milledgeville, received a letter from Senator Hill arguing for acceptance of slave-soldiers, which she forwarded to the *Recorder* to be reprinted on 4 April. "Congress will arm the negroes," Hill informed Miss Evans, "as a dernier resort, but will do so cautiously."[55] Contradicting the arguments of men like Governor Brown and Nisbet, Hill contended that the measure would require no amendment of either the state or Confederate constitutions.[56] During the following week, the *Recorder* printed resolutions from an engineer unit stationed near Milledgeville pledging their lives to fight on for "independence and our dear ones at home": "We consider ourselves willing and able to fight four years longer; and if needs [sic] be, to put the negroes in the ranks."[57] Even after the fall of Richmond, many in Milledgeville still saw the potential to turn the war around with black troops. Indeed, on 18 April, sixty-three-year-old John Smith of Irwinton offered to lead a new crusade: "I offer my services for life, and will command 100 negroes, if put in my hands."[58] Smith envisioned a new southern army formed from the remnants of old armies and augmented by black troops. With this new force, Smith hoped to move North and to "lay it in ashes, dividing all the spoils equally between black and white."[59] Although appearing very late in the debate, these letters reflected the decision by many in Milledgeville that slavery could and should be sacrificed to achieve independence.

In February and March, the citizens of Central Georgia struggled mightily within themselves to determine what sacrifices they must make to win the war. Although the editors of the newspapers in Central Georgia remained divided, the conversion of old opponents like Macon's Samuel Boykin and Milledgeville's R.M. Orme reflected new support for black sol-

---

[55] "Interesting Letter from Senator Hill," *Milledgeville Southern Recorder*, 4 April 1865, 2.

[56] Ibid.

[57] J.C. Wright, "Not Whipped Yet," *Milledgeville Southern Recorder*, 11 April 1865, 2.

[58] John Smith, "How to Stop the War," *Milledgeville Southern Recorder*, 18 April 1865, 2.

[59] Ibid.

diers. In the wake of the failure of the peace conference and Benjamin's speech, the men and women of Central Georgia redefined the cause as southern independence rather than the preservation of slavery. In their letters, these Georgians demonstrated a remarkable willingness to abandon the only social structures they had ever known in order to establish a new nation.

Unlike Central Georgia, Eastern Georgia remained threatened during February and March by Sherman's columns in South Carolina. This Union threat lent an air of necessity to the debate in Augusta and forced the local citizens to seriously consider all options to fill the gray ranks. Ever mindful of this threat, Augusta's *Daily Constitutionalist* highlighted its coverage of the congressional debate. For instance, on 9 February the text of the bill to employ negroes in the army and the accompanying debate filled the center column of the first page in the Augusta newspaper. This article provided a blow-by-blow account of the congressmen hammering out the different provisions and included a list of which legislators voted for and against each amendment.[60] While not exactly riveting, the article illuminated the workings of the usually secretive Confederate Congress on a critical question and put a human face on the debate. On 7 March the paper received word that the measure had passed the House but astutely pointed out that it had failed to address the emancipation question.[61] Finally, on 13 March the *Constitutionalist* reported that the bill passed the Senate by a margin of one vote and chronicled the last-minute change by the Virginia senators to ensure its passage.[62] Not only did the *Daily Constitutionalist* provide the barest snippets from the Confederate Press Association, as did the *Macon Telegraph and Confederate* and the Athens *Southern Watchman*, but the *Constitutionalist*'s editor, James Gardner, placed the pieces in prominent places and with as many details as possible. The strong coverage of the congressional debate provided much-needed perspective to the debate raging among the citizens of Augusta.

---

[60] "Employment of Negroes in the Army," *Daily Constitutionalist*, 9 February 1865, 1.

[61] "Congressional," *Daily Constitutionalist*, 7 March 1865, 2.

[62] "Congressional," *Daily Constitutionalist*, 13 March 1865, 2.

In contrast, Augusta's *Chronicle and Sentinel* provided news coverage for only one side of the debate. On 21 February this paper featured Governor Brown's message, but noted only that Secretary Benjamin and Senator Hunter had given speeches in Richmond.[63] Similarly, on 9 March the *Chronicle and Sentinel* ignored the final debates in the Senate and published the remarks of State Representative Linton Stephens, who termed the bill to arm the slaves an unconstitutional "Trojan horse": "Now if Congress...should put the negro into the army and emancipate him for faithful service—it would be a greater usurpation than ever was proposed in the old Congress."[64] Although noting the measure's passage in the "Telegraphic" column on 15 March, this development drew no immediate comment as the *Chronicle and Sentinel* devoted the next three issues to a justification of Governor Brown's defense of the state in November. Unable to find leaders speaking against arming slaves in Georgia, on 19 March the *Chronicle and Sentinel*'s editor, Nathan Morse, printed the comments of H.W. Hilliard to a band of South Carolina militia recruits.[65] "To train a servile race to the use of arms," Hilliard declared, "is a policy in conflict with our institutions and fatal to our interests."[66] Clearly, the editor of the *Chronicle and Sentinel* crafted his news items to reflect his own views on slavery and presented only one view of the revolutionary debate swirling around Augusta.

Despite the power and logic of Benjamin's address, James Gardner, the editor of the *Daily Constitutionalist*, continued his support for arming the slaves without approving their eventual emancipation. While the debate raged in Augusta, Gardner surrendered the editorial page to a series of letters from prominent men of the city and looked for common themes in the local and national debates. Upon learning of final congressional approval to arm the slaves, he broke a long editorial silence on the issue and celebrated the passage of the measure: "It is a manifestation of our determination to continue the struggle to the bitter end, cost what it may in blood, treasure,

---

[63] "Governor's Message," *Augusta Chronicle and Sentinel*, 21 February 1865, 1.

[64] "Great Speech of Hon. Linton Stephens of Hancock," *Augusta Chronicle and Sentinel*, 9 March 1865, 2.

[65] "Speech of H.W. Hilliard," *Augusta Chronicle and Sentinel*, 19 March 1865, 2.

[66] Ibid.

and the sacrifice of peculiar ideas and prejudices."[67] While the new law did not change the relation between master and slave, domestic slavery, all knew, would be irrevocably changed. Acknowledging this fact, Gardner trumpeted the sacrifice of slavery for independence as a victory of the southern spirit: "We are not so wedded to any single doctrine or political view or life-cherished conviction of right, as not to be willing to yield all, aye, everything for the obtainance of independence."[68] The Augustan recognized and accepted the fact that arming and freeing the slave-soldiers would seal the fate of the whole institution. Although slavery was a high price, Gardner believed independence was worth the cost. Shifting from the triumph of the principle of national independence over the institution of slavery to the new law's practical value, Gardner predicted immediate, dramatic results from the new soldiers: "Doubtless, General Lee will take immediate steps for the enrollment and discipline of a sufficient number of black troops to relieve himself and his grand army of any embarrassment."[69] Finally, on 17 March, he called for the end of the debate in Augusta: "It is law, it is hope, it is help, it is just; let all assist in making it effective."[70] Watching the local debate through the letters in his pages, James Gardner astutely understood the transformation in public sentiment from slavery to independence.

Even after hearing of the failure of the peace conference, Nathan S. Morse at the *Chronicle and Sentinel* refused to accept the end of negotiations and the necessity to consider radical measures. Searching for some alternative to the end of slavery, on 8 February Morse suggested compromising the South's independence: "We might agree to be two peoples politically, and one people commercially. This would secure peace between us. Commerce is a great pacificator."[71] Unfortunately for Morse, few Augustans agreed. As numerous letters appeared in the *Constitutionalist* boldly calling for emancipation, Morse attacked the rival editor for printing the doctrines of Wendell Phillips and Horace Greeley: "Free discussion is one thing. Spreading the

[67] James Gardner, "Arming the Negroes," *Daily Constitutionalist*, 15 March 1865, 2.

[68] Ibid.

[69] Ibid.

[70] James Gardner, "Lead Editorial," *Daily Constitutionalist*, 17 March 1865, 2.

[71] Nathan S. Morse, "Return of Commissioners," *Augusta Chronicle and Sentinel*, 8 February 1865, 2.

doctrine of Abolitionism is another."[72] "Abolitionism is a pernicious evil," Morse declared on 16 March, "and no editor ought to admit [it] in the columns of a paper under his control."[73] Certainly, Morse did not print abolitionist doctrines or even discuss the efforts to put the "Negro Soldier Bill" into force. Despite acknowledging congressional approval of the measure, on 23 March Morse decried efforts to arm the slaves as "calculated to render our cause unpopular, [and] the Confederate Government itself odious." [74] Morse's tenacious defense of slavery appeared amazingly out of touch with the debate raging among the men and women of Augusta.

In the immediate aftermath of Benjamin's speech, a series of thoughtful yet daring letters to the editor took over the editorial page of the *Daily Constitutionalist*. On 22 February "W.W." opened this final phase by clearly defining the state of the debate in Augusta: "While the necessity of employing the negro as a soldier seems generally conceded, there are not a few who express doubts as to the policy of emancipating him."[75] By emancipating the slaves, he argued, the South could win the cheerful cooperation of black men and women at home and on the battlefield, while at the same time proving to many disaffected whites that independence and not slavery remained the primary aim of the war: "Who can tell how many it would bring back of those who have abandoned our cause, as the rich man's war and the poor man's fight?"[76] In a similar vein, "W.L.M." tackled the constitutional problem and argued that if the Confederate Congress had the power to enlist Polish, Italian, and Irish troops, "where is [sic] the prohibitions to the employment of our slaves?"[77] Finally, on 1 March "W.W." realistically argued that the Confederacy must offer the slave freedom because the "sharpest logic and loftiest eloquence about the divinity of slavery and the blessings which it confers...are idle words wasted upon the listless ear of the negro."[78]

[72] Nathan S. Morse, "Who Is to Blame?" *Augusta Chronicle and Sentinel*, 16 March 1865, 2.

[73] Ibid.

[74] Nathan S. Morse, "Radicalism," *Augusta Chronicle and Sentinel*, 23 March 1865, 2.

[75] "W.W.," "Letter to the Editor," *Daily Constitutionalist*, 22 February 1865, 3.

[76] "W.W.," "Letter to the Editor," *Daily Constitutionalist*, 1 March 1865, 2.

[77] "W.L.M.," "Letter to the Editor," *Daily Constitutionalist*, 14 February 1865, 2.

[78] "W.W.," "Letter to the Editor," *Daily Constitutionalist*, 1 March 1865, 2.

In a highly orthodox and diametrically opposed response, "S" wrote on 10 March that slavery remained "a matter of religious trust and duty" and condemned "W.W." as giving up the cause of the war.[79] The cries of the past spoken by "S" found no supporters among the other letter writers, while "Harry South" quickly rose to defend "W.W." On 13 March he declared emancipation an absolute necessity for the survival of the nation: "It will require but a moment's reflection for any man who has the best interest of his country at heart...to give up the institution of slavery forever."[80] "We regard the salvation of the country," "Harry South" further asserted, "in a great degree dependent upon the successful inauguration of this new policy."[81] Mirroring the sentiments at home, an Augusta soldier serving in Richmond wrote and advocated such a policy: "If Congress agrees that the 200,000 negroes ought to be put in, I will fight by them. ... Many of the men wish to see the negroes in the field."[82] Judging from the letters written to the *Daily Constitutionalist*, the overwhelming majority of Augusta's citizens supported arming the slaves, with at least a sizable number approving of emancipation for faithful service.

At the *Chronicle and Sentinel*, Nathan Morse produced no effective response to the debate on emancipation in the *Constitutionalist*. In fact, on 12 March, Morse decried the ideas of the letter writers and suggested that any modification of slavery would plunge the South into a "chasm of ruin": "If these abolition writers and sympathizers are friends to our cause—God save us from their friendship."[83] Although Morse praised the letter of "S," the *Chronicle and Sentinel* received only one letter on the subject during February and March. Morse acknowledged receipt of this letter from "W.W." but stoutly refused to publish it.[84] Instead, Morse declared that "W.W." "proceeds to conclusions which have been justified by no induction sufficiently adequate" and that his arguments "are well calculated to impose upon super-

[79] "S," "Letter to the Editor," *Daily Constitutionalist*, 10 March 1865, 2.

[80] Harry South, "A Man for the Crisis," *Daily Constitutionalist*, 13 March 1865, 2.

[81] Ibid.

[82] "Spirit of an Augusta Boy," *Daily Constitutionalist*, 18 March 1865, 2.

[83] Nathan S. Morse, "Abolitionism in Our Midst," *Augusta Chronicle and Sentinel*, 12 March 1865, 2.

[84] Nathan S. Morse, "The Abolition Correspondent of the *Constitutionalist*," *Augusta Chronicle and Sentinel*, 23 March 1865, 2.

ficial thinkers."[85] In short, Morse found only "S" for an ally, and these two could not match the powerful arguments for black troops and emancipation presented by "W.W.," "Harry South," "Mentor," "W.L.M.," James Gardner, and others in the *Constitutionalist*. The debate about arming the slaves had forced the men and women of Augusta to ask again why they were fighting. The vast majority discovered that slavery could be sacrificed much more easily than southern independence.

As in Central and Eastern Georgia, the failure of the Hampton Roads Conference, Benjamin's speech, and Brown's message added potent fuel to the debate raging in Southwestern Georgia. Numerous news items addressing arming the slaves appeared in the *Columbus Times* and *Daily Sun* and these items formed the backdrop for the local debate. To open this final phase, the *Times* on 14 February printed a brief synopsis of Benjamin's speech: "Mr. Benjamin advocated the immediate employment of negro volunteers to reinforce the armies, and was loudly applauded by the meeting."[86] Although electing not to publish Benjamin's entire address when it arrived, the *Times* continued to cover the issue. On 2 March this Columbus paper reported that Mississippi Governor Charles Clark was now a strong advocate of arming the slaves, though he still opposed their emancipation.[87] Having announced the measure's passage in the Senate four days earlier, on 19 March the *Times* noted initial attempts in Richmond to form black regiments: "Quite a military fever has broken out among negroes employed at the various hospitals here, and...they are already organizing volunteer companies to take the field."[88] Finally, as black men began to don Confederate gray, on 23 March the *Times* printed General Lee's letter to Congressman Ethelbert Barksdale in support of black units: "I do not think that our white population can supply the necessities of a long war without overtaxing its capacity. ... I can only say that in my opinion the negroes will make efficient soldiers."[89] "I think," Lee continued, "those who are employed should be freed. It would be neither just nor wise, in my opinion, to require them to

---

[85] Ibid.

[86] "From Richmond," *Columbus Times*, 14 February 1865, 2.

[87] "Gov. Clark of Mississippi," *Columbus Times*, 2 March 1865, 1.

[88] "The Negroes Arming," *Columbus Times*, 19 March 1865, 2.

[89] "Gen. Lee on the Negro Question," *Columbus Times*, 23 March 1865, 2.

remain slaves."[90] While far from an advocate of arming the slaves, the *Columbus Times* presented full, detailed coverage of the debate rocking the Confederacy.

Benjamin's speech and the final efforts in Congress to arm the slaves produced many news items in the Columbus *Daily Sun*. On 14 February the *Sun* discussed Benjamin's address and featured the Secretary's full text later in the month.[91] Many observers, from both North and South, noted the commitment such a sacrifice would demonstrate. For example, on 22 February the *Sun* reprinted an editorial from the *New York News* that pointed to the "terrible earnestness" of a South willing to give up slavery: "The fierce determination placed thus in proof will undoubtedly satisfy mankind that the issue of the war henceforth is the...sacred right of self-government."[92] Unlike highly partisan papers such as Augusta's *Chronicle and Sentinel*, the *Sun* published the comments of both congressional opponents and advocates of arming the slaves on 16 and 18 February.[93] Although even-handed in its coverage, the *Sun* expressed considerable impatience with the measure's slow progress in Congress, when, on 8 March, the paper reprinted a daring call from Mobile for individual citizens to arm their slaves: "Let the master take down the rifle from his rack, and with the servants who are willing and whom he can trust, volunteer in companies and troops for the defense of the land."[94] Two days later, the paper claimed that Joe Brown, alone, among southern governors, opposed the use of slaves in the army.[95] As evidence of growing support in the army, on 16 March the *Sun* chronicled the efforts of Majors J.H. Pegram and Thomas P. Turner to raise black units in Virginia.[96] In particular, the paper emphasized Lee's instructions to the officers: "I attach great importance to the first experiment. Nothing should be left undone. Make it successful."[97] The news items appearing in the *Daily Sun*

[90] Ibid.

[91] "Telegraphic," *Columbus Daily Sun*, 14 February 1865, 2; and "Secretary Benjamin's Speech," *Columbus Daily Sun*, 25 February 1865, 1.

[92] "Terrible Earnestness," *Columbus Daily Sun*, 22 February 1865, 2.

[93] "Telegraphic," *Columbus Daily Sun*, 16 and 18 February 1865, 1.

[94] "From Mobile," *Columbus Daily Sun*, 8 March 1865, 2.

[95] "The Employment of Negroes as Soldiers," *Columbus Daily Sun*, 10 March 1865, 1.

[96] "Telegraphic," *Columbus Daily Sun*, 24 March 1865, 2.

[97] Ibid.

clearly showed slavery slipping from its preeminent position in the southern mind.

Benjamin's speech and the failure of the peace conference forced J.W. Warren, editor of the *Columbus Times,* to seriously consider arming the slaves for the first time. On 15 February Warren admitted that he had never thought the proposition a practical one and, therefore, had paid it only passing notice: "We have never advocated it, nor have we opposed it directly, with any great degree of earnestness."[98] With the failure of negotiations, Warren realized that black troops would be tried: "It now looks as though Congress intend [sic] to sow the fabled lion's teeth (with the enamel worn off) and gather in a crop of sable warriors."[99] While admitting that a large number of slaves could be spared from agriculture, Warren feared that the white veterans would not accept the new recruits and that the black soldiers would quickly desert. If tried, Warren argued, "We will ourselves, take the best in the country, drill and train them, and then hand them over—ready made warriors—to the enemy."[100]

Having considered the idea briefly, Warren alleged that poor management rather than too few soldiers posed the central problem: "What the country and the cause need, as we conceive, is not negro conscription, but a Secretary of War who will get the men out."[101] As evidence, Warren claimed that Major Allen, the local commissary general, issued 14,000 rations a day, and asked why these men were not facing the enemy. Allen quickly denied Warren's claims and proclaimed on 18 February that three fourths of the rations went to prisoners at Andersonville and the remainder to workers in government factories.[102] Warren's army at home had vanished in an instant. Even as Congress approved the measure, on 1 March Warren declared he saw no necessity for slave-soldiers, but grudgingly accepted the government's decision: "If the bill passed by Congress receives the approval of the Executive we must take it for granted that the emergency demands the sacrifice."[103]

---

[98] J.W. Warren, "Employment of Negroes as Soldiers," *Columbus Times*, 15 February 1865, 2.

[99] Ibid. The parentheses in this quotation appear in the original.

[100] Ibid.

[101] Ibid.

[102] Major Allen, "Letter to the Editor," *Columbus Times*, 18 February 1865, 2.

[103] J.W. Warren, "The Negro Question," *Columbus Times*, 1 March 1865, 2.

Despite finally considering the proposition in depth, Warren could not distinguish a threat so severe that it would necessitate the sacrifice of slavery.

In contrast, William Scruggs at the *Daily Sun* recognized the necessity to arm the slaves and challenged the community to examine its convictions. On 22 February Scruggs assailed Governor Brown's contention that the use of black troops would demean the South: "We fear the Governor is unfortunate in his position on the negro question. The policy of arming slaves against a common enemy in time of invasion is fully justified by the necessity."[104] Although he denied the central government's authority to arm the slaves, Scruggs contended that the states could and should organize black units: "The States may organize military companies, regiments, and battalions, of negro troops, and tender them to the general Government without any violation of the Constitution."[105] Necessity, Scruggs declared, demanded the step: "Between subjugation, with its long train of horrors and attendant evils, and fighting side by side with our slaves in defense of civil liberty, no Southerner would long hesitate."[106] A week later, on 1 March Scruggs announced congressional approval of the measure and compared the revolutionary transformation occurring in the South about the role of the slave to the transition in England about the role of the king at the time of the Magna Carta.[107] Having witnessed the shift in public attitudes and noted the absolute necessity for immediate assistance, Scruggs declared on 22 March that the South could not secure its independence without the slave's help: "It is now evident that the negro slave is to be a sort of balance power in this contest, and that the side which succeeds in enlisting and in securing the active operation and services of the four millions of blacks, must ultimately triumph."[108] Clearly, William Scruggs understood the sacrifice he advocated but confidently chose independence over slavery.

While J.W. Warren contemplated the proposition, many local citizens reacted sharply to the failure of the peace conference and wrote to the *Co-*

---

[104] William Scruggs, "The Governor's Message," *Columbus Daily Sun*, 22 February 1865, 2.

[105] Ibid.

[106] Ibid.

[107] William Scruggs, "Lead Editorial," *Columbus Daily Sun*, 1 March 1865, 2.

[108] William Scruggs, "Policy of Arming Slaves," *Columbus Daily Sun*, 22 March 1865, 2.

lumbus Times to advocate the employment of black troops. On 18 February "AGLA" demanded that the South "strain every nerve" and "lift every arm in defense" to secure its independence: "Perish all other aims but that of national deliverance. ... Let the States promptly donate one hundred thousand negroes...to be trained, well disciplined and held...for national service."[109] The following morning, a letter from a leading peace advocate, Judge P.E. Love of Thomasville, appeared in the *Times*. Having noted Lincoln's tough terms, Love declared that the "delusion" was now passed and he no longer favored negotiations: "I have heretofore been opposed to arming the slaves, but I now yield my objections. Indeed, all I have, negroes, houses, lands, everything, is at the service of the Government, if it wants to prosecute the war."[110] Unlike Judge Love, some correspondents required yet more convincing. For example, "Will Warwick" questioned the necessity of slave-soldiers on 22 February, but as reports of Sherman's march through South Carolina arrived in Columbus, he wrote again and called for black troops: "Georgia and Alabama must. absolutely must! bring one hundred thousand of their men, white and black, into efficient organization."[111] "We meet daily," "Will Warwick" declared, "with men...who are willing to fight and to carry their slaves with them to fight, in defense of their States and homes."[112]

As with "Will Warwick," the threat of renewed attacks in the spring convinced other letter writers to the *Columbus Times* to reconsider their opposition to arming the slaves. As Union forces on the Tennessee River staged for an attack toward Central Alabama, William Samford compromised his opposition to black troops. On 18 February Samford addressed an open letter in the *Times* to Alabama Governor Thomas Watts and suggested he "gather up all the resources in his reach, both white and black," to defend the state: "Opposed as I am to the policy of putting negroes into the Confederate Army, I venture to suggest that they might be efficiently organized into home guard companies, in connection with their masters and overseers,

---

[109] "AGLA," "Mirage of Peace," *Columbus Times*, 18 February 1865, 1.

[110] P.E. Love, "Signs of the Times," *Columbus Times*, 19 February 1865, 1.

[111] "Will Warwick," "Everything for the Cause," *Columbus Times*, 22 February 1865, 2; and "Will Warwick," "Go Farther and Fare Worse," *Columbus Times*, 4 March 1865, 1.

[112] Ibid.

and employed successfully for State defense."[113] Others, more directly threatened than Samford, also wrote the *Times* and requested black assistance. On 8 March a set of resolutions from Thomas's Brigade in Virginia appeared in the *Times*: "Resolved, That when...it shall become necessary to arm a portion or all of the slaves...and make soldiers of them, we will accept it...preferring, as we do, any and all sacrifices to subjugation."[114] A Georgian serving in the 2nd Georgia Battalion also wrote home to Columbus and advocated slave enlistment: "The whole army is in favor of arming the slaves, and I expect it will be done."[115] As in the earlier phases of the debate, the writers of letters to the *Columbus Times* ignored the editor's stout opposition as they discussed the radical steps necessary to secure independence.

Similarly, the correspondents of the Columbus *Daily Sun* chose independence over slavery as their primary war aim. On 19 February a letter from "William Trammell" called for the immediate enlistment of 200,000 black soldiers: "It is better that we should use them in securing our Independence, and give them theirs by gradual emancipation and colonization, than to suffer them to be arrayed in opposition to us, preventing our Independence."[116] The following week, "Iter" proclaimed that the war had irreparably altered slavery: "African slavery, as it existed before the war, let the struggle result as it may, will be numbered among the things that have been."[117] Southerners, "Iter" contended, must follow the lead of General Lee on the necessity of black troops: "If he [Lee] recommends using them as soldiers, the public may rest assured that the exigencies of the times demand such a resort."[118] Finally, on 23 March, a soldier with General N.B. Forrest's cavalry wrote to the *Sun* to call for the formation of black units: "The negroes make first rate soldiers, and whenever you hear a man say he will quit if the negroes are put in, if you will dig around his heart he wants to quit any

---

[113] William Samford, "Thomas H. Watts," *Columbus Times*, 18 February 1865, 2; and William Samford, "Correspondence of the *Columbus Times*," *Columbus Times*, 26 February 1865, 2.

[114] "Thomas' Brigade," *Columbus Times*, 8 March 1865, 2

[115] "Brother Tom," "My Dear Sister," *Columbus Times*, 20 March 1865, 2.

[116] "William Trammell," "What Must Be Done?" *Columbus Daily Sun*, 19 February 1865, 1.

[117] "Iter," "Letter from Iter," *Columbus Daily Sun*, 28 February 1865, 2.

[118] Ibid.

how."[119] Clearly, then, as Confederate fortunes crumbled and hopes for a negotiated settlement vanished, the letter writers of the *Columbus Times* and the *Daily Sun* expressed a growing conviction that slavery must be sacrificed for independence.

After the failure of the Hampton Roads Conference, the small towns of Southwestern Georgia, including Blakely and Albany, earnestly entered the debate over arming the slaves. Although continuing to follow the lead of the Columbus dailies, Blakely's *Early County News* provided considerable space to original news items that addressed the subject of black troops. On 22 February the *News* provided an account of a public meeting in Mobile that concluded that "the government should immediately place one hundred thousand negroes in the army."[120] During the following month, impatience with congressional wrangling appeared in an editorial reprinted in Blakely from the *Mobile Advertiser*: "Whatever is to be done in the arming of our slave population must be done quickly. ... Seize your arms, form companies, and call upon Gens. Dick Taylor and N.B. Forrest to lead you."[121] When news arrived in Blakely that the measure had passed, the *News* announced on 22 March that the president would soon call for up to 300,000 slaves to serve, but noted that Congress had not provided for their freedom: "Nothing in the act is to be so construed as to change the relationship between the owner and his slaves, except with the consent of the owner."[122] Finally, on 29 March the *News* reprinted an editorial from the Augusta-based agricultural journal the *Southern Cultivator* arguing that, with slaves entering the ranks, all Georgians must "do more than double duty" to prevent widespread hunger: "It is now the duty of all farmers, planters, and gardeners in the Confederate States to strain every nerve in making the greatest possible amount of food."[123] As Sherman marched through the Carolinas and the Union grip on Mobile tightened, the news items appearing in the *Early County News* challenged the men and women of Blakely to weigh the value of slavery.

---

[119] G.W. Adair, "Letter from Forrest's Command," *Columbus Daily Sun*, 23 March 1865, 2.

[120] "Mobile, Feb. 14," *Early County News*, 22 February 1865, 3.

[121] "Negro Volunteers—The Duty of the Slaves," *Early County News*, 22 March 1865, 2.

[122] "The Confederate Congress," *Early County News*, 22 March 1865, 2.

[123] "Our Duty Now," *Early County News*, 29 March 1865, 2.

In contrast, the *Albany Patriot* provided only limited coverage of the efforts to arm the slaves. On 23 March the *Patriot* reported the measure's passage in Congress and noted President Davis's displeasure at the late date of the action.[124] All the details of the new law did not appear in Albany until 27 April, when the *Patriot* printed the full text of the bill.[125] A letter from General F.A. Shoup to Senator Gustavus Henry, published in the Albany paper on 13 April, provided the most thought-provoking news item during the period. The old chief of artillery argued that slaves would make excellent soldiers: "The negroes that have served with our armies as cooks and teamsters are as thoroughly enlisted in our cause as their masters; and in many cases have been known to fight as gallantly."[126] The South, Shoup contended, needed the slaves in the field immediately and could not wait for a definite answer on emancipation: "My proposition, then, is to just let the slavery question remain where it is—put into service as many negroes as we can provide with arms and equipment…with all rapidity."[127] Although it published few news items on the subject, the *Albany Patriot* addressed the issue fully in its editorial columns.

While hesitant to espouse slave-soldiers before the failure of the peace conference, editor T.E. Speight of the *Early County News* confidently proclaimed his support for arming the slaves in February. Commenting on the governor's message on 1 March, Speight asserted that Brown had lost touch with the people on the issue of black troops: "Concerning the issue of arming the slaves, the governor joins issue, as a matter of course, with the wisdom and patriotism of the country."[128] Later in the same article, Speight called Brown "a servile minion of the North" and condemned the governor's opposition to all Davis's initiatives: "Gov. Brown opposes every measure which will tend to strengthen our cause and…therefore the arming of the negroes will be injudicious—it will be taking the recruits he is saving for his Yankee friends."[129] On 29 March, when news arrived of the measure's adoption, Speight hailed the decision: "Thus has a new and a great step been tak-

---

[124] "A Bill to Place Negro Soldiers in the Field," *Albany Patriot*, 23 March 1865, 2.
[125] "The Negro Soldier Bill," *Albany Patriot*, 27 April 1865, 1.
[126] "Policy of Employing Negroes," *Albany Patriot*, 13 April 1865, 1.
[127] Ibid.
[128] T.E. Speight, "The Governor's Message," *Early County News*, 1 March 1865, 2.
[129] Ibid.

en in the work of revolution. ... The negro can be made a useful soldier; and we have no hesitation in putting him...in the field."[130] A week later, Speight denounced the "starch-shirt gentry" who sent the poor white to fight but who fought slave conscription: "As there seems to be no chance to get this class to carry muskets, we are glad to know that their 'God-blessed niggers' will have to do so."[131] After the failure of the peace conference, Speight weighed the value of slavery and boldly called for arming the slaves.

Similarly, the unsuccessful attempt at negotiations stirred editor J.W. Fears of the *Albany Patriot* deeply and led him to call for new sacrifices to achieve independence: "The whole country is now convinced that no settlement can be made, except the settlement by strong arms and brave hearts."[132] In January Fears had hesitantly recommended an experiment with 40,000 slaves as soldiers, but after the Hampton Roads Conference, Fears demanded largescale black enlistment: "The circumstance now require [sic] that we should use our negroes. Let them go to the field—about 200,000, (if we can feed them,) and be drilled and put into the fight."[133] Furthermore, Fears suggested an innovative plan to secure the new soldiers' loyalty: "Let it be faithfully promised them that...at the end of the war they shall not only be free, but that to each of them a farm of fifty acres of land shall be given for their services."[134] Such a policy, Fears contended, would draw black volunteers and would give the former slave a stake in the nation he fought to maintain. Unable to understand why others could not see the necessity of the measure, on 23 February Fears questioned the motives of the opponents of black troops, including Governor Brown: "As the Governor is largely interested in land and negroes, it was to be expected that he would protest against making soldiers of the latter."[135] Although a late convert to the cause, J.W. Fears became a powerful spokesman for black enlistment and emancipation during the final phase of the debate. After the failure of the peace conference and Benjamin's and Brown's speeches, the common people of Southwestern Georgia exhibited a distinct transformation in their views.

---

[130] T.E. Speight, "As We Stated," *Early County News*, 29 March 1865, 3.
[131] T.E. Speight, "Several Negro Regiments," *Early County News*, 5 April 1865, 2.
[132] J.W. Fears, "Negroes for the War," *Early County News*, 23 February 1865, 2.
[133] Ibid.
[134] Ibid.
[135] J.W. Fears, "Gov. Brown's Message," *Early County News*, 23 February 1865, 2.

From the letter writers of Columbus to the editors in Blakely and Albany, the citizens of Southwestern Georgia weighed the value of slavery and found that it could be sacrificed to achieve southern independence.

As Confederate fortunes crumbled and hopes for a negotiated settlement vanished, Georgians struggled with each other and within themselves to determine what sacrifices the Confederacy must make to win the war. The debate over arming the slaves forced the common people of Georgia to ask again what was their definition of victory. Although the editors of the newspapers remained divided, the conversion of old opponents like Macon's Samuel Boykin, Milledgeville's R.M. Orme, and Albany's J.W. Fears reflected a rising tide of new support for black soldiers. In their letters, the citizens of Macon and Milledgeville redefined the cause as southern independence rather than the preservation of slavery. In Augusta, the threat of imminent Union attack clearly illustrated the necessity to arm slaves. The *Constitutionalist*'s James Gardner provided a platform for the local debate on his editorial page and the people responded. Judging from the letters written to the *Daily Constitutionalist*, the overwhelming majority of Augusta's citizens favored the employment of black troops, with a sizable number also approving emancipation. Similarly, the letter writers of the *Columbus Times* and the *Daily Sun* expressed a growing conviction that slavery must be sacrificed. In the final phase of the debate, the citizens of Georgia demanded immediate congressional action to place black troops in the field. In so doing, these Georgians affirmed that they would sacrifice everything, even slavery, to achieve their independence.

10

A Last Resort

In February 1865 a traveler from Arkansas penned a revealing portrait of Texas in the Civil War. Unlike Arkansas, which had suffered the ravages of invading armies and numerous guerrilla bands, the Arkansan contended that Texas had not experienced the same fierce conflict: "This place furnishes no evidence of an existing war...War is a myth and it is strongly suspicioned that there are no such places as Richmond and Atlanta or such men as Lee, Beauregard, and Joe Johnston." Although mentioned in the newspapers, few Texans had visited either of the two cities recently, and very few of the men then at home had fought under one of the Confederate chieftains. In fact, the traveler saw few men in San Antonio wearing uniforms but many seemingly able young men pursuing other matters: "Sacks of the precious metal [gold] weighing an [sic] hundred pounds or over are transported about the city upon shoulders unable to bear the weight of a musket. It is strange what a difference there is between fire-arms and specie." The Confederate cotton trade with Mexico produced boom times for a number of cities on the planters' route south to sell their cotton. "Cotton is King," the writer proclaimed, "specie plenty, and San Antonio flourishes despite the war." Confederate and state regulations to the contrary, some of the items purchased in exchange for cotton could not be used against the Union army. Edmund Kirby Smith had little need for fine wines and silk dresses on the battlefield.[1] While the letter writer was obviously being sarcastic, the emphasis he reported in Texas on cotton production, making money, and domestic tranquility rang true. Unlike Virginia and Georgia, life in Confederate Texas remained much as it had in the antebellum period. Union commanders in the Southwest had not adopted the hard war policies so ably employed by William Sherman and Philip Sheridan; therefore, citizens of the Lone Star

[1] "San Antonio," *Dallas Herald*, 23 February 1865, 1.

State had difficulty understanding the desperation evident among the people east of the Mississippi River.

The final phase of the southern debate over whether to arm the slaves began in Virginia during the first week of February 1865. On 3 February Vice President Alexander Stephens, Assistant Secretary of War John A. Campbell, and Senator Robert M.T. Hunter met President Abraham Lincoln and Secretary of State William Seward on a vessel moored off Hampton Roads. Like many in the Confederacy, Texans had been cheered by reports in January that Francis P. Blair, an influential Democrat from Maryland, had visited Richmond and discussed the opening of peace talks. Unfortunately for the weary southerners, Lincoln offered no terms to the Confederate commissioners except submission and reunion. All realistic hope for a negotiated settlement to the war ended at Hampton Roads. Likewise, Duncan Kenner's diplomatic mission offering emancipation in return for recognition had drawn tepid responses in Britain and France. Neither diplomacy in Europe nor negotiation with the northern states proved able to secure southern independence. Torrential rains and the disruption caused by Sherman's march through the Carolinas delayed news of the outcome of the conference reaching Texas until the last week of February. In the Marshall paper the words of Senator Gustavus Henry of Tennessee rang out and expressed the convictions of many disappointed southerners who had hoped for peace. In light of Lincoln's terms, Henry proclaimed that battlefield victories alone could solve southern problems: "Fill up the army! It is the best peace measure after all. Fill up the army—it is the great scheme that will regulate our currency. Fill up the army—it will achieve our independence."[2] Unable to find white men to fill the gray ranks, black soldiers provided the only viable option remaining for the Confederacy. In the final weeks of the war, southerners had to make a frightful choice. They could maintain slavery and accept almost certain defeat or offer a rifle and freedom to their slaves and risk all for independence. In Richmond, in the Deep South, and even in Texas, the discussions over arming slaves took on a new urgency in the final phase of the debate.

---

[2] "Speech of Hon. G.A. Henry of Tennessee in the Senate of the Confederate States," *Marshall Texas Republican*, 3 March 1865, 1.

Fourteen hundred miles from the conference at Hampton Roads, the *Houston Telegraph* and its readers waited impatiently to hear the result. The first hint of the conference's outcome arrived in Houston in an exchanged copy of the *New York Herald* on 20 February. Lacking details of the meeting, Houstonians cursed Lincoln's steadfast resolve for the Union but waited for southern accounts. Two weeks later, on 6 March, portions of speeches made by Confederate leaders in response to the failure of the conference appeared. Portions of the remarks from President Davis, R.M.T. Hunter, and Secretary of State Judah Benjamin appeared in Houston calling for a renewed war spirit. Benjamin specifically pleaded for black troops. As unpalatable as events may have seemed in Houston, the *Telegraph* followed carefully the debate in the Confederate Congress. Similarly, the Houston paper chronicled the transition of other Confederate newspapers from opposition to support for black troops. For instance, the *Richmond Dispatch*'s change of heart appeared in Houston on 13 March: "We hesitate not to say the time has come when negroes should be employed as soldiers, and that they should be offered their freedom, for that purpose." "It is better," the *Dispatch*'s editor reasoned, "to liberate 200,000 negroes, and to put them in the army than to run the risk of losing all."

Support for slave-soldiers also emerged from sources outside Virginia. On 17 March the *Telegraph* published a letter taken from the *Mobile Register* that projected great results from the measure: "Give Lee negroes and food—we have plenty of both—and he will defeat this combination…and still hold Richmond." Three days later the Houston paper published resolutions from a public meeting in Mobile suggesting that Alabamians felt they had no choice but to arm their slaves: "If you refuse to use the negro against the Yankee, the Yankees will use the negro for the enslavement of Southern white men and women. We therefore implore the Confederate Government to authorize the immediate impressment of 100,000 able bodied negro men for the army." On 27 March word arrived in Houston that, two weeks previously, the Confederate Congress had passed a bill to arm the slaves. The *Richmond Whig* trumpeted the defiant step: "Let the despondent take courage. The bill to place negro soldiers in the army passed the Confederate Senate." In contrast, the *Telegraph* did not rejoice. Interestingly, the Houston paper printed the February letter from Robert E. Lee to Ethelbert Barksdale on 31 March, after the question had been decided. Perhaps the

Telegraph feared that Lee's call for emancipated black reinforcements might have tipped the balance in the measure's favor. The tenor of the news reports in Houston reflected the growing acceptance by the southern people of the necessity of the matter.[3]

Rumors and partial Union news reports caused the *Houston Telegraph* and the *Galveston News* to publish conflicting reports of the peace conference during the final week of February. On 27 February reports of the failed Hampton Roads peace conference appeared in Galveston. News reports during this period often arrived in Galveston in the columns of northern newspapers exchanged by island residents with the Union sailors from the blockading squadron. Many Galvestonians tried to disregard unpleasant reports as Yankee propaganda, but most readers came to expect a considerable degree of truth in them. On 3 March a Confederate synopsis of Benjamin's speech delivered in Richmond arrived, but it brought no better tidings. The *Galveston News* did not care for Secretary of State's solution: "Mr. Benjamin presented some disagreeable truths as he said the necessity of using negro soldiers could not be avoided. He...said if the Virginia Assembly would recommend the measure, Lee would be reinforced by twenty thousand in twenty days." In the same issue of the *News*, the arguments of Henry Burnett of Kentucky, John Atkins of Tennessee, and James Orr of South Carolina rang out in detailed accounts of the House and Senate debates over arming slaves. While continuing to follow the debate in the Confederate Congress, the Galveston paper attempted to lead public opinion by choosing its news items carefully. For example, on 10 March the Galveston paper reprinted excerpts from Vice President Alexander Stephens's speech in 1861, in which he declared slavery the cornerstone of the Confederacy. This selection allowed the *News* to argue that calm, rational men had long considered slavery the cause and purpose of the war: "These opinions then," the *Galveston News* argued, "in regard to the true relation of slavery to our government

[3] "The New York Herald...," *Houston TriWeekly Telegraph*, 20 February 1865, 2; "By Telegraph," *Houston TriWeekly Telegraph*, 6 March 1865, 3; "From Latest Papers," *Houston TriWeekly Telegraph*, 13 March 1865, 1; "Late Confederate Papers," *Houston TriWeekly Telegraph*, 17 March 1865, 1; "The following are...," *Houston TriWeekly Telegraph*, 20 March 1865, 2; "By Telegraph," *Houston TriWeekly Telegraph*, 27 March 1865, 3; "Headquarters C.S. Army," *Houston TriWeekly Telegraph*, 31 March 1865, 1; "By Telegraph," *Houston TriWeekly Telegraph*, 29 March 1865, 4.

are not the opinions of a 'mere mad secessionist.'"[4] As prominent Confederate leaders and respected journalists in Richmond, as well as farmers and planters from across the Deep South, endorsed the idea of black troops, the Galveston paper had difficulty locating news items that supported its resolute opposition to arming slaves.

In the final phase of the debate, editor Edward Cushing of the *Houston Telegraph* grudgingly accepted the necessity of arming the slaves. On 6 March he predicted the convergence of Sherman and Grant upon Lee and called on southerners "to put forth all our strength to meet them." "The one central idea," Cushing thundered, "of every man and woman of the Confederacy, must be the duty they owe the sacred cause of independence." Yet, the *Telegraph*'s editor stopped short of questioning slavery. When the slave-soldier bill was defeated in the Senate, Cushing gloried in the failure: "The sentiment of the country has been manifested in the most unmistakable form against the abandonment...of the institution of slavery." As Sherman continued his destructive march through North Carolina, Cushing said little. Finally, on 24 March, he shifted his views ever so slightly. Opening his lead editorial with the assertion that slavery had divine origins, Cushing produced a clear, concise summary of the standard pro-slavery arguments. Slavery, he contended, had been the basis for southern unity and the means to civilize and uplift the "descendants of Ham." Further, he asserted it constituted "the only relation in which the black and white races can coexist in the same community." Suddenly, in the final paragraph, the Houston editor conceded defeat: "It has become our solemn and deep opinion that the course of this war will make it our duty to put the negro into the field as a soldier, with the musket to fight for preservation alike to him and us."[5]

Five days later, on 29 March, Cushing explained his reversal as the result of military necessity and not heartfelt conviction. The *Telegraph*'s editor struggled to accommodate the central government's actions concerning slavery with the constitution: "It is only proper as a military necessity. ... It could only be adopted as a means to preserve the States themselves in virtue

---

[4] "Telegraphic," *Galveston TriWeekly News*, 3 March 1865, 3; "Vice President Stephens on Slavery," *Galveston TriWeekly News*, 10 March 1865, 3.

[5] E.H. Cushing, "We Suppose the Irrepressible Sherman...," *Houston TriWeekly Telegraph*, 6 March 1865, 4; E.H. Cushing, "Lead Editorial," *Houston TriWeekly Telegraph*, 24 March 1865, 4.

of that duty of their common defense, committed to the general government." Cushing also felt the need to bring this radical step in line with proslavery ideology: "If slavery is what we believe it to be—the best form of society—it is not only fitted for peace but for the exigencies of war." True to his principles, he envisioned the new Confederate soldiers fighting to preserve their own servitude without any hope of freedom. He refused to accept the provision that Davis and Lee and many others considered essential for the measure's success. Reassuring himself that slaves appreciated the "blessings" of slavery and would fight to continue it, Cushing proclaimed that the Confederacy had erred in not putting all of their slaves into the army earlier: "It [slavery] is capable of fighting for the defense of society, and not alone for its destruction. We have blundered in this matter. We have not shown sufficient faith and trust in the institution." This conclusion stood in stark contrast with the views of not only southerners in Virginia and Georgia but also with many white Texans.[6]

After sitting on the sidelines for almost a month, on 3 March editor Willard Richardson of the *Galveston News* reported that he had received from thirty to forty letters in response to John Mills's communication that had advocated black troops. Mills's letter, penned in January and published in the *News* in early February, had caused Galvestonians and Texans in general to address the idea of black troops in detail. From these letters written in response to Mills, Richardson deduced, "If we may judge public opinion by the sentiments of our correspondents, the people of Texas are not in favor of lowering themselves to the level of the negro." Richardson blasted the idea of slave-soldiers as the cry of the weak-hearted and disaffected: "To say that we are ready to emancipate our slaves, would be to say, that we are ready to relinquish what we commenced fighting for. It would be an abandonment of principles, as well as a confession of weakness." Emancipation, the editor of the *News* proclaimed, would not bring European recognition: "Slavery, instead of being an element of weakness is one of our principal elements of strength. Instead of having delayed our recognition, its preservation is the only thing that will bring recognition." The self-interested states of Europe, he affirmed, would more eagerly acknowledge a prosperous slave power than a nation without slaves or crops. "We look upon emancipation as an imprac-

[6] E.H. Cushing, "Lead Editorial," *Houston TriWeekly Telegraph*, 29 March 1865, 2.

tical myth," Richardson concluded, "calculated to amuse some ingenious minds…but one that will not receive a single practical recommendation." Despite the failure of the peace conference, the Galveston editor mirrored the letters found in his columns and steadfastly clung to slavery.[7]

When word arrived on 29 March that Congress had passed legislation to allow black Confederate troops, Richardson grudgingly accepted the fact: "We have always had serious objections to employing slaves as soldiers, but we are willing in this as in other matters of a military character to waive our objection in deference to the wisdom of Congress and the matured judgment of such men as President Davis and Gen. Lee."

The Galveston editor drew considerable satisfaction from the lack of a promise of freedom: "We have had some fears that the employment of negroes in the army would be predicated…on their final emancipation. We are glad to see that our Congress has authorized no such change in the condition of the negro." Instead of freedom, Richardson contended that "the greatest boon they [slave-soldiers] can have for faithful service in our armies, will be their future protection from Yankee tyranny and deception, and the heartless neglect and cruelty with which they have been invariably treated." Many southerners hoped that the Union army's indifference to the difficulties facing refugee slaves would convince them that they had been better off living on the plantation. Slaves may have become a bit disillusioned with their liberators, but they had not become so discouraged that they remained on the plantations when Union troops offered the opportunity to leave. Yet, with slavery undisturbed in Texas, many readers of the *Galveston News* clung to the illusion of black contentment. If the Confederacy were to arm black troops, this method—enlistment without emancipation—bothered the citizens of Galveston the least.[8]

After the failure of the peace mission, the *Houston Telegraph* again ran letters concerning arming the slaves in its columns. On 8 March a letter from Bell County, signed "Wiego," reopened the debate among correspondents. "Wiego," whose only son was in the army, called on his fellow citizens

---

[7] Willard Richardson, "Lately we have had…," *Galveston TriWeekly News*, 3 March 1865, 2.

[8] Willard Richardson, "The Negro Question," *Galveston TriWeekly News*, 29 March 1865, 3.

to stick to their principles and not form black regiments. "This would be a sacrilege," he declared, "to the memory of the slumbering heroes, who have perished, fighting for these institutions." Echoing "Weigo's" views, "H" asserted that those who spoke of dernier resorts were not in earnest but had lost faith in the cause: "These men who thus talk assume a greater amount of wisdom…but I fear they are whipped, and this is only a polite way of acknowledging it." Seeking to renew the other side of the debate, editor Cushing attempted to reach "Freestone" again and admitted that he had destroyed the second portion of the letter writer's argument for arming the slaves: "Last sheet lost; also writer's name. Author please furnish another copy." In "Freestone's" absence, on 10 March, "Tom Anchorite" proclaimed, "Slavery is ours, body and sinews; our right, our property, and we should defend it with all our strength." Abandoning the institution, he affirmed, would degrade all southerners: "To yield it now, would be craven cowardice, and an act worthy only of the submissive spirit of a slave." On 10 March Colonel George W. Carter discussed black troops at a public meeting in Houston: "As to the negro, Col. Carter said he…did not begrudge him a more prominent place in this struggle, and for one, was heartily willing, if necessary, to fight by his side." "It is a pitiful thing in us," Carter argued, "who had lived so closely and affectionately with the negro, to affect any squeamishness about fighting with him." Coming well before word of the bill's passage, Carter's words stood in stark contrast to most of the letters in the *Telegraph*. Yet, a few brave southerners took up the call. In a letter written on 19 March, "T.A." called on Texans to give their all: "Let us here not hang back, but on the contrary, when called upon, send forward such of our negro men as can be spared."[9]

Finally, on 7 April, "Freestone's" "Employment of Negroes, No. 2" appeared in the *Telegraph*. Noting that he was in the good company of Robert E. Lee on the issue, the slave owner from Fairfield systematically took on his opponents. First, he tackled the constitutional prohibition against legislating on slavery by boldly asserting that slaves were men as well as property: "Our

---

[9] "Wiego," "Letter to the Editor," *Houston TriWeekly Telegraph*, 8 March 1865, 3; "H," "Letter to the Editor," *Houston TriWeekly Telegraph*, 8 March 1865, 1; E.H. Cushing, "Employment of the Negroes, No. 2," *Houston TriWeekly Telegraph*, 8 March 1865, 3; "Tom Anchorite," "Letter to the Editor," *Houston TriWeekly Telegraph*, 10 March 1865, 3; "Col. Carter's Speech," *Houston TriWeekly Telegraph*, 15 March 1865, 3.

sons, brothers, and fathers are liable to be conscripted and put in the army in virtue of their being citizens, and rational persons; what clause of the Constitution relieves the negro from the same service?" In "Freestone's" view, southern chattel had been transformed into citizens during the war. Second, he flatly stated that the enlistment of black troops would not be a confession of weakness. "Our astute enemies," he declared, "will not be fooled by brave fronts." Instead of denying that they needed black aid, southerners, he affirmed, must strengthen their armies with new black troops. Third, he claimed to doubt that "the negro can better feed the army than fight with it." Dire projections about the crop losses if slaves entered the army, he considered mere speculation. "Georgia," "Freestone" noted pointedly, "has kept her able-bodied men at home working in her corn and cotton fields, making supplies for General Sherman's army." Provisions could not feed the army if the enemy could take them at will. Fourth, he firmly denied that Confederate black troops would inspire northern recruiting efforts: "They are doing all they can to enlarge the fighting material of their armies, and nothing we can do will stop them, unless indeed, it is this very thing of putting the negroes in our own armies, and thus removing them beyond their reach."[10]

Having squarely countered the standard arguments against arming slaves, "Freestone" suggested that the step would be a moral victory: "By putting them in our armies, we teach our enemies that we do not think more of them [slaves] than we do of our sons, brothers, and fathers, and that there is no sacrifice too great, no honorable means to which we will not resort...to attain and establish our right to self government." "We want them for soldiers," "Freestone" concluded, "we want them to fight against Yankee negroes, we want them to increase the manual strength of our armies. ... Let us have them and we will not quarrel as to the mode of getting." Although "Freestone" had produced another strong argument for black soldiers, his enthusiastic support for arming slaves fit better with the attitudes of southerners in Virginia and Georgia than it fit with his neighbors in Texas.[11]

In the final phase of the debate, no correspondent of the *Galveston News* was able to match the fire and eloquence of John Mills or "Freestone."

---

[10] "Freestone," "Employment of Negroes in Our Armies," *Houston TriWeekly Telegraph*, 7 April 1865, 4.

[11] Ibid.

Yet, five more responses to Judge Mills's "emancipation" letter were included in the columns of the *News* in the immediate aftermath of the failure of the peace conference. On 27 February, a private stationed in the Galveston defenses wrote and declared that the discussion of slavery had begun to have ill effects: "The discussion is untimely and fraught with evil; it engenders panic when there is no danger." In addition, "Pelican Private" challenged southerners to call on those who had gone before to steer their course:

> Shall we sell slavery, the legacy of our fathers—a legacy hallowed by the best blood of the Caucassian [sic] race—to purchase independence: Go to the red fields of Manassas, Sharpsburg and Shiloh...and tell their whitened bones that you are *so base, so low, so abject* that you are ready to abandon the cause for which they fell.

On 15 March "Lance Corporal" wrote from the 33rd Texas Cavalry stationed in East Texas. The writer suggested that black troops would be willingly accepted in the army: "All agree that if emancipation should ever be necessary to secure our independence, the sacrifice will cheerfully be made. But only in case such necessity should exist." Stationed as he was along the Red River, "Lance Corporal" could not see that the necessity had yet arisen. One correspondent from Shreveport entered the fray at this point to recommend the adoption of black troops. On 27 February, M. Estis argued that the conscription and fielding of 300,000 black Confederates would have a dramatic moral impact: "It will convince them [northerners] that we are in earnest, in solid earnest, and that we are ready and willing to make any and all sacrifices." The *Galveston News* also reported on the remarks of Colonel George W. Carter at the public meeting in Houston. In contrast to the *Houston Telegraph*'s report, the *News* stressed the speaker's denunciation of slavery-for-recognition schemes and ignored his expressed willingness to fight beside the negro. Finally, a letter from a woman in Central Texas addressed another aspect of the manpower crisis. "Lucy" wrote from Austin and denounced the "hundred able-bodied young men in the civil and military offices of this city, who shirk the service." "Lucy" suggested that similar men infested every city in the state and concluded by urging "every lady to bring her influence to bear in this matter."[12] John Mills's letter had forced the issue of

[12] "Pelican Private," *Galveston TriWeekly News*, 27 February 1865, 3; "Lance Corporal," "(Duff's) 33D. Tex. Cav. Bee's Brigade," *Galveston TriWeekly News*, 15 March

black troops to the surface in Gulf Coast Texas in January, but while the fire of debate no longer blazed as brightly, it continued to burn in March and April. New ideas originating in the discussions of slavery in the East as well as local ideas kept the discussions of black troops smoldering across Texas until the end of the war.

In the immediate aftermath of the peace conference, Gulf Coast Texans discussed a number of proposals to place black troops in the gray ranks. Although Cushing of the *Houston Telegraph* and Richardson of the *Galveston News* maintained their opposition, the correspondents of each paper demonstrated more willingness to consider radical steps. Unlike the letters written to the *News* in response to John Mills during January and early February, a few in the *Telegraph*—like the voices of "T.A." and "Freestone," as well as the remarks of George Carter—rose to support arming slaves. Similarly, "Lance Corporal" and M. Estis made strong endorsements of black troops in the *News*. The breadth of the discussion among the letter writers clearly demonstrated that the citizens of Gulf Coast Texas were seriously weighing the value of slavery. Unthreatened by Union forces and still capable of selling their slave-produced cotton in Mexico, Texans struggled to decide what they must do to attain victory. All the issues discussed in Virginia and Georgia were discussed in Texas. Most Gulf Coast Texans reached different answers than their neighbors in the war-ravaged East, but the serious consideration of black troops illustrates that many, if not all, Texans were coming to the point where they could envision a South without slavery.

Abraham Lincoln's terms for peace—reunion and no retreat from the Emancipation Proclamation—renewed the debate over arming slaves in East Texas. On 24 February the *Marshall Texas Republican* printed the Confederate commissioner's reports and President Davis's patriotic call for new sacrifices at a mass meeting in Richmond.[13] In the same edition, the editor men-

---

1865, 2; M. Estis, "Shreveport Correspondence," *Galveston TriWeekly News*, 27 February 1865, 2; "Col. Carter's Speech," *Galveston TriWeekly News*, 15 March 1865, 2; "Lucy," "Letter from a Lady," *Galveston TriWeekly News*, 10 March 1865, 2.

[13] "Delayed Northern Dispatches," *Marshall Texas Republican*, 24 February 1865, 2. These reports came from a northern paper and were not verified until 24 March when Richmond papers describing the event arrived in Marshall: "The Feeling in the Country," *Marshall Texas Republican*, 24 March 1865, 2.

tioned discussing the situation with a former colleague from the *Quitman* [TX] *Democrat* who had recently returned from Hood's army: "He brings good news of the condition of our armies east of the river. No despondency, or reconstruction, or weak kneed emancipation feeling there." No longer concerned with peace proposals or schemes for recognition, the *Republican* focused on Congressional efforts to fill the ranks. The comments of Gustavus Henry in support of black troops appeared in Marshall on 3 March: "We have men enough who have never been in the service to drive the enemy before us; let us bring them into the field, and give them an opportunity to take part in this great war." Securing the right of self-government, Henry affirmed, warranted the sacrifice. On 17 March the Marshall paper published a southern report that the "Slave-soldier Bill" had been defeated: "The bill was lost in the Senate by a vote of 11 to 10. In official circles this is considered as disposing of the question of arming negroes finally." The Marshall paper looked on the attitudes of its Virginia contemporaries with concern: "The Richmond papers are more frantic than ever. The *Enquirer* calls upon Jeff. Davis to arm slaves without the authority of law." To the surprise of many Texans who opposed black troops, the following week the *Republican* announced that the eulogy had been given too soon and that the slave-soldier was very much alive: "The rebel House of Representatives passed another bill to place 300,000 negroes in the army." Although the report came from a northern paper, no one could misunderstand the step taken in Richmond. Ironically, in the same issue, an appeal from the editor also appeared in Marshall calling for military authorities in Texas to release the impressed slaves then working with the army in order to facilitate spring planting. Subsequently, on 7 April the *Republican* printed the full text of the "Negro Soldier Bill," including the provisions for equal uniforms, rations, and pay for white and black soldiers. In order for the act to pass in Congress—and be acceptable in East Texas—the final provision left the status of the black Confederate soldier in doubt: "Nothing in this act shall be construed to authorize a change in the relation which said slaves shall bear towards their owners." If the slave was to earn his freedom in the army, the master would have to award it to him. In the final phase of the debate, the news items appearing in Marshall came almost exclusively from Virginia. The president, congressmen, and generals in Richmond all strongly supported the radical step and thus demonstrated to the citizens of East Texas that a South without slavery was possible.[14]

As in Marshall, the unsuccessful return of the Confederate commissioners from Hampton Roads sparked renewed interest in Dallas about the proposal to arm the slaves. On 16 March the *Dallas Herald* printed a portion of the Congressional debate over black troops highlighting the opposition of James Leach of North Carolina. In the same issue, the Dallas paper took the front page to speculate on two new Confederate warships and on the likelihood of a French alliance. In Dallas, the slave-soldier issue did not grip the citizens as it did in many communities in Virginia and Georgia. As the slave-soldier legislation wound through Congress, the *Herald* provided a synopsis of events but omitted the names of the advocates on each side. On 6 April word arrived that a bill to place black men in gray uniforms had been approved, and the paper printed the measure in small type but in its entirety. A week later, Davis's frustrations with Congress on the issue became evident in Dallas: "Much benefit is anticipated from this measure, though far less than would have resulted from its adoption at an earlier date, so as to afford time for their organization and instruction during the winter months." The president had recognized the need for black troops much sooner than most southerners. It had taken the entire winter for Congress, like the citizens of East Texas, to understand that they had to choose between independence and slavery. Unwilling to allow themselves to be hurried by the calls of necessity, southerners had discussed the issue fully but reached their choice only after it had become too late to be implemented. An editorial from the *Richmond Examiner*, a very late convert to black troops, cautioned against expecting the new black recruits to relieve the pressure on the white veterans: "Two weeks will elapse before the stress of the campaign will be upon

[14] "Lt. W.J. Sparks," *Marshall Texas Republican*, 24 February 1865, 2; "Speech of Hon. G.A. Henry of Tennessee in the Senate of the Confederate States," *Marshall Texas Republican*, 3 March 1865, 1; "The Latest," *Marshall Texas Republican*, 17 March 1865, 2; "New York, March 4," *Marshall Texas Republican*, 24 March 1865, 2; "The Coming Crop," *Marshall Texas Republican*, 24 March 1865, 2; "The Latest News," *Marshall Texas Republican*, 31 March 1865, 2; "Negro Soldier Bill Passed," *Marshall Texas Republican*, 7 April 1865, 1.

us. Negro regiments cannot be raised in that time, but many white absentees may be returned."[15]

In the wake of the authorization of black troops, the *Dallas Herald* enthusiastically chronicled the formation of the new units. On 22 March a battalion composed of three white companies and two black companies marched down the streets of Richmond before a large crowd. Although the black troops lacked uniforms, one observer asserted that the crowd "generally concurred in the opinion that Sambo could be taught to handle a gun as well as a hoe." Another member of the crowd declared that the drill performed by the new unit would have "done credit to veteran soldiers." On 20 April, the Dallas paper reprinted an editorial from Virginia claiming that slaves hesitated to join the Confederate units because no one could explain the terms of enlistment to the potential recruits:

> The nature of the service which they will be expected to perform, the relations they will bear to the white troops, and the necessity devolving upon them of aiding in the preservation of their own race from extinction, should be expounded in the clearest manner. Let this be done and an army of negro troops will soon be raised.

The ambiguous stance assumed by Congress left enrolling officers without clear direction. The formation of new units rather than the introduction of the black troops into veteran units as replacements led to considerable confusion. No apparatus existed in the Confederate army to assimilate the large number of black recruits expected. On 23 March the *Herald* printed a stylized account of black loyalty to their masters intended to reassure the large number of citizens who continued to have doubts about the prudence of black troops. In this piece, Dick, a slave from Petersburg, was returned to southern authorities with several others "who resisted all solicitations to join the enemy." The author suggested that slaves like Dick, who had seen the Yankees up close and knew their true nature, should form the basis for the new units. Finally, on 27 April, the *Herald* told the story of how

---

[15] "Delayed Telegrams," *Dallas Herald*, 16 March 1865, 2; "Important If True," *Dallas Herald*, 16 March 1865, 1; "By Last Night's Mail," *Dallas Herald*, 23 March 1865, 2; "Negro Soldier Bill," *Dallas Herald*, 6 April 1865, 2; "Important Message of President Davis," *Dallas Herald*, 13 April 1865, 1; "Washington, March 14," *Dallas Herald*, 6 April 1865, 2.

one Confederate general enrolled his own slaves. Nathan Bedford Forrest, the report claimed, "called out twenty-six of his own negro men, and said to them, 'All of you who are willing to become soldiers for the war, step forward and I will give to every one who does so his free papers.'" According to this account, twenty-five men immediately stepped forward volunteering for service and received their freedom. While praising the enlistment of these black soldiers, the *Herald* stopped short of calling for similar steps in Dallas. In contrast to its indifference to the issue early in the debate, after the bill passed, the *Dallas Herald* followed the efforts to form black units carefully.[16]

In Marshall, Robert Loughery welcomed the failure of the peace conference: "It will unite the South. It will put an end to fault-finding and croaking, and misguided men who were sewing the seeds of dissension and discontent in Southern communities." Similarly, he refused to panic at the loss of Charleston and Wilmington, insisting that it would free up fixed garrisons for field service. The loss of Atlantic ports, unlike the potential capture of a Gulf Coast port, alarmed few in Marshall. On 14 April, Loughery announced Congressional approval of black troops and asserted that military necessity had overwhelmed principle: "Looking to the alarming condition of affairs East of the Mississippi River; to the fact that…a majority of Congress has adopted it;…we lose sight of the question itself, in the overwhelming necessity that produced it." Military service, Loughery reasoned, would unfit the black veteran for slavery: "The moment a negro was made a soldier, with arms in his hands and receiving the same pay, rations, and treatment of the white man, that his moral and political status would be changed. … He would never…be such a slave as it would be either profitable or safe to own." Insisting that "instinct, prejudice, and reason" solidly opposed arming slaves, Loughery grudgingly agreed to the experiment: "We seem willing to await the issue of events; to lay aside for the present, reason and prejudice, and let time…pass its verdict on the measure." Two factors, the Marshall editor suggested, would limit the measure's unwanted consequences: "1st, that of

---

[16] "First Parade of Negro Troops in Richmond," *Dallas Herald*, 20 April 1865, 1; "An Intelligent Contraband," *Dallas Herald*, 23 March 1865, 1; "From the *Richmond Whig*, March 22," *Dallas Herald*, 20 April 1865, 2; "Gen. Forrest," *Dallas Herald*, 27 April 1865, 2. The Forrest story is likely a fabrication. Forrest remained committed to slavery and racial supremacy throughout his life. Clearly, the editor is trying to show the practicality of slaves becoming soldiers.

the three hundred thousand negroes that may enter the army, not one-fourth are likely to ever return; and 2nd that, as they are males, the evils consequent upon their changed condition, would last only their lives." Unlike Davis, Lee, and most southerners, Loughery expected the black soldiers to fight to maintain the bondage of their families. Beyond this specific measure, the editor of the *Republican* decried the tenor of Congressional acts and messages originating in Richmond: "Everything emanating from the President recently bears the impress of distrust of our success, if not hopelessness and despair. ... We are ready to endure all things and to hope all things, but a righteous heaven save us from such legislation." As he announced the fall of Richmond and surrender of Lee, Loughery finally called for black troops to be deployed in Texas: "We have at least 75,000 veteran soldiers in the department to place with 40,000 negroes, to be used as the commanders may think best. Better do that than to do worse; and whatever is done;...must be done quickly." The necessity to arm the slaves only emerged in Loughery's mind once all the Confederate armies east of the Mississippi had been destroyed.[17]

As in earlier phases of the slave-soldier debate, editor John Swindells of the *Dallas Herald* failed to provide a short, concise statement of his opinions but, rather, employed the words of others to express his sentiments. On 23 March Swindells printed a speech given by his longtime ally and friend, Senator Louis T. Wigfall. Refuting the idea of a rich man's war and a poor man's fight, the Texas senator declared that the poor man had the most to fear from the loss of slavery and Confederate defeat: "He would inevitably be crushed, while the man of wealth and talent, and distinguished officers would buy or demand and obtain protection in any part of the world." Only the poor white, Wigfall argued, would be left to compete with the emancipated slave. Judging by the steady stream of men deserting from the southern armies, few Confederate soldiers accepted this logic. When word of the

[17] Robert Loughery, "The Telegraphic Intelligence," *Marshall Texas Republican*, 24 February 1865, 2; Robert Loughery, "The News—The Prospect," *Marshall Texas Republican*, 24 February 1865, 2; Robert Loughery, "The Negro Conscription," *Marshall Texas Republican*, 14 April 1865, 2; Robert Loughery, "The President's Message," *Marshall Texas Republican*, 14 April 1865, 2; Robert Loughery, "The intelligence which we publish...," *Marshall Texas Republican*, 7 April 1865, 2; Robert Loughery, "The Change of Policy," *Marshall Texas Republican*, 21 April 1865, 2.

disastrous Battle of Five Forks arrived, Swindells assured his readers that the accounts were simply Yankee propaganda. "It will be seen," he projected, "that the Yankee dispatches are again flying to the breeze rumors of peace, based upon the downfall of the rebellion. … We don't place any reliance in any such reports." Later in the same edition of the *Herald*, the editor praised the "good conduct" and "bravery" of the slave population in general and commended one slave in particular for rescuing two children from a fire. Swindells included such pieces to reassure the white residents of the loyalty of their black neighbors. On 27 April Swindells reprinted an editorial from Mississippi chastising the Richmond press for its self-absorption and its radical ideas: "Richmond is not the Confederate States; nor do the Richmond journals with all their praise worthy love of the grand and glorious Old Dominion, correctly expound Southern popular sentiment." Further, the Meridian editor bridled at the Virginian editors' attempts to lead public opinion: "Richmond papers seek to excite jealousies between Middle and Gulf States, because as they allege, the latter are unwilling to convert slaves into soldiers." Angrily, the Mississippian asserted that there was no difference of opinion between the regions: "The supposition is baseless. Our Congressmen do not properly represent their constituents. Let the negro go. If he will make a soldier, the Gulf States will furnish half a million negroes." As the nation crumbled and President Davis called for black troops and a resort to guerrilla warfare, the *Herald*'s editor praised Davis's "godlike conduct" in comparison to the "party hacks" who ruled in Congress. Swindells was willing to go the full distance with the Confederacy. He never clearly avowed support for black troops, but he consistently chose and prominently placed editorials and news items that furthered the debate. These pieces openly and consistently advocated the enlistment of black Confederates, a step the editor could not bring himself to take in his Dallas columns.[18]

In the wake of John Mills's bold proposals during the second phase of the debate, Robert Loughery attempted to set the tone for East Texas letter writers in late February: "It is evident to every well informed reflecting man,

[18] John Swindells, "Speech of Mr. Wigfall," *Dallas Herald*, 23 March 1865, 2; John Swindells, "Our Houston papers…," *Dallas Herald*, 20 April 1865, 2; John Swindells, "Good Conduct," *Dallas Herald*, 20 April 1865, 1; John Swindells, "The *Richmond Enquirer*…," *Dallas Herald*, 27 April 1865, 1; John Swindells, "The Last Days of Congress…," *Dallas Herald*, 27 April 1865, 1.

that emancipation, either immediate or remote, while it would degrade our people and destroy the prosperity of our country, would not be of the slightest benefit to us in the pending struggle." In response, "Old Soldier" spoke for many small slaveholders as he penned a stinging indictment of the government's use of slaves impressed into the army: "When I see my country bleeding at every pore, and our officials misapplying the resources, viz: to cleaning up ballrooms and waiting on those on temporary service here…when my sons are doing the menial service of the camp, I feel that all our sacrifices are of no avail." If Confederate leaders had not employed impressed slaves wisely, the writer seriously questioned how these same generals would utilize an army of slaves if slave owners sacrificed the institution. Hundreds of idle acres, "Old Soldier" concluded, might be put into provision crops for soldiers' families if the army would release these underemployed slaves. A soldier from Tennessee traveling through Texas had little sympathy for such complaints: "My erring citizen, let me whisper a few words in your ear. Never have your daily avocations been disturbed by the presence of the enemy; you have been allowed to work your fields in peace, and have for the last two years been blessed by abundant crops. Your prosperity…has not been swept away." Texans had been inconvenienced by the war, the Tennessean decided, but had never known the war as other southerners had. In a different column of the *Republican*, C.S. West of General Smith's staff stopped short of advocating revolutionary measures but echoed many of the Tennessean's complaints: "The truth is our people are asleep! they are dreaming of gold and of cotton! dreaming of peace! instead of preparing vigorously for prolonged, earnest, unrelenting, merciless war!" Arguing that hard war might lead to frightful choices, West proclaimed, "I will however take any of them [emancipation or foreign alliance] as a dernier resort; yea, abolition itself, rather than lose our independence."[19]

These varied responses to the idea of slave-soldiers led Loughery to publish two strong arguments from prominent citizens against arming slaves. On 17 March a letter from Ashbel Smith appeared in the *Republican* and

[19] Robert Loughery, "The Communication of Col. Gillespie," *Marshall Texas Republican*, 24 February 1865, 2; "Old Soldier," "For the Texas Republican," *Marshall Texas Republican*, 3 March 1865, 1; "A Follower of Forrest," "I'm ruined! I'm ruined!", *Marshall Texas Republican*, 10 March 1865, 1; C.S. West, "For the Texas Republican," *Marshall Texas Republican*, 3 March 1865, 1.

questioned the idea that emancipation would have any impact on Confederate foreign relations. Having negotiated recognition with Britain and France for the Republic of Texas, Smith ridiculed all who thought slavery was the reason Europe failed to recognize the Confederacy: "The poor simpletons, why, slavery in its moral aspects, has never delayed recognition for an hour, nor would its abandonment now hasten by one hour our recognition." Self-interest and not any moral ideal, he averred, guided the European powers. Further, Smith asserted that Mills had accepted the ideology of the abolitionists if he believed that the world was set against slavery: "They have adopted the stereotyped cant of the vilest section of the black republican party in the United States. They abandon the fundamental principles of the South, and have taken up the cry of Wendell Phillips." Similarly, on 24 March Loughery printed the charge of Judge C.A. Frazier to a grand jury sitting on a treason case. "Is not the…advocacy of either reconstruction or emancipation a treasonable adherence to them and their cause? Is it not aiding the enemy to engraft that faith, and those opinions, and principles upon the hearts of the people?" All classes in white society, Frazier contended, benefited from the institution: "The rich and the poor, the enlightened and the illiterate, all have a vital interest in the institution. … Slavery is a source of income to the master, and the barrier that stands between thousands of our fellow citizens and their [slaves'] condition." Emancipation, Frazier affirmed, would bring subjugation and not independence. On 24 March, as Lee teetered on the edge of defeat, Frazier boldly declared that Texans did not have to choose between independence and slavery: "The preservation of our institutions is as sacred a duty to ourselves and our posterity as that of establishing our independence as a nation. Indeed they are one and inseparable." Although the judge saw no need to arm slaves, he resolutely called for southerners to give their all for the cause. If we cannot gain our independence on our own terms, Frazier concluded, "let us place all in one funeral pile and fall together in the common ruin." Smith had a national reputation as a diplomat and Frazier exerted considerable local influence. These two prominent citizens forcefully rebutted Mills's contentions that emancipation might strengthen the southern cause on the battlefield and abroad. Unlike the soldiers who had written to the *Republican*, these wealthy slave owners had seen little of the war and, therefore, could not envision a Texas without slavery.[20]

Since John Mills's January letter had appeared in the *Galveston News* and in the *Marshall Republican*, soldiers, planters, and old politicians had all taken turns jousting with him. His name, long a prominent one in Texas political circles, had become synonymous with emancipation. On 1 March, Mills broke and recanted his letter of 20 January. "The object which I had in writing," Mills declared, "has been accomplished." The revolutionary ideas found in the letter, he assured his neighbors in Marshall, were not his own: "In my letter I embodied...the opinions I have so frequently heard expressed by loungers about town, railroad travelers, and much to my surprise, by some large and intelligent slaveholders. ... To give impetus to such discussion, I assumed, for a time, to entertain these opinions." The resulting discussion of slavery, Mills believed, had been quite profitable as it caused Texans to examine the institution, the concept of independence, and the relationship between the two. Mills suggested that the strawman he created in January had allowed prominent Texans to avert a popular call for emancipation. Declaring the numerous replies to his letter "perfectly satisfactory," he contended that the debate in Texas had unified rather than divided the citizens. "Never since the war began," Mills concluded, "have I doubted our ability to maintain our independence without humiliating concessions to Yankeedom, or any of the rest of mankind, on the subject of slavery or any other." Whether an administration official inspired the initial letter or Mills undertook it on his own, the judge had paid a high price. In his second letter he acknowledged "denunciations thick and heavy" in response for the positions he had taken. Any hope for a renewed political career was gone.[21]

Despite a surface plausibility, Mills's explanations for his earlier position do not ring true. First, if he only wanted to create a strawman, the judge would have been well advised to employ a pseudonym, thus allowing the ideas to surface without sullying his name. The only advantage of using his real name was to give the ideas expressed more legitimacy. Second, the re-

[20] Ashbel Smith, "Letter from COL. ASHBEL SMITH," *Marshall Texas Republican*, 17 March 1865, 1; C.A. Frasier, "Charge of Judge C.A. Frazier," *Marshall Texas Republican*, 24 March 1865, 1.

[21] John T. Mills, "Robertson County, March 1st. 1865," *Marshall Texas Republican*, 17 March 1865, 2.

traction letter from Mills did not reflect the same strong arguments buttressed by keen insights into the situation of the nation that distinguished the first letter. The finely developed ideas in the first communication illustrated the care expended in its production. If it was a strawman, it was one built with golden prose. Finally, the timing of the retraction, just after the failure of the peace conference, suggests that Mills saw the end coming and did not want to be counted as one who had advocated radical yet unacceptable measures. Perhaps he had lost faith in the Confederacy or, as likely, had given up on his fellow Texans, fearing that they would never be willing to make serious sacrifices. In short, he appears to be a politician backtracking quickly from an exposed position that the public failed to embrace. Interestingly, no other Texas newspaper printed Mills's letter renouncing his previous views.

In East Texas, the debate over arming slaves produced fruit in March and April. While Robert Loughery in Marshall stoutly refused to accept the need for black troops, others like John Swindells in Dallas probed the concept in detail. Despite Swindells's willingness to print a number of pieces concerning black troops, no letters on the topic made it into the columns of the *Dallas Herald*. In contrast, the correspondents of the *Marshall Texas Republican* produced a clear picture of a dynamic local debate focused on the reward given to the black veteran for faithful service. Few in East Texas reached the depth of discussion seen in Virginia and Georgia, where southerners accepted the need for black recruits gained by an offer of emancipation and, therefore, spent the last phase of the debate considering the role of the emancipated slave in a post-war, independent South. Yet, the slave-soldier debate as it developed in Marshall and Dallas clearly demonstrates that Texans seriously considered the use of black troops and the long-range implications of the step. A distinct minority of East Texans boldly advocated the move to arm slaves, but the range of views expressed in opposition indicates a community thoroughly reassessing its values.

The failure of the Hampton Roads Conference and the speeches of prominent men in Richmond added potent fuel to the debate over slave-soldiers that smoldered in Central Texas. On 1 March the *State Gazette* printed the president's and the commissioners' reports of the peace conference. Agreeing with the Richmond leadership that the situation called for absolute unity, the Austin paper decried class divisions as it printed an item from Mobile that questioned the planters' faith in the cause: "It is the fear of losing property, the dread of exile from their homes, the lack of nerve to face and endure the privations and trials that have overtaken so many of their countrymen...that causes so many to despond." Other reports in early March suggested that the army ranks were not as thin as often reported. "There may be less ardor," a *Richmond Whig* editorial boomed in Austin, "but there is perhaps more determination." Throughout March and into early April, items appeared in the *Gazette* discussing the impact of Confederate emancipation upon French and British policy. None of these articles discussed the impact of emancipation on the South, but focused instead on the step's importance in winning European recognition. Long after other newspapers had abandoned the idea, the *Gazette* continued to speak enthusiastically of a diplomatic path to independence. Finally, on 29 March the Austin paper noted the debate over arming slaves in the Confederate Congress. In the same issue, the *Gazette* reported that the Virginia legislature had intervened and instructed the state's senators to change their votes to ensure passage of the "Negro Soldier Bill." On the same page, the paper proclaimed the North Carolina legislature's opposition to the measure. As late as 10 May, over a month after announcing the first enlistment of black troops, the Austin paper questioned what had become of the constitutional protests raised by the Carolinians. Unlike papers across the South, the *State Gazette* reported the Congressional debate only in its final stages and provided no information on how individual leaders had voted. Reports of black men in gray uniforms filled the columns of many southern newspapers, but the Austin paper resolutely refused to follow the tide. In early May the *Gazette* partially explained its reticence: "We hold that the people are entitled to know everything about their government; though it is not probably at all times prudent that every act of those in authority should be made public." Williamson Oldham, an 1860 resident of Austin, had introduced the bill authorizing black troops in the Confederate Senate, but the Austin paper did not pass the word to their readers. Clearly, the editor of the *State Gazette* did not think the citizens of Austin needed to know the depth of the slave-soldier debate that blazed through the Confederacy.[22]

---

[22] "The Very Latest News," *Austin The Weekly State Gazette*, 1 March 1865, 2; "The following from the *Mobile Advertiser*...," *Austin The Weekly State Gazette*, 1 March 1865,

In Bellville, news of the failure of the Hampton Roads Conference struck somber chords. The account from the wire service appeared on 28 February and left little question about the immediate future: "Both sides denominate the attempt to negotiate, an utter and complete failure; and both announce a vigorous prosecution of the war as the only road to peace." Twice in the next month, *The Countryman* printed reports of General Lee's support for black soldiers and his conviction that he could make valuable soldiers of the former slaves. "I would but give to them the certainty of freedom and a home when they shall have rendered efficient service," the Confederate commander declared. When the measure came before the Confederate Senate, Osterhout noted Texas senators Louis Wigfall's opposition and Williamson Oldham's support for the measure. After announcing Lee's surrender on 25 April, *The Countryman* attempted to ignore Confederate efforts to raise black replacements. For example, on 16 May the paper printed under a large headline the new conscript bill, which detailed efforts to get every white man into the army. In the next column, the Bellville paper placed the full text of the bill to arm the slaves, but instead of a similar headline, Osterhout hid it in smaller type under the heading, "From the *Richmond Whig*." The "Negro Soldier Bill" that Congress passed gave Osterhout exactly what he had desired in February—slave-soldiers without a guarantee of freedom—but he never crowed that his ideas had been adopted or commented on the efforts throughout the South to implement the measure. With the Confederacy crumbling, the editor in Bellville saw little incentive to tamper with slavery.[23]

2; "The *Richmond Whig*, Jan 6th," *Austin The Weekly State Gazette*, 1 March 1865, 1; "The New Plan," *Austin The Weekly State Gazette*, 1 March 1865, 1; "By Sunday's Mail" and "By Friday's Mail," *Austin The Weekly State Gazette*, 29 March 1865, 1; "A Continental Policy for America," *Austin The Weekly State Gazette*, 5 April 1865, 1; "The Legislature of North Carolina," *Austin The Weekly State Gazette*, 10 May 1865, 2; "By Friday's Mail," *Austin The Weekly State Gazette*, 12 April 1865, 1; "To the Public," *Austin The Weekly State Gazette*, 3 May 1865, 1; "A Bill to Provide for Raising 200,000 Negro Troops," *Lynchburg Virginian*, 15 February 1865, 2. The Marshall and Galveston papers carried some remarks on the state of the country during this period, but like the *State Gazette*, neither journal trumpeted Oldham's proposal.

[23] "The Peace Mission," *Bellville Countryman*, 28 February 1865, 1; "Gen. Lee on the Use of Negroes in the Army," *Bellville Countryman*, 14 March 1865, 1; "From the *Richmond Enquirer*," *Bellville Countryman*, 28 March 1865, 1; "The News Condensed,"

In LaGrange, the *Patriot* printed a number of news items concerning slavery and the government, but most pieces conformed to the paper's "states' rights" position. Again noting the stance of Governor Brown of Georgia, the *Patriot* decried the central government's employment of slaves and tax-in-kind policies: "The present policy is the surest mode to diminish the armies, exhaust the Treasury, break down the spirits of the people, and drive them to despair." Closer to home, on 18 March the LaGrange paper provided an account of a public meeting in Austin and highlighted the remarks of Lieutenant Governor Fletcher Stockdale. Unwilling to believe that Sherman's movements had produced real despondency, Stockdale blamed the "Richmond papers who seem willing to invoke foreign aid at the sacrifice of our domestic institutions." On 8 April the *Patriot* presented a synopsis of President Davis's 13 March message to the Confederate Congress, which asked in part for black troops. This portion was omitted from the account that appeared in LaGrange, but an adjoining column provided Lincoln's views of black men in gray. "I have in my lifetime," the U.S. president asserted, "heard many arguments why the negroes ought to be slaves; but if they fight for those who would keep them in slavery, it would be a better argument than I have yet heard." Contending that slaves could not fight and produce provisions at the same time, Lincoln said it made little difference how the slaves were used. After the news of Lee's surrender arrived on 29 April, no more items concerning slave-soldiers appeared in the *Patriot*.[24]

Far from the climactic events in Virginia, David Robinson clung to his principles and struggled to find some way to keep faith in the cause without making tough choices. On 1 March and again on 5 April, the *Austin State Gazette*'s editor predicted salvation in the form of an alliance between the Union and Confederate forces in order to expel the Europeans from Mexico. Even as he grasped at such straws, he refused to publish Davis's final address to Congress. Citing space considerations, Robinson printed portions of the message on treasury notes, supplies for the army, and military exemptions,

---

Bellville Countryman, 21 March 1865, 1; "Bad News," *Bellville Countryman*, 25 April 1865, 1; "From the *Richmond Whig*," *Bellville Countryman*, 16 May 1865, 1.

[24] "New Orleans, February 24," *The LaGrange Patriot*, 18 March 1865, 1; "We acknowledge our obligation…," *The LaGrange Patriot*, 18 March 1865, 2; "President's Message—Synopsis," *The LaGrange Patriot*, 8 April 1865, 2; "Mr. Lincoln's Speech," *The LaGrange Patriot*, 8 April 1865, 2; "Telegraphic," *The LaGrange Patriot*, 29 April 1865, 1.

but omitted a central portion that demanded passage of the slave-soldier legislation. On 12 April the editor noted the formation of black units in Richmond but made only the slightest editorial comment: "From all accounts Sambo can as readily be taught the use of the musket as the hoe. Several companies were drilled in the streets in Richmond and are said to have presented a very creditable appearance." Such a step appeared counterproductive to Robinson, who had other plans for the slaves. "No supplies can be obtained from abroad," he contended, "for the army or the people, save through the medium of cotton." New Conscription Bureau regulations announced by W.J. Herbert in April limited production to subsistence crops only, as the government's grip on manpower tightened: "Exempted Farmers are required to raise grain and provisions exclusively. Farmers detailed or exempted, having less than fifteen hands, are required to select companies for assignment." Even as the Confederacy imploded in April 1865, Robinson proclaimed the crucial importance of cotton production, denounced all moves to take the slave from the plantation, and championed the interests of the slave owner while saying nothing of the non-slaveholding farmer who suddenly found himself sent to the army. In Robinson's view, the Confederacy had made all the wrong moves. Congress had made soldiers of slaves and now the army sought to end cotton production. The revolution had gone badly wrong in the Austin editor's eyes.[25]

Having accepted the idea of arming the slaves without emancipation in February, John P. Osterhout at *The Countryman* stoutly refused to move any further. On 28 February he chastised the *Quid Nunc* of Crockett for discussing black freedom: "It is much to be regretted that this apple of discord should have been introduced into the struggle. It can do no good." Twice, in March, Osterhout called for the end of all details and exemptions: "Shall we yield? Never! No, Never! We say rather, let every man to the front, without regard to age, occupation, or exemption." In neither appeal for "all" to go forward to battle did he mention black troops either as slaves or freemen.

[25] David Robinson, "Alliance," *Austin The Weekly State Gazette*, 1 March 1865, 2; David Robinson, "In Another Column…," *Austin The Weekly State Gazette*, 5 April 1865, 2; David Robinson, "The Message of President Davis," *Austin The Weekly State Gazette*, 5 April 1865, 1; David Robinson, "Recruiting negro troops…," *Austin The Weekly State Gazette*, 12 April 1865, 2; David Robinson, "Cotton," *Austin The Weekly State Gazette*, 5 April 1865, 2.

Finally, on the day the "Negro Soldier Bill" appeared in the Bellville paper, Osterhout printed a two-column biblical defense of slavery. Alexander Gregg, the Episcopal Bishop of Texas, described discussions of emancipation as manifestations of moral weakness and against the laws of nature. In the final crisis of the war, the editor of *The Countryman* chose the preservation of slavery over his oft expressed hopes for southern independence.[26]

An argument with Edward Cushing, the editor of the *Houston Telegraph*, forced William McClellan of the *LaGrange Patriot* to openly declare just how far he was willing to go in support of the Confederacy. On 4 March McClellan printed Cushing's charges against him. Specifically, the Houston editor accused him of being a pre-war opponent of states' rights, having openly discussed emancipation while in Kentucky, and having been a strong opponent of secession in 1861. "He who publickly [sic] urges that the impressment laws are unjust, unnecessary, and unwise," Cushing asserted, "must secretly (at least) believe that the cause to sustain which they are imperatively demanded, is unjust, unwise, and its success unnecessary." Cushing had received significant criticism for his grudging support of Davis's centralizing measures such as impressment, conscription, and taxes. Therefore, when the *Patriot* questioned Cushing's faith in states' rights, the Houston editor exploded. Cushing had strongly supported the states' rights and proslavery positions generally accepted in the South for over fifteen years. To be accused by McClellan, who had openly opposed secession, of being unfaithful to southern principles struck Cushing as too much. McClellan conceded that he never believed in the right of secession, but he strongly refuted the Houston editor's other assertions. First, he claimed that he had always considered slavery a matter subject exclusively to state control: "Once surrender its [slavery's] control to either a Federal or a Confederate authority, and its doom, sooner or later, and at no distant period at that, is sealed forever." Second, he affirmed that his belief in states' rights extended to the point that he thought a state could take steps no other body should legitimately take: "Each State now has the right, if it is deemed best, to dedicate every slave

---

[26] J.P. Osterhout, "The Quid Nune," *Bellville Countryman*, 28 February 1865, 1; J.P. Osterhout, "The Failure of Lincoln to Make Peace," *Bellville Countryman*, 21 March 1865, 1; "Cyrus," "A Plan for the Election of Civil Officers of the State," *Bellville Countryman*, 7 March 1865, 1; J.P. Osterhout, "Bishop Gregg on Slavery," *Bellville Countryman*, 16 May 1865, 1.

within its borders to the upholding of this war, whether they employ them as soldiers, camp servants, engineers, teamsters, or in any other capacity." In conclusion, he argued that the key point was not whether slavery survived but whether the government acted in accordance with "the principles of our institutions." Black men in gray might be necessary, he admitted, but the sacrifice must be made by the people of the states and could not be made by the Richmond government: "If so, let the people, according to the true forms and principles of their government, resolve upon and declare it. Theirs is the right, theirs is the sacrifice, and they have the right to make it." Upon receipt of the news that Congress had approved black troops, on 8 April McClellan vowed to make the best of it. Asserting that the new policy "set aside, and forever, the dogma upon which we originally staked the issue," the LaGrange editor argued that he could see no necessity for the measure: "The situation East of the Mississippi may present a demand for the military services of the negroes which, we on this side, cannot well appreciate." Further, he proclaimed, "We feel certain that the time has not come for the enrollment of negroes—slaves or freemen—in the Confederate armies, here in Texas." William McClellan, despite the decision of the civil and military authorities east of the Mississippi, simply refused to accept the change in policy.[27]

Two powerful if contradictory letters appeared in the *State Gazette* during the final phase of the debate. In an appeal to the citizens of Texas on 3 May, Governor Pendleton Murrah admitted the severity of the crisis but called upon Texans to remember that the defeat at the Alamo was followed by victory at San Jacinto. Murrah argued that they must rely upon God and themselves and not upon fanciful ideas: "You cannot look for relief to emancipation, nor to those other weak and wicked delusions—reconstruction and a foreign protectorate. The men who would distract you with such treasonable proposals are unworthy of your confidence." Condemning the national government, he called upon Texans to remain true to the original aims of the war. "When a nation forgets the principles which led her into revolu-

[27] E.H. Cushing, "The *LaGrange Patriot*...," *The LaGrange Patriot*, 4 March 1865, 2; William McClellan, "We shall certainly not quarrel...," *The LaGrange Patriot*, 4 March 1865, 2; William McClellan, "We copy below...," *The LaGrange Patriot*, 8 April 1865, 2; William McClellan, "We have noticed...," *The LaGrange Patriot*, 22 April 1865, 1.

tion," the governor proclaimed, "she ceases to be the same Nation." In the same issue of the *Gazette,* a letter from General Thomas C. Hindman presented a diametrically opposed view. Stationed in San Antonio, the wounded officer suggested that the "Negro Soldier Bill" offered "the remedy for the misfortunes east of the Mississippi." Hindman, who was present when Pat Cleburne placed his memorial before the officers of the Army of Tennessee, suggested that if it had been implemented at that time, Sherman could not have succeeded in his 1864 campaign. Noting the absence of a guarantee of freedom in the measure adopted by Congress in March, the general proclaimed the promise essential: "It seems improbable that any considerable number of slaves will volunteer, in good faith, to fight for our freedom without the stimulus of thereby winning their own freedom also." Now was the time for action: "Every march and battle, every day and hour add to the tremendous hazards of delay." Echoing the call of General Lee, Hindman further argued that the southern states must promise a home to the emancipated veterans. In his introductions to the two letters, the editor simply said that the authors addressed "matters of present public importance" but endorsed neither position.[28]

Central Texas as represented by Austin, LaGrange, and Bellville provides an intriguing opportunity to examine how far white southerners were willing to go to modify slavery without the impact of hard war to influence their decision. The pro-cotton and pro-slavery positions of David Robinson at the *Austin State Gazette* militated against a full local debate. Far from the Union armies in Virginia, Georgia, and the Carolinas, such a position made sense. International market forces still operated in Texas with numerous reports of cotton selling for more than forty cents per pound. McClellan in LaGrange and Osterhout in Bellville provided more discussion of the slave-soldier issue, but both stopped short of attempting to overturn the slave system that continued to work so well. The vast distances to the key battlefields and consistent, strong economic forces in large part explain why the citizens of Central Texas differed from their brothers and sisters in Virginia and Georgia, and even from fellow Texans on the Gulf Coast and in East Texas.

---

[28] Pendleton Murrah, "To the People of Texas," *Austin The Weekly State Gazette*, 3 May 1865, 3; Thomas C. Hindman, "Letter from Gen. Hindman," *Austin The Weekly State Gazette*, 3 May 1865, 3.

In February, March, and April, Texans received repeated reports of the Confederacy crumbling. The failure of the peace conference complemented by Sherman's march through the Carolinas, and finally compounded by Lee's surrender, painted a portrait of national destruction. These Confederate misfortunes led Texans to discuss arming slaves fully. Yet, none of these dire events touched the citizens of Texas directly. Enemy soldiers were not burning their barns, and their slaves remained quiet as they still produced marketable cotton. Intellectually, many white Texans realized that some dramatic step must be taken to avert utter defeat, but no overwhelming necessity for black troops emerged in Texas. In contrast to Robert Durden's conclusions in *The Gray and the Black,* Texans did not lack the "intelligence, imagination, and moral courage" to sacrifice slavery but, rather, never understood the depth of the crisis. John Mills, William Sledge, "Freestone," and others produced strong arguments and innovative ways to place black men in gray uniforms. Even so, most Texans did not heed the writers' warnings but, rather, clung to slavery. The Civil War in all its intensity and brutality never reached Texas; therefore, these Texans represented the ideas of southerners about slavery without the revolutionary impact of war. While many in Virginia and Georgia openly discussed not only armed slaves but the role of the emancipated slave in the post-war South, such a debate would not have occurred without the absolute necessity to place more men in the field. Acceptance of the idea of black Confederate troops was directly related to a region's immediate experience of the death and destruction resulting from hard war. The reality and perception of military fortune shaped this significant social and political debate. Because Texas was far removed from the active theaters, its citizens responded to the military crisis very differently than did southerners nearer the battle lines.

Conclusion

11

Independence or Slavery?

From November 1864 to April 1865, Jefferson Davis conducted his final and most critical campaign. In it, he hoped to gain significant popular support for revolutionary steps intended to make independence, rather than the preservation of slavery, the central tenet of the Confederate cause. The battlefields for this campaign were the hearts and minds of ordinary southern men and women. Davis recognized that the Old South and the institution of slavery had been mortally wounded during the war. Rather than accepting Confederate defeat, Davis attempted to transform the contradictory war aims of 1861 into a clarion call for a New South founded on independence rather than slavery. The president had seen his world transformed by the war and he hoped that the South more broadly had been transformed as well. To launch his campaign, he set the stage for serious discussions of the slave's role in the war effort by asking for additional black laborers for the army who would receive freedom as a reward for their service. Having broached the idea that the slave had an obligation to the state as a person as well as property, Davis orchestrated a campaign to ensure that newspapers across the South would discuss the idea that the time had come to arm slaves. Although Secretary Benjamin and General Lee played important public roles in this effort, Davis conducted the campaign behind the scenes with great skill. The resulting slave-soldier debate afforded common southerners the opportunity to express what slavery and the "southern way of life" meant to them.

In response to Davis's efforts, the Confederacy and its citizens conducted an open, thorough debate concerning the introduction of the slaves into the Confederate army. In the process, they weighed the value of slavery and defined the sacrifices they could make to achieve independence. After all the editorials and all the letters had been written, had a real transformation in people's views of slavery taken place? Were congressmen from occupied areas who had no constituencies the only ones to vote to arm the slaves? Would the veteran white regiments accept the new recruits? Had it all been merely a theoretical discussion? Did the common people of Virginia, Georgia, and Texas have the "intelligence, imagination, and moral courage" to abandon slavery and place black troops in the field?[1] By comparing the depth, sincerity, and significance of the debate concerning arming the slaves in Virginia, Georgia, and Texas, a clearer picture of the importance of slavery in white southern society and of the strength of Confederate nationalism emerges.

Unparalleled in its depth, the Confederate debate over arming slaves reached across region and class lines to produce a thorough discussion of the merits of slavery. The debate was not limited to political leaders, editors, and a few thoughtful commentators in the capital, as Robert Durden suggested in *The Gray and the Black*. Soldiers, editors, and common citizens from all three regions entered and fully participated in the discussions over the role of slaves in the war effort. In Richmond, Jefferson Davis and Judah Benjamin astutely recognized that they could not radically transform the social relations between white and black southerners without gaining the approval and, for it to be successful, the enthusiastic support of the vast majority of both slaveholding and non-slaveholding whites. Therefore, they contacted influential local leaders across the South and asked them to energize local discussions of arming slaves. These administration efforts and the startling Union victories at Nashville and Savannah brought forth a tremendous number of responses from common citizens attempting to find a path to victory.

Southerners in all sections of the Confederacy—Upper South, Deep South, and Trans-Mississippi West—seriously considered the introduction of black men into the army. Virginia, Georgia, and Texas provide an interesting and informative comparison. Ulysses S. Grant's powerful army pressing ever closer to Richmond, as well as the proximity of Philip Sheridan's cavalry to the Roanoke and Shenandoah Valleys, provided a keen sense of urgency to the debate in Virginia. Union positions stretched from the James River at Richmond over twenty-five miles to Petersburg. Artillery fire could be heard often in the capital, reinforcing the critical position of the Confederacy. The arrival in Lynchburg of refugees fleeing from the Federal troops in the Shenandoah Valley and the city's crucial location on the last rail line

[1] Durden, *The Gray and the Black*, 287.

into Petersburg produced a clear picture of the situation and reinforced the significance of the manpower crisis.

William T. Sherman's march through Georgia in November and December and his subsequent operations in South Carolina kept Georgians firmly focused on the immediate need to increase the strength of the Confederate armies. The arrival of decimated units from Hood's once-proud army left little doubt in Georgia that the situation was serious. In contrast, without an immediate Union threat in the Trans-Mississippi, most Texans were unable to conceive the enormity of the manpower problem. Within each state, sub-regions emerged in which people framed the debate differently based on their perception of the Union threat. For instance, Augusta, in Eastern Georgia, remained threatened by Sherman much longer than other areas of the state. Some of the first and most poignant letters came from this threatened city. Similarly, Galvestonians viewed the debate differently because they could see the Union navy just off the island and knew that at any point a large Union force might land on their beaches. Not surprisingly, the most open and heated discussions of slavery's merits in Texas occurred on the pages of the *Galveston News*. Virginians and Georgians observed the destruction all about them and over time their attitudes on a number of topics, including slavery, shifted. In contrast, the men and women of Texas saw little of the war and, therefore, struggled to grasp the magnitude of the issues leading their neighbors in the East to consider radical steps. Unquestionably, the closer a person was to the Union army, the more likely they were to express interest in arming slaves. Yet, even in the most unthreatened areas of Texas, southerners took the question seriously and discussed the implications fully.

Distinct rumblings of unrest between slave owners and non-slave owners appeared in some newspapers, but this schism never quite became a sharp division on the issue of arming slaves. The voices of rich slave owners could be heard, but so, too, were the opinions of yeoman farmers and even poor whites. Governor Joseph E. Brown of Georgia and Senator Louis T. Wigfall of Texas feared a rupture along class lines and took great care to reassure poor whites and non-slaveholding immigrants that they had much to lose if slavery fell. In all three states, too many slaveholders offered to send their slaves to join the army for the issue to become simply a contest between the two classes. Yet, remarks like those of Charles Button of Lynchburg, Virginia, and "Freestone" of Fairfield, Texas, chiding those willing to sacrifice their sons but not their slaves spoke to serious rifts in the old southern orthodoxy that had been exposed by the war.

Women rarely appeared, at least clearly identified as women, in the newspapers, but they discussed the issue fully in their diaries and private correspondence. A white woman asking for the protection of a black soldier would have transgressed so many social conventions that most women never entered the public debate. "Celestia" of Macon, Georgia, and "Lucy" of Austin, Texas, wrote to the newspapers and made some references to arming slaves, but these two women stood nearly alone. Yet, the letters of Mary Akin, Mary Chesnut, Dolly Burge, and others clearly demonstrate that southern women were not only aware of the issues at stake but also held decided opinions about arming slaves. Encompassing both slaveholders and non-slaveholders, a few women as well as many men, and regions and subregions that framed the debate differently, the Confederate discussions concerning black soldiers attained tremendous depth. The critical military situation played a role in this discussion, but desperation never became the overriding factor.

From the first, many commentators have questioned the sincerity of southerners who agreed to sacrifice slavery in the hope of gaining independence. How could a society built upon a foundation of slavery and racial inequality elect to abandon slavery? Yet, Davis, Benjamin, Lee, and a host of common citizens expressed what a New York paper described as a "terrible earnestness" to do just that.[2] By examining the vote of each state's congressional delegation, the efforts of military units to fill their ranks with black troops, and the attempts to form new black regiments at home, the depth of the change in public views about the importance of slavery shines through.

The actions of Virginia's legislative bodies concerning arming the slaves provide an interesting case. With the national government located within the confines of the state, most Virginia legislators had relatively frequent contact with their constituents; therefore, one would expect these congressmen would best reflect the opinions of their constituents. In the early stages of the debate in the House, Thomas Gholson, a wealthy businessman from Petersburg, led conservative efforts to prevent any measure to arm slaves.

[2] "The newspapers of the enemy…," *Richmond Enquirer*, 30 January 1865, 1.

Although Williams Wickam introduced a measure for slave laborers in November, most of the Virginians in Congress remained silent on the issue. On 20 February, the bill to arm the slaves came to a vote and the Virginia delegation split six to four in favor of arming slaves. David Funsten from Alexandria; John Goode, Jr., representing Lynchburg; Robert Johnston from Clarksburg; Fayette McMullin of Wyethville in Southwest Virginia; Samuel Miller of Charleston; and Charles Russell of Wheeling all voted to arm the slaves. On the other side, John Baldwin from Staunton, Gholson of Petersburg, Frederick Holliday of Winchester, and Wickam from Richmond voted against the measure.[3]

Individual motives for decisions are always complex, and the choices made on this issue were no different. Four of the six Virginians who voted to arm the slaves represented areas long occupied by the Union. As important in determining their motives, two of these men owned no slaves at all and none of the others owned more than eight. Although some of these men from overrun districts may have felt they had nothing to lose by arming slaves (Thomas Alexander and Richard Beringer have suggested as much), the interests of the areas they represented might just as well have influenced their decisions. All six of the Virginians who voted to arm the slaves came from the mountain sections of the state where slavery had never been strong. This region had supplied large numbers of private soldiers but few general officers to the Confederacy, a fact that concerned some in Western Virginia. In addition, until Philip Sheridan raided the Shenandoah Valley in the fall of 1864, it had largely fed the Confederate armies in Virginia. In short, these six men represented areas that suffered much for the cause in blood, treasure, and in misery from Federal occupation. These factors, along with their own lack of slaves, provide as convincing an answer for their motives as the idea that they had nothing to lose.[4]

The four Virginians who voted against arming slaves have more varied backgrounds. Baldwin and Holliday represented areas in the Shenandoah

---

[3] *Journal of the Congress, 1861–1865,* Vol. 7, 612–13; Gyula Pauer and B. Reed Durbin, *The Historical Atlas of the Congresses of the Confederate States of America, 1861–1865* (New York: Simon & Schuster, 1994).

[4] Thomas Alexander and Richard Beringer, *The Anatomy of the Confederate Congress: A Study of the Influences of Member Characteristics on Legislative Voting Behavior, 1861–1865* (Nashville: Vanderbilt University Press, 1972) 248–53, 354–89.

Valley and probably had a similar experience of the war to those from the Valley who had supported the measure. Gholson and Wickam represented cities in the heart of the wealthy, tobacco-growing regions of the state. Neither of the districts was overrun, but both Petersburg and Richmond had suffered significant losses in runaway slaves and in slaves impressed by the army. Plantations no longer functioned well anywhere in Virginia, and any hope of producing products with slave labor must have been faint. Only one of these four owned fewer than ten slaves, yet none owned more than sixteen. No clear common reason for opposition emerges, although strong faith in slavery as a divine institution appears to have figured prominently in Gholson's decision.[5]

Decisions by Virginia's senators were also interesting. Allen Caperton from Peterstown, owner of 43 slaves, and Robert M.T. Hunter, owner of 116 slaves, had considerable money and prestige invested in slavery. Of some interest, Caperton's hometown was not only occupied but had also been incorporated into the breakaway state of West Virginia. Although both generally supported the war effort, Hunter had spoken out against a number of radical steps suggested by Davis. On 21 February, Caperton and Hunter both voted against a bill to provide 200,000 slave-soldiers for the army. At this point, the House of Delegates intervened and, on 4 March, enacted binding instructions for the two Virginia senators to change their votes to support black troops. The legislature went even further and provided for raising black regiments even before Congress had approved the idea. From the shift in the votes of the two senators, it appears that Caperton and Hunter may have represented the large slave owners of the state better than they did the majority of the people as reflected in the legislature.[6]

In January and February 1865, the citizens of all three regions of Georgia demanded immediate Congressional action to place black troops in the field. Georgia's Congressional delegation quickly responded to the rising tide of popular support for slave-soldiers. In January, Warren Akin of Northwest Georgia; Hiram Bell of Northeast Georgia; Mark Blandford, representing Columbus; George Lester, representing Atlanta; and John Shewmake, representing Augusta, all supported a bill to experiment with

[5] Ibid., 354–89.

[6] Ibid.

40,000 black troops. Joseph Echols, representing Athens; Clifford Anderson, representing Macon; and James M. Smith, representing LaGrange, had opposed the measure. Julian Hartridge of Savannah and William E. Smith of Albany did not participate in this vote. As the spring campaign neared and the manpower crisis deepened, the congressmen again addressed the issue. On 20 February, Warren Akin proposed that if the president could not raise enough troops to "maintain...the independence of the Confederate States, then he is hereby authorized to call on each State...for her quota of three hundred thousand troops...irrespective of color." Initially, the measure failed, but Akin, Clifford Anderson, Hiram Bell, Mark Blanford, James M. Smith, and William E. Smith all voted for Akin's amendment. Union forces occupied none of the districts thus represented. Julian Hartridge, alone among the Georgians present, opposed the measure, and he represented the only occupied area in the state. A few moments later, Charles Conrad of Louisiana resubmitted Akin's motion, and this time it passed.[7]

Finally, just prior to the session's end, on 20 February, Thomas Foster of Alabama called for a vote on the main bill to arm the slaves. Unlike Akin's amendment, this measure explicitly directed the president to enlist 300,000 slaves immediately. Facing the final test of the war, Akin of Northwest Georgia, Anderson of Macon, Blanford of Columbus, and William E. Smith of Albany voted to sacrifice slavery for independence. Hartridge of Savannah, Bell of Northeast Georgia, and James M. Smith of LaGrange found that they could not totally abandon slavery and voted against the measure.[8] Significantly, early proponents of slave-soldiers, like Shewmake of Augusta and Lester of Atlanta, had already left Richmond and did not vote.[9] Assuming the continued opposition of the absent Joseph Echols of Elberton, the Georgia Representatives favored the enlistment of black soldiers by a majority of six to four. Similarly, the two Georgia senators divided on the issue, with Herschel V. Johnson voting against the measure on 8 March.[10] Meanwhile, Senator Benjamin Hill accepted the necessity to arm the slaves,

[7] James Sledge, "The Negro Question in Congress," *Athens Southern Banner*, 15 February 1865, 1.

[8] Ibid.

[9] Ezra J. Warner and W. Buck Yearns, *Biographical Register of the Confederate Congress* (Baton Rouge: Louisiana State University Press, 1975) 150, 218.

[10] "Congressional," *Augusta Daily Constitutionalist*, 13 March 1865, 2.

but he had already left Richmond in early March and did not vote. Instead of leading the fight in the Senate, he stumped the state, trying to rally Georgians for the Confederate cause and to counter Governor Brown's attacks on the Davis administration.[11] Although military necessity doubtless played a large part in the congressmen's decisions, the Union occupation of a district appeared to have only a limited influence on how they voted. Rather, the congressmen from Georgia voted for black troops because they heard the cries of common Georgians demanding the sacrifice of slavery in order to achieve independence.

Texans in Congress showed few of the divisions seen in the delegations from Virginia and Georgia. John R. Baylor, alone among the Texans, voted to arm the slaves. As a non-slave owner and the former Confederate Governor of the Arizona Territory, Baylor was willing to accept extreme measures to continue the fight. Anthony Branch of Huntsville, Caleb Herbert of Colorado County, Franklin Sexton of St. Augustine, and Stephen Darden of Gonzales all opposed black troops. All of these men owned slaves, with Herbert and Sexton owning from forty to eighty. With slavery working well in Texas, it must have taken considerable courage for Baylor to vote to arm the slaves. Surprisingly, Williamson Oldham of Austin introduced a bill to arm the slaves in the Senate on 10 February and voted for similar measures throughout the final days of the session. Louis T. Wigfall, the other Texas senator, opposed the ideas of his colleague with great vehemence. Oldham often expressed reservations about administration policies, but on this one issue, he firmly supported the administration.[12]

In Virginia, Robert E. Lee struggled to command his army, while at the same time he directed efforts to form black units in Virginia. Two days after the bill passed in Congress, Lee ordered J.W. Pegram and Thomas P. Turner to raise the first unit and issued orders for them to begin recruiting. On 17 March the *Lynchburg Virginian* announced the plans underway: "Recruiting offices will be opened immediately all over the country and the slave-holders of Virginia, especially, will, we trust, respond promptly. Let

[11] "Interesting Letter from Senator Hill," *Milledgeville Southern Recorder*, 4 April 1865, 2.

[12] *Journal of the Congress of the Confederate States of America, 1861–1865,* Vol. 4 (Washington: U.S. Government Printing Office, 1905) 543.

Virginia in this emergency show…that no sacrifice is too great to make for the holy cause of freedom." The following day the *Virginian* printed an appeal from Pegram and Turner for slave owners to bring their slaves in to enlist. A week later, the newspapers reported that five hundred black troops, recruited from slaves already working for the army, had paraded in Richmond: "The interest of the occasion was lessened by the failure to uniform and equip the negro soldiers. They were armed with muskets." In addition to uniform and equipment shortages, considerable confusion arose concerning whether the state or Confederate authorities should run the instruction camps. On 24 March, Governor William Smith wrote to Davis asking why Lee had not requested the troops the state had begun to form. As late as 30 March, General James Longstreet selected soldiers to be sent to other states to begin recruiting new black units. With Lee abandoning Richmond on 2 April, few if any of these black soldiers ever made it into the trenches. Yet, in the last issue of the *Richmond Whig*, on 3 April, the editor praised the battalion created by Pegram and called on slave owners for more black troops: "Every master should encourage his slaves to enlist, and not refuse to let them defend a country in which they have a common interest with the white citizens; the example would be extremely valuable."[13]

Based on the appeals in the Virginia papers, it appears that black recruits did not flock to see the enrolling officers and that the army was poorly prepared for those who did. Even so, the common people of Richmond and Lynchburg had pursued the idea of black soldiers with considerable zeal. The lists of slave owners' names who had offered their slaves to the army demonstrated that a number of Virginians were ready to live up to their word. Interestingly, Charles Button, editor of the *Lynchburg Virginian*, had drawn considerable notice for supporting black troops early in the debate. As black soldiers paraded in Richmond, the *Richmond Whig* reprinted a letter from twenty-seven citizens of Lynchburg strongly advocating Button's candidacy for the Confederate congress. Although he had never run for elective office, Button's stance on slavery had won him broad support in the western

[13] *Official Records*, Series 4, Vol. 3, 1093; "Gen. Lee is now accepting…," *Lynchburg Virginian*, 17 March 1865, 1; "Colored Troops," *Lynchburg Virginian*, 18 March 1865, 1; "Parade of Negro Troops in Richmond," *Lynchburg Virginian*, 23 March 1865, 2; "The City: Drill of Colored Troops," *Richmond Whig*, 3 April 1865, 1.

portion of Virginia. Black troops had come too late to aid the South militarily, but Virginians from all areas of the state had genuinely tried to place their slaves into the army.[14]

Despite the claims of several opponents of the measure, veteran Georgia units quickly accepted the idea of black comrades and developed plans for their introduction into the army. For example, on 15 March, the men of the Forty-Ninth Georgia Regiment proclaimed their willingness to admit black soldiers into their ranks: "When in former years, for pecuniary purposes, we did not consider it disgraceful to labor with negroes in the field...we certainly will not look upon it in any other light at this time, when an end so glorious as our independence is to be achieved." Not content with mere words, the men of the Forty-Ninth proposed a plan to ensure a quick and efficient transition to a multi-racial unit: "After the negroes have been conscribed, an officer or enlisted man from each company be sent home to select from the negro conscripts such who may have owners...in the company, or who from former acquaintance with the men, may be deemed suitable to be incorporated in those companies." Through this procedure, the veterans hoped to "create, or rather cement, a reciprocal attachment between the men now in service and the negroes." Just prior to the fall of Petersburg, General Lee praised the unit's initiative and granted permission for them to implement it. Clearly, the men of the Forty-Ninth Georgia Regiment took the idea of black comrades seriously and developed a strong, practical plan to integrate the new troops into their ranks.[15]

Meanwhile, back in Georgia, other veteran military units sought new black recruits. On 14 April, Thomas Key, the commander of an artillery battery stationed in Macon, called for Georgians to "show your faith" by allowing their slaves to enter active service.[16] Having seen the unit suffer enormous losses with the Army of Tennessee, Key hoped to rebuild the unit with black soldiers: "I propose to take my present command as officers and non-commissioned officers...to receive, organize, drill, and discipline a battalion

---

[14] "The Right Spirit," *Lynchburg Virginian*, 24 March 1865, 2; "Correspondence," *Richmond Whig*, 1 April 1865, 1.

[15] George B. Davis, Leslie Perry, and Joseph Kirley, *The War of the Rebellion: A Compilation of the Official Records of the Union and Confederate Armies,* Series 1, Vol. 46, Part 2 (Washington: U.S. Government Printing Office, 1895) 1316–17.

[16] Thomas Key, "Countrymen, Show Your Faith," *Albany Patriot*, 27 April 1865, 1.

of negroes for artillery service." The South, Key argued, must have more men immediately: "It is the physical strength that we need, and it makes little difference whether he has a black or white skin. ... Bring in your negroes promptly, as now is the crisis and the time for action." Furthermore, the young captain asked the owners to emancipate the new soldiers, to provide for their families, and to promise them a home upon their return. Through such steps, Key believed he could release the military potential of the former slaves and form an efficient unit of artillerymen from the new recruits. Far from a theoretical abstraction, Key astutely perceived that black soldiers offered the only ray of hope for southern independence.

As Key formed his new black battalion in Macon, courageous Georgians broke with the past and endeavored to build a new army. Although the bill that armed the slaves did not free them, army regulations that accompanied the measure required the manumission of the soldiers prior to enlistment.[17] As slave owners sent their slaves to the army, they announced their own emancipation proclamation. On 17 April, the citizens of Early County met "for the purpose of organizing Companies of Negroes for the defense of our country."[18] Captain J.T. Henderson and J.S. Powell took the lead as the men and women of Blakely and Early County proclaimed their preference for independence over slavery.[19] During the following week, the *Albany Patriot* praised the efforts of Congressman William E. Smith to raise a regiment of black soldiers from Southwestern Georgia.[20] Even in this southwestern region of the state, where no Union boot had tread, Georgians yielded their slaves in the hope that such a sacrifice would assure their independence. Even staunch opponents of black troops relented and gave up their slaves in the final weeks of the war. For example, Howell Cobb maintained his opposition to black soldiers throughout the debate, but, on 15 April, Cobb's son offered to supply a company of black men to the Confederate army.[21] Clearly, Georgians had meant what they said in their editorials

---

[17] "Government Orders to Carry into Effect the Act Arming the Slaves," *Columbus Daily Sun*, 15 April 1865, 1.

[18] "Blakely, Ga., April 17, 1865," *Early County News*, 19 April 1865, 2.

[19] Ibid.

[20] "Negro Troops," *Albany Patriot*, 27 April 1865, 2.

[21] John A. Cobb to David C. Barrow, 15 April 1865, Barrow Papers, cited in Mohr, *On the Threshold of Freedom*, 285.

and letters. When forced to choose between slavery and independence, these Georgians overwhelmingly chose independence and formed black military units.

In Texas, no effort was made to form black military units. Rather, after they reported the fall of Richmond, most newspapers avoided all references to arming the slaves. On 27 April, Governor Pendleton Murrah published an address to the state and counseled continued resistance. "Recall the convictions upon which you entered this contest," Murrah advised. "When a nation forgets the principles which led her into revolution she ceases to be the same nation." Even as he acknowledged the collapse of Confederate armies in the East, the governor suggested that Texas constituted an "Empire in herself" and, with her great resources, could continue the struggle and "redeem" the other Confederate states. Despite the state's dire position, Murrah refused to accept radical steps: "You cannot look for relief to emancipation, nor to those other weak and wicked delusions—reconstruction, or a foreign protectorate. The men who would distract and divide you with such treasonable proposals are unworthy of your confidence." Weary veterans returning to Texas from Lee's and Johnston's armies in early May signaled the end for all who cared to see. Even so, most Texans remained in a state of collective denial until the end of May, when Confederate leaders surrendered to Union commanders in Louisiana.[22]

The debate over arming slaves in Virginia, Georgia, and Texas illustrates well the dramatic impact of hard war on southern society. The debate in the newspapers had not been a mere theoretical discussion. The news items, editorials, and letters to editors appearing in the newspapers all demonstrated the slow, steady transformation in public opinion during the debate. The news reports added a wider perspective to the arguments advanced and formed a backdrop for the formation of local opinion. Richmond editors like Nathaniel Tyler and John Daniel set the tone for many with powerful editorials that were widely reprinted across the South. These editorials ushered the public into the discussion in October and proved influential until the fall of Richmond. Initially, many editors in Georgia and Texas attempted to use their editorials to stifle the debate, but with the military disasters at Nashville and Savannah, they could no longer suppress the cries for

---

[22] "To the People of Texas," *Dallas Herald*, 11 May 1865, 1.

change. In contrast, James Gardner in Augusta, Georgia, and John P. Osterhout in Bellville, Texas, encouraged open debate, but soon found public opinion racing far ahead. Newspaper columns set the stage for a dynamic, wide-ranging debate of slavery.

While news reports and editorials set a tone, the opinions of the local citizens appear clear indeed in the letters to editors. Although fairly divided about the advisability of arming the slaves in November, military necessity led the overwhelming majority of the people in Virginia and Georgia to support the concept of black troops by early March. In particular, the resolutions from military units and the accounts of public meetings in both states point to the gradual shift in public opinion. In contrast, Texans expressed little interest until January, when John Mills and William Sledge wrote to the Gulf Coast papers and advocated black troops. In all three states, the letter writers became the strongest advocates for black troops.

As the Confederacy faced its final crisis, Virginians and Georgians not only advocated the measure in letters to editors, but also struggled mightily to form black military units. After five months of soul-searching debate, the common men and women of Virginia and Georgia proclaimed that they would sacrifice everything, even slavery, to achieve their independence. The citizens of Virginia and Georgia readily accepted black troops even if they continued to differ on the black veteran's status in a post-war Confederacy. The continuation of the cotton trade in Texas through Mexico provided a powerful incentive to maintain slavery at all costs. With efficient, lucrative plantations still running smoothly, it appeared to many premature, if not unwise, to arm the slaves. The cessation of significant Union military activity in the Trans-Mississippi region after the spring of 1864 provided a strong sense of security in Texas. The vast distances to the key battlefields and consistent, strong economic forces in large part explain why the citizens of Texas differed from their brothers and sisters in Virginia and Georgia. These Texans represented the ideas of southerners about slavery without the revolutionary impact of war. In short, acceptance of the idea of black Confederate troops was directly related to a region's immediate experience of the death and destruction resulting from the war, and not from pre-war ideas.

Judging by the votes of the Virginia, Georgia, and Texas congressional delegations and the efforts of military units to enlist black comrades, a significant transformation had occurred in the mind of many Confederates.

Virginians and Georgians acted upon their words and tried to trade slavery for independence. The war may have begun as a conservative attempt to avoid change, but the hard war both sides adopted in the final years of the conflict revolutionized not only battlefield tactics but also the objectives of the war. Efforts to arm slaves in Virginia and Georgia show that weary men and women who had seen destruction all about them were willing to make any and all sacrifices that might lead to victory. In contrast, far from the battlefields in the Upper South and Deep South, Texans could not envision a situation that would demand such a sacrifice. The selection by Virginians and Georgians of independence rather than slavery as the primary war aim illustrates well the transcendent power of warfare to change the views of individuals and nations.

Jefferson Davis's final campaign to arm slaves offers a window into the very depths of southern society. His goal was not simply to find more men for Lee's army but, rather, to create a new Confederate identity based in the experience of war rather than in the shades of the Old South. Few editors, and even fewer of the men and women who wrote into the newspapers, describe sacred ideas or institutions. Converts to Davis's ideas were looking forward to a new nation rather than returning to an idealized past. Independence at all costs was the watchword in Virginia and Georgia by the spring of 1865. The Confederacy as Virginians and Georgians had come to understand it meant far more than the preservation of slavery. The conservative revolution of 1861 had, in fact, become a true revolution. The decision to place black troops in the Confederate ranks was the ultimate step toward a new South defined by the war rather than antebellum conceptions. As Jefferson Davis had surmised, the vast majority of Virginians, Georgians, and even some Texans discovered that slavery could be sacrificed much more easily than southern independence.

Was President Davis's final campaign a success? Davis's efforts did not lead to largescale black enlistment in the Confederate army. All of the steps taken to place black men into the army came far too late to alter the course of the war or even to delay southern defeat by a single day. If this is the measure for success, then he failed in this last campaign. In a deeper sense, Davis did achieve dramatic successes. He sparked and then shaped the most dynamic discussion of the value of slavery in southern history. The master-slave relationship was much discussed but so, too, was the relationship between the large slave owner and the yeoman farmer. Families who had sent fathers, husbands, and children to war could not understand why their rich neighbors would not also send their slaves. Significant differences remained within white society even as the Confederate Congress authorized the enlistment but not the emancipation of the prospective black troops. As Bruce Levine and Chandra Manning have suggested, a number of planters and political leaders continued to cling to the old values of racial supremacy. Even so, planter resistance to change had to be tempered by the vast numbers of plain folk who would see any hesitation to arm black slaves as positive proof that the struggle was a rich man's war and a poor man's fight. Grudgingly accepting the necessity for black military assistance, these southern leaders may well have agreed to black troops hoping to thus limit the economic and social damage caused by the end of slavery. The problem is that these reluctant leaders were not the only southerners with a voice in this critical moment of Confederate soul-searching. Jefferson Davis had invited all white southerners into the debate. Many Georgians and Virginians saw black men in Confederate gray as their best hope for a brighter future. While some, like Samuel Boykin, embraced the idea of emancipation and argued for full black citizenship, others doubtless wanted to weigh the value of black assistance before making fulsome promises of equality.

This complex picture of Americans struggling to shift racial ideals mirrors the varied ideas expressed by other Americans two years before. Abraham Lincoln, like Jefferson Davis, could lead people only so far in his efforts to bring about racial change. It would take two additional years after the Emancipation Proclamation and numerous instances of heroic battlefield action by African-American troops for Lincoln to develop white support for the 13th Amendment. If the Reconstruction Era proves nothing else, the Union victors remained quite hesitant to award full equality to the black veteran and his family. Jefferson Davis did not have the same period for his new ideas to grow and develop. It would be grossly unfair to expect the Confederate leader to have developed greater consensus on racial issues than Lincoln had in attaining victory, and yet that is what most historians have done as they dismiss Davis's efforts. Jefferson Davis waged his most dynamic political campaign in the final months of the Civil War and demonstrated exceptional skill and vision as he sought to save the Confederate nation. In this six-month process, the Confederate people answered the president's call to rethink their most deeply held convictions and demonstrated an earnest commitment to a new Confederate South shaped by the Civil War.

Bibliography

VIRGINIA NEWSPAPERS

Lynchburg Republican
Lynchburg Virginian
Richmond Enquirer
Richmond Examiner
Richmond Sentinel
Richmond Whig
Rockingham Register
Staunton Vindicator

GEORGIA NEWSPAPERS:

Albany Patriot
Athens Southern Banner
Athens Southern Watchman
Augusta Chronicle and Sentinel
Augusta Daily Constitutionalist
Columbus Daily Sun
Columbus Times
Early County News
Macon Christian Index
Macon Southern Confederacy
Macon Telegraph and Confederate
Milledgeville Confederate Union
Milledgeville Southern Recorder

TEXAS NEWSPAPERS:

Austin The Weekly State Gazette
Bellville Countryman
Dallas Herald
Galveston News
Houston Telegraph
LaGrange Patriot
Marshall Texas Republican

BOOKS

Akin, Warren. *Letters of Warren Akin: Confederate Congressman*. Edited by Bell I. Wiley. Athens: University of Georgia Press, 1959.

Alexander, Thomas, and Richard Beringer. *The Anatomy of the Confederate Congress: A Study of the Influences of Member Characteristics on Legislative Voting Behavior, 1861–1865*. Nashville, TN: Vanderbilt University Press, 1972.

Andrews, J. Cutler. *The South Reports the Civil War*. Pittsburgh: University of Pittsburgh Press, 1970.

Ayers, Edward. *In the Presence of Mine Enemies: The Civil War in the Heart of America, 1859–1864*. Reprint edition. New York: W.W. Norton, 2004.

Beringer, Richard E., et al., editors. *Why the South Lost the Civil War*. Athens: University of Georgia Press, 1986.

Blair, William. *Virginia's Private War: Feeding Body and Soul in the Confederacy, 1861–1865*. New York: Oxford University Press, 1998.

Brewer, James H. *The Confederate Negro: Virginia's Craftsmen and Military Laborers, 1861–1865*. Durham, NC: Duke University Press, 1969.

Burge, Dolly. *A Woman's Wartime Journal: An Account of the Passage of Sherman's Army on the March to the Sea*. Edited by Julian Street. Macon, GA: J.W. Burke, 1927.

Confederate Congress. *Journal of the Congress of the Confederate States of America, 1861–1865*. Volume 7. Washington: Government Printing Office, 1905.

Davis, Jefferson. *The Papers of Jefferson Davis*. Volume 11. Edited by Lynda L. Crist, Kenneth H. Williams, and Peggy L. Dillard. Baton Rouge: Louisiana State University Press, 1999.

———. *The Rise and Fall of the Confederate Government*. Volume 1. New York: D. Appleton and Co., 1881.

Durden, Robert F. *The Gray and the Black: The Confederate Debate on Emancipation*. Baton Rouge: Louisiana State University Press, 1972.

Elliot, Claude. "Union Sentiment in Texas, 1861–1865." *Southwestern Historical Quarterly* 50 (1947): 449-77.

Escott, Paul. *After Secession: Jefferson Davis and the Failure of Confederate Nationalism*. Reprint edition. Baton Rouge: Louisiana State University Press, 1992.

Faust, Drew Gilpin. *The Creation of Confederate Nationalism: Ideology and Identity in the Civil War South*. Baton Rouge: Louisiana State University Press, 1989.

———. *Mothers of Invention: Women of the Slaveholding South in the American Civil War*. Chapel Hill: University of North Carolina Press, 1996.

Freehling, William. *The South vs. the South: How Anti-Confederate Southerners Shaped the Course of the Civil War*. New York: Oxford University Press, 2001.

Gallagher, Gary. *The Confederate War*. Cambridge: Harvard University Press, 1997.

Gorgas, Josiah. *The Journals of Josiah Gorgas 1857–1878*. Edited by Sarah W. Wiggins. Tuscaloosa: University of Alabama Press, 1995.

Gowan, Gilbert E., and James W. Livingood. *A Different Valor.* New York: Konecky and Konecky, 1956.

Jones, John B. *A Rebel War Clerk's Diary.* Edited by Early S. Miers. Baton Rouge: Louisiana State University Press, 1958.

Jordan, Ervin, Jr. *Black Confederates and Afro-Yankees in Civil War Virginia.* Charlottesville: University Press of Virginia, 1995.

Key, Thomas, and Robert Campbell. *Two Soldiers: The Campaign Diaries of Thomas J. Key, C.S.A. and Robert J. Campbell, U.S.A.* Edited by Wirt A. Cate. Chapel Hill: University of North Carolina Press, 1938.

Lale, Max S. "Robert W. Loughery: Rebel Editor." *East Texas Historical Journal* 21, no. 2 (October 1983): 3-15.

LeConte, Joseph. *'Ware Sherman: A Journal of Three Months' Personal Experience in the Last Days of the Confederacy.* Berkeley: University of California Press, 1937.

Levine, Bruce. *Confederate Emancipation: Southern Plans to Free and Arm Slaves during the Civil War.* New York: Oxford University Press, 2006.

Manning, Chandra. *What This Cruel War Was Over: Soldiers, Slavery, and the Civil War.* New York: Knopf, 2007.

Martinez, Jaime Amanda. *Confederate Slave Impressment in the Upper South.* Chapel Hill: University of North Carolina Press, 2013.

McCurry, Stephanie. *Confederate Reckoning: Power and Politics in the Civil War South.* Cambridge: Harvard University Press, 2010.

McPherson, James. *Battle Cry of Freedom: The Civil War Era.* New York: Ballantine, 1988.

———. "Foreword." In *Divided Houses: Gender and the Civil War,* edited by Catherine Clinton and Nina Silber. New York: Oxford University Press, 1992.

Meade, Robert D. *Judah P. Benjamin: Confederate Statesman.* New York: Oxford University Press, 1943.

Mohr, Clarence. *On the Threshold of Freedom: Masters and Slaves in Civil War Georgia.* Athens: University of Georgia Press, 1986.

Nisbet, James C. *Four Years on the Firing Line.* Edited by Bell I. Wiley. Jackson, TN: McCowat-Mercer Press, 1963.

Pauer, Gyula, and B. Reed Durbin. *The Historical Atlas of the Congresses of the Confederate States of America, 1861–1865.* New York: Simon & Schuster, 1994.

Sanders, Charles W., Jr. "Jefferson Davis and the Hampton Roads Peace Conference: 'To secure peace to the two countries.'" *Journal of Southern History* 63 (1997): 803-26.

Sparks, Randy J. "John P. Osterhout, Yankee, Rebel, Republican." *Southwestern Historical Quarterly* 40/2 (1986): 111-38.

Symonds, Craig L. *Stonewall of the West: Patrick Cleburne and the Civil War.* Lawrence: University of Kansas Press, 1997.

Thomas, Emory. *The Confederacy as a Revolutionary Experience.* Reprint edition. Columbia: University of South Carolina Press, 1992.

———. *The Confederate Nation, 1861–1865.* New York: Harper and Row, 1979.

———. "Rebel Nationalism: E.H. Cushing and the Confederate Experience." *Southwestern Historical Quarterly* 73 (1970): 343-55.

Toombs, Robert. *The Correspondence of Robert Toombs, Alexander Stephens, and Howell Cobb.* Edited by Ulrich B. Phillips. Washington: US Government Printing Office, 1913.

Tyler, Ron, et al. *The New Handbook of Texas.* Austin: Texas State Historical Association, 1996.

United States War Department. *The War of the Rebellion: A Compilation of the Official Records of the Union and Confederate Armies.* 70 volumes. Washington: U.S. Government Printing Office, 1880–1901.

Vinovskis, Maris. "Have Social Historians Lost the Civil War? Some Preliminary Speculations." *Journal of American History* 76 (1989): 34-58.

Warner, Ezra J., and W. Buck Yearns. *Biographical Register of the Confederate Congress.* Baton Rouge: Louisiana State University Press, 1975.

Watkins, Sam R. *"Co. Aytch": A Side Show of the Big Show.* Columbia, TN: Columbia Herald, 1882.

White, Harry K., editor. *Official Records of the Union and Confederate Navies in the War of the Rebellion.* Series 2, Volume 3. Washington: U.S. Government Printing Office, 1922.

Index

15th Regiment Alabama Volunteers, 189-90
A Bonded Man, 145
A Soldier, 160-61
A Virginian Officer, 104
Abraham, 40, 77,136, 172, 208
Adair, G.W., 225
AGLA, 224
Akin, Mary, 132-33, 264, 266-67
Akin, Warren, 54-55, 131-33, 136, 151
Alabama Legislative Proposal, 8-9
Albany Patriot, 61, 66, 150, 226-28
Albany, GA, 47, 60, 131, 141, 149-150, 267 270-71
Alexander, Peter W., 50-51, 60, 64,155
Allen, Henry W., 23-24, 30-31,156,159-60
An East Tennessean, 113-14
Anderson, [slave], 170-71
Anderson, Clifford, 131, 267
Anderson, George T. Georgia Brigade, 208
Anderson, Joseph R., 8
Anderson, Patton, 12
Annan, S., 147
Athens Southern Banner, 52, 130-31, 209-11, 267
Athens Southern Watchman, 52-53, 128-30, 208-10, 215
Athens, GA, 47, 55-56, 67, 123, 131, 136, 208-9, 267
Atkins, John, 110, 117, 124, 168, 233
Atlanta, GA, 23, 30, 46, 80, 100, 123, 131, 230, 266-67
Augusta Chronicle and Sentinel, 56-7, 59, 67, 136-37, 139-41, 216-19, 221
Augusta County, VA Meeting, 198, 200
Augusta Daily Constitutionalist, 56, 58-60, 67, 130, 136-37, 139-41, 210, 215-17, 219, 273
Augusta, GA, 5, 28, 46-7, 100, 119, 131, 136, 143, 151, 215, 220, 226, 229, 263, 266-67
Austin The Weekly State Gazette, 68, 84-5, 87, 173-74, 176, 179, 250-54
Austin, TX, 68-69, 71, 79, 87, 154-55, 181, 239-40
Austin, TX City Meeting, 253
Bagby, George W. "Pan", 65, 146-47
Baldwin, John, 265
Banks, Nathaniel, 153
Barksdale, Ethelbert, 192-93, 212, 220, 232
Barnes, W.H., 125, 136, 151,
Bate, William, 12
Baton Rouge, LA, 24
Baylor, John R., 268
Bedford County, VA Meeting, 197, 200
Bell, Hiram, 131, 267
Bellville Countryman, 85-86, 88, 174, 176-77, 179, 181, 252, 254-55
Bellville, TX, 5, 71, 84-85, 88, 90, 174, 176-81, 252-54
Benjamin, Judah P., 9-10, 13, 17-18, 26, 96-98, 112-14, 121, 158, 186-89, 201-4, 207-8, 210-11, 215-16, 218, 220-22, 228, 232-33, 262-64,
Berringer, Richard, 3, 265
Beta Omega, 83
Blair, Francis P., 111, 185, 231
Blair, William, 200
Blakely, GA, 5, 47, 60-61, 66, 149-50, 226, 229, 271
Blandford, Mark, 131, 266
Blockade, 68-9, 71, 78, 154
Boyce, William W., 78-79, 81
Boykin, Samuel, 49-50, 126, 205-7, 215, 229, 275
Bragg, Braxton, 98
Branch, Anthony, 268
Breckinridge, John C., 193
Broaddus, A.S., 180-81
Brother Tom, 225
Brown, Albert, 129, 138, 143, 186, 188, 194
Brown, Joseph E., 28, 57, 122, 128, 178, 203-5, 207, 211, 214, 216, 220-21, 223, 227-28, 253, 263, 268
Burford, Nathaniel, 83
Burge, Dolly, 55, 264
Burnett, Henry, 123, 138, 143, 168, 194, 233
Butler, Benjamin, 7, 86, 114
Button, Charles, 27, 39-40, 43, 117-18, 120, 197, 263-64
Caleb Cutwell, 163-65
Camillus, 54

Campbell County, VA Meeting, 197, 200
Campbell, John A., 203, 231
Caperton, Allen, 194, 196, 266
Carlos, 68-9
Carter, George W., 237, 239-40
Cedar Creek, battle of, 38, 40
Celestia, 264
Chambers, Henry, 36
Chambersburg, PA, 42
Charleston Courier, 145
Charleston Mercury, 62, 124
Charlottesville Chronicle, 62
Cheatham, Benjamin F., 13, 95
Chesnut, Mary, 264
Chicago Times, 61-63, 72, 74, 85, 157
Christy, John, 53, 57, 67, 128-130, 136, 210-11
Clark, Charles, 28, 113, 220
Clayton, Samuel, 150-51
Cleburne, Patrick, 10-15, 31, 106
Cleburne's Memorial, 11-14, 257
Cobb, Howell, 99, 106-7, 122-23, 131-32, 136, 151, 158, 209, 271
Columbus Daily Sun, 61-66, 143-48, 151-52, 220-21, 223-25
Columbus Times, 61-65, 142-44, 146, 220, 222-25
Columbus, GA, 5, 47, 65-67, 131, 141, 145-49, 151-52, 223-26, 229, 266-67
Conscription, 8, 18, 28, 49, 53, 57, 69, 74, 82, 84, 88, 107-10, 112, 122, 124, 132, 138, 146, 222, 228, 239, 254-55
Convention of the States, 78-79, 111, 128, 130, 206,
Cox, T.J., 147-49
Cushing, Edward H., 74-75, 158-61, 165-66, 179, 181, 234-35, 240, 255-56
Dad Burnitt, 64-65
Dallas Herald, 80-83, 167-73, 230, 242-46, 250, 272
Dallas, TX, 71, 83
Daniel, John, 36-37, 99-100, 102-3, 111-12, 114, 195, 202, 272
Darden, Stephen, 268
Davis, Jefferson, 13-14, 98-99, 111, 169-79, 178, 185, 190, 193, 198, 200-2, 227, 235-36, 245-46, 253, 261-62, 264, 274-76
Davis, annual address Nov 64, 15-17, 31-33, 42-43, 52, 55, 72, 84, 86
Davis letters to officials, 96-98, 121-23, 157-58
Davis, Joseph R. Mississippi Brigade, 191
Detailed soldiers, 6, 8, 40, 53, 76, 132, 254
Durden, Robert, 2, 258, 262
Draft Exemptions, 2, 42, 49, 51, 58, 63, 84-85, 88, 124, 131, 133-34, 141, 143-44, 205-6, 253-54
E, 131-32
Early County News, 61, 66, 149-50, 226-28, 271
Early, Jubal, 38, 40
Echols, Joseph, 131, 267
Elberton, GA, 54, 132-33, 267
Ellis, J.W., 114-15
English Church and State Review, 61
Evans, Augusta J., 214
Estis, M., 239-40
Fears, J.W., 66, 150, 228-29
Female soldiers, 89-90, 149
Flash, Henry H., 48-49, 51, 57, 67, 123-26, 136, 204-6, 208
Foote, Henry, 37, 72-73
Forshey, Caleb G., 162
Forsyth, John, 40-41, 98-99, 123, 158
Fort Bend, 163
Fort Fisher, 119, 126, 155, 181
Fort Valley, GA Meeting, 208
France, 9-10, 102-3, 113-14, 157-58, 171, 175, 231, 248
Frazier, C.A., 248-49
Frederick the Great, 109, 117
Freestone, 160, 238,
Funsten, David, 265
G.W.D.,
Galveston Tri-Weekly News, 73-78, 86, 89, 156-60, 162-65, 171-72, 177, 180-81, 233-36, 238-40, 249, 252,
Galveston, TX, 5, 70-71, 154, 180, 263
Gardner, James, 56-58, 67, 137-39, 151, 215-17, 220, 229, 273
Gettysburg, 7, 8, 14
Gholson, Thomas, 129, 189, 264-66
Gillespie, Clayton C., 172, 247
Gilmer, Jeremy F., 193
Gilmer, John H., 103
Goliad Meeting, 164
Goode, Jr., John, 265
Gordon, John B., 191
Gorgas, Josiah, 24-25, 30, 33,
Grant, Ulysses S., 7, 10, 16, 18, 23, 30, 33, 41, 44, 46, 68, 90, 95, 109, 116, 159, 177, 234, 262
Gray, Peter W., 69, 166

Great Britain, 9-10, 102-3, 113-14, 174-75, 231, 248
Greeley, Horace, 79, 217
Grouby, E.H., 66, 149-50
H, 163
Haiti, 118, 163
Hampton Roads Conference, 17-19, 69, 111, 176, 185-86, 191, 197-8, 202, 203-4, 213, 220, 226, 228, 231-33, 242, 250, 252
Harris, Isham, 12-13
Harrisonburg, VA, 40, 42-43, 119-20, 199-200
Harry South, 140-41, 219-20
Hartridge, Julian, 131, 267
Henry, Gustavus, 37, 187, 227, 231
Herbert, Caleb, 268
Herbert, W.J., 254
Hill, Benjamin, 205-6, 209, 214, 267-68
Hilliard, H.W., 216
Hindman, Thomas C., 13-15, 257
Holliday, Frederick, 265
Hood, John B., 72, 82, 87, 95-96, 98, 118, 156,158,162, 164-65, 169, 173, 176, 241, 263
Hotze, Henry, 9-10
Houston Tri-Weekly Telegraph, 17, 71-77, 155-56, 158-59, 160-61, 165-67, 179, 181, 232-38, 255-56
Houston, TX, 5, 70-71, 78, 173, 239
Hunter, Andrew, 104-6,192
Hunter, Robert M.T.194, 196, 203, 216, 231-32, 266
Huntsville Item, 85-86, 89, 175, 268
Impressment, 14, 44, 57, 68, 78, 99, 100, 193, 232, 255
Iter, 66, 147, 225
Jim, 64
J.L.D., 128
J.L.G., 165
J.T.M., 77-78
Jackson Mississippian, 142, 149
Janus, 127
John Hampden, 127
Johnson, Herschel V., 78, 209, 267
Johnston, Joseph E., 12-14, 98, 106, 191-92, 230, 272
Johnston, Robert, 265
Jonah, 77
Jones, John B., 186-87
Jordan, Ervin, 4
Justitia, 65-67
Kenner, Duncan & Colonial Proposal, 102-4, 113-14, 130, 134-35, 147, 157-58, 163, 167, 171-72, 175, 185-86, 231
Key, Thomas J., 204, 270-71
LaGrange Patriot, 69, 86-87, 90, 175, 177-78, 253, 255-57
LaGrange, TX, 71, 84, 179-81
Lance Corporal, 239
Land, Nathan, 54-55
Larkin, 59-60
Lee, Robert E., 7, 29-30, 33, 37, 41, 46, 51, 62, 68, 72, 80, 95, 98-101, 109, 121, 124, 138-39, 146-47, 149-51, 155, 164-65, 167, 177, 186-92, 194-98, 201-2, 204-7, 212, 217, 220-21, 225, 230, 232-37, 245, 248, 252-53, 257-58, 261, 264, 269-70, 272, 274
Lee, Letter to Andrew Hunter, 104-7, 129, 145, 168
Lester, George, 131, 266-67
Levine, Bruce, 4, 275
Lincoln, Abraham, 6-7, 36, 40, 44, 46, 82, 85, 87, 95, 108, 111, 136, 160, 172, 175, 179, 185, 195, 198, 203, 224, 231-32, 240, 253, 275
LeConte, Joseph, 141-42
London Times, 48, 116-17, 155
Longstreet, James, 51, 269
Loughery, Robert W., 81-82, 166, 169, 171-72, 244-48, 250
Louisiana Native Guards, 6-7
Love, P.E., 224
Lucy, 239, 264
Lynchburg City, VA Meeting, 197, 200
Lynchburg Republican, 27
Lynchburg Virginian, 26-27, 38-41, 116-17, 120, 186, 192, 194, 196-98, 252, 263-64, 268-69
Lynchburg, VA, 5, 30, 44, 118, 199, 202, 262, 265, 269
Macon Christian Index, 49-50, 126, 128, 205-7, 214-15, 229
Macon Southern Confederacy, 123-28, 133
Macon Telegraph and Confederate, 47-49, 50-51, 67, 77, 123-27, 134, 136, 169, 204-7, 215,
Macon, GA, 5, 47, 55-56, 100, 131, 136, 203, 211, 229, 264, 267, 270-71
Madison, 141
Mallory, W.A., 147

Marshall Texas Republican, 69, 78-83, 155, 157, 167, 169, 171-72, 181, 231, 240-42, 244-45, 247, 249-50, 252
Marshall, TX, 5, 68, 71, 79-80, 166
Martinez, Jamie, 6
Mason, James, 112-13
Maxwell, Augustus, 137-38, 168, 194
McClellan, William, 89, 175, 177-78, 180, 255-57
McMullin, Fayette, 265
McDonald, James, 35-36, 109-11
Memphis Appeal, 13, 86, 124, 142
Mentor, 141, 220
Mexico & Cotton Trade, 68-69, 75, 85, 87, 90-91, 154, 166, 176, 181, 230, 240, 253, 273
Miles, William P., 29-30, 105, 129, 192-94
Milledgeville Confederate Union, 133-36, 151, 211-13
Milledgeville Southern Recorder, 134-35, 212-15, 229, 268
Milledgeville, GA, 47-48, 55-56, 133, 214, 229
Miller, Samuel, 265
Mills, John T., 157-58, 160-66, 171-72, 177, 180-81, 235, 238-40, 246-50, 258, 273
Mobile Evening News, 73
Mobile Advertiser and Register, 40-41, 98, 123, 137, 204-5, 226, 232, 251
Mobilia, 127
Mohr, Clarence, 3-4, 271
Monroe, John, 27
Morse, Nathan S., 57-59, 67, 138-40, 216-20
Murrah, Pendelton, 154-55, 175, 256, 272
Nashville, TN, 17-18, 82, 87, 95, 99-100, 108, 116, 120, 122-25, 144-45, 151, 153, 165, 167, 174-76, 181, 262, 272
Native Georgian, 46
New Orleans, LA, 6-7, 24, 27, 70, 153
New York Herald, 74, 232
New York News, 41, 80-81, 221
New York Times, 47-48, 72
New York Tribune, 143
New York World, 143
Nisbet, James C., 12
lNisbet, Joseph, 134-36, 151, 211-14
Nomen, 53
North Carolina State Journal, 149
Old Soldier, 247
Oldham, Williamson, 194, 196, 251-52, 268
Orme, R.M., 135, 212-13, 215, 229
Orr, James, 137-38, 168, 194, 233
Osterhout, John P., 88-89, 176-77, 180-81, 252, 254-55, 257, 273
OrrOzina, 135-36
Parrhesia, 180
Pegram, J.W., 196, 201, 221, 268-69
Pelican Private, 239
Petersburg, VA, 16, 18, 23, 33, 38, 44, 46, 68, 76, 96, 116, 159, 177, 181, 189, 199, 202-3, 212, 243, 262-64, 266, 270
Porcher, Frederick A., 96-99, 158
Porcupine, 162
Prentice, George D., 117
Press Assoc. of the Confederate States, 52, 56, 123, 215
Preston, J.T.L., 201
Preston, James S., 99
Price, Sterling, 71, 80, 110, 153-54, 165-66, 181
Pugh, James, 142
Q, 126
Raleigh Confederate, 52
Raleigh Standard, 39
Ramsey, James, 129
Randolph, [Macon, GA], 51
Randolph [Marshall, TX], 172
Reynolds, Thomas C., 80
Rhett, Barnwell R., 85
Richardson, Willard, 75-76, 86, 89, 159-60, 164, 166, 236-36, 240
Rich Man's War, 2, 51, 53, 77, 110-112, 114-15, 140, 152, 164-65, 177, 179-80, 187, 207, 227-28
Richmond Dispatch, 62, 232
Richmond Enquirer, 25-26, 31, 33-34, 39, 44, 73, 102, 108-9, 117, 121, 134, 137, 149, 167, 189-90, 246, 252
Richmond Examiner, 36-37, 99-100, 102-4, 112-14, 190, 195, 202, 242,
Richmond Sentinel, 27, 34-35, 107, 121, 167-69, 185, 191-92, 194-95
Richmond Whig, 27, 35-36, 73, 109-11, 113-14, 232, 251-52, 269
Richmond Whig numerical study, 101-2, 119, 121, 124, 142, 155
Richmond, VA, 5, 8, 16, 29, 33, 39, 42, 44, 48, 60, 69-70, 80, 96, 99, 111, 158, 164, 186-87, 199, 214, 219, 220, 230-

31, 240-41, 243, 245-46, 254, 262, 265-66, 269, 272
Roanoke County, VA Meeting, 197, 200
Robinson, David, 87, 174, 176, 181, 253-54, 257
Rockingham County, VA Meeting, 199-200
Rockingham Register, 41-43, 119-20, 199-200
Roundabout, 60
Russell, Charles, 265
S, 219-20
Samford, William, 65, 224-25
Saltville, VA, 116, 118
Savannah Morning News, 41, 62,
Savannah, GA, 17-18, 82, 95, 100, 118, 122-25, 142, 156, 167, 175-76, 262, 267, 272
Scruggs, William, 63-64, 144-45, 151-52, 223
Seddon, James A. 13, 32-33, 46, 96, 99, 106-7, 132, 158
Sexton, Franklin, 268
Shelbyite, 173
Sheridan, Philip, 38, 40-41, 43-44, 46-47, 116, 118, 156, 199-200, 262, 265
Sherman, William T., 10, 18, 23, 39-40, 90, 100-1, 118, 135-37, 149-50, 153, 156, 159, 174-76, 181, 186-87, 191, 215, 224, 226, 230-31, 234, 238, 253, 257-58,
Sherman's March to the Sea, 18, 54-55, 67, 68, 95-96, 98, 122, 132-33, 135-39, 144, 169, 179, 263,
Shewmake, John, 131, 266-67
Shreveport, LA, 71, 83,153-54, 239-40
Simms, William, 138
Sire and Son, 207
Slave laborers with the C.S. Army, 6, 8, 10, 13-14, 24, 28-29, 154-55
Slave laborers, Proposal for 40,000, 31,33, 35-37, 43-44, 48, 52-53, 56-58, 62-63, 65-66, 72-73, 75-76, 79-81, 84-85, 112, 131, 146-47, 150, 158-59, 167-69, 172, 178, 185-86, 192-93, 211, 262, 265
Slave Soldier Bill, 186-86, 194-96, 200-1, 209-12, 215-18, 221, 227, 233-36, 241, 243, 251-53, 255, 257, 264-69,
Sledge, James A., 52-53, 130-31, 136, 210-11, 267
Sledge, William, 160-62, 166, 179-81, 258, 273,
Slocum, Henry, 63
Smith, Ashbel, 154, 173, 248-49
Smith, Edmund Kirby, 109-110, 153-54, 230, 247
Smith, George W., 69
Smith, James M., 131, 267
Smith, John, 214
Smith, Richard M., 34-35, 107,
Smith, William, 28-29, 37-39, 48, 52, 143, 193, 269
Smith, William E., 131, 267, 271
Soldier, 163
Solon, 126-27
Southern, 163
Speed, Jno, 197-98
Speight, T.E., 150, 227-28
St. Louis Republican, 61
Staunton Vindicator, 41-43, 118-19, 198-99
Staunton, VA, 40-41, 198-99, 265
Stephens, Alexander, 2, 78-79, 81-82, 122, 145, 176, 180, 185, 203, 231, 233
Stephens, Linton, 216
Stevens, Clement, 12
Stockdale, Fletcher, 253
Stringfellow, John W., 115-16, 121
Swann, William, 37, 56
Swindells, John W., 82-83, 169-71, 245-46, 250
Sydney, 51
T.A., 76-77, 237, 240
Taylor, Walter H., 29-30
Terry's Texas Rangers, 76
The Liberator, 130
Thomas, E.L. Georgia Brigade, 208, 225
Thomas, George 13, 18, 95-96, 122, 175
Tom Anchorite, 237
Trammell, William, 225
Traveler, 77
Troup County, GA Meeting, 208
Turner, Thomas P., 196, 201, 221, 268-69
Tyler, Nathaniel, 25-26, 33-34, 100-2, 108-9, 272
Tyler [TX] Confederate Journal, 170
Upson County, GA, 127
Vance, Zebulon, 28, 56-57, 73
Vest, George, 138
Vicksburg, 7, 8, 14-15, 173
Vidette, 207-8
Villeré, Charles, 36-37
Virginius, 146

Volunteer of '61, 207
W.L.M., 218
W.W., 60, 79, 140-41, 218-20
Walker, William H.T., 12-13
Warren, J.W., 63, 144-46, 222-23
Wartmann, John H., 42-43, 119-20, 199-200
Washington, George, 7, 30, 104, 172
Watkins, Sam R., 95
Watson, John, 138
Watts, Thomas, 28, 56, 62, 224
West, C.S., 247
Wickam, Williams, 36, 265-66
Wiego, 236-37
Wigfall, Louis T., 81, 106, 138, 192, 194, 245, 252, 263, 268
Wiley, Bell, 3
Will Warwick, 224
Wise, Henry A., 212
Wise, Henry Virginia Brigade, 190
Woodside, 164
Wright, J.C. 214
X, 114
Yost, Samuel M., 41-43, 118-19, 198-99